"TORCHERED" MINDS

"Torchered" Minds

Case Histories of Notorious Serial Arsonists

Ed Nordskog

To order additional copies of this book, contact:
Xlibris Corporation
1-888-795-4274
www.Xlibris.com
Orders@Xlibris.com
103280

This is for my colleagues-the detectives, special agents, and arson investigators-worldwide who work every day to identify, track down, arrest, and convict those most cowardly, sick, and devious of all criminals. It is an extraordinarily difficult task that on a daily basis is fraught with pitfalls and rife with myths and misconceptions. It is doggedly carried out by men and women who are routinely assailed by critics, stymied by bureaucrats, second-guessed by chair-warming administrators, avoided by many prosecutors, and eviscerated by defense attorneys, "learned" psychologists, and other hired guns.

If it was easy, anybody could do it. It's not, and they can't.

—Ed Nordskog, Detective, 2011

CONTENTS

ACKNOWLEDGMENTS

The following special people shared their insights, knowledge, and investigations with me. A major investigation of any crime is a very personal quest by the involved investigators, and they tend to develop a sense of ownership with their case. It becomes part of them and its successful resolution becomes seared into their psyche forever. I want to thank those very generous people for sharing a piece of their experience with me. Det. Rich Edwards, Det. Enrique Velazquez, Det. Michael Digby, Det. James Gonzales, Lt. Julio Salcido, Det. Sgt. Ron Ablott, Det. Rich McClellan, Det. Sgt. Craig Anderson, Det. Larry Lewis, Det. Mike Cofield, Det. Todd Anderson, Det. Sgt. John Ament, Det. Sgt. Mike Costleigh, Det. Sgt. Derek Yoshino, Senior Criminalist Phil Teramoto, Det. Sgt. Ed Huffman, Chief John Graham, Investigator David Liske, Investigator David Westfield, Supervising Investigator Joe Konefal, Supervising Investigator Jim Allen, Investigator Chris Vallerga, Capt. Tom Oldag, Chief Keith Mashburn, Investigator Chris Klein, Senior Special Agent Ron Michel, Supervising Special Agent Mike Matasa, Special Agent Mike Hidalgo, Special Agent Dan Heenan, Special Agent Scott Fulkerson, Investigator Bob Luckett, Special Agent Ron Huxman, Special Agent Dan Briot, Chief John Kabala, Deputy District Attorney Mike Cabral, Deputy District Attorney Ron Smalstig, Deputy District Attorney Susan Schwartz, Deputy District Attorney Sean Carney, Dr. Dian Williams, Dr. John DeHann, Dean Beatrice Yorker, JD, and Mr. Matt Hinds-Aldrich.

I want to give special acknowledgment to the man who taught me the secret world of fire investigation, Det. Don Powell, and also to the best detective I ever met and who spent thousands of hours teaching a young, eager, wide-eyed, Midwestern boy how to "read crooks" and solve even the most intricate crimes in Los Angeles, Det. Sgt. Michael "Edge" Forst.

The Arsonists Speak . . .

"Arsonists are typically loners and losers, like serial murderers, but the arsonist sneaks around behind people's backs to do his crimes." (John Orr in his book *Points of Origin*)

"Ever since I can remember I've always loved fire. I'll tell you something. I just didn't pick it up overnight. Ten years I've been doing them and I'll tell you it's bloody hard to stop when you get the urge." (Bruce George Peter Lee)

"I set hundreds of fires when I was a child. Many of them were not serious, but the Fire Department had to be called. I also did this myself, I had no motive except I loved to cause the excitement. I *never* got caught." (David Berkowitz)

"Some days I wake up with such a strong urge that I have to talk myself out of setting fires."(John Dominguez)

"I (sic) been doing fires since I was a little kid. See, the little fires don't excite me, you know. Only big fires excite me . . . The bigger the fires, the more I get excited." (Ottis Toole)

"A fact-based work that follows the pattern of an actual arsonist who has been setting serial fires in California over the past eight years . . . As in the real case, the arsonist in my novel is a firefighter." (John Orr in a letter to publishers and agents describing his book *Points of Origin*)

"I liked the attention from setting fires; the Blue + red lights flashing from the firetrucks + police cars, the rushing of firefighters hooking up the hoses to put out the flames and people gathered to watch." (Thomas Sweatt)

"I like to see firefighters working. It's nice to see how they fall into the fire." (Cayetano Godino)

"See, I could build a fire and burn up anybody I wanted . . . piss me off and I'll burn you out" (Pat Russ)

"I done this because of my destitute circumstances and because I was sore at the world in general." (Robert Driscoll)

"About this time I began to try to figure out some way to punish those who punished me. The only thing I could figure out was to burn down the building . . . I had fully decided when I left there just how I would live my life. I made up my mind that I would rob, burn, destroy, and kill everywhere I went and everybody I could as long as I lived." (Carl Panzram)

"I once worked as a fireman-there is a bit of arsonist in all firemen . . . I would be quite happy to burn the world down." (Colin Ireland)

The Experts Speak . . .

"Fire setting is not a urethral-erotic problem. It's a problem with expressing aggression. If you have delinquent tendencies and you're really assertive and someone bugs you, you confront them. You either talk to them or punch them out. But it's direct. Fire setting is usually very indirect. It's a symbolic way of getting back at someone you believe has hurt you." (Dr. Kenneth Fineman, psychologist, University of California, Irvine)

"Arsonists are people who can't deal on an interpersonal basis. They strike out at society because they feel rejected, unloved. They have low self-esteem." (Anthony Olen Rider, criminologist and Supervisory Special Agent for the Federal Bureau of Investigation)

"Thrill seeker fire setters . . . enjoy the risk of setting fires and the powerful idea of 'getting away with' a crime. Arson is a validation of their intellectual superiority over other individuals, other men, in particular." (Dr. Dian Williams, arson research fellow and internationally recognized expert on juvenile arson activity)

"Arsonists are nocturnal in nature . . . are voyeurs and burglars . . . have histories that often include theft, prowling, trespassing, peeping, lewd behavior, and vandalism . . . operate with a great deal of deception and sneakiness." (FBI Profiler William Hagmaier)

"The truth is very little is known about arsonists because so few arsons are solved." (Dr. Joel Dvoskin, American Board of Forensic Psychology)

"Arson . . . is the crime of a coward. It is perpetrated by a person who wants to strike out but does not have the courage to face his intended victim nose to nose." (FBI Profiler John Douglas, the *Mindhunter*)

PROLOGUE

Who the hell am I to write a book and offer my expert opinions about serial arsonists? In 2006, shortly after the deadly Esperanza Fire in San Bernardino County of California roared up a mountain and killed five firefighters, it was declared an arson event by the handling investigators. A few days later, task force members investigating that fire would arrest a local mechanic named Raymond Lee Oyler and charge him with a series of arson fires and murder in the first degree. The prosecutors sought the death penalty against Oyler, and many months later, he would in fact be convicted of multiple arsons and the murder of those firefighters. He would be the first person in United States history that would receive the death penalty for setting a wild land fire.

During this fire event and the ensuing trial, I would occasionally hear from "experts" in the field of arson as they gave their paid opinions for local and national media. Included in this ongoing parade of "experts" would be nationally known "criminal profilers," psychologists, criminologists, psychiatrists, and several fire chiefs. These same people always pop up on the news/entertainment shows after every major arson story these days. I have personally bumped into several of these "experts" at various training functions and conferences in the fire investigation field over the years. After listening to them and evaluating what they were saying in comparison to my actual experience in the field, I came to the conclusion that either (a) they didn't know anything about the subjects of serial arson, fire investigation, and what truly motivates arson attacks or (b) the opinion and profile they gave was so vague and "boilerplate" that it would fit almost every criminal for every conceivable criminal event . . . the standard "disenfranchised and angry lone male, with relationship problems, a troubled childhood, and the inability to cope with stress."

After my very first serial arson case in 1997, I began to study this field a bit and came to the conclusion that there was very little serious documentation of the crime of serial arson. The studies conducted by researchers and scholars

---

seemed somewhat ancient and small in scope and quite often lumped serial arsonists with every other convicted arsonist. Most were based in the statistics gathered by fire departments and police agencies, and I knew for sure that those statistics were (and continue to be) completely unreliable. As I began getting more experience in the field of serial arson cases and fire investigation in general, I learned that there were many different types of arsonists, all of who committed their acts for their own particular reasons. I learned that even in the very small niche of serial arsonist behavior, there were many subsets. I also learned that almost nothing I had ever been taught in any major arson school proved to be true regarding serial arsonists. By reading more and more studies and behavioral assessments, I learned that there were indeed some consistent generalities in the field, but each case was so different and unique that it was often impossible to label or categorize most offenders.

In 2005, I had a mind-numbing experience. I was in a jury trial with a sophisticated serial arson offender who paid $2 million dollars for a very skilled defense team. To help counter his defense and bolster our case, the prosecutor and I consulted with an "arson profiler" who was then working at the national level. After several phone conversations and an exchange of written material, both the prosecutor and I were stunned at how little this "national expert" seemed to actually know about the subject material. We opted not to use that "expert" as his knowledge level was clearly well below that of several arson investigators in our own area.

My triggering event for writing this book came in 2009, when I was asked to be part of a State of California panel to study, evaluate, and rewrite the state's Arson and Explosives Investigation Course. That "blue ribbon" panel was originally made up of a group of about thirty longtime "experts" in the arson and bomb investigation fields. One of those members was a very vocal gentleman who had long claimed to be an "expert" on serial arsonists. I had experienced that "expert" in a courtroom setting and personally knew him to be a man with over forty-five years of experience in the arson investigation field. During our lengthy meetings and documentation reviews, that "expert" forcefully gave strong opinions on how serial arsonists acted, appeared, thought, and what their motives were. He maintained that most serial arsonists were sexually motivated men, who liked to match wits with investigators, usually used a sophisticated delay ignition device, always watched their arson events, and specifically targeted firefighters for injury or death during their arson schemes.

The rest of the panel, including me, was extremely skeptical of that guy's views, and we challenged him on them. We forced him to back up his statements with actual case evidence to support them. Surely, in forty-five years of working and teaching in the field, that expert had some case evidence to support his theories. Nope. That "expert" was not able to produce a shred of real case evidence to support his arguments. He only maintained the usual mantra: "Well, everybody knows that serial arsonists act this way or that way." We tossed him off the panel, and from that point on, we only accepted information and theories that were backed by real case histories and evidence, and not by the usual firefighter lore and psychological babble that seems to permeate and infest the world of arson investigation. The biggest problem with this field of study is that the guy we kicked off the panel had been an instructor in arson investigation for over thirty years and had also been a recognized "expert" by the courts. Even more alarming was that many of us in the room had initially been trained in arson investigation by that guy as he was one of the few instructors in California at the time. More than one generation of fire investigators had received bad information from that one "expert."

So, by 2009, after having been personally involved in over fifteen serial arson cases and discussing dozens more with colleagues, I came to the realization that many of these "experts" really didn't know what they were talking about. It is doubtful that many of these "experts" have ever conducted a serial arson investigation, done research into the serial arsonist's background, monitored his behavior during a surreptitious surveillance, or have sat across a small table in an interview room with one in his most vulnerable period . . . those first few hours after his arrest. I further recognized that nobody had ever compiled a reasonable book on the analysis and comparison of major serial arson case histories. My "research" had led me to study hundreds of case histories and conduct my own analysis of the offender and his motives. From this mixture of personal contacts with (now over twenty) serial arsonists, my research into hundreds of other serial arson cases, and my personal contacts with several investigators who have conducted their own serial arson investigations, I am able to present what I believe is a more "real world" view of serial arsonists.

Detective Ed Nordskog

CHAPTER 1

The Background

A good laymen's definition of arson is to unlawfully start a fire with the malicious intent to destroy the property of another.

The word "arsonist" is one of the most misused terms in the criminal investigation field. The mere mention of this term or one of its more colloquial cousins such as pyromaniac, firebug, spark, or torch conjures up the image of a wild-eyed maniacal man in a tattered trench coat who wanders through the night compulsively setting fires to peoples' homes as they sleep. Our firefighting brethren often have the very strong opinion that arsonists have it in their foremost intentions to injure or kill firefighters. Armchair investigators, of course, always believe that arsonist behavior is absolutely a byproduct of sexual deviation and that arsonists actually derive erotic gratification from their fire setting activities.

While most of these beliefs are based on antiquated pseudo psychiatric opinions and Hollywood over-dramatizations, as in the Donald Sutherland character in *Backdraft*, the truth about why people set fires is quite a bit more mundane. According to just about every study on the subject, the number one motive for arson is the spite/revenge motive. This is most often manifested in a domestic or personal dispute. In short, when someone is really, really mad, they may start a fire to destroy something of value. A very close number two motive for arson is financial gain. Crime concealment arson, most often following a murder, is another fairly common motive. Juvenile arson activity is mostly a form of vandalism with little intention of starting a serious fire. All of the above motives are generally singular acts and are usually not part of an ongoing fire setting pattern of behavior.

I acknowledge that this particular bit of information clashes with the published results of the only known major study of *serial arsonists*. This study, undertaken in 1997 by FBI and ATF behavior analysts from the National Center for the Analysis of Violent Crime (NCAVC), consisted of interviews of a fairly small sampling of eighty-three convicted serial arson offenders. While I would agree with the methodology and results of this study as it pertains to convicted serial arson offenders, I would offer my very strong opinion that we in the arson investigation business seldom identify and catch the clever arsonists. If they are professional fire setters, say for instance persons working for organized crime entities and have refined their *modus operandi* to a level of sophistication, then I submit that we seldom even identify their efforts as incendiary acts.

With that in mind, the concern of this book is the peculiar activity of the serial arson offender or more gently "the multiple fire setter." The National Fire Protection Administration (NFPA), along with most credible sources, describes a serial arson offender as a person who is involved in three or more separate fire events, with a cooling off period between events. This description is used to distinguish a serial offender from a spree arsonist. A spree arsonist is best described as an offender who sets several fires in a very short period of time with no cooling-off period. Most arson fires in the United States are set by one-time offenders for the previously described motives, and not by serial or spree offenders. To this end, a serial arsonist is a fairly rare and unique criminal offender.

With that in mind, it is my contention after a lengthy career in this business that the most sophisticated arson attacks are done by persons in furtherance of insurance fraud. It is during these events that investigators find sophisticated time delay ignition devices. It is during these events that investigators uncover the elaborate "staging" of scenes, and it is during these events that evidence is revealed of long-term planning by the involved parties.

Another group of arsonists that are extremely difficult to identify and catch are the internal extremists. Most often called "domestic terrorists," these groups, which for the most part are identified with environmental and animal rights movements, comprise well-educated and highly motivated zealots, who operate in small cells and routinely practice counter surveillance and counter-intelligence activities. These "eco-warriors" use extensive planning and target selection methods, conduct detailed pre-raid reconnaissance, and can defeat modern security systems. They use pre-assembled incendiary delay devices that are simple in design and fairly reliable. Their targets are chosen by the cell group itself, and there is little information gleaned by law enforcement before the event. These fire events tend to be carried out as well-organized paramilitary operations. The fires that are caused by these groups tend to be large dramatic events with extensive financial impact to the targeted victim. Typical targets include universities, research labs, commercial animal farms, various industries, large construction projects, and luxury car dealerships. In recent years, these groups have begun to conduct personal attacks on the homes and vehicles of executives and officials within the above targeted institutions. These groups have the ability to operate nationwide and sometimes worldwide, and it is difficult for local authorities to track and identify the members. Due to their skill and planning, the members of these groups are seldom prosecuted for these incendiary attacks.

Put simply, we usually only catch the young, disorganized, emotional, violent, mentally impaired, and drug/alcohol-addled arsonists. It is my experience that the preplanned events are too difficult to recognize and prove, and thus, the skilled or smarter arsonists get away with it all too often. This would absolutely skew the stats in favor of the disorganized arson offender.

The other major fact in my disagreement with this study is that a vast majority of arson units across the United States simply don't investigate "nuisance" fires. These are often trash and vegetation fires, where items of little value are burned. In my experience, fire chiefs do not want to waste precious resources on these minor events. This is a very sad circumstance indeed. Even the authors of the 1997 serial arson study concede that fire agencies overlook many "nuisance" fires, when it is clear that these are the exact fires that the vast majority of serial offenders commit. As we shall see in this book, it is a rare serial offender indeed who targets inhabited structures.

Dr. Dian Williams is a foremost researcher and expert on juvenile fire setting activity. This author has consulted her on one case and has read all or most of her research findings, and believes that she has some of the most learned and credible opinions on fire setting behavior. In her lifelong studies, she believes that at a minimum, juveniles are responsible for at least one-half of all arson fires and probably many more than that. Unfortunately, Dr. Williams is aware (and this author agrees) that a large number of juvenile fire setters are merely counseled for their acts and are seldom documented or placed into the criminal justice system. That large number of criminal fires goes unrecorded and the offender is seldom registered or given the proper treatment. With this in mind, a vast number of juvenile-related fires are also not counted as "arson" events in the various reporting systems. Likewise, many juvenile offenders who are having repetitive issues with fire setting or may actually be serial arsonists are simply dismissed by the fire investigation community and allowed to re-offend for years.

Lastly, many if not most fire agencies do not investigate automobile fires. The rationale most often cited is that these are insurance matters, and public resources should not be wasted on this small crime. This is the biggest problem with arson statistics. My own investigative experience shows that over 75 percent of the vehicle arsons in my jurisdiction (Greater Los Angeles area) are in fact owner-involved insurance fraud events. By not including car fires, trash fires, vegetation fires, and juvenile-related fires into reported arson statistics, fire agencies are not giving analysts the proper foundation for research and reporting. With that, I would make the bold statement here that most of the arson statistics nationwide are completely invalid because properly trained fire investigators are not examining every fire in their jurisdictions.

The Motives

Most credible sources, including the NFPA, National Fire Administration, and the FBI's National Center for the Analysis of Violent Crime (NCAVC), cite several possible motives for arson behavior. The most common motives cited include.

1. Spite or revenge
2. Financial gain or profit
3. Crime concealment
4. Excitement—power, vanity (hero fires)
5. Vandalism
6. Extremism/terrorism/political/religious
7. Curiosity (juvenile fire setting)

Serial arson motives are much more complicated and often include a combination of motives, personal stressors, alcohol and drug use, and mental health issues. In recent years, most investigators and psychoanalysts have gotten away from the term pyromania, which connotes an uncontrollable urge or compulsion to start fires. Additionally, the notion that arson is always a sex crime has also been diminished in recent years. In the end, the two most commonly cited motives for serial fire setting are revenge and excitement/vanity or a combination of the two.

From this investigator's empirical research, personal experiences during 1,600 arson investigations, his close association with several dozen other experienced arson investigators, and through his review of several dozens of case histories, a rough "profile" of a serial arson offender is offered. Although there are no absolutes here, there are some trends that seem to arise in many serial arson investigations. To look at these trends, it is recognized that serial offenders are generally divided into two main groups. The groups are classified as organized arsonists and disorganized arsonists. These are the same traits that are highlighted in the NCAVC study.

Organized Serial Arsonist

1. Almost all are male adults
2. More likely to use a device of sorts
3. Ignition scenario and target are preplanned
4. Severity of fire and results are planned
5. There is usually some effort used to access target
6. This offender has unlimited mobility
7. This offender may operate in daylight hours (wild land arsonist)

Some personal characteristics of this type of arsonist include:

1. A conscious indifference to society
2. Egocentric
3. Manipulative
4. Methodical and cunning
5. May live some distance from the scene
6. Has chameleon personality

The organized serial offender is much rarer than the disorganized offender. Examples of this type of offender would be a hired arsonist or "torch" who does work for insurance fraud, gang/mob activities, or for some sort of financial gain. The extremist arsonist or the "eco-warrior" is another organized offender. A close match to this would also be the ideological arsonist. This person would have an almost religious fervor to their act and would target things such as abortion clinics, vice targets, including massage parlors and strip clubs, or even churches. A final example of the organized arsonist would be a firefighter arsonist in the vein of John Orr, a person who will be discussed in depth in the following chapters.

Disorganized Serial Arsonist

1. Most are male adults and juveniles.
2. Most offenders light the vast majority of their fires in and around the areas where they live, work, go to school, or have some other personal connection.
3. Most serial offenders are loners with few friends.
4. Most are nocturnal in their behavior.
5. Most have issues with drugs or alcohol.
6. Most pick random targets.
7. Most use available materials at the fire scene.

8. Most have limited mobility and usually access scenes by foot or bicycle.
9. The most common form of ignition is open flame via match or lighter.
10. Most events are unplanned and set at an impulse.
11. Most events lack cunning and sophistication.
12. Most of these offenders have predictable times within which they usually light fires. These times are related to the convenience of the offender, such as when he gets off work or out of school or when his parents or spouse are not around.

Common Traits

In 2008, this author attended a seminar for homicide investigators in Las Vegas, Nevada. As part of this, a lecture on serial offenders was offered by noted FBI behavioral analyst and author, William Hagmaier. In that venue, Mr. Hagmaier spoke about his many years of studying and classifying serial offenders of all types. He had some pointed remarks regarding serial arsonists. Hagmaier said that while each case was decidedly different, his studies showed many similarities among serial arson offenders that may prove useful to investigators. Among their many traits were that many serial arsonists were males with effeminate tendencies. These included a high degree of fastidiousness and general neatness in appearance. He believed that many had some form of obsessive compulsive disorder (OCD) and were preoccupied with things that were messy or disorganized.

Another trait that Hagmaier noted among serial arson offenders was that they were generally non-confrontational. They tended to "turn the other cheek" during interactions with people, but then would wait and plot out their revenge. This type of offender might wait days, weeks, or even months to attack the persons or institutions they believe have wronged them in some way. Hagmaier said that in his opinion, most arsonists are generally cowards, who settle all grudges by attacking when people are most vulnerable.

Hagmaier also stressed that serial arson offenders were generally nocturnal in all of their activities and operated with a great deal of deception and sneakiness. He said that many were "voyeurs and burglars." He said that almost all were involved in theft or burglary, and that many had past arrest histories for odd crimes such as vandalism, prowling, petty theft, trespassing, burglary, and theft from fire houses. Many also might have some sort of illegal sexual activity in their background, including public indecency, solicitation of prostitution, annoying children, lewd conduct, etc. Additionally, many who were engaged in excitement or thrill-based arsons had numerous contacts with police as "victims" or callers to the 9-1-1 emergency system (Hagmaier, personal communication, February 2008).

This author has reviewed numerous serial arson case histories from local sources in the California area and has noted other consistent traits. Most of the serial arsonists had some form of prescription medication or illegal narcotics use in their background. Many abused alcohol. Many had been involved in incidents where they falsely reported emergencies or fires and/or maliciously pulled fire alarms. Many were well known to firefighters and police officers in their area as "oddballs" or "weirdos," prior to being identified as serial arsonists. The majority had some form of physical or mental impairment. Almost all had threatened or attempted suicide at least once. Most had been institutionalized in some manner at least once. A last odd trait manifested itself in the male offenders who actually drove a vehicle. To a man, almost all of them were known by their friends or the police as extremely aggressive drivers.

Profiling

This book will give examples of all of the various types and sub-types of serial arsonists. Some as you will see, have multiple or mixed motives and are difficult to classify. Others have an evolving motive and level of sophistication. They could have been disorganized in their early fires but at some point evolved into a somewhat more organized fire setter. The end result of this writing is that it should be made clear that there is no singularly apt description of a serial arsonist. Each case is somewhat unique with various oddities thrown in just to skew a clean profile. Each is also so bizarre that even Hollywood's most imaginative writers could not create a character that would surpass some of the true offenders. So, despite decades of popular belief, even among criminal profilers and fire investigators, there is not currently an adequate singular "profile" that includes all or even most serial arson offenders.

Some of the arsonists described here are nationally known, very notorious people. Others are more of the norm in this field. They are just locally known offenders who for a short period of time terrorized a region and then were caught and hopefully sent away.

The author points out here a notable fact with this writing. Serial arson is still a crime with very little credible documentation. There are countless books, movies, and reams of studies regarding serial murderers and mass murderers, but precious little in the serial arson field. If the truth be known, it would be a logical conclusion to assume that many serial murderers have some degree of serial fire setting in their background. It is only because the murders are so much more shocking and serious that the suspect's arson activity (if any) gets overlooked. With this caveat, your author recognizes that not all of the below listed information has been professionally vetted by researchers and analysts. Most has to be taken at face value from books, biographies, newspapers, internet accounts, court records, or brief mentions during other related criminal investigations. Some of the older cases involve sole source references based on statements or confessions from the offender, with little or no corroboration from investigative or academic sources. The author in some of the below listed cases makes his "detective analysis" based solely on the limited sources available. The author apologizes in advance to the involved detectives and investigators for any errors or omissions in the telling of their casework. Of course some facts will be missed as only the investigator and the arsonist know for sure what really happened in a case.

The Investigators

The sole motivation in studying and compiling these cases is for the benefit of my brethren in the fire/arson investigation community. The arson investigation field is a much maligned profession, which has (sometimes deservedly) come under tremendous scrutiny in recent years for unprofessional work and botched investigations. This author has over twenty years' experience as a criminal investigator covering almost every facet of crime and can attest to the fact that fire/arson investigation is the most difficult, complex, and technical investigation there is. The degree of damage, loss of evidence, and the other dynamics of the fire scene far outclass the difficulties encountered at most homicide scenes. The complexities of a typical arson for profit scheme or insurance fraud case are some of the most challenging in the criminal investigative field. Additionally, arson investigation and the follow-up criminal prosecution are encumbered with countless erroneous assumptions and myths in the minds of the prosecutors, defense attorneys, judges, juries, and the public as a whole. These myths and assumptions are massive obstacles that need to be overcome to successfully bring an arsonist to justice.

The arson/fire investigation field is also an emerging science and, as such, is filled with numerous toys, gadgets, and other gimmicks designed and marketed by companies as the means with which to solve cases. There are current trends to rely on accelerant detection K-9's, mechanical carbon detectors, heat sensors, polygraphs, tracking systems, computer modeling, arc mapping, fire scientists, behavior analysts (profilers), spatial and temporal mapping, and other investigative tools. While all of these items have some degree of value as aids to the investigator, they seldom solve a crime by themselves. The astute reader will note in most of the following case histories that the offender was identified, tracked down, and arrested by a motivated and intelligent investigator or team, who doggedly studied their quarry, painstakingly followed leads, conducted interviews, collected and analyzed forensic evidence, and eventually linked the suspect to the crime. The truly brilliant (or perhaps lucky) investigators in this bunch were able to achieve a rapport with the arsonist and get him to open up and talk about his activities. These are the time-tested methods of criminal investigation that continue to be the most successful and lead to the most prosecutions of the serial arsonist. These stories are assembled and retold here to pass on the lessons learned from these heroic investigators to other professionals in the field so that a better understanding of how to identify these offenders is reached.

During the research for this book, I read dozens of articles, books, and papers from highly respected psychologists, psychiatrists, behavior analysts (profilers), and others in the academic fields surrounding criminal investigation. It is interesting to note the wide variety of opinions and studies that have come from these individuals concerning the topic of serial violent crime, including fire setting. As has been discussed already, very few of these learned professionals agree with each other and with previously published studies.

One particular professional in the field makes a refreshing admission. Dr. Elliot Leyton, a criminal anthropologist from Canada and writer of true crime books, notes in his 1986 work *Hunting Humans* that "the police, who are commonly regarded as stupid and brutal, often appear in these pages to possess more intelligence and insight into the killers than do the "professionals." Leyton further points out that many psychiatric professionals readily admit that their diagnoses are "trivial . . . and meaningless." In a glaring case that precisely illustrates the point, Leyton states that a noted prison psychologist reported to a parole board that the prisoner "is an extremely intelligent young man, who is intact psychologically." He then recommended parole for the prisoner. Sometime afterward, the "young man" would be arrested for possession of burglary tools. At the time, a mere sheriff's deputy would note that the "young man" was "the strangest man I've ever met . . . It's just a gut reaction. This man's into something big." The strange "young man" referred to here in this anecdote is a young Ted Bundy, who would go on to be known as one of the most famous and prolific serial killers of all time. This example illustrates the idea that oftentimes the "street sense" of the officer or investigator far outweighs any academic credentials possessed by learned psychologists and psychiatrists in the field.

The reader will see that there are no easy profiles and no apt descriptions of any of the following offenders. As professionals, we can only gather as much information as is available and make our best opinion from there. Of course as always, only the arsonist knows who he is and why he did it.

CHAPTER 2

The Serial Arsonist Murderers

The vast majority of serial arson offenders do not commit murder. In fact, you will shortly see that a serial arsonist/murderer is the rarest of all the rare offenders. That being said, it has been "common knowledge" since the 1980s that serial fire setting has been popularly known as one leg of the homicidal triad. Noted FBI Profiler John Douglas writes in *The Anatomy of Motive* that animal cruelty, bed wetting, and fire starting as a juvenile are the main common denominators in almost all serial murderers. But Douglas is quick to note that research shows that many, many offenders who are not murderers also dabbled in fire setting as a juvenile. His studies did not focus on arson or fire setting, but he was quick to realize that fire setting was one of the first crimes that many serial offenders committed. The men in this chapter are the most dangerous arsonists ever identified, and you will see that most if not all can link their crimes back to their youngest years.

Peter Dinsdale a.k.a. Bruce George Peter Lee: Serial Mass Murderer/Serial Arsonist
Period of Activity: 1973-79, Hull, England

Around midnight on December 4, 1979, in Hull, England, a fire started at the only outside doorway to an apartment occupied by the Hastie family. As a result of this fire, three sons: a fifteen-year-old, a twelve-year-old, and an eight-year-old, all perished. Arson investigators found spent matches, burned newspaper, and an amount of liquid paraffin on the floor just under the mail slot at the door. They concluded that an unknown suspect had poured the paraffin through the mail slot onto the floor and had lit it with the matches and newspaper. A forensics investigator uttered a poignant opinion at the scene, commenting that the act appeared to be the work of someone with experience at starting fires. This investigator would prove to be quite a sage at a later juncture.

An exhausting investigation produced many theories and multiple leads, none of which panned out for investigators. Hull was a gritty, blue-collar industrial port city, and the Hastie family was considered a band of thugs by other residents and the local constabulary. Needless to say, few neighbors were cooperative, and save for the investigators, no one really cared that much. The area was rife with hooligans, street thugs, drug dealers, and prostitutes.

After six months of investigation and running out of plausible leads, Det. Supt. Ron Sagar and his team began interviewing a group of young male prostitutes in the area known as "rent boys." They felt that those boys, who were constantly on the street, would have heard something. This proved a bit fruitful as one of the young men claimed to have had an illicit sexual relationship with one of the deceased Hastie boys. This nineteen-year-old "rent boy," formerly known as Peter Dinsdale, was an odd chap who had recently changed his name to honor martial arts legend Bruce Lee. Taking a chance, Det. Supt. Sagar confronted that boy, now known as Bruce George Peter Lee, with an investigative ruse or bluff. Sagar informed him that he was aware that Lee had started the Hastie family fire. The stunning reply from Lee was simply, "I didn't mean to kill them." Lee then gave the investigator intimate knowledge of the fire scene that only the arsonist and investigators would know. He eventually said he was mad at fifteen-year-old Charlie Hastie for threatening and extorting him after they had engaged in an "indecency" (mutual sexual act). Lee also said he felt scorned and ridiculed by the Hastie family due to his physical and mental handicaps.

Bruce George Peter Lee had led a difficult life. He was born in 1960 and never knew his father who had abandoned his mother. His mother was a prostitute and gave him up to his grandmother when he was just six months old. Because of physical deformities and occasional epileptic seizures, his grandmother referred to him as "the freak" and virtually disowned him. He ran wild in the streets and had almost no supervision. By the time he was in his teens, he was dirt poor, resided in various state homes, and had a low level of intelligence. He had a deformed right arm and leg; he walked with a pronounced limp and held his arm across his chest in an immobile manner. He was clearly undernourished, poorly dressed, and had resorted to occasionally selling his body to men in order to survive. He was introduced to homosexuality while living in "care homes" throughout his teen years. From there, he joined the "rent boys" prostitution network.

After his arrest for the Hastie family fire/murders, a police sketch of Lee was released to the newspapers. A shocked woman named Mrs. Fenton recognized the sketch as a boy she had called "daft Peter." This woman had been the victim of a near fatal fire in her home a year earlier. She had seen "daft Peter" on her porch and yelled at him to go away. A bit later, a fire had erupted just inside her doorway on the floor. She later believed that Peter, whom she described as a local "half wit," had poured something through her mail slot and ignited a blaze. She and her daughter were trapped in the burning home and were only rescued at the last instant by firefighters. As a result of the fire, she miscarried a child. In the weeks following the fire, Mrs. Fenton was too ill to make a clear statement to police about the incident, and in the absence of her information about "daft Peter," arson investigators concluded that the blaze was due to someone carelessly leaving a lit cigarette on her carpet.

Mrs. Fenton alerted Det. Supt. Sagar about Lee, and the investigator went back to talk to Lee about the Fenton fire. His reply was that he had indeed lit the fire at her home as a favor for someone else. He also offered, "I like fires, I do. I like fires." After further questioning, Lee shockingly admitted that he was a "fire raiser" and that "I killed a little baby once."

Lee then admitted to breaking into a home, sprinkling paraffin on a sofa and the floor, and igniting it. He said a little baby died in the fire. A records' search confirmed just such an incident in 1977 when six-month-old Katrina Thacker died in a house fire as the rest of her family barely escaped with their lives. Arson was never suspected in the blaze, and it was blamed on a spark from the fireplace. Lee admitted to being an onlooker in the crowd to this event. After that admission, the Thacker case was reopened, and the Thacker family acknowledged they knew Peter Lee and had had an altercation with him just days prior to the fire.

Lee then admitted to even more fatal fires. He claimed he had killed a boy from his school several years prior after igniting that boy's home. Most alarmingly, Lee claimed to have started a fire at an old age home in 1977, during which eleven elderly men perished. He said he went out on his bicycle looking for a place to burn. He found the "old blokes home" by chance and kicked in a window. He entered a room where a man was sleeping and poured from a can of paraffin he had been carrying around the man's bed. He then used some paper and lit the fire. Lee discarded the empty can in a nearby river. The next day he read in the papers about eleven old men dying in the fire. This information was confirmed by the investigators after Lee took them to the scene. Like the other fires, the original investigation had wrongly concluded that the fire was an accident due to a plumber working with a blowtorch on a boiler in the building earlier that day. This incident occurred when Lee was but sixteen years old and was one of the worst mass murders in British history. A woman who was caring for Lee at the time of the event later testified that he told her after the fire, "That was no accident . . . I know."

The same day Lee directed detectives to the "old blokes' home," he led them to another nearby house and told them he had committed his first murder there when he was just twelve years old. Lee said that he lit the fire in the home of a schoolmate who was also handicapped. He found out the next day that the schoolmate died as a result of the fire. After this admission, the investigators were able to confirm that six-year-old Richard Ellington had died in a house fire in 1973. Firefighters had found his burned body in the home after ten other family members managed to escape. Lee gave no real reason for this fire, and it had never been classified as arson.

A picture of Lee's life was developed through his admissions and from statements made by acquaintances. He realized by age nine that he was fond of fires. A childhood friend admitted to accompanying Lee to burn a lumberyard. Lee later admitted to burning a shopping center. Because of his deformities and poor circumstances, Lee was often made fun of and ridiculed by other kids. However, despite this he was seldom seen to get upset and was later described as quiet and a loner.

Although of lower intelligence and education, prosecutors would later describe him as having developed an "animal cunning" and was extremely street savvy. That allowed him to commit at least thirty known major arson fires for which he was never even suspected.

In statements to the investigators Lee told them, "My master is fire." He said he felt his fingers tingled just prior to lighting fires. He also told them that he hated people and especially hated people who had homes because he never had one. Lee eventually claimed to have killed twenty-six persons during his arson attacks.

In 1973, he said he was wandering the streets at night with a can of paraffin when he found a home with an open window. He entered and set a fire. A seventy-two-year-old invalid died as he was unable to escape the fire.

Two weeks later, the thirteen-year-old Lee said he lit the home of another disabled man. That man and Lee had had an earlier dispute over pigeons, and Lee entered his home and poured paraffin on him while he was asleep in a chair. Neighbors were horrified to hear screams and see the man running into the street with his clothes on fire. In this case, arson was not suspected, and the fire was blamed on the man's clothes being too close to an open fireplace. A few days after the fire, Lee returned to the home and killed all the deceased man's pigeons.

When he was fourteen, Lee said he entered a disabled women's home and lit a fire on the bed where she was sleeping. After she died, the fire was blamed on her smoking in bed, despite her family's insistence that she did not smoke in her bedroom. Lee gave no motive for this killing.

In 1976, the sixteen-year-old Lee said he entered a home and poured paraffin under the stairs. The fire eventually killed a thirteen-month-old baby, and the fire was blamed on a five-year-old son who had "confessed" to the investigators. When he was older, the five-year-old recanted his confession, and there was no physical evidence that he had lit the fire. Lee's confession years later solved that "accident."

In 1977, Lee claimed to have entered another home where several people were sleeping. He poured petrol and lit a fire in the living room at 3:00 a.m. Two young children died in that fire, and investigators later blamed one of the adults for leaving an unattended cigarette. Lee's confession matched the scene and solved yet another "accidental" fire.

In 1978, Lee claimed to have been walking randomly around with a squirt bottle filled with paraffin hidden on him. He said he "felt fire in my head" and squirted the liquid into the mail slot of a home. He then lit newspapers and pushed them into the slot. A witness reported a circle of fire in the living room around several young kids followed by an explosion. The fire killed an adult and her three young sons. A coroner's inquest put the blame for that event on the victims playing with lighter fluid.

A later review of the case would show that Lee had an extraordinary talent for remaining hidden in plain view. He was a common character in his neighborhood and was always at the scene of the fires; yet he was never suspected of any involvement, nor for that matter were any of those incidents ever suspected as being criminal acts. Hull in those days was a very poor area, and living conditions were less than perfect. Many homes used open fireplaces. Furnishings and furniture were cheap and easily combustible, and few residences had any sort of fire alarms or warning systems. Smoking inside was very acceptable, and house fires were a fairly common occurrence. Most were considered to be accidents. Arson was never a consideration until Lee's final fire.

In 1981, Lee eventually struck a plea bargain in that case and was convicted on twenty-six counts of manslaughter based on "diminished responsibility." He also admitted during that plea to eleven counts of arson. Lee was sentenced to an indefinite period of incarceration at a maximum security mental hospital for those crimes. He remains there until this day.

Investigator Analysis

Bruce George Peter Lee is an anomaly in the world of serial arsonists. He is at the very high end of the danger spectrum and is truly a unique character. While serial arson is a rare crime, those that do it seldom target structures. Of those few rare ones who target structures, few if any target structures that are occupied. The rarest of the rare actually enter the occupied structure to commit the act. This alone makes Lee probably the most unique and dangerous known arsonist in history.

Lee has a mixed motive as do many arson offenders. His motive appears to be a mixture of revenge and excitement. He wanted revenge from a society that had scorned and ridiculed him all of his pathetic life. He was indeed dealt a bad hand in life and grew up resembling the crippled Kevin Spacey character in *The Usual Suspects*. By his own admission, he became excited by fire or at least the power of terror that it gave him.

Like most serial offenders, Lee's *modus operandi* (MO) appears to have evolved in sophistication as he grew older. He started out by breaking windows and forcing entry into homes, while he openly carried marked containers of petrol and paraffin. There is no doubt over the years that he was noticed or stopped for carrying that obvious evidence, and he later resorted to carrying the paraffin secreted in a squirt bottle in his clothing. Additionally, it is probably reasonable to speculate that his choice of fuel, paraffin, was learned over the years to be less volatile than petrol (gasoline) and safer to use. I am quite sure that he probably burned himself a time or two with the petrol. His method of delivery also developed as his later fires were less risky and involved him squirting the fuel through the mail slots as opposed to actually entering the home.

Like most serial arsonists, Lee traveled by foot or bike and capered in areas where he felt familiar and comfortable. He was able to blend quickly into a crowd after starting the fire and aroused no suspicion from neighbors.

Of note in this case is the fact that Lee had an adversarial connection to many of his victims. Oddly though, like Lee, many of the victims suffered some sort of handicap or disability. It is unknown if this aspect had any influence on Lee's target selection. The sentencing judge noted that every one of Lee's murder victims was hampered in their ability to escape the fires by their age (young or elderly), physical disabilities, or the fact that they were asleep. Some observers opined that Lee may have been targeting persons who were disabled like him.

The final analysis of these events is only too common in the world of arson investigation. Almost every fire that Lee was suspected of lighting was classified as a "misadventure" (accident of some sort). In only one fire was arson suspected. Therein lies the main problem with catching a serial arsonist. Investigators seldom realize that a crime has even occurred. Lee seemed to revel in the information that he had fooled the firemen. He made several comments during his interrogations that the fire service personnel never recognized his fires as criminal events. The investigating officer noted that Lee seemed pleased about that.

As readers will note in some of the following serial arson cases, Lee's claims were met with great skepticism and disbelief by local fire administrators. In fact, for seven years after he pled guilty, there were commissions and court hearings suggesting great disbelief by community leaders and politicians that a disabled young boy of low intelligence could have set all those murderous fires without ever having been detected. The lead criminal investigator in the matter was accused for years of fabricating the evidence and falsifying Lee's confessions. Finally, eight years after Lee's final fire, the courts and public were satisfied by a detailed hearing that Lee's claims and confessions were factual, despite the former fire chief's insistence to the contrary. What was made clear during that period was that there was not an effective investigative procedure in place that coordinated investigative efforts between the fire and police services. This lack of coordination caused events like those to slip through the cracks between the two disciplines. Readers of this book will find that this situation is not unique to Hull.

Lee also was aware of how dangerous certain fuels could be. He claimed to have learned through his fire setting that paraffin was safer than petrol (gasoline) and would start the fire slower, giving him a chance to safely escape. He learned how to properly spray the liquid in a manner that would give him a short bit of delay time in which to safely steal away.

Lee was a loner most of his life with no family to rely upon. Like many of the worst offenders in this book, Lee spent part of his youth in one institution or another. He was never married, nor did he have close friends. Lee worked an odd variety of unskilled jobs.

Lee is a disorganized offender, who as he matured developed a safer and more organized manner of ignition. However, he remains in the disorganized arena as his target selection is somewhat random and his activities remained impulsive and reckless.

Lee lit thirty known fires and killed twenty-six persons as a result of his attacks. He is one of the few serial arsonists who actually intended to commit murder while setting his fires. It is likely that he lit hundreds more fires of a lesser nature in his lifetime. His years long death toll makes him the most dangerous serial arsonist ever identified.

John Leonard Orr (Glendale Fire Department, Captain/ Arson Investigator):Mass Murderer/Serial Arsonist Period of Activity: 1975-91, Southern California

John Orr is the most significant (known) serial arsonist in United States history. He earns this lofty title for many reasons, foremost being the fact that he was not only a firefighter arsonist, but was in fact a well-respected arson investigator. His story is akin to a big city homicide investigator becoming a serial murderer and then joining in the hunt to capture himself. John Orr was the stuff that movies are made of, and of course, since his crimes surrounded the Hollywood area, they did immortalize him on film more than once.

John Orr's notorious exploits are well documented in at least two books. One, *Fire Lover* by noted police writer Joseph Wambaugh, expertly details the intricacies of John Orr and the laborious investigations and court cases that took place around him. A second less professional but just as interesting book was *Points of Origin* written by John Orr himself before he knew he was a suspect in an arson/murder investigation. This book, according to the investigators and prosecutors who hounded him for years, is cited as a virtual confession by Orr of his psychotic serial fire setting activity.

Your author also has unique insight into this case study. Your author worked for twelve years alongside one of the lead investigators in the John Orr murder investigation, Det. Richard Edwards. Your author has also had numerous personal conversations with other investigators on this case, including lead ATF investigators, the local prosecuting district attorney on the arson/murder, two former partners, and a friend of John Orr. Some of the following information and analysis is derived from those conversations.

On October 10, 1984, a massive fire broke out in the Ole's Home Center business in South Pasadena, California. At about 8:00 p.m., the large store was open for business and there were numerous employees and customers scattered in the open warehouse. The fire started and spread so quickly that several people were trapped inside, with some barely making it out alive. In the aftermath of that event, two employees, seventeen-year-old Jimmy Cetina and Carolyn Krause, along with two customers, Ada Deal and her grandson Matthew William, were all dead. Among the many investigators, firemen, and law enforcement personnel who showed up at that scene was off duty Glendale Fire Department Investigator John Orr. In fact, he was observed, while the fire was still actively burning, to be wearing civilian clothes and snapping photos. (This author has viewed many of the original photos taken by John Orr at that fire scene.) After much debate and several differences of opinion, the lead investigator responsible for that scene called it an accident. Oddly, John Orr who volunteered to assist in the fire scene investigation adamantly insisted even after that that the incident was an incendiary act or arson. He also opined that an incendiary delay device had been used in that incident and at two other incidents in the immediate area that night.

Arson fires in businesses that are open are extremely rare events. The night of the "Ole's" fire, there were two other fires at nearby businesses. One occurred in a grocery store simultaneously and just blocks away from "Ole's." The other in another grocery store just a few miles away happened an hour before "Ole's" and originated in a rack full of potato chips. The local investigator on that scene knew that John Orr was the "most accomplished arson sleuth" in the area. He summoned Orr to his fire and noted that, despite being off duty and living in another city, Orr showed up very quickly. Orr then gave the local investigator a lengthy opinion on the high volatility of potato chips and their oils and asserted that that was most likely the work of an arsonist. Still, despite those additional two rare arson events happening in such close proximity, the "Ole's" fire remained classified as an "accident" for several more years.

A few days after the "Ole's" fire, a similar fire started in another large home supply store in nearby North Hollywood. This occurred in some poly foam materials within the store. The remains of an incendiary delay device were found at that event.

Two months later, still another fire occurred in another nearby "Ole's" store. This one was classified as arson after an incendiary delay device was found in the debris. This fire mostly failed, and the minimal damage revealed a cigarette wrapped in a rubber band holding three matches.

These events were not atypical in the Los Angeles basin during those years. For a four-year-period prior to the Ole's event, an increasing number of brushfires were occurring in the foothill region surrounding the cities of Glendale, Burbank, and Pasadena. John Orr, as the sole Glendale arson investigator, had stated several times to the media and to other investigators his belief that all of these fires were the work of the same serial arsonist. He proposed training and a joint effort into investigating these fires. As part of this large-scale arson investigation, several fire agencies had formed an ad hoc group called the Foothill Arson Task Force to combat that phenomenon. The Foothill Arson Task Force mainly comprised investigators from the smaller fire agencies in the Los Angeles area. They focused on the arson series in the cities of Glendale, Burbank, Pasadena, and other nearby communities. The most respected investigator among this group was John Orr, and he assumed a leadership role within the Foothill Arson Task Force. As part of his duties, he was able to gain access and monitor the progression of other fire and law enforcement agencies into the ongoing arson investigations. He had intimate knowledge of all of those brushfires and became aware of the emerging series of retail business fires.

John Leonard Orr was a different breed. In retrospect, most casual observers would say that he was obviously an arson suspect based on his behavior and background. A more experienced observer though will comment that his behavior was not that much different from thousands of other cops, firefighters, and the "wannabe" types that aspire to be them.

Born in 1949, Orr grew up in suburban Los Angeles. His mother left the family when he was sixteen, and Orr lived alone with his father. At some point, he decided he wanted to be a fireman. At eighteen, he joined the air force in hopes of avoiding Viet Nam and of getting experience to become a firefighter in Los Angeles. He eventually was assigned as a firefighter in the air force but led an uneventful life.

After his discharge at twenty-two years of age, he made several attempts to be a police officer or firefighter with various agencies in Los Angeles. A big disappointment for Orr at that time was when he was refused hiring by the Los Angeles Police Department on failing the psychological screening test. He was also denied employment by the large Los Angeles Sheriff's Department. Orr was later hired by the Los Angeles City Fire Department but flunked out of their academy for both academic and physical problems. By his own later admission, Orr was heartbroken over those failures. What was learned only years later at his trial was the reason for Orr failing the LAPD psych test. He was described in their evaluation as having a very passive and "schizoid" personality, who "may have sexual confusion in his orientation." His official but secret diagnosis at the time was "personality trait disturbance. Emotionally unstable personality."

John Orr has been described as a "serial marrier" with four marriages. His hobbies included camping, street racing in "muscle cars," and drinking in bars until late at night. He took up a series of jobs at fast food restaurants, including Kentucky Fried Chicken and a 7-Eleven store. He also began a career in writing.

Like nearly all organized serial arson offenders, John Orr was notable in his looks for his very ordinary appearance—not too old or young, not too tall or short, not handsome, not ugly, just ordinary. He was always soft and chubby appearing, but not overly fat. According to the investigators who knew him, he was also slightly effeminate in appearance and mannerisms.

In 1974, John Orr was finally accepted and hired by the Glendale, California, fire department, which at the time was one of the lowest paid agencies in Los Angeles. He began attending college in his off hours and studied criminal justice and police science topics. While working in the 7-Eleven off duty from the fire department, he began making dozens of "arrests" for shoplifting. He soon began making arrests and detentions of crooks and thieves while off work on his personal time. Several times he chased down and tackled thieves and other petty crooks for various crimes. He began seeking employment off duty as a security guard and was miffed that most stores only hired off duty policemen, not firemen. He eventually was hired by a Sears store and was their most productive security guard, arresting or detaining over fifty suspects in just his first few months. Despite these impressive arrest stats, Orr would become irritated when the local cops would roll their eyes and act annoyed every time he brought in a shoplifter. They snickered behind his back that he was an overzealous super cop in the mode of TV cop Barney Fife.

During this early period with the fire department and because of his security work, Orr sought and received permission to carry a concealed firearm. By that time, he began to hang out at "cop bars" and mimic the badge heavy swagger of local policemen. He was well known as a "cop wannabe" by both the police and fire departments in Glendale. He was thought of derisively by the local cops who referred to him as a one-man crime crusader or "Dirty Harry." He even went "undercover" to catch shoplifters and kids who pulled fire alarms.

Orr soon got tired of the boring firefighter duties and requested and got assignment to work at a fire patrol position. That was a job that let him go out by himself in a pickup truck to conduct fire prevention patrol. That job included brush abatement duties and looking for arsonists. Orr was notable in that position as he often did "stakeouts" for arsonists and was chastised several times for overaggressive enforcement of brush abatement issues.

One really crazy incident occurred when Orr, who was driving a bright yellow fire department pickup truck and carrying two pistols, started an unauthorized vehicle pursuit of two suspected burglars. That was followed by Orr chasing one of those men in a subsequent unauthorized foot pursuit. Never in great physical shape, Orr ended the chase by vomiting on the fallen suspect. Orr was always disheartened after those events as he never felt he got as much credit as he deserved. Instead, he usually got heckles and criticism from other firefighters and the police.

During that time period in the mid-1970s, a small arson series was occurring in Glendale. Two fires in that series were at a department store near the Sears where Orr worked as security. In one, the fire was set during business hours in a pile of boxes. Orr just happened to be passing by from his security job and helped the responding firemen fight the large fire for two hours. That series of fires was never solved. Years later, it would be linked in "signature" to John Orr's other fires.

By the early 1980s, a new series of fires was plaguing Glendale. An arsonist was setting fire to the brush-covered hillsides that surrounded the city. Other firefighters noted that Orr always responded to those scenes, even when off duty. It was noted several times that he was more zealous in his duties than any other employee. Orr told other firemen that he was "profiling" the scenes to "put himself in the arsonist's head." John impressed a battalion chief by actually finding a cigarette/matchbook delay device after a devastating brushfire.

The Glendale fire marshal decided at that point that the fire department needed a full-time arson investigator. Coincidentally, Orr was taking arson investigation courses at a nearby college. He eventually applied for and got the job as the department's arson investigator. He almost immediately began submitting written articles to various fire magazines for publication. Included in these submissions was an article discussing the mind-set of serial fire setters. Apparently, nobody at the time thought that that could be a bit heady of a subject for a brand-new arson investigator with very little experience or training.

During that time period, the city of Glendale appeared to have more arsons than any other jurisdiction. By 1984, John Orr had become heavily involved in the California Conference of Arson Investigators (CCAI) and actually sponsored and hosted training for many small agencies. He soon gained a strong local reputation among the investigators in neighboring agencies for his expertise in the investigation of brushfires. He frequently was able to "read" a fire scene and find incendiary delay devices after several other investigators had missed them. Because of that, he soon began responding to neighboring jurisdictions to assist in their brushfire problems. He also developed training courses in locating origins and ignition sources for brushfires.

A natural progression of his expertise led Orr to become very active in the CCAI training seminars, which were hosted twice a year in Northern or Central California. In 1987, Orr attended the January training seminar in Fresno, which is in the Central or San Joaquin Valley of California, about three hundred miles directly north of Los Angeles. During that three-day seminar of arson investigators, three arson fires occurred in open retail businesses on successive nights. Delay devices consisting of matches and a cigarette were found in two of the fires, and all three occurred in racks holding poly foam materials. On the last day of the conference, in the city of Tulare, which is about one hour south of Fresno, arson fires occurred in two retail businesses. The fires were again in racks of poly foam materials. A cigarette and matches delay device was found at one of the scenes. This time a suspect was described. A later investigation would show this description to be very close to John Orr.

A couple of hours after the Tulare fires, the most significant fire in this story occurred in Bakersfield, which was another hour south of Tulare. A fire broke out in a floral and craft store, and the local arson investigator was able to recover a fairly well-preserved incendiary device comprising a cigarette, some matches, and some yellow legal paper. Within minutes, that same investigator got called to another arson fire in a nearby fabric store in a bin of foam rubber. Witnesses described the same suspect as in the Tulare fire. The next day, investigators from the three jurisdictions compared notes and came to the conclusion that the same suspect had lit seven fires at similar retail businesses with the use of similar devices placed in bins of highly volatile materials. All of the fires had occurred along the same highway corridor, Route 99, which was the main road linking Fresno to Los Angeles. All of this occurred in the four-day period surrounding the arson investigator's training conference.

The Bakersfield fire investigator, Capt. Marv Casey, was able to get one quality fingerprint off the incendiary device and at that time started thinking that it was someone associated with the arson investigator's conference. No other investigators would agree with him at that point.

In March 1989, there was another CCAI conference, this time on the coast in Monterey, California. John Orr also attended that conference. Two days prior to the conference and two driving hours south in the town of Morro Bay, an arson fire erupted in a rack of poly foam pillows in a retail store. The next afternoon, the day prior to the conference, another arson fire started in a foam pillow display in a retail store in Salinas, just nineteen miles away from the conference.

The day following the end of the conference and two hours south of it in Atascadero, an arson fire broke out in some foam padding in a home improvement store. A cigarette/matches/yellow paper delay device was discovered in the aftermath. Two hours later in the same town, an arson fire erupted in some foam rubber in another retail store. Within the hour and slightly south, a third fire started in some poly foam material in a hardware store. Several hours later, a fourth fire occurred still further south in San Luis Obispo. This arson fire occurred in a retail party supply store that was packed with numerous employees and customers. Like the previous series in the Central Valley, all six of these retail store arson fires occurred during the dates surrounding an arson investigator's conference. All thirteen fires occurred along the only major highway connecting the conference sites to the Los Angeles area. John Orr was one of the ten people from the Los Angeles area who had attended both conferences.

The original fingerprint found in the Central Valley series was run through a California statewide database with negative matches.

By 1990, John Orr had been promoted to Captain and had begun writing a novel entitled *Points of Origin*. On June 27 of that year, with the temperature at over 110 degrees and the Santa Ana winds howling, the massive College Hills fire broke out in the Glendale foothills. This was the same area that had been experiencing the increasing arson problem over the previous six years. Coincidentally, John Orr had been the Glendale arson investigator for the same period of time. The fire seemed to have originated at numerous locations all at the same time. On that day, witnesses would later describe Orr's behavior as extremely erratic. He was found at the scene of several of the ignition points *before* the first fire engines had arrived. At one point, he directed an assisting investigator to the origin and showed him an incendiary device he had found. It was a butane lighter modified to remain lit. This assisting investigator was extremely impressed how Orr was able to find that small item in hundreds of acres of burned grass and brush within just minutes of the fire starting. A witness to the scene later gave a police detective a description of a possible arsonist that closely matched John Orr.

The College Hills fire was the largest in Glendale's history with the destruction of sixty-seven homes, and John Orr, who was notorious for his rabid work in following up other arsons, spent almost no time trying to solve this case. By all accounts, he fairly well kissed it off.

From late 1990 to early 1991, the Los Angeles basin was hit with a new wave of arson fires in open retail businesses. This arson series had some odd quirks. In the City of Los Angeles, the Hollywood, and San Fernando Valley areas, the Los Angeles City Fire Department (LAFD) was examining a series of fires in grocery, fabric, and convenience stores centered among display racks of potato chips. This unknown arson suspect was given the name "potato chip arsonist." Still, in other parts of Los Angeles and in several South Bay cities, a suspect was lighting fires in fabric stores among racks of poly foam materials. The Los Angeles Sheriff's Department (LASD) and LAFD were conducting a joint investigation into an unknown subject dubbed the "pillow pyro arsonist." All of these fires were occurring in open retail businesses in the late afternoon or early evening hours. During two of those investigations, detectives were able to locate an incendiary delay device constructed of a Marlboro cigarette, a small piece of yellow legal paper, and three paper matches, all wrapped together with a rubber band. This fairly sophisticated device would give up to fifteen minutes of delay time for the arsonist once the cigarette was lit. This device was a virtual clone of the device found three years earlier in Bakersfield.

By April 1991, the ATF had gotten involved and was beginning to follow old leads. Among them, they took the Bakersfield fingerprint and brought it to the more modern sheriff's lab in Los Angeles. The lab analysis matched the latent print to John Orr's LAPD application prints from twenty years prior. Over the next few months, agents showed Orr's photo to numerous witnesses at fire scenes. Several of the witnesses were able to identify him as being at their business prior to the fire.

By mid-1991, investigators had obtained a copy of Orr's novel and recognized it as a literal diary of the fires they were investigating. Soon, another brief spate of arson fires linked to John Orr occurred in the fall of 1991. These included the College Hills fire and an arson fire at Burbank Studios. By that time, John Orr had been deemed a suspect in at least five different arson series. He was considered the prime suspect in the "Potato Chip Arsons" in Los Angeles, the "Pillow Pyro Arsons" in the South Bay and San Gabriel Valley, the "Highway 99 Arsonist," the "Highway 101 Arsonist," and the "Foothill Brushfires Arsonist."

John Leonard Orr was eventually arrested and charged with numerous arson fires. Upon his arrest, investigators located police badges, incendiary delay devices, and dozens of photos of some of the fire scenes under investigation in that case. He also had video footage of several of the scenes prior to fire engines arriving. Orr denied committing any crime and refused to speak to the federal investigators.

In July 1992, after a jury trial, John Orr was convicted in the federal court for three of the Central Valley arsons of 1987. In 1993, he pled guilty in the federal court in a plea bargain agreement to arson fires in the 1989 series on the Highway 101 corridor and to fires in businesses in the City of Los Angeles and the South Bay. He was sentenced to several years in the federal prison.

In 1998, John Orr went on trial in the state court for the College Hills fire, Burbank Studios fire, and the Ole's arson murder of 1984. That case was reopened and reclassified as arson ten years after the event. On June 26, 1998, Orr was convicted of four counts of murder in the first degree for the "Ole's" fire and was also convicted of the College Hills fire. He was acquitted of the other incidents. John Leonard Orr was sentenced to four life sentences without the possibility of parole.

The aftermath of this case was devastating to the firefighting community. Even after being convicted of fires from several different series, with those convictions representing *hundreds* of non-tried fires, many firefighters and some fire investigators still feel that John Orr was not a bad guy.

The investigators who took him to his final trial revealed some compelling statistics. In the years he was an arson investigator in the foothill region, the area averaged sixty-seven brush arson fires per season. In the years after his incarceration, the same area averaged one brush arson fire each year. Likewise, there are similar statistics in the Los Angeles basin for arson fires occurring in retail stores during business hours. Those same investigators have the strong opinion that John Leonard Orr was responsible for 1,200 to 2,500 arson fires over his lifetime.

Investigator Analysis

John Leonard Orr truly is the most unique serial arsonist ever identified. He is first and foremost a rare breed in that he is one of the few organized serial offenders on this list. To that extent, he fulfilled nearly every aspect of the FBI's Behavior Analysis Unit's list of traits of an organized serial arsonist. He was highly mobile and spread his crime wave through dozens of jurisdictions over a four-hundred-mile distance. He scouted and preselected his targets, and he pre-selected and pre-built his unique incendiary delay devices. The investigation also showed the startling fact that Orr would photograph some of his targets one year and then torch the area a year or two later. He selected his fuels based on his knowledge of how fast they would spread the fire. He took dangerous risks to physically enter arson targets and expose himself to countless numbers of witnesses. He was extremely ordinary in appearance and was able to commit hundreds of crimes without suspicion. He was believed to have used disguises and posed as either a police detective or press photographer on several occasions. He was extremely cunning and was able to interact among the very investigators who were seeking him. He had a conscious indifference to society and set fires with the intent of causing massive damage and at considerable risk to human lives. He continued to set those tremendously dangerous fires for years even after at least one of his fires (Ole's) caused the deaths of four people. To this day, he has never acknowledged his crimes or shown any remorse for the deaths and damage he caused. John Orr was a heavy user of alcohol, but many of his fires were set when he was presumably sober and on duty. One of the more unique aspects of Orr that defies most arson profiles is that his fire setting activities were not nocturnal. Most of his known fires occurred in broad daylight, in large metropolitan areas, or in busy retail businesses,

While this author is by no means a psychiatrist, John Orr presents a veritable cornucopia of theories for armchair shrinks to discuss. He was obviously picked out early in life by LAPD psychologists as having a schizoid personality. For possibly the same reason, he was turned down for employment by other police agencies. However, for the entire time he was employed as a fireman, he kept requesting assignment to more police-oriented duties. He sought the right to carry firearms and drive police-looking vehicles. He referred to himself as a detective rather than as an investigator as most fire investigators go by. He carried multiple large or exotic handguns with him and frequently engaged in dangerous or unauthorized off duty police-type activity. He routinely and over aggressively enforced minor laws and zealously pursued petty offenders. Upon his arrest, he was carrying both a firefighter's badge and a home-made but similar police detective badge. He was over-the-top macho in his appearance and mannerisms, drank heavily at cop bars, drove his car everywhere at dangerous and excessive speeds, and responded to fire scenes even on his day off. He was the ultimate form of the police "wannabe."

Another, even darker aspect of John Orr arose after his arrest. Task force detectives following up on his bizarre activities began to suspect he may have been involved in at least one rape/murder. It was learned that many street prostitutes recognized photos of Orr, and he had identified himself to them as an undercover vice detective from Los Angeles. Serious investigative attempts by more than one detective in the area attempted to link Orr to missing or murdered prostitutes. No cases were ever connected to him.

John Orr wrote a book that was basically about him catching himself or at least his two alter egos taunting and chasing each other. His book is a fascinating study of bad, breathless, and lurid descriptions of a hardened detective wearing mirrored shades, speeding down dirty alleys in a "souped-up" muscle car, carrying massive .45 caliber automatics, catching bad guys, downing whiskey, and bedding highly impressed busty broads. He obviously spent a lot of hours fascinated by 1940s detective noir. Based on my conversations with those who knew, drank, and worked with him, he actually fancied himself in that very context.

Orr also appears to possibly be dealing with sexual identity issues. Indeed, one of the original investigators on the case learned through interviews that John Orr was linked, at least anecdotally to a group of firefighters from various agencies in wife swapping and possibly homosexual group activities at a large park in Los Angeles. Orr was married four times and was a serial philanderer even by his own admission.

Orr is obviously a frustrated cop "wannabe" and fits into a group of literally thousands of others in the same field. In this vein, he can be classified as a vanity or hero arsonist. He committed those crimes to bring much wanted attention to himself and further his reputation as an arson expert. Indeed, a check of the archives for the *Los Angeles Times* newspaper from that era shows numerous stories written about arson activity in the Glendale area, with detailed quotes from "Lead Investigator John Orr." He routinely called reporters and gave them information on cases he was working on, including what was generally considered confidential details about the evidence found at the scene. That was quite different from the norm in the arson and homicide investigation world where the vast majority of professional investigators are quite mum about the facts and details of their cases. Orr was clearly eager to share his "inside information" with the media.

From the investigator standpoint, vanity arsons occur more frequently than most people realize. A case in point was the massive Universal Studios fire which occurred in Los Angeles in 1993, where a security guard lit a fire for the purpose of putting it out and reporting it to his supervisor. That was not the first time that the guard lit a fire for that purpose, but in that case the fire got too large and eventually consumed almost the entire back lot of the studios, causing nearly fifty million dollars in damage. There are dozens of similar examples of vanity fires by security guards, police officers, forest rangers, wardens, military personnel, ambulance drivers, tow truck drivers, arson watch volunteers, and just about any other profession that is involved with or dabbles in the emergency responder field. Quite often, many of these offenders who have lit multiple fires have come from the ranks of volunteers, reserves, cadets, explorers, or other part-time or newer employees.

Within this group is the touchiest subject of them all—the firefighter arsonist. Just a brief Internet search will show the most ardent defender of the fire service that this is not a rare problem, nor is it a new problem. There are hundreds of cases of firefighter arsons and firefighter serial arsons dating back nearly a century. It should be pointed out that these numbers are minuscule compared to the number of firefighters who actually work in the United States. But let's not forget the fact that investigators probably identify and apprehend only about 10 percent of the offenders in the arson field. This would indicate that the number of firefighter arsons and serial arson is most likely still a relatively small number, but probably much higher than is actually known.

John Orr is of course the extreme example of the firefighter arsonist. However, his case does differ from the "norm" in even this small genre. In most of the known cases of firefighter arson, the offender is fairly young or a newer member of the unit. The offender is often a part-time volunteer, or a "call" firefighter, and in most cases not a full-time professional firefighter. The offender most often uses available items at the scene to commit his offense and usually picks random targets. The offender almost always uses an open flame (match or lighter) to effect a "hot set" of his target. The offender almost always strikes at night and usually in the area where he works.

John Orr's motives, like everything else about his case, appear to be unique to him. An argument can be made that John Orr lit the brushfires in his area early on for the sole purpose of showing his city that it needed a full-time arson investigator, namely him. That would give him a financial incentive for his arsons. As his fires continued, Orr began gravitating toward businesses. One could argue that he was a thrill seeker in that he physically entered his targets in full view of witnesses to commit his crimes. This would point to an excitement motive. Based on his psychological history and anecdotal accounts of his sex life, some argument could be made that he was one of the very rare sexual offender arsonists. But probably, his main motive is very clear. He was never allowed to be what he really wanted—a police detective, so he set his fires for the purpose of creating a huge event into which he would then insert himself as a hero and expert in the field of fire investigation. By many accounts, John Orr was not shy of cameras or publicity and was frequently fond of making statements to the press. His foremost motive was probably closer to the vanity/hero motive than any other one.

A final interesting observation about Orr's motives came to me when I was looking at the photos he took the night he responded off duty to the Ole's fire. The "expert" investigator failed to follow the basic rules of investigation that he taught other investigators. His scene photos from that night don't show shots of the building as a whole or what section of the building the fire was in or, even more important to an investigator, crowd photos in hopes of capturing the arsonist. Orr's photos were mostly of firefighters pulling hoses off trucks, entering the structure, and putting water on flames. He took many photos of fire equipment and firemen in action, but almost none of the scene. This would tend to show Orr's desire to capture the excitement of the event and not to be concerned with the investigative aspects of the event. After reviewing his entire case history, I am convinced that Orr never learned to be a good investigator and probably solved very few cases other than the ones he set.

In this most unique of all cases, probably one of the more peculiar effects of Orr's actions is the way his crimes have tainted the fire investigation field. If the truth be told in investigative circles, many investigators have grown to suspect firefighters or even other investigators in any odd rash of arson fires, particularly in wild land fire cases. This author has a unique perspective in that I joined the arson investigation field just as John Orr was being convicted of his arson/murder case. After attending hundreds of hours of arson investigation training since, I have noted that every class regarding the *modus operandi* of arsonists and serial arsonists stresses heavily upon the use of delay incendiary devices by these offenders. Hours of training time are spent creating and employing the "most common delay incendiary devices." But studies have shown, along with dozens of local case histories, that the documented use of incendiary delay devices is almost non-existent in serial arson cases.

John Orr, through his training efforts and by his actions, was able to convince an entire generation of fire investigators that delay incendiary devices are in fact the norm. The data and case history reviews strongly suggest otherwise. In fact, while John Orr had impressed others with his expertise on serial arson offenders, he appears to be wrong on many accounts. It is this investigator's opinion that Orr transformed himself into the serial offender he may have seen in a bad Hollywood movie or read in a lurid crime novel as a kid. In the end, because everything he did defied the norms for a serial arsonist, John Orr was probably only an expert on himself.

For those of you looking for his redeeming values or that maybe he was a good guy who "cracked under the pressure," please remember that John Orr has never expressed any remorse for his fires or the victims. He appears to have lit fires from the day he started as a firefighter. He has scoffed at the investigators who tracked him down and continued his dangerous fire setting activities for years after he killed people in the Ole's fire. He appears extremely narcissistic with little empathy for any others.

John Orr is classified as an organized offender based on his intelligence and cunning, his use of exotic delay ignition devices, pre-selection of targets for maximum destruction and effect, and his ability to carry out his attacks for years undetected. He is believed to have lit over twelve hundred arson fires and killed at least four persons during his attacks. Some detectives who worked on his case believe his arson total to exceed twenty-five hundred.

Thomas Sweatt "D.C. Serial Arsonist": Murderer/Serial Arsonist
Period of Activity: 1980-2005, Washington, D.C.

Another popular misconception of a serial arsonist is that they are all sexual offenders. This is probably the rarest offender of them all. However, some arsonists do have a sexual motive behind their fire setting. Thomas Sweatt is one of these very rare birds.

On a cold January night in 1985, in the northeast area of Washington, D.C., a chance encounter between two thirty-year-old black men who passed each other on the sidewalk led to a major house fire and the death of a mother in the flames. Thomas Sweatt was walking home from work late at night and spotted what he considered to be an attractive man passing him on the sidewalk. After they passed, Sweatt turned and began to surreptitiously follow the man who eventually walked to his nearby home and went inside. Sweatt was smitten with that man and just had to see him again soon. Sweatt would later write down his thoughts of that night. He knew he had to see the man at least one more time, "but the only way would be through fire."

Thomas Sweatt was excited and rushed to his own apartment. He changed clothes and then gathered the makings of a crude incendiary device. Late that same night, Sweatt drove his car back to the man's home, poured gasoline under the front door, and then placed a towel at the base to hold the gasoline inside. He ignited the gasoline with a match and stood back as flames and smoke soon began to seep out of the top of the door.

Sweatt then got back into his car and circled the block. His hopes were realized when he returned to the home and found the object of his desire standing on the front porch in his underwear as the home was furiously burning. Sweatt couldn't tell at the time, but the man was in shock from severe burn injuries. As Sweatt was debating whether to jump out and "save" the man and his screaming family, he heard the sound of approaching fire engines and decided to flee the scene. What Sweatt found out the next morning was that several family members were injured in the large fire and the mother, Bessie Mae Duncan, died due to fire and asphyxiation. This wasn't Sweatt's first fire, but it was his first murder. The funeral for Miss Duncan occurred on a rainy day. It is doubtful any of the mourners paid much attention to the solitary thirty-year-old Thomas Sweatt who stood outside of the funeral home in the rain that day to view the proceedings. Sweatt did not see the man who he had followed home that night, when he was at the funeral parlor. During the funeral, the deceased woman's husband, thirty-year-old Roy Picott was fighting for his own life in a hospital, trying to recover from the serious burn injuries of the fire. He would lose that fight two months later when he finally succumbed to his injuries.

An investigation of the fire scene ensued, and the investigators wrongly concluded that the fire was related to a carelessly discarded cigarette in a back bedroom in the upper story of the home. The case was classified as an "accident" and closed. Family members would always be puzzled by the ruling as they knew that no one smoked cigarettes inside the home. Twenty years later, an arson task force comprising ATF agents and local investigators would reopen this case and positively clear and solve this latent arson and double murder. This followed the arrest of Thomas Sweatt for a series of arson fires and his startling confessions and descriptions of his lifelong fire setting behavior.

Thomas Sweatt would later describe much of his adult life to the investigators who had arrested him. He also gave a detailed account of many of his fires to a reporter in Washington, DC, after his arrest and conviction. This account was described in a series of letters between the two, which was later published by the reporter, Dave Jamieson. This author has met with the two lead investigators on the case and gleaned some of this material from them. ATF Special Agent Scott Fulkerson and Fire Investigator Bob Luckett were two of the lead investigators on the "DC Serial Arson Task Force," and both spent many hours conducting detailed interviews with Sweatt.

Thomas Sweatt was raised in a large, loving, and fairly normal family in the South. Unlike many other arsonists, he regularly attended church all of his life and maintained close family contacts until his arrest. However, by his own admission, he knew from a very young age that he had several bizarre obsessions. While his brothers were fascinated with toy cars and sports, he was more interested in dolls and playing "dress up" in feminine clothing. By his early teen years, he was a compulsive masturbator and would remain that way for the rest of his life, often masturbating more than a dozen times a day. He developed an extreme sexual obsession for odd items, including men's shoes, men's clothing, military and police uniforms, and locations where men frequented, like barbershops. He soon recognized that he was gay and spent the majority of his time trying to find a way to be around places where men would congregate.

Thomas Sweatt remained off the arrest records for most of his life, save for a grand theft arrest for stealing jewelry from a man he had picked up on the street. The case was never prosecuted, and Sweatt continued to operate well below the radar of the police.

Sweatt was fascinated by anything military and attempted to join the navy when he was about twenty-one years old. He was turned down after a physical and later admitted that it had disheartened him for years. Later, he confided that his lifelong career obsession was to be a United States Marine. Hardly the marine type, Sweatt was always described as being very meek, polite, soft, pudgy, who spoke with a very soft voice. He later stated that he liked all men in uniform, but was not very fond of police officers. He felt that they were nice to look at, but that they made fun of his soft voice and effeminate qualities. Among his other obsessions, Sweatt fantasized regularly about bus drivers and men wearing uniforms and shiny black shoes.

By the 1980s, Thomas Sweatt had relocated to the Washington, DC, area and had started his lifelong employment in fast food restaurants. For several years, he had no car and frequently walked the streets of that rough black neighborhood. He had few long-term relationships, but occasionally picked up men off the streets or from gay bars. His favorite areas to hang out were among the military clubs near large installations.

Thomas Sweatt worked many hours in various chicken restaurants and was highly regarded as a good cook and hard worker who kept his work area spotless. His fastidiousness and hard work was noticed immediately, and he began to climb the ladder in this industry. After several years, he became a highly regarded manager of a Kentucky Fried Chicken restaurant. Sweatt would later say that despite his stellar job performance, he never liked working in the fast food industry and was constantly reminded by family members that it was a failure as a career. Sweatt hated the stress and headaches the job caused him.

In his off hours, Sweatt and his sister had a side business where the two would renovate and furnish homes and vacant apartments. He was known as having a very good eye for detail and a high sense of fashion and decorating ability. He was also highly skilled in light construction and renovation work.

But in the few hours when he wasn't working, Thomas Sweatt had another, much darker obsession. As soon as he settled into his neighborhood, the area became heavily involved in arson activity. Sweatt began setting fires to various items for different reasons. If he didn't like the way an old car or building looked, he burned it. If he was mad at someone for some perceived slight, he burned their car or business. If he coveted a vehicle or nice house, he burned that. If he desired a man, he burned his car or office to attract his attention. Thomas Sweatt used fire as his means of connecting with people or venting his anger at someone.

Sweatt torched the garage behind his apartment, homes, and businesses in the area, and even torched a barbershop after a bad haircut. After the barbershop was rebuilt, he noted transients and drug addicts loitering around it, so torched it again. Thomas Sweatt claimed to have lit dozens of fires on the east side of DC throughout the late 1980s and early 1990s and was surprised that he was never suspected as an arsonist. During that same decade, the arson squads in the area were investigating about two hundred structure arsons per year. After Sweatt's arrest in 2005, the same area would average about sixty-five structure arsons per year. A later analysis of the spatial relation of these fires would show that they clustered heavily in the areas around Sweatt's home and work sites.

During those nighttime forays, Thomas Sweatt began to use various forms of a crude incendiary device. He often used light plastic gallon containers (usually milk, water, or juice jugs), which he filled with gasoline. He used a piece of cloth or towel at the top to use as a wicking material. He then lit the wick or poured the gas at the scene.

Thomas Sweatt was also involved in high-risk voyeurism. His fetish for the military in general and marines in particular caused him to carry out bizarre surveillances and nighttime raids. He often parked outside marine recruiter's offices and filmed the young, fit recruiters in their crisp tan uniforms with blue pants. He masturbated in his car and later again when he would watch the film. He broke into recruiters' cars and stole any items of uniform or paraphernalia he could find. He would then order additional military items from a catalog at home and would dress up as a marine in his apartment, marching around and masturbating furiously. He later claimed to have set fire to several recruiting offices in the DC area.

Sweatt was also heavily involved in another form of masochistic voyeurism. After detectives found some bizarre tapes in his home, Sweatt explained their meaning. Sweatt would often call a local marine recruitment office and ask for a recruiter to come and speak to "my nephew" about joining the Corps. Invariably, a young, muscular black marine recruiter would show up at Sweatt's door wearing his distinctive uniform. Sweatt would then explain that "my nephew" wasn't home from work yet, but would the recruiter please sit down and wait. At some point, Sweatt would sit close to the recruiter and often reach over and fondle the shocked man. In many cases, the recruiter's predictable reaction would be to jump up, beat the hell out of Sweatt, and then flee out the door. Sweatt would clandestinely video the entire event and, despite the beating he often took, would replay it later many times for sexual gratification. Sweatt would later tell the investigators that these moments captured on tape were some of his favorite possessions.

Another extremely bizarre ritual that Sweatt practiced would be to lay out an entire marine uniform on his bed and then literally attempt to have intercourse with the flat uniform, frequently ejaculating on the dress blue pants. Sweatt confided that he often ejaculated onto uniforms and into military-style shoes.

A true firefighter aficionado, Sweatt would often call in false fire alarms just to see the trucks arrive so that he could film them. He lingered around or returned to the scenes of several of his arsons and filmed the firefighting activity so that he could later masturbate to it.

His feelings were not the same toward cops as he felt their badges, guns, and squad cars represented the power that he didn't have. He wanted to capture that power, so he claimed to have lit dozens of police cars around the city. Sweatt later said that he felt extremely powerful after he had torched a police cruiser.

Sweatt also had a deep sexual obsession for members of the Metropolitan Transit Authority or bus drivers. He was aroused by their dark blue uniforms and shiny black shoes. He often stalked the younger, more athletic black male drivers and filmed them as they arrived for work. Once they had entered their buses and driven away, he placed his incendiary devices under their personal cars. He told investigators that he got much more of a sexual thrill out of that if the cars were sporty and sexy. A victim of one of these fires was found years later and confirmed to investigators that he and several coworkers all had their cars torched in the parking lot near their work site. A local liquor store owner was also contacted, who confirmed that he had witnessed dozens of burned cars over the years in a lot near his store, which was used by bus drivers.

Sweatt went on to ignite hundreds more fires that were never connected to him until he confessed to them. Among his targets was the house of one of his boyfriends. Sweatt's explanation for the fire was that he was so obsessed with the young, athletic man that he decided to burn his home.

Years later, a reporter would send Sweatt photos of homes that he had allegedly burned. Sweatt had an amazing recall for the specifics about each home and yard and gave the reporter reasons why he burned specific structures. In many cases, he had passed the home and saw a muscular, young black man in the yard. Other times, he saw a well-kept classic or sports car and just knew that a mechanically minded man lived there, so he burned the home hoping to see the man emerge. On other occasions, the very yard or style of home piqued his interest. He favored burning wood or aluminum exterior homes as opposed to brick as they made a much larger fire and caused more excitement.

In 2001, Sweatt purchased a used car and began using it to extend his arson activity beyond his home and work areas. One night, he placed one of his incendiary devices in a partially constructed apartment complex, burning the entire million-dollar site to the ground. Sweatt later stated he was very pleased with that massive fire and was surprised that it was classified as an "accident" by fire authorities.

By the early 2000s, Sweatt had developed a fairly consistent method of operation or signature to his fires. He would go out at times without a specific target in mind, but with the knowledge that he was going to ignite something. Once he had decided on a target, he scouted and stalked it for a short period and then would employ his device at a late nighttime period, usually after the residents had gone to sleep.

Sweatt began to fine-tune his incendiary device and his method of employment. He evolved into using the plastic gallon jug, filled with gasoline and placed in a plastic grocery-style bag for discreet carrying. In most cases, he used a piece of his own clothes as a wick. Sweatt would usually approach a target home and place the device on the wooden porch area or at the back door. He frequently sat or lingered on the porch for many minutes fantasizing about the impending fire and excitement. After he ignited his device, he would return to his car and watch the fire grow from a distance. Sometimes he would circle the block. Sweatt liked to wait around for the fire trucks and often filmed their activity. The next day, he scanned the newspapers for a report on the incident and usually cut out the article to save. He would then record the event in his diary.

In 2003, a chance meeting and idle conversation between two fire investigators would start the downfall of Thomas Sweatt. The investigators were from neighboring jurisdictions and were swapping stories about odd fire series in their respective jurisdiction. Both soon realized that they were talking about identical fire series. They soon compared notes and found that they had several fires with a similar MO. The fires all occurred late at night, on the porches or at the doors of occupied homes. The investigators linked up with the ATF and their lab and got positive confirmation that an identical incendiary device was found at four of the fire scenes. Additionally, they found fifteen other recent fires that fit the exact same pattern. With this confirmation, the "Metro DC Arson Task Force" was formed in July 2003 to investigate these fires.

After plotting the fires on a map, the investigators noticed two patterns that were widely apart. The spatial or geographic profiling was not much help at first, but would later prove very compelling. A look at the victims showed that they had no relation to each other and had no factors before the fires that would point to them as victims. The victims and target selection appeared to be totally random.

The task force's first real description of the arsonist would come in September 2003, when a black male was seen sitting on a victim's porch at 3:00 a.m. He was confronted, and he mumbled that he was lost. After he left, the victim found the unburned incendiary device he had left, and the lab was able to get a DNA sample off a human hair found in the bag with the device. They also had a vague description of the arsonist. That fire event failed, but the device matched the four others at the lab. An FBI/ATF psychological profiler would opine that the suspect was most likely "lonesome, anxiety-ridden, and hobbled by a deep sense of failure." After his arrest, Sweatt would confirm that to be a pretty accurate profile of him.

As the task force began to plow forward with its leads, the senior members opted to announce their activities in the media via frequent press conferences.

Like all similar entities, its spokesman implored the arsonist to give up before more people were hurt. Of course, Sweatt, who rabidly monitored everything to do with the hunt for the arsonist, loved the power he was feeling. What the task force members soon find out was that Sweatt had already killed with his fires and on more than one occasion.

The task force started to look at past fires that matched the current series they were investigating. The found a structure fire that occurred in June 2003, which had killed eighty-six-year-old Lou Edna Jones. A review of that fire proved it to match their series, and at that point, the task force knew they had a murder case on their hands. Sweatt would later recall the fire in a letter to a reporter. He said he was drawn to the home because he had seen a young, muscular, and handsome black male retrieving mail from the mailbox. Later that night, he returned with his incendiary device and just sat on the porch for over thirty minutes contemplating the upcoming fire. He said he hoped to see the young male jump out of a window from the burning home and run into his arms for help. Sweatt finally lit the fire at around 4:30 a.m. and was extremely pleased and excited to see how large it got. He said he was saddened by the death of Ms. Jones but still recalled the fire very fondly.

Upon his arrest, Thomas Sweatt confided in investigators that he had maintained a massive video library of many of his voyeuristic events and had kept a detailed diary of many of his fires. He said he always followed the press coverage of one of his fires and was delighted to learn that an arson task force had been formed in 2003. He said he knew by sight and by name all of the task force leaders and loved to watch them in their uniforms and medals as they gave frequent press conferences and updates. Sweatt said that in the weeks prior to his arrest, he was contacted by detectives on the task force, and he destroyed his diary out of fear of discovery. He later told a reporter that he still had a written record of many of his fires hidden away.

As the months wore on, Sweatt enjoyed the attention of the task force. He followed them in the media and saw them several times on the street. At its peak, the task force had over fifty-five investigators combing the neighborhoods most affected by fire. Soon Sweatt began to really push his luck and go into areas where he knew the task force could be lurking. In October 2003, he lit another home on fire within just a few blocks of a stakeout team. They later learned that they had missed Sweatt by mere seconds as he fled the area before they could close all the streets. Sweatt also noted that task force agents had started staking out convenience stores near his work and even came into his restaurant for a meal. He made sure that he spoke to them and walked very close to them.

By November 2003, Sweatt began to expand his fires out of the DC area and into Northern Virginia. One of his devices was found at a house fire in that area. Soon the task force began to examine fires in all neighboring jurisdictions. Sweatt later admitted that he was toying with investigators and trying to throw them off the trail in DC. His vehicle was filmed at a fire in Virginia as it was flashing its lights at a passing fire truck. Although the image was never made very clear, Sweatt later confirmed that he had been taunting the firemen as they went to put out one of his fires.

By early 2004, Sweatt had lit a few more homes on fire. In February, he lit a fire in the stairway inside an apartment building, nearly trapping several people inside. His actions were getting more dangerous and occurring at an increasing frequency. This particular fire, however, left Sweatt's DNA on the cloth wick. Investigators could scientifically link many of the fires, but they still had no suspect.

Soon leads began to dry up, and the frequency of the fires abated somewhat. The task force did not hear from the "DC Serial Arsonist" for several months. The task force started using really innovative and exotic techniques to identify the source of the materials in the devices. They were able to confirm that the bags that held the devices were only sold at a certain type of convenience store in the DC area, and they began a program to try and track the bags. They visited and staked out many of those stores and later learned that one store in particular that they staked out shared the parking lot of Sweatt's KFC restaurant.

In December 2004, Sweatt's own gamesmanship and attempt to be clever finally gave investigators a clue they could use. Sweatt, in a further attempt to throw off the task force, again drove down into Virginia and lit a home on fire in Arlington. At that scene, he planted some evidence as a "red herring." He left a Marine Corps cap and pants near the fire scene. DNA was found on the pants matching the DC arsonist, and the task force then approached the Marines to find out if they had an arsonist in their rolls. The Marines had no active clues to arsonists within their ranks and had no database for DNA of their personnel. However, as a by-product of the meeting with the Marine investigators, the task force learned that the USMC did have a good lead on a male who had been identified as a suspect in some arson fires to vehicles outside of a barrack. The suspect had been identified by his vehicle plate. That plate was registered to Thomas Sweatt. Even better, Thomas Sweatt lived right around the corner from one particular convenience store that the task force had identified as being linked to their arsonist!

Task force investigators then went to the KFC to interview Sweatt. He denied involvement in any arsons, but for some reason, he agreed to give them a DNA sample. After the investigators left, Sweatt went home and destroyed his diary of fires. A few days later, the lab confirmed that Sweatt's DNA did match the DNA recovered off the Marine pants and the devices found at several fire scenes. The task force finally had a name and face to go with their fires.

Thomas Sweatt was arrested on April 27, 2005, and interviewed by Agent Fulkerson and Investigator Luckett. After ninety minutes of denials, Sweatt finally gave in and admitted his activity as the "DC Serial Arsonist." He then gave a several hours' long confession of hundreds of fires he had set over the previous thirty years. His only request at the time was that he wanted to meet and shake the hand of task force spokesman Blackwell, who had been the face of the task force at all of the televised press conferences.

Investigators spent the next few frenzied days searching Sweatt's apartment, reviewing his video library, and then returning to interview him about what they had found. Among many items, they found a newspaper article referencing a fatal fire in 2002. When they asked Sweatt about that incident, he admitted to starting the fire that killed eighty-nine-year-old Annie Brown. He also admitted to the killing in 2003 of Lou Edna Jones.

Girding for a lengthy and intense trial, investigators were shocked when, within two weeks, Thomas Sweatt's attorney approached them and said Sweatt would plead guilty to all of the fires if he was spared the death penalty. Thomas Sweatt was sentenced to two life sentences plus an additional 136 years in federal prison. As part of that plea agreement or "proffer," Sweatt was to give full admissions to all fires he had ever lit with the agreement that he receive immunity from prosecution. Eventually, Sweatt would go out for four total days with detectives pointing out locations of all of the fires he could remember. As a result of that, many months of follow-up investigation were required to track down and confirm those claims. In the end, investigators positively identified and cleared out 353 arson fires that Thomas Sweatt had committed, dating back to the 1980s. As in many arson cases, most of Thomas Sweatt's arson fires were never considered to be criminal events at the time of their occurrence. Many were never reported to the police, and records for a large number of his arson fires were never validated.

Both the investigators and reporter noted that Thomas Sweatt really enjoyed talking about all of his fires. He was very happy to be driven around to revisit old fire scenes or view photographs of the locations. They also noted that he seemed very relieved to unburden himself of the secret that he had kept for thirty years.

Thomas Sweatt has expressed remorse several times for the injuries and deaths he caused due to his arson activity. However, to this day, he appears to have no qualms about reliving the incidents and openly discussing the details.

The investigators on this case believe that Thomas Sweatt lit well over one thousand fires in his lifetime. They have confirmed that he killed no less than four people with his fires. They suspect that he had killed another person earlier in life, but Sweatt refuses to discuss certain aspects of his youth.

Investigator Analysis

Thomas Sweatt is the ultimate example of the excitement-based, sexually motivated arsonist. A true rarity, his fires were based on pure excitement, power, and sexual thrill. He is also one of the few people in the world who have admitted this. His rareness in the world of criminals is so startling that it caused one of the lead investigators to unabashedly remark, "I still have a million questions for him. My only regret is that I came across him when I was in my fifties, as opposed to my twenties. He was that unique to the world." This author would have to agree. Finding someone this deviant and this open about himself is truly a bonanza in the small world of arson investigation. He would be a well spring of knowledge as to how certain offenders think, plan, fantasize, and carry out their acts. Any professional arson investigator with an interest in learning would give his right arm to spend a week picking the brain of Thomas Sweatt.

Thomas Sweatt's devices were extremely reliable in that they almost always functioned as designed and seldom left identifiable evidence. They were crude and simple in design and were only built for one reason: efficiency. They were not designed as delay devices and did not have nearly as many failures as most incendiary delay devices tend to have. His placement of the devices was extremely high risk and no doubt added to his thrill of the event. He usually placed them on the porches of homes where people were asleep. The fact that this occurred in a heavy urban environment with potentially hundreds of witnesses in the area makes his actions all the more daring. In an amazing revelation, he told investigators that he sometimes sat on the porch for upward of forty minutes just savoring the moment before the excitement started. He had no use for a delay system as he was a voyeur at heart and needed to be close by to see the fire, hear the excitement and screams, and watch the approaching fire units.

Like John Orr, Thomas Sweatt would be a psychologist's dream to attempt to analyze. Again, this author is not a psychiatrist and would not even pretend to understand all of the peculiarities of Thomas Sweatt's emotional makeup, but suffice to say that some laymen's observations can be made for the sake of criminal profiling.

It would be difficult to find any other serial arsonists with as many sexual obsessions as Thomas Sweatt. He had a bizarre sexual obsession with inanimate objects. Those included shoes, uniforms, cars, certain types of homes and garages, and certain buildings like barbershops and recruiting offices. His interest in voyeuristic activities and surveillance operations was just as important to him as his interest in fires. He had sexual and excitement interests in military men, police—and firemen, bus drivers, barbers, his own male family members, and eventually, even in the investigators who arrested him. This author was told by one of the lead investigators that they had to deal with Sweatt's obvious sexual excitement on several occasions when they were interacting with him. He developed a fondness and sexual attraction for some members of the investigative team.

Thomas Sweatt, like many (but not all) serial arson offenders, was obsessed with neatness and tidiness. He was fastidious in all aspects of his home, work, and life. He was basically a "neat freak." There is no doubt that many of the items he burned were unsightly vehicles, trash, or other debris in the area where he lived. Most neighbors say that he seemed to love to clean the building in which he lived and was often seen doing lawn and other beautification chores.

Sweatt, again like almost all arsonists, was always described as a loner who was fairly meek, quiet, and unassuming. There is almost no record whatsoever of him ever having confrontations with any persons. Like many arsonists, he solved his disputes indirectly by attacking his victim's homes, cars, and businesses after a perceived slight.

Again, like many serial arsonists, Thomas Sweatt was also a burglar and a thief. There is one criminal case where he stole items from a boyfriend. However, his admissions show that he often stole items of military, police, fire service, and bus driver paraphernalia from the vehicles of these people. He would use those items later as props in his own sexual fantasies.

Another aspect of Sweatt that is consistent with other arsonists is his voyeuristic or Peeping Tom-type activity. He stalked his victims for short periods and no doubt peered into their windows and spied on them at work. The act of sitting on their porch or entering their rear yard to place a device was another means of getting intimately close to his victims. Sweatt was obviously fairly careful and clever at that as there are very few, if any, records of him ever having been detained or arrested for such acts.

He was nocturnal in his activities and prowled the streets every night on his way home from work, looking for men or for potential targets of his fire setting.

The background of Thomas Sweatt does differ greatly from the majority of serial arsonists in one significant aspect. There is no record of severe childhood trauma or a severely disjointed family structure. Perhaps it occurred, and Sweatt never wanted to talk about it, or perhaps Sweatt was just one of those really odd guys in the world who was wired differently from the rest of society at birth. In its apparent normality, Sweatt holds a childhood similarity to both David Berkowitz and John Orr (both of whom psychologists have opined had gender or sexual identity issues). There is no doubt that his sexual identity was a huge factor in all of this.

Thomas Sweatt also possessed similar traits to other famous arsonists like Paul Keller, Pat Russ, and Bruce George Peter Lee. They all committed fires wherein multiple victims died. Later, they would confide to investigators that they felt sorrow for their victims after each fatal event. However, each of these individuals also continued to light fires for months and years after their fatal fires. This behavior demonstrated a callous disregard for human life, and even though they professed some degree of remorse, it was obviously overridden by their need to fulfill their fire setting behavior. Sweatt, like the others, was able to emotionally distance himself from his murders and continue his acts of arson without looking backward.

Thomas Sweatt started out in life as a disorganized serial arson offender. At some point, he developed his method of operation in his device and deployment technique to the point where he developed a signature. His signature started with his target selection and continued to his device, the method and time of emplacement, and the savoring of his illicit act through his desire to remain in the area and view the results of the fire. He was highly mobile, and his fires were designed to cause the maximum amount of damage. His one true point of disorganization is that he went out at night with the intention of starting a fire, but he had to hunt for the right target and opportunity. To this point, he is still probably classified as a disorganized offender, but came very close to refining himself into an organized offender.

Very similar to John Orr, Sweatt was able to effectively lead a double life for over two decades. He was consumed by his fire setting and voyeurism, but he had developed enough skill to hide it from even his closest family members and maintain a high degree of production in his regular job. Also like Orr, he seemed to enjoy interacting with the very investigators who were chasing him. It is no doubt a very intense thrill to actually talk to investigators who are on a stakeout trying to catch you. Orr and Sweatt also shared some other traits. Both had worked at Kentucky Fried Chicken, and both expressed that they had been frustrated with their boring jobs. Both were chubby and non-physical, and both hung around their events to view the excitement they had caused. Another person very similar was David Berkowitz.

In this vein, this author places Thomas Sweatt alongside of John Orr as one of the most unique and dangerous arsonists on this list. The two of them set the gold standard in the United States for severity of crimes, amount of activity, and the ability to carry on that double life in plain view of everyone. Both were in love with the excitement of their acts and the resulting press coverage of the events. Both were also no doubt completely thrilled with the prospect of being hunted by task forces in their respective areas.

Addressing the circumstances of Sweatt's arrest, this investigator has to give credit where it is due. The identification and apprehension of Sweatt was a fantastic example of good old-fashioned detective work. While the task force comprised many persons from many jurisdictions and some of the things they did were probably not high percentage methods of apprehending a serial offender, the main thrust was their decision to focus on the device and its forensic value as the crux of their investigation. In the end, cold, hard forensics from the device and matched to a potential suspect was the key element in this investigation. That, coupled with the fantastic job of establishing a rapport and conducting a productive interrogation of Sweatt, was the key ingredient in solving this series. This is probably one of the best overall investigations this writer has reviewed as it relates to hunting a serial arsonist. Because of his random choice of targets and the skill level he had developed over his hundreds of events, it is doubtful Sweatt would have ever been caught with just the use of eyewitnesses or surveillance operations.

One dark sidelight of this investigation is that the task force was beset with problems involving media leaks and some power struggles. Task force leaders, because of a leak in their information security, were forced to hide some of their critical information from members who were believed to be giving or selling it to the local media. This sort of behavior is becoming more commonplace in many law enforcement investigations.

Thomas Sweatt is one of the most prolific known arsonists in U.S. history and was confirmed to have lit 353 fires and murdered at least four persons. A more likely number of arson fires attributed to Sweatt is probably well over one thousand.

Paul Kenneth Keller "Seattle Serial Arsonist": Murderer/Serial Arsonist
Period of Activity: 1992-93, Seattle, Washington

For a five-month period in 1992 and 1993, fire investigators in the northern Seattle area knew that they had a huge problem on their hands. Someone was setting structure fires at a tremendous rate. Sometimes the fires occurred several times a night and then nothing for a couple weeks, and then there was another spree of fires. There was very little evidence at the scenes—no unique ignition devices, no accelerant residue; in fact, little to no evidence at all was found at the scenes.

The Sno-King Arson Task Force (the fires were spread over Snohomish and King Counties) was established by Seattle Fire Department Lt. Randy Litchfield and ATF Agent Dane Whetsel. As the fire series progressed and spread outward, this task force would eventually involve thirty-five federal, state, and local agencies. The efforts of this unit would be monumental, but would not come to fruition until the early morning of February 6, 1993. On that day, they would arrest a twenty-seven-year-old advertising salesman named Paul Keller. This arrest would be Keller's first contact with law enforcement during his entire life. What would follow his arrest would be his startling revelations about the secret double life he had been living.

The first spate of fires occurred on August 6, 1992, when an arsonist set fire to three homes under construction in a neighborhood. Keller would later admit that he had been drinking and smoking marijuana and happened upon the small construction site. He said he used his lighter to ignite some exposed tarpaper on the outsides of the unfinished homes and was amazed at how quickly the flames spread. The three buildings were demolished in the fire.

Within the next week or so, the same area would have six arson fires to churches, causing major damage to some of the structures. At the time, investigators had advised one of the church's reverends that it was likely the arsonist was someone connected to the church. The cleric was shocked months later when that proved true as the entire Keller family were heavily involved in the church. Other targets soon followed, including a bakery, lumberyard, and some occupied homes. There was really no rhyme or reason to these attacks, and the variances in the target selection baffled investigators.

As soon as the media got wind of that arson spree, the attacks increased in their frequency. By September, the task force had identified eleven structure fires having the unique signature of the arsonist. In mid-September, the serial arsonist was speeding up his activity. On September 20, he torched three homes; by the next week, he had torched three more. The main benefit of press coverage in this series was that the public was acutely aware of the problem and was actively sending tips to the task force. Task force leaders were able to channel a bit of that media hype and obtained a $25,000 reward for information on the case. Additionally, it inspired local agencies to spend money (foolishly in this author's opinion) on a thermal imaging device for their patrol helicopter, in hopes of detecting the arsonist at work in the dead of night. Lastly, the task force decided to give their quarry a code name and dubbed him "Specter."

In the middle of this spree, a watershed event occurred in this case. On September 22, 1992, a suspicious fire occurred at the "Four Freedoms" retirement home. In that blaze, three elderly women residents, Mary Dorris, Bertha Nelson, and Adeline Stockness, perished as the flames destroyed the structure. This fire was a bit different than the fires in the arson series, as this one had originated in a room within the home. At first, this fatal fire was classified as "suspicious" and not as "incendiary" and was not immediately connected to the current arson series. A second fire a week later at another retirement home in the area was classified as part of the arson series. This second fire was extinguished by sprinklers with very little damage. However, significant physical evidence was located at this "fizzled" fire, including evidence of a window screen being pried open and a pair of fingerprints being recovered. These two very significant fires indicated that if they were in fact related to the series, then Specter had taken an enormous leap in his danger level by actually physically entering his arson scenes where people were sleeping. He was becoming more dangerous by the minute.

The month of October did not slow down the arsonist. On October 3, three occupied homes were torched, and the families sleeping in them barely escaped with their lives. By that time, the arsonist had graduated from burning homes under construction and empty buildings like churches and warehouses to igniting homes where people were sleeping. The danger level of his attacks continued to escalate in an exponential manner.

The first part of October was extremely frenetic for the arsonist. On the sixth, the arsonist set fire to the large "Vancouver Door Company," causing a massive amount of damage. The next night he destroyed two more homes. A week later, he lit nine fires in two nights, destroying three homes and five carports. The local media was going insane over these events, and the press coverage was relentless.

The task force, despite being a collection of many agencies, was noted for the deliberate and systematic way in which it went about this case. Each fire scene was processed in a similar fashion, and basic police and arson investigative work was conducted. Tire and footprints were located, witnesses were interviewed, and exhausting house-to-house canvassing took place. The results of this work soon manifested itself in the development of possible suspect descriptions. Several witnesses, including responding firefighters, had reported seeing an unexplained person in the area of several of the fires. That person, who did not at all fit anyone's portrait of a serial arson offender, was described at times being around the fire scenes after the events. Several tips had come in describing possible odd persons around the areas both before and after the fires. One of these persons described kept reappearing in various locations. It was a thin, white male, well groomed, possibly in business attire. This subject was seen in and around various fire scenes possibly carrying a mobile telephone (fairly rare in those days) and/or a portable radio. Another tip that was recurring was an American model four-door car, plain in color, with the appearance of a "fleet" vehicle. While the investigators worked on that person's description and drew up several possible sketches, a team of analysts began working up a psychological profile of the arsonist. At that time, the task force leaders opted to keep the information confidential and not give it a general release. As it was, the task force's tip line was overwhelmed with hundreds of obscure and bizarre tips. Many task force hours were spent tracking down and eliminating those tips. Most were just people settling old scores or sending the police after a cheating spouse.

Further, in a testament to their professionalism, the task force began to develop and refine the arsonist's fire scene profile or signature. They examined the choice of targets, items or fuels first ignited, time of event, and method of ignition. They soon refined that to a point where they immediately recognized the "signature" of the arsonist when they arrived at a scene. That would help in differentiating between the serial arsonist's fires and any other of the "normal" arson fires that typically occurred in a large suburban area.

The arson signature for this arsonist was fairly simple. He attacked all his targets late at night. He left no matches, device, or accelerant at the scene, so his ignition scenario was just an open flame of some sort, most likely a lighter, to the combustible material at the scene. He lit his fires at chest height or higher. His target selection was a bit varied, but most had some sort of combustible material protruding at the point of ignition. The homes he lit had highly combustible fiberglass or tarps somewhere near the point of origin of the fires. Again, the task force kept that information close to the vest, lest the arsonist changed tactics or they poisoned a possible future confession with that information.

One of the more important things that the ATF agents on the case did was to refer this "Specter" case to the FBI behavioral analysts in Quantico, Virginia. Soon the case landed among a group of profilers headed by the famed "Mindhunter," John Douglas. Douglas, who was one of the original group of "profilers" developed by the FBI, would become the most famous due to his cases being highlighted in books (*Mindhunter* et al.), television shows, and movies (*Silence of the Lambs*, et al.). In 1999, John Douglas would co-author a book along with Mark Olshaker called *The Anatomy of Motive*. He would devote an entire chapter of that book to the fire setting activity he found common among the serial murderers he interviewed as a profiler. In that book, he wrote fairly extensively about the Paul Keller case, even though he did not personally interview Keller.

Among the many aspects his group "profiled" about Specter prior to his identification and arrest as Paul Keller, Douglas relates that they believed that Specter was possibly a traveling salesman or someone of that field. They discerned that through the appearance of a "fleet"-type vehicle, a neat and tidy business appearance, and the fact that the fire series soon spread to some very distant locales. The "profile" also indicated that Specter had some major triggering incident in his life near the start of this series, but probably had relationship problems throughout his entire life. Douglas and associates believed that the triggering event was most probably a loss of a job or love or even a combination of both.

Specter also probably was a failure in life or at least viewed himself as a failure. Specter was probably quite proud of his fires and the power they gave him, as he probably was unable to exert any power in other aspects of his life. The profilers did predict that Specter would start to branch out in his fires and expand his area of operations. Additionally, as the hype grew and he became more skilled and emboldened by his early fires, Specter's future fires would probably be larger and more devastating, with a much higher potential for death. They described Specter's future fires as an escalation of his ability to exert his power over people. They predicted, based on his skill level, that he would have been lighting fires since his youth and would have grown in sophistication over the years. Based on the current level of his fires, they predicted his age to be in his late twenties to mid-thirties.

Additionally, the profilers added in the usual tendencies they seemed to assign to most offenders. They predicted the arsonist would have a history of cruelty in his background, probably to animals or younger siblings. They also said he was most likely a police or fire buff and had possibly applied for either profession in an active or auxiliary status. He would of course be an emotional loner with failed relationships with women. He would have been considered an oddball in his past and would have been non-athletic and probably a disruptive person in school and at work. He would have problems with his temper and would most likely be neat, tidy, and overly fastidious. He would seldom take responsibility for his actions and would be quick to blame others. He would likely have an interest in rough pornography and may have an interest in bondage and fetishism.

By October, the tip line finally produced its first promising return. A tipster had called and given a description of a suspicious vehicle near one of the arson scenes. The vehicle was a 1992 Dodge Shadow, four-door sedan, blue in color, with no current plates, but bearing the paper plates of an advertising company. Task force investigators spoke to the owner of that company, Mr. George Keller, and asked him for his help in locating the car. Immediately, George Keller's heart sank as he realized it was an exact description of the car his twenty-seven-year-old son Paul was currently using. He also realized that his son had been acting a bit odd lately as well. For some reason, when the investigators came to see him, the license plate they wanted to identify did not match the type on Paul's car, and George Keller breathed a huge sigh of relief. That tip seemed to reach a dead end as so many had before.

During the holiday months of November and December, the serial arsonist's pace seemed to slow slightly. A total of sixteen fires were attributed to him during that time period. Those fires did produce several consistent witness sightings of a man matching the original description of Specter. Unbelievably, one of those events caused a witness to call in a tip of a well-dressed white male in a newer model Chrysler Sedan loitering in an area where a fire later broke out. Soon a police officer spotted the man and his car as it pulled into an Exxon gas station. As the well-coiffed and well-dressed young man exited his car, the approaching officer decided that he did not resemble an arsonist (the patrol officer's image of an arsonist, at least), and the officer made the decision not to contact and identify him. That officer would months later recognize Paul Keller as the well-dressed man he had seen at the gas station that night. More than one witness would describe a similar-appearing male standing nearby as the firemen worked on the fires. Soon several police composite drawings were generated through witness descriptions. Those composites were all fairly similar.

Still, the fires continued and the tip lines produced no workable leads, and the task force was becoming frustrated. Over the course of January 1993, the task force debated on their next course of action. They did notice an unexpected shift in the fires though. For some odd reason, four fires bearing the unique signature of the Seattle area arsonist sprang up in Eastern Washington, over one hundred miles away. The investigators had no explanation for that event, but didn't think it was a copycat, since they had not released the "signature" information to the press.

Part of the profile provided by Quantico would advise the task force to at some point go proactive with the case and plant ideas into the subject through the media. The profilers believed that someone near the suspect would recognize him or his behavior. By late January, they decided to take that bold step, and they scheduled a massive press conference for the twenty-seventh. During the conference and at the behest of the profilers back in Quantico, they picked an investigator to speak about their suspect. They released the composite sketches and had ATF Agent Whetsel purposely describe him as having no self-esteem and having come from a dysfunctional family. Agent Whetesel revealed that the task force was seeking any information on a white male between thirty and forty, who had a neat appearance, wore his hair short and well coiffed, had a neatly trimmed mustache, was slightly built, and had a gaunt and angular face. He was well dressed in a coat and a tie and had the appearance of a businessman. This was the profile the task force had developed, who had been seen at some of the arson scenes loitering about and even talking to firemen and some police officers.

Along with this information, the task force profilers described the suspect as being a low performer in school with bad grades, few friends, and generally bad at relationships and peer acceptance. They revealed that the arsonist probably had some major setback in his life in July.

The press conference was watched by tens of thousands of people, but two in particular were completely shocked by it. Ben Keller and his father,

Mr. George Keller, a fifty-one-year-old advertising executive, were stunned at how the composite sketches looked identical to their brother and son, Paul Keller. The physical description was also an exact match. The psychological profile, as generic as it was to many arsonists, also seemed to fit Paul as well. George Keller was in turmoil. A completely dedicated family man who had strong Christian beliefs, he began to believe his son was the notorious Seattle serial arsonist. George, like many people in the Seattle area, had been closely following the arsonist case in the media. He knew a way to check and see if his son Paul had been involved. He was aware that a group of fires had occurred many miles away from the Seattle area in eastern Washington. Both of his sons worked for him in the advertising agency, so George had his other son Ben check Paul's whereabouts on the day of the arsons. Sadly, they learned that Paul had been working in the area of the arsons on the day they occurred and had even purchased gasoline with a company credit card less than two blocks from some of the fire scenes. They also found that his cellular telephone bills placed him near the scenes of several of the fires. Lastly, they were aware that the company vehicles he drove also matched the description shown on television.

George Keller was devastated! He called an immediate family meeting (without Paul) and consulted his wife Margaret, and the two made an extraordinary decision. In an incredible display of ethics, morals, and citizenship, the Kellers decided to go to the task force with their suspicions about their son Paul. They didn't hesitate and contacted task force investigators the very day of the press conference. What the family told the task force investigators shocked them. They said that Paul had a lifelong fascination with the fire service and knew where every fire station in the Seattle area was located. They confirmed that when the arson series started in July 1992, Paul had just finalized his divorce (the only relationship he ever had with a woman which lasted just under two years) and had filed for bankruptcy. At the same time, Paul learned that he had been turned down for employment by a fire agency for the second time. He would never fulfill his dream of being a firefighter. The family also said that Paul had been involved with at least two fires in his past, had uncontrollable bouts of anger, and frequently carried around a police/fire scanner. Paul Keller seemed to fit the task force profile exactly.

The Kellers also gave task force investigators a bit of a background on their son. Later information was to emerge during the sentencing phase of Paul Keller. Paul was born to the Kellers on January 6, 1966. From his first moments after his birth, Paul was plagued with problems. His umbilical cord detached at birth and caused him severe stress and trauma in the first few days of his life. His parents would later point to that medical issue as the root of all of Paul Keller's later problems. Paul was raised in a loving and religious home along with a younger brother and sister. The parents were attentive and involved in their children's life. Their Christian religion was an extremely important part of their life, and they regularly attended church as a family. Paul was active in church and sang in the choir until his arrest. The family had a good income and had all the advantages of the upper middle class.

However, there was a dark side to Paul Keller. While his siblings grew up virtually trouble free, Paul was a constant source of trouble and conflict. He was hyperactive and frequently engaged in disputes, arguments, and fights with his siblings. He was abusive and rough with his younger siblings and caused them injuries on more than one occasion. As a result, he was frequently harshly disciplined by his parents. His siblings would later describe him as extremely aggressive and violent toward them, both physically and verbally.

When he was nine, Paul was sent to a neurologist because of his aggressive behavior. The neurologist described him as being hyperactive and prescribed some medications which seemed to have no effect. He later told the Kellers that they were destined to be "long-suffering parents" because of Paul. A more true prediction has never been heard.

By the time he was nine, Paul had been in trouble for setting fire to a vacant home. He was later detained for shoplifting. When the misbehavior continued, the Kellers sent Paul to a private church school for similar children. That school also applied vigorous discipline to these problem children. In school, Paul was considered extremely bright, but a low performer with his grades. He seemed bored and unchallenged by schoolwork and consequently did very poor academically, despite being considered highly intelligent. He was not athletically inclined and did not make or keep friends easily. His parents could never recall him having a girlfriend until he was twenty-five when he abruptly married a girl from their church. Their marriage unraveled within eighteen months.

Paul did have one overriding passion. He loved firemen and the fire service. A close family friend was a firefighter and frequently took Paul to the fire station. Paul grew up hanging around the fire stations in the area. His parents and friends would later recall that he spent all summer responding to fire calls on his bicycle throughout the Everett, Washington, area. They would even realize that it was an ongoing joke with the firefighters that Paul would frequently beat them to fire scenes. Even as an adult, Paul was seen frequently at fire scenes. He almost caused accidents a few times trying to get to them. He was also known as a very aggressive driver who received frequent traffic tickets for his overly aggressive driving.

That passion did not abate once Paul was an adult. He began collecting firefighting equipment and clothing. He had a large collection of sirens, axes, and other paraphernalia. Upon his arrest, investigators found an active fire department radio scanner, full firefighter "turn out" gear in his car, and dozens of other fire department items. Paul amazed investigators and interviewers with his in-depth technical knowledge of obscure firefighting equipment, gear, and tactics. He could recite intimate details of the history of local Seattle area fire departments and rescue services.

Once he was an adult, Paul's life seemed a bit rocky, but then appeared to improve. He held a job briefly as a security guard and then as a bookkeeper. He lost the second job after a mysterious fire erupted under his desk one day. Soon his father came to his rescue and hired him as a salesman for his company. He showed talent as a salesman, and soon his life seemed to have the outward appearance of success. He was considered a very high achiever in the advertising business. He was active in church and at twenty-five years old was married. Later, Paul would reflect on his life as a complete fraud which obscured his many personal failures. He said he hated the type of work he did and had always wanted to be a firefighter. He was rejected twice by fire agencies in the year before the arson spree. His brief marriage collapsed in 1991, and he declared personal bankruptcy just a month or two before the arson spree began. He said he began having extramarital affairs, smoking pot, and drinking alcohol. He also admitted to hanging out at adult bookstores and at massage parlors. This activity was in direct conflict with his family's strong Christian values. He kept these activities and the rest of his failures hidden from his family. After his wife left, he felt his life was completely out of control. In the summer of 1992, just weeks before the arson spree began, he sought out psychological help. He never followed up on his original effort.

After speaking to the Kellers, the task force began to plan their next step. They followed and studied Paul Keller for the next ten days and tried to get a feel of how he led his life. They wanted to interview him with a lot of background information in hand. They knew that the best way to convict him would be to get a full confession. To facilitate that, they staged the scene and time of his arrest with great care. They knew that Keller was nocturnal and that he would be most vulnerable in the early daylight hours. They wanted to shake him up by taking him "out of his cycle." They chose his arrest time for 6:20 in the morning of February 6, 1993. They used his affinity for the fire service as a tactic and showed up at his home in a formal manner with many police cars and fire trucks on hand. He was spoken to in a very official manner and then led to the task force headquarters for critical interrogation.

The task force then employed their most critical tactic. The first person Paul Keller saw when he entered the interrogation room was his father, George Keller. George implored him to do the right thing—tell the truth and start the process of healing. That tactic worked as Keller immediately told them, "I have set some fires."

Within just a short period, Paul Keller admitted to fifteen fires. Over that day and subsequent days, he told investigators about his targets and method of ignition. Those details were an exact match to the many fire scenes the task force had attended. Keller surprised them by admitting to several fires that they were not aware of or had been called accidents. Then, in a show of cooperation, Keller took investigators to as many scenes as he could remember and walked through the arson event with them. Prudently, the investigators taped all of these re-creations for later use in court.

Keller told investigators and later makers of a documentary film that he had no real reason for starting fires. He blamed all of the fires as spontaneous, unexplainable acts that occurred only after he drank alcohol or smoked marijuana. He said he was always drunk when he lit fires. Investigators noted, however, that he had an uncanny ability to remember the exact details of events where he claimed to be drunk.

He declared that his target selection was random and that he had nothing personal against the occupants or owners of buildings. He said he would see some highly combustible material extending from a building and just light it with his cigarette lighter. He favored cardboard boxes, plastic, paper, tarps, fiberglass panels, and any other product or attachment to a structure that would ignited and spread quickly. He never brought items with him other than a lighter and did not use any liquid accelerants. He said when he saw something that he knew would ignite quickly, he "lit it and left" and never looked back. He did not know why he lit the fires but just stated that "my brain clicked and said, light it." Investigators were surprised at some point during his admissions that Keller had the gall to actually blame some of the victims for their fires. He said it was their fault that they had left combustible materials out in the open.

During his confessions, Keller always stated that he "had no desire to hurt anyone for any reason" and had no idea why he lit fires at homes where people were sleeping. He believed in his mind he was "just a spectator" to an event and wasn't really involved in the massive horror and destruction. He could only speculate that his fires were "child's play, without real purpose." After his arrest, he stated that he had always contemplated turning himself in and that upon being arrested he "was glad it was over and done."

Keller also asserted on film that although he was highly interested in the fire service, that interest had nothing to do with the fire setting behavior. He was very adamant that the fires were due to alcohol and drugs and that "I'm not a nut."

Shortly after his arrest and at his parent's urging, Paul Keller agreed to a plea bargain with the prosecutors in this case. He admitted to and was convicted of thirty-six arson fires in the recent spree. He also admitted to an additional forty arson fires, but they were dropped as part of the deal. He threw himself at the mercy of the court and awaited his sentencing.

Before his sentencing, he, his parents, and his attorney began an aggressive campaign to mitigate the damage. Through the recovery of long hidden hospital records, his family learned that at birth Paul had an umbilical cord problem for several hours, which reduced oxygen to his brain. He was diagnosed with "fetal distress syndrome" as a result of that. His parents emotionally claimed that they had no knowledge of that and felt angry that the hospital hid that from them. They said that "injury" was the root of all of Paul's later issues. A psychologist also told the court that, throughout his life, Paul had been suffering from undiagnosed attention deficit disorder (ADD), which could have been controlled with the prescribing of proper medication. His attorney argued that those two treatable issues had shaped his erratic behavior and caused the fire setting activity. To be fair to Keller, there could be some credence to that argument. That those two issues shaped his life is arguable since he grew up in the exact same environment of his siblings and they had no obvious behavior issues. The result of that was that his attorney argued that Paul Keller, properly treated with prescription drugs, was not a danger to society and that his sentence should be minimal. He suggested something to the order of two to five years in prison.

Another aspect of Keller's childhood that emerged upon conviction was his assertion that at age twelve he had been forced at gunpoint to perform sexual acts on an adult male firefighter. Keller, who had the lifelong love of the firefighting service, would tell his therapist later that that forced sexual abuse continued for two years and affected him the rest of his life. He said he felt pressured by his reputation as a troublemaker to keep this sexual assault to himself and not report it.

The prosecution argued that Keller was extremely dangerous and that he only reluctantly admitted to his crimes after being confronted with compelling evidence. They said that his admissions were minimizing in their extent and were very self-serving. They noted the discrepancy that he always blamed drunkenness for his fires, yet months later could recite exact details of each event. The prosecution believed that Keller was hiding numerous arson events from them and argued for a seventy-five-year sentence in prison.

During that phase, Keller's attorney allowed him to participate in a documentary film about the case where Keller admits his guilt and blames drugs and alcohol. His family appears in the film and discusses his problems at birth. The film *Portrait of a Serial Arsonist* was done as a bit of a legal gambit to try and get a reduced sentence. It did give reviewers a good idea of the type of person Paul Keller was. He was not shy or reticent when speaking on camera. He appeared extremely intelligent, bright, and very comfortable talking about his crimes. He almost seemed to enjoy talking about the arson series. He displayed almost no emotion and very little real compassion for his victims. He was also careful to point out that he was sorry for any injuries he had caused and was adamant that he had never killed anyone with his fires. Lastly, he stated that his fire setting career was very short in duration and that there were no other fires other than the seventy-six he had admitted to.

The court was not impressed. On May 7, 1993, Paul Keller was sentenced to seventy-five years in state prison for the thirty-six fires he had admitted to starting. After sentencing, the task force still had a few more chores. They were examining potential fires dating back several years to when Paul Keller was ten years old. They also had one more fire that they had never resolved. After his conviction, the crime lab matched Paul Keller's fingerprint to another large arson scene. In December 1993, they filed murder charges against Paul Keller for the "Four Freedoms" retirement home fire of the previous year. Keller subsequently pled guilty to that event and received a ninety-nine-year sentence to be served concurrently. He admitted to entering a bedroom in the facility and igniting a bed with his lighter.

Over the years, Paul Keller has been the subject of much speculation regarding many other unsolved fires. After one brief interview, he and his attorney refused all calls for statements. In 2007, a Seattle newspaper wrote an article naming Keller as the possible suspect in a 1987 arson murder, wherein an elderly couple named Monte and Gladys McCaughey had died. That same night, three other unsolved arson fires burned near their North Seattle home. This was in a year with numerous other unsolved arson fires in the area. At the time, Paul Keller was twenty-one years old and working as a security guard in the area of the fires. In original interviews, Keller had denied any involvement in those fires. However, the murder fire bore his unique signature. It was set at night in a carport among some paint and wood scraps that were stored there.

His claims notwithstanding, detectives have always believed that Keller has only admitted to a few of the fires he has done. Seattle Fire Lt. Randy Litchfield, one of the original task force leaders, maintains that Keller's "got a truckload of fires he won't talk about." The lieutenant said that Keller was not nearly as forthcoming as he appeared on video. He strenuously denied involvement in each event until confronted by irrefutable evidence. Only then did he admit, begin crying, and "go the Christian route." He described Keller as a smooth pathological liar who refused to discuss his childhood fire setting. Investigators maintain that he set fires as early as nine years old, when he tried to ignite a vacant house. He later lost his job as a bookkeeper when his desk mysteriously caught on fire.

Investigators say they are still looking into Keller as a suspect in the 1987 arson murders. He will not be eligible for parole until 2078, when he will be 112 years old.

Investigator Analysis

News stories have quoted several Seattle area prosecutors, detectives, and fire investigators as describing Paul Keller as the "most prolific arsonist in U.S. history." That appears to be a bit of an overstatement, but not by very much. At the time of his arrest, he was indeed in that category. Shortly though, he was surpassed by both John Orr and Thomas Sweatt in both the amount of known arson activity and the number of deaths caused by that activity. However, Keller is no slouch and reigns alongside those two as the three true heavyweights in the field of known American serial arsonists.

The identification, arrest, and conviction of that man were by no means fluke or happenstance events. He did not leave much forensic material at his scenes like John Orr and Thomas Sweatt. He did not use a signature device. His victims appear to be mostly random targets of opportunity. Without the efforts of the task force, the odds of catching this guy were extremely slim. This case illustrates another very important point that still seems lost on some arson investigators. These types of cases are not "made" by flooding potential target areas with surveillance units of arson investigators. They are not "made" by staging dramatic press conferences imploring the suspect to do the right thing and give himself up. They are not "made" by spending countless dollars on expensive technology and gear as many administrators are so fond of doing.

On the contrary, these types of cases are "made" by running a well-organized investigation, where each fire scene is methodically and systematically processed as an individual event. Any forensics is located, collected, and then analyzed by experts. Then, the area of each event is heavily canvassed by seasoned detectives who are astute at asking the right questions of people. The information, no matter how small, trivial, or seemingly unimportant, is then coalesced into a central information system or computer for later retrieval, analysis, or action. Tip lines are staffed with reliable people, and a list of clues is formed and acted upon.

Outside resources, including psychological profilers; temporal and spatial relation experts to graph, chart, and analyze patterns of activity; and police sketch artists, are employed. If a suspect is identified, then seasoned surveillance specialists such as major crimes or narcotics detectives are brought in to run a professional surveillance operation on the subject. On a case of this magnitude, it would simply be foolish to bring in a bunch of unskilled police officers or fire investigators to attempt to conduct surveillance on this man.

When a subject is identified, then a massive effort to study his background and tendencies is undertaken, all in preparation for the seminal point in any serial arson investigation—the interrogation. Generally, investigators have one decent chance at that, and if they use the wrong tactic, wrong information, wrong personnel, or as usually happens, too many personnel, then that golden opportunity is lost forever. This is the "money shot" of every case. If the truth be told, we as investigators want and need a successful interrogation. Firstly, investigators, despite all their work, always question themselves. They need positive confirmation from the arsonist himself that what they have believed throughout the case is true. Secondly, they need to know the exact specifics of each arson event. They need that as a learning tool for future arson cases, and they need that as closure to confirm whether they missed some evidence or whether their opinion on the ignition scenario is accurate. No matter how seasoned or skilled an arson investigator may be, only the arsonist himself truly knows how and why he started a particular fire. His confession almost always fills in the missing gaps or gives surprising answers about the sequence of events.

From an outsider's perspective, the Sno-King Arson Task Force did an incredible job on all facets of that investigation. They located and processed what little forensic evidence was found at the scenes. They maintained good case integrity and were careful not to divulge critical "hold back" information to the public or media. They used nearly every available asset and tool in an investigator's kit, including profilers, "tip lines," outside experts, surveillance operatives, and the media itself. They made tactical decisions on how and when to release sensitive information. Lastly, they made the correct assessment on how to arrest and interrogate Paul Keller for the maximum results.

They needed to use all of those things effectively as Paul Keller was not your typical arsonist. He was highly mobile and extremely intelligent. He had no criminal history and did not usually conduct himself in a manner that would bring him to the attention of the police. He was well dressed and very plain in appearance and likely would not have come to anyone's attention as being a "suspicious person." His method of attack was simple, quick, and efficient. He spent very little time at the target location and carried away his ignition source, a lighter, which would not attract anyone's attention even if he had been stopped. He did not use accelerants and did not have to deal with any issues regarding them or the containers they were in. He did not use a signature delay incendiary device that investigators may have located forensics on.

However, Keller had one weakness in his activities that eventually led to his identification. He was the ultimate firefighter "wannabe." He had the dangerous (for him) tendency to linger around after some of his fires and engage witnesses in conversation. He even took the great risk at times of interacting with the police and firefighters working the scene of one of his arson fires. In that, his desire for excitement and inclusiveness in the event caused him to be identified not as a suspect but as an "odd" person at several scenes. This ultimately led to his downfall.

Based on that investigation, there is little doubt to most investigators that Keller had been involved in fire setting since his earliest years. His admissions were self-serving and his alibi of being addled by alcohol and drugs is most likely a face-saving gesture toward his religiously inclined family. I would have to opine that young Paul Keller probably set a few of those fires that he was the first responder to on his bicycle in his teen years. It defies the odds and logic that he could be at so many fire scenes prior to the firefighters themselves.

Additionally, he worked part-time as a security guard, which is always a high-risk field for fire setters. This fact also makes him a prime suspect in all those unsolved fires in 1987 when he was twenty-one years old.

The investigators and prosecutors on the case list a "triggering event" for the start of Keller's arson spree in 1992. His recent divorce and personal bankruptcy were obviously heavy factors that were involved. However, it is just as likely that his two rejections from fire agencies were just as strong factors. Lastly, two really unique things were going on in 1992 in the arson world. First, in April, the massive Los Angeles riots broke out, and for two weeks straight, the nation was treated to endless footage of hundreds of buildings in Los Angeles burning at the hands of arsonists. The dramatic footage also included, of course, the endless police and firefighting activities related to those riots.

A second event may have been more to the point. The major newspapers were running an ongoing story that spring and summer about Glendale, California, Fire Investigator Capt. John Orr, who was on trial in California for the first of his four major arson series. His first conviction for a series of arsons in Central California rocked the firefighting world. Being obsessed with the fire service, there is little doubt that Paul Keller was aware of that earthshaking case and the ripples it caused in the fire service. While this is of course pure speculation, it is possible that up to that point Keller had just dabbled in fire setting behavior over the years. Along with his personal upheavals, the press coverage surrounding the John Orr case may have had a direct impact on why Keller decided to take his arson behavior to a mercurial level.

There is no doubt that Paul Keller is a classic excitement-motivated thrill arsonist. He may have had a bit of spite or revenge in him also as he lit a church on fire that he was related to. His actions were fairly spontaneous and disorganized. He chose a simple ignition source and spent very little time or effort at his scenes. It is safe to say that there are probably a few hundred lesser fires that Paul Keller lit that have not been attributed to him. Because

---

of that, it is difficult to assign a number to his arsons, but something between three hundred and five hundred seems reasonable. What is noteworthy about him that puts him in the same class as both John Orr and Thomas Sweatt is that he attacked occupied buildings. He even was so bold in at least two cases (nursing home arsons/murder) to physically enter the structure to start the fire. Despite his pleas at remorse, he was a clear-thinking man who continued to light his fires for a long time after he had already killed some people. This note, again like Orr, Sweatt, and George Peter Lee in England, puts Paul Keller's danger and evil levels well above most serial arson offenders. The potential for additional arson deaths by this suspect was unlimited.

Paul Keller is among the most dangerous of all known arsonists and has admitted to seventy-seven structure fires that have killed at least three people. He is a suspect in a dozen more fires and possibly the deaths of at least two more people. He is serving a ninety-nine-year sentence in state prison.

Pat Russ: Mass Murderer/Serial Arsonist
Period of Activity: 1960-71, New York and Southern California

During the summer of 1977, a pair of serial arsonists was busy setting over one hundred fires in the Los Padres National Forest in Santa Barbara County, California. As a result of the heavy fire activity of that pair, the forest service mounted a massive surveillance and investigative operation in that area. Two teenagers were eventually caught and convicted for that arson series. Officials often wondered why the area was always plagued by a massive number of incendiary fires. Ten years after that pair was arrested, the most notorious serial arsonist of them all, John Orr, ignited a series of blazes with incendiary devices just a few miles down the road. Six years prior to the pair's destructive summer, still another serial arsonist ignited one of the largest and most destructive fires in Santa Barbara County history, the Romero fire.

Pat Russ was driving up the Pacific Coast Highway 101 to visit his estranged wife on October 6, 1971. In what he would later describe as an overwhelming urge, he stopped and placed an incendiary device at the base of a steep slope in some dry brush, near the town of Goleta. That was one of three similar devices Russ placed that day. That small incendiary blaze, ignited in the late afternoon during a hot Santa Ana wind condition with humidity at 9 percent and the temperature at a hundred degrees, soon exploded into the massive Romero fire. That fire burned for nine more days, destroying over fourteen thousand acres and five homes and killing four forest service firefighters. The men, Richard Cumor, Delbert Deloachage, Thomas Klepperich, and Leonard Mineau, were part of a crew operating bulldozers as part of the firefighting effort when they were overrun by flames. Two other crewmen were seriously burned but survived the event.

Although that fire was a suspected arson, nobody could link Pat Russ to it until two years later when he was arrested for another arson fire in Orange County. Inexplicably, after his arrest and incarceration in Atascadero State Hospital, Russ told his parole officer that he wanted to confess to investigators about several arsons. During that interview, Russ confessed to setting the Romero fire and similar brushfires near Los Angeles. He described to investigators how he had constructed an incendiary device out of a baby food jar filled with gasoline and toilet paper with an extended fuse. There is no record of that device having ever been recovered.

Pat Russ was arrested and indicted on that arson murder on April 13, 1973. After much legal wrangling, Russ was found not guilty by reason of insanity for the crime of murder. He was sentenced on the arson charges to a state prison mental hospital and was freed from prison by 1977.

After that amazing confession, Pat Russ befriended the fire investigators who put him away. When he got out, he did a unique thing by allowing himself to be interviewed on film for educational purposes. He believed he had a sickness similar to drug abuse or a sexual offender and felt that talking about it was therapy. In 1987, he even gave an interview to a *Los Angeles Times* writer. During all of the sessions, he described himself as a lifelong arsonist who, when he became an adult, started to do fires as a living. He described a life of contract arsons for crime groups, which eventually landed him in Attica Prison in New York. He said he spent over a decade being paid to set fires to restaurants, warehouses, and other businesses. He eventually gravitated to doing some paid torch jobs in Southern California. By the late 1960s, he was married and had obtained legitimate employment. He claimed to have stopped lighting fires during that time period. Russ said that his failing marriage was his motivation for starting a new string of wild land arsons in the early 1970s. During that same time, Russ was also suspected of setting fire to the house in which his wife and children were sleeping. He was never arrested for that incident.

Pat Russ was a man of short stature who walked with a limp. He would later describe himself as a "cripple." He had a really bizarre family life. He started out being one of eighteen kids. In a cruel twist of fate, he was the product of his grandfather molesting Russ's mother, thereby making his grandfather also his father. He would later become sexually abused by another family member. He later described a deep hatred for his mother who told him that she would have been happy if he had died at birth.

Despite the freakish circumstances of his birth, Pat Russ grew very fond of his grandfather/father. The man worked for a trash business and at the very early age of about two or three years old began taking Pat along with him to work. Part of that work entailed burning items in an open incinerator. Pat Russ at forty-seven years of age admitted that as a child the incinerator had been very comforting to him as he felt he could burn all his troubles away with the flames.

Russ said that he remained close to his grandfather/father until the man died when Pat was eight years old. He said that a local Catholic priest tried to comfort him during the wake and funeral and told him that his grandfather was just resting. When Russ later learned the truth about death, he was so angry he decided to show the priest what he thought of his attempts at comfort. Russ said that his first real arson fires occurred at that age of eight when he torched the priest's church, rectory, and school. Russ then began a several-year spree of fires. He said he lit the vast majority of his fires at that age because he had such anger at his mother, family, and society in general. He said that the fires were fantasies that helped him "burn his mother" if he wanted to. By the time he was twelve, Russ had endured several years of familial abuse, sex abuse, and frequent beatings. He said that each time he received a beating for setting a fire he would go back and set a bigger fire. He dropped out of school in fourth grade being nearly illiterate, and his mother described him as a "retard." He was sent to a juvenile work farm at that age. He would later say that his stay in the work farm was a way for him to take his rage against his family and turn it on society in general. He said he developed a deep hatred for everything in society because it had turned its back on him.

After his stay in the juvenile system, Russ continued his fire setting behavior. Somewhere in that time frame, he realized that besides venting his anger, fire setting began to give him a sense of power, which he had never obtained in his life. He said he learned at a fairly young age that he could make money from setting fires. He would later claim to have lit over five hundred arson-for-profit fires in the Rochester, New York, area in the 1950s and 1960s.

Just prior to starting his 1971 arson series in Southern California, Russ's seemingly stable family life dissolved as his wife had an affair with Russ's own brother. Russ would later lament that throughout his life he had always "been dealt a losing hand." He said he felt that someone should pay for that, and as a result he developed a lifelong philosophy, "You piss me off, I'll burn you out."

Pat Russ would later admit to committing over eighteen hundred arson fires, with five hundred or so as a paid "torch." He claimed that his fires caused in excess of $80 million in loss. He is a two-time convicted arsonist and was last known to be living out of his truck in Southern California. He hasn't been heard from since the late 1980s.

Investigator Analysis

Pat Russ is one of the very few organized offender arsonists on this list. A review of his history shows that he most likely, through sheer volume of activity, evolved from a disorganized to organized offender. He readily admits that most of his youthful fires were due to his hatred of those who he believed did him wrong in some fashion. In a weird twist, he was able to translate a youthful urge or need (fire setting) into a means of income. He gravitated toward being a professional "torch" or paid fire setter and thereby was forced by circumstances to use planning, transportation, and delay devices in order to prevent injury and facilitate his escape. His devices were designed for a specific target and were made to ensure maximum damage of that target.

Like many of the others on this list, he was a drifter and loner with few friends. When last heard, he was residing in a camper in the Los Angeles area. He was unable to make the one marriage in his life a success and his work record (other than arsons) is that of an unskilled laborer.

Like the only other organized offender arsonist on this list, John Orr, Russ committed at least some of his arsons in the daytime, albeit in remote wilderness type locations. This fact brings up another arsonist anomaly. Serial fire setters who set wild land fires often differ from urban fire setters as they tend to set blazes during daylight hours. This occurs for several reasons. It is difficult to travel and find good target areas at night, the optimum conditions of high temperature, low humidity, and strong winds are usually during the afternoons, and there is no necessity to use darkness to cloak one's activities since the rural domain tends to have few people and an infinite number of places to caper unseen.

This author viewed a videotape made of Pat Russ in the 1980s. This tape, entitled *An Arsonist Talks—about Juvenile Firesetters,* is an informal panel discussion of the causal factors of juvenile fire setting. It is hosted by a retired president of the United States Fire Administration, who is a former fire chief of many years. The other two panel members are a firefighter/arson investigator and a counselor for the probation department, both from the San Bernardino area of Southern California. These last two members were considered to be "experts" on juvenile fire setting behavior and prevention. Pat Russ was the final member of the panel.

Despite the poor quality of the video and the dated clothing, this "discussion" is "must see material" for any professional arson investigator. It is an exact demonstration of how not to interact with a serial offender of any ilk, let alone a unique subject like an arsonist. The host, who quickly states that he has over thirty-five years in the fire service, barely conceals throughout this tape his disgust and hatred for Pat Russ. Although seated alongside of Russ, the host routinely turns his back to Russ and dismisses his answers and explanations as "cop outs and alibis." He often lectures Russ, and his inquiries are more accusations than questions. He and the other panel "experts" practically scoff at Russ's explanations for his behavior as "crazy" and then give their own explanations for his behavior. Although the tape is just over twenty minutes long, the well-meaning "experts" succeed in making Russ visibly angry, as they basically tell them that they know what caused his behavior and he doesn't.

The tape is almost painful to watch, as the panel did not apparently want to ask Russ questions or get his opinion on the subject matter. They were more interested in telling him their clinical views of his behavior.

On his part, Russ is hardly the meek, mild, and timid arsonist that is often described by investigators. He is militant, agitated, and argumentative with the panel. He practically fumes with anger and disbelief at the assertions of the panel and is extremely agitated by the time the tape ends. There is little doubt in my mind that Pat Russ left that taping so agitated and upset that he most likely lit a fire somewhere nearby. The tape is highly recommended viewing on how not to interview a suspect in any criminal case.

This tape was mentioned as it is a glaring example of one of the many problems affecting arson investigation. To be fair, the host of the tape was not an investigator but was a nationally known former fire chief. It is my opinion that many fire chiefs, and to an extent their arson investigators, have a deep emotional hatred for arsonists, particularly those involved in the death of firefighters. This hatred often clouds a professional and non-biased investigation and discussion into the facts and causes of an arson event. Many chief officers are of the strong opinion that arsonists set fires with the sole intent of injuring firefighters. I can find no documented case where this was the motive of the arson offender; however, this perception exists today at many investigation seminars and training meetings. As is demonstrated in all of the included case studies, the motives and rationale of the serial arsonist are so diverse and latent that truly only the offender himself probably knows why he lit the fire.

Pat Russ is another unique guy in that he is one of the few paid arsonists or "torches" on this list. The "torch" has been popularized numerous times in movies, books, film noir, and adventure magazines. In the fire investigation field, the paid arsonist has existed in the past, mainly on the East Coast of the United States and mainly related to organized crime syndicates. A strenuous review of the available crime data shows very little mention of any persons associated with multiple "torch jobs." This author has personal information of an organized arson ring in Southern California in 2002. Other than these few mentioned cases, the professional "torch" remains an enigma as there is little verification currently available to confirm his existence.

Raymond Lee Oyler "Esperanza Arsonist": Mass Murderer/ Serial Arsonist
Period of Activity: 2004-06, Riverside County, California

On the morning of October 26, 2006, this author was in Henderson, Nevada, at a seminar for the International Association of Arson Investigators. Among the many subjects being taught there, I was providing a lecture and case history of a massive arson-for-profit ring to about eighty other fire investigators from Nevada, Arizona, and California. Early that morning, a fire investigator in the audience, who was employed by Cal Fire, the state firefighting agency in California, stood up and announced that a large fire had broken out in the Cabazon area during the middle of a blistering Santa Ana wind condition. He maintained phone contact with his partners throughout the next few hours and by that afternoon tearfully announced at the seminar, "It looks like we've lost some firefighters."

Riverside and San Bernardino counties are large swaths of desert, mountains, and some small cities spread over a large portion of Southeastern California, about two hours east of Los Angeles. Where the two counties meet in the Riverside area is a zone where the coastal region ends and the massive Southern California desert region begins. This area is dominated by San Jacinto Mountain, which looms nine thousand feet above the desert floor. Nestled at the base of this mountain is the community of Cabazon. A few miles east are the posh communities of Palm Desert and Palm Springs. To the north is the linear San Bernardino mountain range. Because of the topography of this region, along with the desert influence, the area is known for an ongoing pattern of high winds through all the local mountain roads and passes. Because of the perpetual wind conditions in the region, massive "farms" of giant windmills line all the mountain passes in the area. The largest of these farms is in the Cabazon area just west of Palm Springs. During the Santa Ana wind condition which occurs at least twice a year in the fall, the winds drastically switch direction 180 degrees and blow blast furnace hot toward the west for about a three—or four-day period. The bulk of these winds whip down through the natural topographic funnel that runs east to west through the area. This funnel is defined on maps as the Interstate 10 corridor, along which most of the desert towns are aligned. It is also known as the San Gorgonio pass or more often locally "the wind tunnel."

In late October 2006, Santa Ana winds were howling, and the winds were at gale force speeds in the mountain passes. Shortly after 1:00 a.m. on the twenty-sixth, a fire erupted at a bend in the road of the semi-remote Esperanza Avenue, in the southwestern part of the town of Cabazon. The origin was among the dry grass and brush that surrounded a pile of tires and other debris at the base of the slope. Because of the tinder dry conditions, single-digit humidity, and the high temperatures, the fire quickly grew in size. The road runs along the base of Mt. San Jacinto, and the terrain on the south side of the road was almost straight uphill for several thousand feet. This fire literally exploded up the side of the mountain, with flame lengths of nearly hundred feet. Crowds outside of the large Morongo Indian Casino just a few miles away across the ten Freeway were able to watch the fire race up the nine-thousand-foot mountain in the darkness.

Southern California fire agencies, as they always do during these conditions, had numerous prearranged strike teams available to fight the blaze. Those teams came from a combination of local fire departments, state agencies, and several federal agencies. By dawn, the fire had grown exponentially in size and was beginning to threaten small mountain communities several miles away. One of the many crews who were called in to fight this blaze was U.S. Forest Service Engine no. 57 based out of the nearby mountain town of Idyllwild. This crew comprised Capt. Mark Loutenhiser and Firefighters Jess McLean, Daniel Hoover-Najera, Jason McKay, and Pablo Cerda. By five fifteen that morning, those five men were staged near a road junction to conduct structure protection operations in the mountains above the approaching fire. They deployed in darkness and took up defensive positions around an empty vacation home that had good views of the valley and a large swimming pool from which to draw water. They were well above the fire and did not report any activity in the darkness. Even as dawn broke that day, the darkness remained as the fire below was pushing smoke and ash in front of it.

What the firefighters did not know was that the home they were guarding sat above a hidden chute or natural funnel in the mountain. Shortly after 7:00 a.m., their sister crew, stationed just a few hundred yards away, reported that a wall of flame had exploded out of the chute and had completely overrun the crew of Engine no. 57. At the time, the winds were roaring uphill at over 50 mph, and the accompanying smoke, ash, and firebrands had completely obscured the vision of everybody in the area. The crew had almost no warning whatsoever, and the firefighters were barely able to flee more than a few yards before they were engulfed by the flames. Four of the men died almost immediately, and the fifth died a few days later from massive burns. Responding firefighters found the bodies of their mates still burning when they arrived to help a few minutes after the fire had roared through. The twelve-hundred-degree heat of the firestorm had completely destroyed everyone and everything in its path.

The deadly blaze dubbed the "Esperanza Fire" by officials burned for four more days after that and was not contained until October 31. Besides killing the five firefighters, it consumed over forty-one thousand acres of brush and forest, destroyed or damaged fifty-four homes and ranches, and destroyed a large number of livestock. Within a day of it starting, investigators had located the area of origin and had determined that the fire was an act of arson. More importantly, they had located a cigarette and wooden matches delay incendiary device within the area of origin. Upon finding it, investigators immediately recognized the device, as they had seen some like it before.

The San Gorgonio Pass area of Southern California had been having its share of fires over the past six months. Many, of course, could be written off as accidental fires due to equipment and vehicle problems. However, as early as June 2006, investigators had noted numerous unexplained fires occurring just off the rural and semi-rural mountain roads in the area. A review of the fire history in that area showed that that particular region of Southern California had been plagued with more than its share of wild land fires for several years. The area spanning from the I-15 Freeway to the west, which generally marks the start of the Los Angeles basin, to the town of Palm Desert on the east routinely had several hundred fires each year. While most of those were accidental events, many could not be explained or were outright arsons.

To make matters worse, there were other factors at play in that area. A dirty secret in the firefighting community was that forest service investigators had long suspected a local forest service fire captain of being a possible serial arsonist. They had even conducted more than one surveillance operation on that man over the past few years and believed that he could have started several dozen fires in the forests north of Los Angeles and lately in the San Bernardino area. That man had never been arrested for the fires, but was aware that he was being followed and had in fact "burned" more than one surveillance team as it tried to track him on the lonely mountain roads. That person would pose a significant problem to investigators and the prosecution in the future**.

By June, the stakes had changed, and the suspicious fires in the area had increased. Along with that came the alarming discovery of a delay ignition device found at two fire scenes. The device, a classic "layover" style delay device consisting of a filtered "Marlboro" cigarette with five to seven matches lying over it at a ninety-degree angle, had been found near the origins of both fires. The crime lab would later find the same person's DNA on the cigarette butts of both devices. It was clear by mid-summer that at least one serial arson offender was working in the area. At seven arson scenes in the area, investigators had located similar cigarette and matches delay ignition devices. Investigators took the drastic step of installing "pole cameras" at various locations in the area. These were static surveillance cameras, surreptitiously hidden on utility poles. The stakes were getting higher as by October, sixty unsolved arson fires had occurred in that area. Later in the summer, still more ignition devices were found, but those differed in design. Those latter ones were more of the "John

Orr" style with matches surrounding a single cigarette and secured by a rubber band. Investigators believed that either there were two arsonists in the area or there was one arsonist who was experimenting with his devices.

On October 22, a fire broke out on Mias Canyon Road. At that fire, a suspicious vehicle was seen on the pole cameras. That vehicle, a Ford Taurus, was linked to a mechanic from the local town of Beaumont. The mechanic had a fairly active criminal history and was currently wanted for failing to appear in court on a matter. His name was Raymond Oyler.

When the Esperanza blaze broke out four days later, investigators had yet to interview Ray Oyler regarding the Mias Fire. A day after the firefighters were killed in the mountains above Cabazon, a massive arson task force was assembled consisting of local, state, and federal investigators. A reward, which eventually reached $500,000, was posted for information leading to the arrest of the arsonist. One of the first things that task force members did in the investigation was to go to Beaumont and interview Ray Oyler. At that time, they were able to get a voluntary DNA sample from him.

A "monkey wrench" was thrown into the investigation early, as investigators located a known and registered arsonist who lived very close to the area of origin of the Esperanza Fire. He was questioned by task force members, and he also submitted a DNA sample. DNA was also taken from other family members, including his brother. Eventually, the "monkey wrench" was dealt with through a thorough investigation, and the arsonist who lived near the origin was eliminated as a suspect in that event.

On October 31, the same day the final firefighter from Engine 57 succumbed to his injuries, Ray Oyler was arrested and charged with arson for the two fires that occurred in June. His DNA matched the DNA recovered on the two cigarette/matchbook devices found at those events. He was also classified as "a person of interest" in the Esperanza Fire.

Upon his arrest, task force investigators served a search warrant at his home and recovered several digital cameras, a number of cigarette butts and an "afro style" wig. Another sinister item was also found in his car—a copy of the underground revenge manual called the "Anarchist's Cookbook."

During a "bail enhancement" hearing shortly after the arrest, task force investigators revealed to the court that the cigarette and matches devices they had found during the June fires which had Oyler's DNA on them were nearly (but not quite) identical to the matches and cigarette device found at the origin of the Esperanza Fire. They considered those to be "signature devices." Unfortunately, for the prosecution, lab experts were not able to recover anyone's DNA off the Esperanza device.

Following his arrest, thirty experienced prosecutors and investigators reexamined the evidence, and all unanimously agreed that Oyler had started the Esperanza Fire. He was subsequently charged with five counts of murder and eleven counts of arson, which included eight other fires that had occurred since June 2006.

Ray Oyler, thirty-six years old at the time of his arrest, was a heavily tattooed man who had had several run-ins with the law. He had done an eight-month stretch in state prison in 2001 for a drug charge. He also had a 1995 arrest and conviction for auto theft. Not much is known about Oyler's early life. He grew up in the San Gorgonio Pass area where he resided most of his life. When he was sixteen years old, he fathered a daughter. The mother of that child was fifteen years old, and she and Ray never married. Oyler had been briefly married from 1997 to 1999 to another woman. His ex-father-in-law described Oyler as a "violent lowlife" who had been involved in the sale and use of drugs. His ex-wife later died in a traffic accident, but investigators were able to locate public records of her and Oyler's marriage. A review of her petition for divorce from Oyler describes him as "violent, unpredictable, and paranoid." She also described that he was heavily into drugs. At the time of the Esperanza Fire, Oyler was working as an auto mechanic and was living with his twenty-four-year-old girlfriend. The two had a seven-month-old daughter together. Upon his arrest, coworkers expressed disbelief and told authorities that Oyler was a chain smoker and maybe "accidentally" lit the fires. It is interesting to note that neighbors described him as nocturnal, in that he was often spotted awake late at night doing things around his home.

An important side note to this case was that there is some evidence that earlier in his life Ray Oyler trained as a firefighter. While never hired, he was known to have taken courses in fire science and having applied at more than one fire agency in California.

The Esperanza murder trial began in 2008. Leading up to this, more details emerged about the case. Investigators revealed that upon first being interviewed, Oyler had given them distinctly different alibi stories as to where he had been and what he was doing on the night of the fire. A witness who stood next to Oyler as the pair was viewing the fire from a distance heard him remark, "It's burning just as I expected it would." A relative came forward and told the task force that Oyler was upset with the county animal control agency for taking his dog, and he had stated that he was going to burn the mountain as a diversion so that he could free his pit bull. That relative also stated that Oyler claimed to have lit two other fires on the day the dog was impounded. That was the same day as the Mias fire. A check revealed that his dog had in fact been impounded just one week prior to the Esperanza fire. Other evidence that puts Oyler "out and about" during the incident was his image on a security camera at a convenience store, where he purchased cigarettes. When later interviewed by detectives about his cigarettes, Oyler lied about the brand that he usually smoked. All of those factors weighed heavily against Oyler at his trial.

During the trial, the prosecution upped the stakes and charged Oyler with twenty-three wild land fires, seventeen of which were started with delay incendiary devices somewhat similar to the two with Oyler's DNA on them. The prosecution acknowledged that some of these devices differed from others, but that was because Oyler was experimenting with different ignition systems. The prosecutor noted that each fire got progressively larger and that it appeared that Oyler was trying to perfect his fire setting activities to have one large and major event. Spatial mapping showed that Ray Oyler's apartment was dead center in the middle of all of the fires.

The defense team acknowledged that Oyler was a serial arsonist and that he in fact did use ten identical delay devices called "layover" devices to set only ten of the fires. They disputed Oyler's involvement in the other thirteen fires, including the Esperanza fire. They described his devices as five to seven matches set at right angles to and lying over a cigarette. They established the defense theory that at least one more serial arson offender was working the area and then tried to introduce evidence pointing at a former firefighter in the area as a serial arsonist. After a lengthy hearing, the trial judge would not allow that evidence into the trial. A defense expert testified that Oyler's devices were his signature and that the Esperanza device did not fit his signature. The prosecution dramatically countered that Oyler's signature was "destruction, chaos and fire."

The trial lasted for a month. Finally, in early March, the jury found Oyler guilty of nineteen counts of arson, sixteen counts of possessing incendiary devices, and five counts of first degree murder. Two weeks later, after just one day of deliberation, a jury sentenced Raymond Lee Oyler to death for the murder of five firefighters. Oyler was sent to California's death row in 2009, still protesting his innocence for the Esperanza fire.

** Author's Note

The Raymond Oyler case was concluded not without its share of controversy. In January 2009, defense attorneys tried to introduce evidence into the trial that a second serial arsonist had been at work in the very same area where the Esperanza fire had occurred. The prosecution fought that evidence from being heard by the Oyler jury, and a hearing was conducted by the trial judge to determine if that "evidence" was relevant to the case. Of course, that hearing was out of the presence of the Oyler jury, but it was open to the public and reported in the local media.

Defense attorneys called to the stand a formidable witness, recently retired United States Forest Service Investigator Ronald Huxman. During a lengthy hearing, Huxman related that he had been conducting a several years long investigation into a man named Michael McNeill. McNeill had been employed for several years by the forest service as a "fire prevention technician." He had even been promoted to the rank of battalion chief. His duties included driving around in patrol vehicles looking for fires and looking for areas overgrown with brush and ripe for massive fires.

Investigator Huxman related that McNeill had a history of odd and bizarre behavior and had been moved to three different forests in the state of California over a several-year period. In each area that he moved into, a rash of arson fires would erupt. Delay incendiary devices were found at some of the sites. The delay incendiary devices were similar to the device found at the Esperanza fire origin, a bundle of wooden matches held together with a rubber band, surrounding a cigarette. That device was somewhat different from the "layover device" that Oyler's attorneys admitted that he favored. The devices suspected of having been placed by McNeill were a very close copy of the devices used twenty years earlier by the notorious John Orr, another fire captain.

Huxman first noticed McNeill when he worked in the Angeles National Forest in the Los Angeles region. McNeill seemed to have a gift for "discovering" fires. Under suspicion by his coworkers, McNeill mysteriously left the forest service for a year or so and was employed by the Bureau of Land Management. By 2006, McNeill was hired back with the forest service and was promoted to the rank of captain. Later, McNeill was transferred to the San Bernardino area, where he made numerous claims to being an expert in arson investigation. Shortly after his arrival, that area seemed to have a spate of suspicious and arson fires. At that time, Huxman notified his cohorts in the San Bernardino area with his suspicions about McNeill. Surveillance operations were mounted, and soon investigators realized that McNeill was aware that he was being followed, as he routinely played games with investigators and faked suspicious activity to see if they would confront him, which they did on occasion. This "cat and mouse" game went on for months until a month before the Esperanza fire. Investigators realized that McNeill was on to them and again abandoned their surveillance of him.

However, by that time they had begun to suspect that McNeill had possibly faked many of his qualifications and did not appear to be a competent arson investigator. He was unable to write simple reports and was unwilling to show up at scenes of arson fires, despite being observed in the area at the time of the fires.

The arson investigation into McNeill soon fizzled as it was obvious that he was playing games with investigators. During the investigation, it was learned that McNeill had lied on his original background information when applying for his forest service job and was in fact a convicted felon. He had prior felony convictions for burglary and for making terrorist threats against a girlfriend. He also had a misdemeanor conviction for falsely reporting an emergency. Additionally, there was evidence in at least two police reports that McNeil had both fabricated evidence and attempted or threatened suicide. Lastly, at least two police agencies had determined that McNeill had falsely identified himself as a firefighter and had produced fake identification and badges. McNeill had also checked himself into a psychiatric facility.

All of that criminal and suspicious activity had occurred in the years prior to McNeill being employed by the forest service. A deeper probe into McNeill's background showed that he had in fact been fired from his very first firefighting job in rural Utah, when the fire chief suspected him of placing a delay incendiary device at a brushfire. In true John Orr fashion, McNeill, then a twenty-two-year-old rookie firefighter, had ceremoniously marched into a burning field and "found" a delay incendiary device. When confronted by his chief about this suspicious act, McNeill did not deny his guilt, but simply left the fire company without saying a word. Somehow all of this obvious historical information had eluded forest service administrative personnel, and he had been hired and remained employed for several years. Upon confirming this information in 2007, the forest service finally terminated McNeill's employment.

The McNeill saga did not end there. In 2008, McNeill came to the attention of investigators from the Los Angeles Sheriff's Department, when he reported himself as the victim of an arson attack. A bizarre and lengthy investigation ensued and resulted in the sheriff's investigators accusing McNeill of staging that attack and another arson attack with a "Molotov cocktail." When confronted with his staged incidents, McNeill went on the offensive and began "planting" digital evidence against his former wife, along with investigators from the sheriff's department, US Forest Service, and the ATF. He additionally began threatening judges and elected officials and warned of committing murders and of setting off "a dirty bomb." As it turns out, McNeill was an expert with computers and was able to forge documents and send fake e-mail messages to investigators, administrators, and even to courts. McNeill was arrested by undercover sheriff's investigators while literally at the keyboard of a computer sending threats and fake e-mail messages. A search of his home by ATF agents revealed that he had forged certificates and documents from dozens of federal schools and agencies, falsely declaring him an "expert" in fire and bomb scenes, narcotics, and many other disciplines. By 2008, McNeill was in jail in Los Angeles on dozens of felony charges and was facing a twenty-year-sentence if convicted. His bail stood at $2.8 million.

Despite his incarceration, McNeill still did not go away quietly. In September 2009, the largest brushfire in Los Angeles County's history raged for several weeks across the Angeles National Forest, destroying over 100,000 acres, hundreds of structures and homes, and killing two Los Angeles County firefighters. This fire, known as the "Station" fire, was determined to be an arson event by forest service investigators, and the murder/arson investigation was turned over to the Los Angeles Sheriff's Department. Several weeks into the massive manhunt for the arsonist, sheriff's homicide investigators got a letter and phone calls from McNeill who was being held at the county jail. McNeill demanded to speak to investigators as he claimed to have "intimate knowledge" about who set that massive Station fire.

Your author, as part of the investigative task force into the Station fire, accompanied a homicide detective to interview Michael McNeill. We listened to McNeill speak for almost two hours and concluded that he did not have any personal knowledge of the Station fire event. However, we were struck by how clever and sly he was as he reiterated many events that had already been in the local media, and he was able to tell in a convincing manner that would lead a person to believe that he in fact did have personal knowledge of the fire. McNeill came off as a very skilled conman and placed the blame for the Station fire on the very investigator, Ron Huxman, who had been dogging him for years. In telling his story, it was evident that McNeill was an aficionado of John Orr as he had intimate details and knowledge of Orr's fire setting activities. He claimed in the interview that the series of suspicious fires surrounding him (McNeill) for several years was in fact a cunning plan by the forest service to blame him and thereby cover up the fact that several forest service arson investigators were in fact serial arsonists. McNeill claimed that he was "onto the true arsonist" and that federal officials wanted to silence him. He also claimed to be a "leading expert on arsonists" and to have formed a Riverside area arson task force. Both claims proved to be complete fabrications.

McNeill's assertions were soon discredited, but he displayed the traits and knowledge of a serial fire setter to me, and it would be a difficult issue for the court to deal with in regards to McNeill's involvement in any of the Oyler fires. On a final (and satisfying) note in this bizarre story, Michael McNeill pled guilty in early 2011 to numerous counts of making terrorist threats against public officials. He was sentenced to nineteen years in state prison. He has adamantly denied any involvement in any wildfire arsons or the two staged arsons at his home.

(The above information was compiled through court records, newspaper accounts, a personal interview of McNeill, letters sent by McNeill to investigators, and personal conversations with several investigators from the Los Angeles sheriffs, ATF, USFS, and Cal Fire)

Investigator Analysis

Ray Oyler is the first person in the United States ever to be sentenced to death for murder for starting a wild land fire. This landmark case has opened legal grounds for several impending arson cases.

Ray Oyler was a serial arson offender who was in the process of perfecting his fire setting activity with the hopes of achieving greater and greater results. His devices were simple and easily constructed and afforded him a several-minute delay to get away from the area of origin. His brief background in the fire service no doubt gave him the knowledge of how to build incendiary devices. This case is a nice illustration of a question that has bothered me for years: why do we in the fire investigative field continue to teach aspiring firefighters how to build incendiary delay devices? I find it akin to teaching a citizen how to commit the perfect murder.

CHAPTER 3

The Serial Murders and Arsonists

Five of the previously cited men, Bruce Peter Lee, John Orr, Thomas Sweatt, Paul Keller, and Pat Russ, represent the true heavyweights of the serial arson world. All of these men were convicted of multiple arsons and multiple murders. In their cases, it is clear that arson is their primary motivation and that they are arsonists who happen to have murdered as a result of their arsons. The following group of offenders is almost the opposite. This group of extraordinarily heinous individuals comprises serial murderers who also happen to be serial arsonists. Their main focus is more obviously on the murder aspect than of the fire setting. Many are quite famous for their murder sprees and are not well known for their incendiary acts.

According to former FBI behavioral analyst William Hagmaier and almost all of his colleagues, most serial killers they have studied have very similar backgrounds. Among their shared traits is the fact that the vast majority have a history in their youth of extensive bedwetting, animal torture or abuse, and extensive juvenile fire setting behavior. Of course, all of this is almost always related to horrendous childhoods which include physical and sexual abuse, neglect, and possibly some physical or mental abnormalities. Hagmaier, during a lecture attended by this author, stated that almost every serial killer he personally studied showed a history of arson activity. Among the more well-known killers who have a history of arson were Ted Bundy, who was executed in Florida and suspected of at least thirty-three murders. Bundy's fire setting activity was never fully investigated due to the intense investigations surrounding his multi-state murder spree, but he did admit prior to his death to a childhood history of arson. Arthur Shawcross, a.k.a. the "Genesee River

Killer" who died in prison in New York in 2008, was convicted of thirteen murders and was suspected in another. His ex-wife revealed to investigators that she was appalled by his acts of animal torture and frequent fire setting during their marriage. He had at least one arson conviction on his record. Another famous criminal who had at least two arson convictions on his record was the notorious Charles Manson. In post-World War I Germany, serial killer, Peter Kurten, a.k.a. the "The Vampire of Dusseldorf," while committing his string of child rapes, murders, and attempted murders also produced at least one conviction for arson. In the same era, Germany also produced a mass murder spree arsonist named Ernst Wagner.

The most prolific serial killer ever identified in the United States was Gary Ridgway. For a twenty-year-period from 1982 to 2001, he escaped justice while amassing a body count of at least forty-nine young women. That man, more famously known as Seattle's "Green River Killer," admitted after his arrest to the usual serial murderer childhood trilogy of animal torture, bedwetting, and serial arson activity. He has been sentenced to over forty life sentences for his murders.

It should be noted that while the majority of the serial killers who have spoken to the "profilers" have admitted to arson activity, there is very little documentation to support their statements, since their murder investigations greatly overshadowed any other behavior. Below are a few of the more prolific serial murderers who are also serial arsonists.

Ottis Elwood Toole: Serial Murderer/Serial Arsonist
Period of Activity: 1957-82, Florida, Many Western States

Almost all serial arson offenders are distinct loners, with few friends and relationships that seldom last. Ottis Toole is the one person in this book who defies some of the rules of a serial arsonist. This should be no surprise since he defied almost every rule in society and for that matter nearly every rule as a civilized human. Among his many claims to infamy, the label of serial arsonist is down the list a bit from Toole's more notorious labels. Ottis Toole is probably the most deviant person on this list, and if his litany of claims is to be believed, he is one of the most deviant persons in American history. Before his death on Florida's Death Row in 1996 (of natural causes, not execution), Ottis Toole was accused of and freely admitted to being a child rapist, serial murderer, mass murderer, serial arsonist, necrophiliac, practitioner of bestiality, and serial cannibal. Famous among his many notorious claims is that he openly admitted to kidnapping, raping, and killing six-year-old Adam Walsh, the son of TV host John Walsh, who would later dedicate his life and career to hunting "America's Most Wanted."

Ottis Toole is one of the few serial arson offenders who had a partner. For the last six years of his freedom, Ottis Toole partnered with a man named Henry Lee Lucas. The pair claimed to have killed up to six hundred persons across several states. Although that number appears to be highly exaggerated by the pair, experts believe that a number that is around hundred victims is more likely. No matter the actual number, their grisly tale of murder and depravity far outweighs any arsons committed by Ottis Toole as an individual.

Toole was raised in bizarre and despicable circumstances in Jacksonville, Florida. There is little doubt that the events of his childhood shaped him into the monster he became fairly early in life. His alcoholic father fled the home when he was just a baby, and his mother was a religious zealot who often forced him to wear girl's clothes and kept him supplied with narcotics. At the same time, his grandmother actively practiced satanic rituals. Toole's grandmother reportedly involved him in her satanic rituals while he was a child, which included self-mutilation and robbing graves for body parts. He later stated that he was raped by an adult male at age six and then later introduced to sex at age ten by his elder sister. Not surprisingly, this hellish childhood caused Ottis Toole to be a frequent runaway when he was young. By twelve, he was involved in a homosexual relationship with a neighbor boy.

In addition to these environmental plagues on his childhood, Toole was also maligned by numerous physical and mental ailments. He was described as having an IQ of around seventy-five, or just slightly above retardation. Many experts later opined that his IQ was probably higher, but that he performed very low on the tests due to several learning disabilities. He was diagnosed with dyslexia and ADHD and grew up illiterate. He suffered physically from epilepsy and had frequent grand mal seizures. At one of his later murder trials, psychiatric experts would describe Toole as having paranoid schizophrenia.

Toole said that in this early stage of his life, he got his only relief out of setting things on fire. He would later state, "I been doing fires since I was a little kid. See, the little fires don't excite me, you know. Only the big fires excite me." By the age of fourteen, Toole took to dressing as a female prostitute and luring male customers for sex. He killed his first man at this age by running him over with a truck. That same year he strangled a woman. He often frequented gay bars in his early teen years. Despite all of these factors, Toole was not arrested for any crime until the age of seventeen, when he was jailed for loitering.

For the next few years Toole survived as a transvestite prostitute, selling his body to men. He also continued his fire setting behavior. By his early twenties, he had been arrested and convicted for the crime of arson.

From 1966 until about 1973, Toole dropped off the radar and was believed to have been drifting around the American southwest. He survived by panhandling and prostitution. By 1974, Toole had become a prime suspect in the murder of a twenty-four-year-old female in Nebraska. He left Nebraska and stopped in Boulder, Colorado, where within a month he became a suspect in the murder of a thirty-one-year-old woman. Accused but not charged in either crime, Toole left the area and headed back to Jacksonville, Florida.

By 1976, he married a woman who was twenty-five years older than him. She left him three days later when she learned that he was a homosexual. That same year, Toole met Henry Lucas in a Florida soup kitchen. The two soon developed a sexual relationship and learned that they both had similar horrific childhoods. The two remained partners in murder and in love for the next six years. Toole admitted to over 108 murders while with Lucas. Lucas later gave varying accounts of up to six hundred murders, many of which are now in considerable doubt by investigators. While in prison, both Toole and Lucas gave dozens of explicit confessions and interviews detailing countless acts of arson, murder, decapitation, necrophilia, and cannibalism.

In 1981, Toole (acting alone) kidnapped and murdered young Adam Walsh. On January 12, 1982, Toole locked a sixty-four-year-old man in his own home and set fire to the house, killing him. In February 1983, Toole murdered a nineteen-year-old girl in Tallahassee. He was subsequently arrested for both crimes, and in 1984, he was convicted and sentenced to death for that arson murder. That same year he was convicted and received a second death sentence for the nineteen-year-old-girl's murder. Both sentences were eventually commuted to life in prison. While in prison, Toole also admitted to four additional murders and was given four more life sentences. Toole died in prison of liver failure in 1996. He was forty-nine years old.

Investigator Analysis

Ottis Toole was included into this writing for a specific reason. He is a very well-known serial murderer, but much lesser known serial arsonist. There are very few records available to link him to a specific number of arson events. The only real documentation available about his serial arson behavior is his admissions during several videotaped interviews. As in many of these cases, there is very little corroborative evidence. However, he has at least two convictions for arson and one of them is for a deliberate arson/premeditated murder. This evidence alone can make the inference that he was involved in many more arson events for which he was never arrested.

The main reason Toole's arson activity has never been explored is because the other crimes he was involved in were so horrific in their scope and number that arson was probably not a very important subject to the investigators trying to track him.

Toole's case very much mirrors the activities of serial murderer/serial arsonist Carl Panzram of fifty years earlier. Both were products of a bestial childhood who suffered greatly as the victims of both physical and sexual abuse. Both claimed to have been introduced to homosexuality by violent means, and both later adopted that same violent sexual behavior themselves, no doubt reinforced by their early years in prison. Again like Panzram, Toole vanished from the public records for a number of years as he wandered, roamed, and tramped the Western United States. This nomadic lifestyle makes it very difficult for law enforcement agencies to track serial criminals, and this no doubt facilitated Toole's ongoing criminal lifestyle.

Like many of the arsonists in this writing, Toole had severe physical impairments (epilepsy, seizures) along with social and mental deficiencies. Also burdened by learning disabilities, Toole was a ripe candidate from the outset to be a serial fire setter. His own descriptions that fire setting was his only outlet as a youth show that it was his only sense of power at that time. Toole freely admitted that he drew excitement from fire setting and that the bigger the fire, the more the excitement it caused in him. Most of the available literature on Ottis Toole describes him as being sexually aroused by fire. This author believes that that is an unsupported argument with little medical or academic documentation. It is more likely that his fires were caused by the mixed motives of power, excitement, and probably revenge. The revenge aspect is similar to his other crimes in that he did horrible things in retaliation to the horrible things that were inflicted upon him as a child.

Ottis Toole also shares a distinction for accomplishing what very few serial arsonists are able to do. He actually killed someone in a structure with one of his arson fires. It is extremely difficult to commit premeditated murder by arson, mainly due to the vagaries of fire and the relative slowness by which it progresses. Most arson/murder victims are in some way incapacitated or asleep before the event and are unable to flee the flames.

Ottis Toole was a disorganized offender arsonist, who chose his targets at a young age for their convenience and opportunity. There is no evidence that he used any sort of device or delay system to start his fires. He most likely used available materials at the scene and an open flame, most likely matches, as an ignition source. While there is no way to gauge an accurate number of his arson events, it is probably very safe to speculate that they were in the hundreds or even up to a thousand.

Cayetano Santos Godino: Serial Murderer/Serial Arsonist Period of Activity: 1900-13, Buenas Aires, Argentina

Although they may achieve more notoriety, serial offenders are not solely based in the United States. Other than the United States and England, however, there appear to be few public records listing serial arsonists. One name that does stand out is an evil little man who is as notorious for his murders and attempted murders as he is for his fire setting activity.

Like most subjects in this book, Godino was cursed from birth. He was born on Halloween in 1896 to two Italian immigrants in Buenas Aires. The couple had seven other children to care for, and Godino's father was a child/ wife abuser and a raging alcoholic. To complicate matters, he had syphilis when Godino was conceived and passed on severe health problems to his son as a result. These health issues persisted and caused some visible physical abnormalities to Godino. He was extremely small in size, well under five foot tall as an adult, and had extraordinarily large ears. These physical oddities no doubt added to his rage in life as he obtained the uncomplimentary nickname of the "big-eared midget."

This childhood trauma no doubt was the major factor in this man's violent future. At a very early age, his mother observed him torturing and killing birds and cats. He soon began playing with fire on a routine basis. He was extremely violent and not at all interested in education. Because of this, he was quickly moved from school to school by worried officials.

At just seven years old, Godino committed his first serious crime. He lured a small two-year-old boy to a secluded area and beat him over and over until the boy collapsed. He then threw the boy into a nearby ditch. A passing policeman observed some of this activity. Just over a year later, he lured another two-year-old child to an abandoned building and began beating her with a rock. Again, a nearby police officer intervened and saved the girl. Godino was not prosecuted due to his young age.

By the time he was ten years old, he was a compulsive masturbator and abuser of animals. His actions were so out of control his parents sent him to a state-run reform school. At twelve years old, he was seen attempting to strangle a two-year-old boy. He was released from jail almost immediately and a week later tried to maim another young boy by setting fire to his eyelids. After that final event, his parents brought him to the juvenile authorities where he was incarcerated for three years.

In 1911, Godino was released from juvenile hall at the age of fifteen years old. Within a month of his release, his activities skyrocketed. On January 17, 1912, he set an arson fire to a large warehouse. Upon his arrest, he told the cops he loved to see firefighters working and liked it when they fell into the fire. Nine days after this arson, a thirteen-year-old child was found dead in a nearby abandoned house. Godino would later be charged with that murder.

Two months later, Godino set fire to the clothes of a five-year-old girl. She would later die as a result of her burns. He was subsequently charged with that murder several months later.

In September 1912, Godino torched a railway station. Six weeks later, he was arrested after he tried to strangle an eight-year-old boy. He was released back to his parents while awaiting trial for the attempted murder. A week later, a police officer saw him hitting a young girl. Four days after that, he attempted to kidnap a little girl and was caught after she began screaming. Later in November, he set fire to two large outbuildings.

By the first week of December 1912, Godino was coming to the peak of his orgy of violence and fire. He lured a young boy to a secluded building by promising candy. Once there, Godino beat him and tried to strangle him with his belt. When that didn't work, he used the belt to hog-tie the young boy and began beating him mercilessly. After a while, he decided to hammer a nail into the young boy's head. He went out looking for a nail and was confronted by the boy's father who was looking for the child. Calmly telling the father that he had not seen the boy, Godino continued on his quest for a nail. He found one and returned to the scene and hammered the nail into the boy's skull, killing him. Later, he went to the child's wake and poked at the skull where he had hammered the nail. Godino was soon arrested, and he gave a full confession to all of his crimes. He eventually admitted to the murders of four very young children, the attempted murders of seven other children, and the arsons of seven structures.

At the age of sixteen, Godino entered a reformatory. He soon tried to kill some of the other juvenile inmates. A court later declared him insane and shortly sent him to an adult prison. He had numerous problems with other inmates and was hospitalized for a severe beating he took after he killed some cats belonging to other inmates. By 1944, after many years of bad health in prison, he died under suspicious circumstances.

Investigator's Analysis

Cayetano Godino never had a chance in life, nor did any of his victims. What little documentation there is of this man shows that he was cursed before he was even born. In most cases, syphilis can be passed down and has a history of attacking certain portions of the brain. There is little doubt his exposure to this disease caused his birth defects and any brain defects there might have been. Additionally, growing up in an abusive home also set the stage for what was an inevitable ending.

Early warning signs of many serial murderers and many arsonists include animal torture, compulsive juvenile fire setting, and compulsive masturbation. These three items are sometimes known as the "building blocks" for serial murderers. This case varies little from the lives of Carl Panzram, Bruce George Peter Lee, Pat Russ, and Ottis Toole. All of these men had tremendously traumatic childhoods and then spent years in juvenile facilities. Each emerged from their stay in the state-run homes even more angry and violent. Each went on unspeakable rampages after their initial release from incarceration.

Godino, being an extremely small person, targeted the weakest and smallest members of society. He attacked extremely young children and was very brutal in the attacks. He no doubt stalked his targets for a short time, but was not an organized offender.

Although there are only seven structure fires attributed to Godino, the reports of his fire compulsion at a young age would safely put his fire totals in the hundred. He murdered at least one person with fire and attempted to murder a second child with fire.

Colin Ireland "Gay Slayer": Serial Murderer/Arsonist Period of Activity: 1970-93, Essex, England

On July 19, 1993, Colin Ireland approached a lawyer in Essex, England, and advised him that he had been with a recently murdered man and was wanted for questioning by the police. Shortly after that he was presented to the local police where he gave a statement denying his involvement in the murder. Unfortunately for him, the police had his fingerprints at more than one homicide scene and arrested him for the murders of two gay men over the previous few months. One month later, Ireland gave a full confession and admitted that he was in fact the "Gay Slayer" that police had been searching for in the sadistic bondage murders of five gay men. He pled guilty without a trial and was sentenced to prison for life. Once there, he gave a detailed history of his life and crimes to a writer named Anna Gekoski. She later made these details public in an online format "Crime Library on truTV.com."

Gekoski's account reflects that Colin Ireland grew up very poor and in a broken home in lower class England in the 1960s. He and his mother moved numerous times in his youth and he never fit in. He was always behind in school and was numerous times the subject of bullying and teasing by schoolmates. Among his more humiliating experiences was the time when he and his mother were forced to live in a homeless women's camp which he described as worse than any prison.

By the time he was twelve, Ireland had several brushes with pedophiles. Because he was so poor, there were several occasions where grown men in restrooms or at arcades would offer him money for sexual favors. While he did not take up the offers, he later revealed he was emotionally scarred by those events. He hung out with other poor young men who because of their dire circumstances were forced to provide services to men in order to survive. Those lads were known as the famous "rent boys" or street prostitutes found throughout many cities in England in the 1960s and 1970s. Those events would foment a very strong hatred within Ireland when he got older.

When he was in his teens, he began getting into trouble with the law by committing an ongoing series of minor offenses. He started a lifelong series of stints in state-run homes and prisons. Among his first serious crimes was when he was sixteen years old and in a state school for running away. Another ward in the school picked on him to the point that when the boy was asleep, Colin burned up his belongings with an arson fire. He was immediately transferred out of that institution. In later years, he would admit a lifelong fascination with arson and burning things, although he never states exactly how many fires he had been involved in. Colin admitted that he had recurring fire dreams and that he was enthralled with the fire service and fire equipment.

As he grew older, he developed a few heterosexual relationships and was even married a couple of times for short periods. However, his constant trips back and forth to prison and jail broke up any serious relationships. By his late twenties, he had gone to prison for a couple burglaries and a car theft. This pattern continued for most of his twenties and early thirties. His first wife left him because she was worried about his increasingly aggressive behavior. He walked out on his second wife after just four months of marriage.

By his late thirties, Colin Ireland had dabbled at several lower-level jobs. These included manual labor, homeless shelter manager, and working at pallet yards. He was also able to get some short-time employment as a volunteer firefighter, but for an unknown reason, that career did not last long. Because he had grown fairly large in size, he also worked on occasion as a bouncer in gay clubs, although he has always maintained that he was not gay.

By 1993, and approaching forty years of age, Colin Ireland did not have much to show for his life. He had no serious employment, hadn't accomplished much, and had no family. His one enjoyment was that he was fascinated with crime dramas and loved television, books, and movies about forensics and serial killers. He would later claim that at that age he made the conscious decision to see if he could pull off the perfect series of murders.

Because of his lifelong association with gay men (although continuing to maintain that he was not gay), he knew that a local club in the Essex area was a very likely place to "hook up" with a partner for the evening. On March 8, 1993, he entered that club with the intent of finding a murder victim for the evening. He eventually located a man who identified himself as a masochist or someone willing to accept sexual punishment. Ireland was careful to leave with that man via a rear door to the bar as he was aware that there were security cameras covering the front. The pair made it to the victim's apartment, and Ireland was easily able to convince the victim to submit to being bound. Once that occurred, Ireland produced a pair of gloves from a "murder kit" he had brought with him and began to beat the victim severely. He then suffocated the victim with a plastic bag and staged props around the victim's body for the police to find. Those props included stuffed animals arranged in the sexual "69" position. He also did a curious act, and using a lighter, he burned the pubic area of the victim. Prior to leaving, he completed a detailed anti-forensics sweep of the apartment and patiently waited for hours to leave so he would blend with other pedestrians.

Ireland waited two months before returning to the club for another victim. This next man just as easily agreed to be bound, and this time Ireland robbed him of his ATM pin number. After getting the number, Ireland beat this victim severely, burned his testicles with a lighter, and then suffocated the man with rags stuffed down his throat. Again, Ireland completed a detailed anti-forensics cleaning of the apartment and staged dolls and stuffed animals in a "69" position around the victim's body.

Six days after this event, Ireland struck again. This time he picked up the very wealthy son of a U.S. Congressman at the club. Once the man was tricked into being bound, Ireland robbed him and then strangled him with a noose. He staged a doll on the body in a "69" position and completed his anti-forensics sweep.

Because he had not heard of his exploits in the press, Ireland waited only three more days to murder again. In a clone of the previous case, he strangled the victim with a noose after robbing him of his pin number. In burglarizing the apartment after the murder, Ireland found that the victim was HIV positive and became incensed. He returned to the body and began burning various parts with a lighter. He also killed the man's cat and posed the cat's body on the victim by placing the cat's mouth on the victim's penis and the cat's tail in the victim's mouth or a "69 position" of sorts. Finally, because of these oddities, the police linked at least two of the crime scenes to the same unknown suspect. Another major break was that during his "anti-forensics sweep" after the murder, Ireland missed one of his fingerprints on a window frame.

During this brief series, Ireland had called the media and police on at least two occasions to tell them about the crimes. After this fourth murder, he directly called the local police and told them that he had committed all four murders which to this point they had not linked. He called another agency with the same information. Of course, he did not identify himself in either case.

After placing those two calls on June 12, 1993, Colin Ireland stalked and murdered his final victim from the same club. This time he convinced the victim to be handcuffed. As soon as that occurred, Ireland placed a noose on his neck and demanded his pin number. He then strangled the man with the noose. It was during this attack that he decided to take his fire setting to a new level. He turned on the natural gas within the apartment and lit a fire with the hopes of incinerating the entire block. He then left. The fire burned itself out and was not noticed for a day or so.

After his arrest and subsequent confessions, Colin Ireland was asked about this final fire. He stated, "I once worked as a fireman—there is a bit of arsonist in all firemen." He also told them, "There is something in me that's highly destructive. In some moods I would be quite happy to burn the world down."

Ireland never explained why he staged the crime scenes in a sexual manner, but only said he wanted to shock the people who found the body. He also has maintained that he never engaged in homosexual acts and did not even take his clothes off or touch the men in any of those assaults. He said his sole motivation in those attacks was to get enough murders to qualify himself as a serial killer. He succeeded.

Investigator's Analysis

Colin Ireland became a serial killer as a lark. He intended to commit those crimes and stop after reaching a degree of notoriety. He obviously chose gay men as they were vulnerable and he was familiar with them and their habits. He never fully explained his fire setting peculiarities. Obviously, some of what he did was anti-forensic in nature, but some of his burnings were definitely related to some psychological need. A telling statement about his fire setting was the quote where he made reference to burning the world down. It is easy to imagine him having lit dozens if not hundreds of smaller fires in his past.

There is very little usable information about Ireland, but his case can be considered a mixture of sexual need and anger.

Carl Panzram: Serial Murderer/Serial Arsonist
Period of Activity: 1905-30, Western United States (Primarily)

To illustrate just how diverse serial arson offenders can be from each other, one only has to examine the case of Carl Panzram. Unlike the majority of the offenders listed in this group, Panzram was a career criminal whose entire life was an ongoing wave of violent crime. While the vast majority of serial arson offenders are non-confrontational, cowardly, almost passive persons, Panzram was the epitome of brutal, in-your-face violence. To Panzram, arson was almost an afterthought with crimes of rape, murder, robbery, and sodomy being his foremost pursuits. The case of Panzram was not well known at all until his story was first printed in the late 1960s. By that time he had been dead for over thirty years and had been long forgotten by all except for one person. Because of his complete lack of notoriety, this analysis of Carl Panzram has to rely on a single source document entitled *Panzram: A Journal of Murder* by Thomas E. Gaddis and James O. Long.

Carl Panzram was born in Northern Minnesota as the sixth child of German immigrants in 1891. His family can only be described as hard working, but ignorant and poor. His mother was a strict religious woman and his father was a drifting dreamer. By the time he was ten years old, his father had deserted the family and left him to be raised by brutal elder brothers and his mother. When he was twelve, he rebelled against the harsh rules and hard work of home and attempted to flee to the West to seek his fortune. Caught almost immediately, he was sent to the Minnesota State Training School for boys for the next two years. He would later describe his stay in that institution as the most significant education he had during his lifetime. He would state until his dying day that what he learned in that school trained and shaped his values and morals for the rest of his life.

The school, like most juvenile facilities in the early 1900s, was run by a religious organization. Panzram would later write that the school had but two rules to live by: Christianity and brutality. He claimed he was beaten and tortured on a near daily basis and forced to undergo intense religious indoctrination. From that, he learned to despise all religions and learned that he was able to absorb massive amounts of physical abuse. By night, he was educated into the world of force, fear, rape, and sodomy. From the other wards, he learned the lifelong lesson that it was better to be the aggressor than the victim. He learned to distrust and despise all persons and that the weak will always be the victims of the strong. Panzram lived that code the rest of his days.

In 1905, Panzram at the age of twelve claimed to have lit his first fire, wherein he burned down a large administrative building at the institution. He later wrote that it was done in hatred of the administrator of the facility. Although the fire was never suspected as being arson, state records do report a large fire at that facility that year. After noting with satisfaction the results of that blaze, Panzram vowed from that point on to continue to burn and destroy any persons or institutions who he felt wronged him.

Upon his release from the juvenile facility, Panzram again left home for the West, riding the rails and sleeping in hobo encampments. During that trip, at the age of fifteen, Panzram was gang-raped by a group of fellow tramps on a train. He later wrote that from that point on he vowed to repay every other traveler in kind. That same year he met up with an accomplice who taught him the finer arts of robbery and burglary. The two claimed to have broken into and burgled dozens of rural churches. After successfully stealing any valuable, Panzram always torched the structure. He said later that he did it not to hide his crime, but in fact because of his hatred for the institution.

On a whim, he joined the army at age sixteen. Within two months of joining, he had been disciplined a dozen times and was finally sent to the army prison at Fort Leavenworth, Kansas, for a three-year sentence. In the brutal conditions of hard work, beatings, bad food, and alleged torture at that prison, Panzram learned to despise the army as much as religion. He claimed to have set fire to a large prison shop in about 1908 by using a candle and oily rags as a delay device. Prison records would later show that a large fire of "unknown origin" had destroyed their large shoe shop building. Panzram left the army prison in 1910 and in his words left the only bit of good that remained inside of him. He said that the three years of beatings, punishment, torture, and bestial hard work convinced him once and for all that he would take out all his hatred on society in general. He left that institution with the sole intent of causing as much harm as he could to society.

Panzram began wandering around the West, aimlessly seeking opportunity and short time employment. He was invariably fired shortly from nearly every job he took. He fought on a daily basis and stole whenever the opportunity arose. He claimed to have set fire to a large circus tent at the Missouri State Fair in 1912. Months later, he claimed to have set fire to dozens of farm buildings in Arizona after he burglarized them. He said he burned every rural structure he came across, and when he couldn't find one, he burned the grass and prairie. During the same spree, he carried two stolen guns and would shoot any horse or cow he came across for the fun of it. Panzram at that time rode freight cars across the southwest and eventually into Oregon. He said he committed armed robbery, sodomy, and assault on dozens of other hobos or vagrants.

Panzram developed a flair for breaking out of jails as he had been arrested numerous times in small towns, but he escaped almost as many times. In one escape in 1912, he set fire to a town jail in Idaho. By 1914, Panzram had been arrested in Oregon for a burglary. Upon learning that he had been tricked by police into confessing and accepting a plea deal, he set fire to a county jail he was held in. Prison records later confirmed that incident. Partly as a result of that fire, Panzram was sent to one of the worst prisons in the nation in Oregon to do a seven-year stint.

In that prison was where Panzram really stood out. He had many fights with guards and several escape attempts, each ending with his capture, a severe beating, and then torture. During one escape attempt, he set fire to a prison shop as a distraction. During a second incident in 1916, Panzram, after taking steps to disable fire hoses, was seen setting fire to a prison industry building. Several months later, Panzram did effect an escape and fled to a distant town where he was recaptured after a shootout with local police. After he was sentenced to an additional ten years for that crime, Panzram eventually fashioned a successful escape from the Oregon prison several months later. He was never rearrested for that crime.

Fleeing the West, he ended up on the East Coast and then spent some time as a seaman in South America. He was eventually hired by an oil company in that area, and after being fired for fighting, he set fire to an oil rig by using an improvised delay device of rags, grease, and petroleum. Again, later records of the "Sinclair Company" confirm a massive oil well fire in the region during that time period. Panzram then tramped around Central America and Europe for a couple of years before again ending up on the East Coast of the United States. He returned back to a life of burglary and robbery, and in one unique case, he burgled the home of former U.S. President William Howard Taft. Among the items he stole were a large amount of bonds and the former president's personal .45 caliber pistol. By 1920, Panzram had killed his first men. He was living aboard a yacht in New York harbor. Every few nights he would go into town, recruit a few sailors to help him with his boat, and then get them drunk. After he would rob and sodomize them on his yacht, he would shoot each in the head with President Taft's pistol and dump their bodies in the ocean. He claimed to have killed ten men in this manner over a three-week period.

After a few months more of crime and jail in the States, Panzram shipped out to Europe and Africa. In the Congo, he raped and killed a small boy with his bare hands. A week later, he murdered six Africans who he hired to take him on a hunt for crocodiles. Returning to the United States a year later, he began a string of burglaries, robberies, and rapes that eventually landed him in a New York prison. In that institution, he set a large fire and attempted to set off a "time bomb" in order to cover an escape attempt. He only succeeded in falling thirty feet during the attempt and damaging his legs for the rest of his life. After that event, he attempted to murder another con in that prison with a hammer and then spent the rest of his five-year sentence in solitary confinement, broken up only by torture and physical punishment by the guards.

Upon his release, Panzram again shipped out across the ocean, and when months later he returned to the United States, he began a new, even more sinister series of crimes. Panzram claimed that in the final year or two of his freedom, he raped and murdered an eleven-year-old boy by beating his brains out. He would later confess to a friendly guard that he had raped and killed three small boys within that time period.

In August 1928, Panzram was arrested for a routine house burglary in Washington, DC. Inexplicably, when he was informed of the reason for his arrest, Panzram snorted derisively and told the detectives that he had "killed too many people" to worry about that little charge.

While in the District of Columbia jail, Panzram, ever recalcitrant, began trying to escape from his cell. Upon discovering his efforts, the jail guards brought Panzram to a basement area and physically tortured him for several hours. During that session and later on his own volition to a friendly guard, Carl Panzram admitted to a string of murders that no one was even had occurred. Authorities at first did not believe him and believed the admission to be empty boasts by a lifelong criminal, but eventually reporters who heard his story linked him to several unsolved killings.

Over the next few months, while communicating with a friendly guard, Panzram began documenting his life on paper. He was unique in that he was unapologetic and without remorse for his self-admitted life of crime. He admitted to and described thousands of burglaries, rapes, forced sodomy, hundreds of arsons, and twenty murders. While he felt no pity for his victims, Panzram did try and justify his actions in his writings. He claimed that from his earliest incarceration, the juvenile justice and prison systems created him and made him the most despicable man in the world. He said at the time of his arrest he had been contemplating any number of mass murders, including derailing trains, gassing trains in tunnels with poisonous gas and explosives, mass poisoning of food and water supplies, and others. Panzram felt that he had evolved to the point where he didn't want to live and didn't think anyone else deserved to live either.

In an odd predicament, the authorities who held Panzram were unsure of where to send him to face the murder charges since they were spread through numerous states. He made their decision very easy about a year after his arrest, when after admitting his guilt on the burglary charge he was sent to Leavenworth Federal Prison. Within just a few short months, he murdered a prison worker after warning staff for weeks that he was going to do that very act. He soon pled guilty to premeditated murder, acted as his own lawyer (as he always did), and was sentenced to death. Panzram then refused all appeals on his behalf and demanded to be immediately executed. His wishes were granted on September 5, 1930, when he was hung by prison authorities.

Investigator Analysis

Carl Panzram is part of a small group of serial arsonists who are also serial murderers. However, in his case there is no record or even suspicion that any of his fires killed anybody. His arsons and murders were separate definitive acts of destruction and hate.

Panzram also differs from many other serial arsonists in that his physical description and mannerisms are opposite of what one might expect. Most often, serial arsonists are thought of as cowardly, meek, and non-confrontational. In many of the cited cases in this writing, they are often physically described as soft, somewhat effeminate, fastidious, and very non-threatening in stature.

Panzram was always described as extremely physical, overly muscular, imposing, aggressive, fierce, and hardened.

He was also different in that he was no stranger to law enforcement. He was a well-known and oft-arrested career criminal, specializing in burglary and robbery. However, nowhere does it show that he was ever associated by investigators with the crime of arson. The reasons for this are fairly simple to see in hindsight. In Panzram's time, formal law enforcement agencies were just beginning to evolve. He was a drifter his entire life and probably left an area in the wake of one of his fires. To further complicate things, the West was filled with drifting men just like him, so it was easy for him to get lost in the sea of wandering men. Panzram was also fond of using aliases, which no doubt further helped him avoid detection. Lastly, when Panzram was committing his arsons in jail, he was surrounded by thousands of other potential suspects, who would never cooperate with the staff. This fact would make it impossible for penal authorities to place the blame of any arson on a particular individual.

Panzram is one of the earliest arsonists we have in this study. The main reason for this is that there simply are very few documents available today that have addressed this criminal field before the 1970s. Because of this problem, it can be difficult and problematic to put an exact tally to the total number of Panzram's fires. Most of the information regarding his arson activity came directly from his confessions and must be taken with that in mind. There is not enough corroborative evidence in the one book available about this man. However, this author has scoured that book and notes that the authors did painstaking research and have actually confirmed that many of the major fires claimed by Panzram did exist.

Like most arson stories, the original events were seldom attributed to an individual, and many were not even called criminal acts. There is good reason for that. Fires of every origin were just more common ninety years ago than they are today. Many buildings had no fire safety considerations whatsoever. Most materials used in furnishings, furniture, clothing, etc., had no fire resistance properties. Open flames were more commonplace in the form of candles, lanterns, open fires, open stoves, etc. Smoking in every form was also more common, and as a result of all of these factors, structure fires were not looked at as rare events. It would be easy to see why Panzram's arson claims, if true, were not attributed to him, even though he was easily recognized as a career criminal.

Regarding motive, this one is simple since Panzram himself describes his reasons for everything he did. He is the ultimate form of the revenge-based arsonist. In his case, he lit fires in order to get revenge from the very institutions he felt had wronged him all of his life. His target selection was clear in that he specifically targeted the various penal institutions he hated. Most of his confirmed acts of arson were within jails, juvenile facilities, and prisons. According to his confessions, his favorite target for revenge was churches. He estimated that he and sometimes a partner torched dozens of churches in their crime wave across the American West. Again, the choosing of those churches as a target was based on all the wrongs Panzram believed the Christian religion had done to him. For some other less defined reason, he also bragged about torching virtually any barn, outbuilding, or ranch property they came across. At the same time, Panzram also claimed to have randomly killed the ranch or farm livestock that he came across for no particular reason. One can only speculate that he had grown up with nothing and probably hated others for their successes. The last major fire that Panzram claims was to an oil rig in Central America. He admits that that was lit as revenge for being fired from his job on the rig.

Panzram's level of sophistication appears to have evolved as he matured. He obviously was not the most skilled criminal in the world as he was arrested dozens of times. However, similar to the Bruce Peter Lee case in England in the 1970s, Panzram was a student of the street. His skills and "animal cunning" no doubt developed over the years and he learned from his early failures. He claims to have used rudimentary materials found at the scene (grease, rags, torches, etc) to fashion devices of a sort that would mask the original origin of the fire. Like many street criminals, Panzram's MO evolved through the years, and there is probably little doubt that his latter arson events were much more successful than some earlier events.

Panzram also has some other dangerous and unique traits. Some other criminal types that are close cousins to arsonists are the bomber and the poisoner. While both types are even rarer than the arsonist, Panzram admits in his writings that he dabbled and planned in both of those pursuits. He admitted to small-scale poisoning of food at a juvenile facility when he was but twelve years old. Just prior to his final arrest, he was fantasizing about large-scale poisonings and bombings of trains.

As far as his personality traits were concerned, Panzram was generally a loner all his life with very few friends. He had no contact with his family, and other than a crime partner or two, he seldom shared his misdeeds with anyone.

Carl Panzram may go down as one of the most hate-filled and dangerous men who ever lived, but his arsons are much less dramatic. He is classified as a disorganized offender (with some semi-organized traits), based on his main motive—pure hate. He self-admittedly burned many targets as he happened upon them, using whatever materials he came across. His devices, when used, were made from available materials found at the scene and were fairly crude in their design. Based solely on his own admissions and the few verified accounts available, an approximate number of arson events associated with Panzram would be between five hundred and one thousand.

David Berkowitz ".44-Caliber Killer"; "Son of Sam": Serial Murderer/Serial Arsonist
Period of Activity: 1965-77, New York City

In the summer of 1977 in Yonkers, New York, Craig Glassman, a detective with a local sheriff's office, was dealing with a string of oddities. He had moved into an apartment at 35 Pine Street a few weeks prior and had soon received several threatening notes at his door and his mailbox. The notes mentioned "Satan" and "demons." The notes continued for several weeks until the early morning hours of August 6. Detective Glassman awoke to find a fire burning outside his apartment door. That would be the last in a string of hundreds of fires lit by a disturbed man known as David Berkowitz. Berkowitz was arrested amid media frenzy four days later, but not for the arson.

Berkowitz was a very soft, almost feminine-looking twenty-four-year-old, who looked just like the nice Jewish boy next door, which he was. He was a nonconfrontational person who was an army veteran and had successfully held several jobs. He was working in a postal facility at the time of his arrest. Neighbors would later describe Berkowitz as that nice, innocent-looking, shy boy who lived alone in an apartment and didn't bother anyone.

Like almost all serial arsonists, Berkowitz was a loner who hid a very dark and disturbing side of his persona during the day. At night, he frequently walked and drove about the city, attempting to control his demons. He wasn't always successful.

Berkowitz was born in 1953 in New York. He was later told that his natural mother died at birth and that there was no record of a father. Three days after his birth, he was adopted by a loving Jewish family from the Bronx and lived a fairly uneventful life with them. From his earliest years, both his mother and father realized that David was a bit of a sneak. He was very adept at doing things behind his parents' back and getting away with them. His adopted parents realized there was something a bit odd about him, but they could never really put their finger on it.

After his arrest and conviction, Berkowitz detailed his secret life in a series of dozens of interviews and lengthy letters with the psychiatrist assigned to his case by the court, Dr. David Abrahamsen. Abrahamsen, one of the foremost authorities on the criminal mind, later described Berkowitz's story in many seminars, papers, and a book *Confessions of Son of Sam.*

Berkowitz said he learned at a very young age to be sneaky and sly. He was extremely innocent looking, and he took great delight in doing some small crime and having his parents wonder who could have done that, certainly not that young innocent child. Berkowitz was prone to overeating and indulged in sweets and desserts. He soon gained a soft, almost feminine appearance with innocent blue eyes and curly hair.

Sometime in his preteen years, Berkowitz started developing his deviant behavior. There was a bird his mother kept that always bothered him. Over the course of a week, he slowly slipped poison to the animal until it died. He loved to capture and torture insects and small rodents, often burning them with matches. He disliked dogs and cats and frequently accosted all the animals in the neighborhood. Conversely, dogs seemed to dislike him as they often barked at him. A week before his final fire, Berkowitz shot and killed a neighbor's dog. He later said of himself, "I killed and tortured thousands of bugs . . . I was killing, maiming, and destroying since I was a child."

During that same period, Berkowitz started experimenting with fire and vandalism. He often wandered about his home and apartment building, burning small things and breaking items. He did that for no particular reason other than to see if he could get away with it. By the time he started going to school, he was frequently pulling the fire alarm and had set dozens of small fires in trash bins on the school property. He would later say he compulsively vandalized for no reason whatsoever. He broke car antennas and windows and destroyed maintenance and construction equipment. He vandalized his apartment building by staging floods, tearing out elevator controls, and spilling paint. He stole items on a daily basis and took things he didn't even want.

He frequently played truant or feigned illness to get out of school. His mother was naive and overprotective and always fell for his fake illnesses. While walking to and from school, David began lighting fires in large trash bins, piles of boxes in alleys, vegetation, and rubbish heaps. He was fascinated by firefighters and their equipment and often stayed around to see if they would show up. He later guessed that he had lit several hundred such fires in his teens and had never been caught or even suspected. David grew quite adept at hiding his activities. He later said he became very enthralled and self-satisfied by his ability to cause all that commotion and get away with it completely.

In all his thousands of devious acts, he acted alone. He grew up a true loner and one who was proud of his ability to avoid suspicion. He had few friends to confide in, and those few had no idea of his secret life. In other words, he was the perfect serial arsonist. Berkowitz would later state that his forays into the neighborhood to commit arson, vandalism, or thievery gave him a sense of "power . . . even omnipotence."

David grew up never having a girlfriend or having sex with a female. His only sexual adventures were in Korea during his army stint, where he gave and received oral sex with the prostitutes. However, by his own admission, he was an obsessive masturbator who did the deed numerous times a day. He has denied to his biographers that he has ever masturbated before, during, or after a fire event. Berkowitz's psychiatrist would later opine that David was most likely struggling with his sexual identity throughout his life and was probably homosexual. A differing opinion on this paragraph comes from profiler John Douglas who writes in *The Anatomy of Motive* that he personally interviewed Berkowitz in Attica Prison. During the interview, Douglas asserts that Berkowitz admitted that he frequently masturbated while watching fires that he had set. If that is true, it is one of the few documented instances of such an act that has long been believed to be commonplace.

Ever fascinated with fire, David told his psychiatrist that ever since he was a young boy he had wanted to die a hero's death while fighting fire or stopping crime. He later joined both the local fire department and the police department in an "auxiliary" status. Not satisfied with that, he joined the army in a spirit of patriotism in 1971 and asked to be sent immediately to Vietnam where he could lose his life as a hero. Oddly, after being sent to Korea, Berkowitz became staunchly anti-war and refused to carry a weapon.

When Berkowitz left the military in 1974, he began a furious three-year-period of intense fire setting. Detectives later found notebooks or "diaries" in his apartment detailing 1,488 fires from 1974 to 1977. The fires were carefully documented as regards time, place, type of fire (trash, car, building), and responding units. The local fire departments would later greatly dispute that number as their records did not match Berkowitz's diaries. In his book *Multiple Fire Setters*, author (and fire investigator) Brett Martinez cites an FBI study that indicates Berkowitz was responsible for at least 2,000 fires and an additional 137 maliciously pulled fire alarms between the years 1974 and 1977. Berkowitz even dubbed himself during this period as "The Phantom of the Bronx."

Eventually, David's arrest made national headlines and led to dozens of newspaper stories for months to come, numerous court decisions, several psychiatric papers, books, and at least a couple of television programs or movies. He was forever immortalized in the annals of American crime for his serial spree that year, yet almost no arson investigators or anyone else recognized David Berkowitz for his string of fires that totaled conservatively over two thousand.

Berkowitz was never identified as an arsonist until months after his high-profile arrest. In early 1977, Berkowitz stated he was obsessed with a string of demonic messages sent to him by a neighbor's dog. David made dozens of calls to the police and other agencies reporting that dog and his owner, Sam Carr, to no avail. David suggested that the dog caused him to carry on a string of more famous crimes that year. Eventually, David shot the neighbor's dog, calling attention to himself and bringing to close the thirteen-month spree of shootings of eight persons and the murders of six young New Yorkers. That all came to a head at the end of the summer of 1977, known forever as the "Summer of Sam."

Almost no one knows David Berkowitz as an arsonist. Nor does anyone know him by his birth name, Richard Falco. However, he is easily recognizable by his adopted name David Berkowitz or even by his nicknames "The .44 Caliber Killer" or more famously "The Son of Sam."

Investigator Analysis

More than anyone else in this writing, David Berkowitz personifies all the difficulties that fire investigative agencies have in recognizing, tracking, identifying, and arresting serial arsonists. By all rights, his arson events should have been detected years before his arrest. His activities occurred in a large, modern, high-density urban environment where he lived a fairly stable life and stayed in a small geographic area. His environment had large, modern police and fire agencies with presumably competent investigators. By his own admissions, he committed arson thousands of times in a heavily populated area, during both the day and the night, and was never even considered a suspect. He was not a drifter and did not disappear from the area after igniting his fires. In fact, his own diaries and letters indicate that he stood by, engaged firefighters in conversation, and later noted down specific details about each fire. He also later claimed to have reported several of the fire incidents and to have contacted the fire department and told them that there was an arsonist loose in their area. In retrospect, he probably stood out to the firefighters as an overly enthused, nerdy fire service aficionado who got in their way and pestered them with lots of questions. To be fair to the firefighters, there are lots of these types of persons who do appear routinely at fire scenes and act in a similar fashion and are not involved in fire setting. If an investigator was to query the fire stations near Berkowitz's home, it is a good bet that he would have been regarded as a regular visitor to them.

Because of the highly sensational and serious level of Berkowitz's murder series, which was totally unrelated to fires, nobody bothered to spend the time inquiring into the specifics of his fire setting, other than to note that it was one of the cornerstones of many serial murderers. The fire departments in the area have long maintained that his diary appears to be more fantasy than reality and cannot confirm, nor do they believe, that he set the fires he claimed.

After reviewing dozens of serial arson cases, my opinion is quite the opposite. Berkowitz's activities are highly consistent with an excitement-based serial arsonist. He spent his entire life engaged in sneaky and surreptitious behavior and by his own admissions reveled in the fact that he was very adept at never being suspected of committing crimes. The other crimes he also admitted to was the abuse, torture, and poisoning of animals; vandalism sprees; and theft for the purpose of excitement. Each one of those crimes is also highly consistent with serial fire setting behavior for excitement.

Additional evidence of this is his attraction to the police and fire service, where he held auxiliary positions in both fields. He obviously had an attraction to oversized firearms as his gun collection upon his arrest was quite impressive. He had assault style weapons and committed his murders with an oversized .44 caliber revolver. This caliber had been made famous just a few years prior in the *Dirty Harry* movie starring Clint Eastwood. Your author notes here that it is not uncommon for these "wannabe" types to favor massive, almost ridiculously large firearms. Recall that John Orr also had a penchant for multiple large firearms.

Berkowitz also had a love for the military and enlisted with the hope of "dying in Vietnam." He had a self-described "hero complex" and had always pictured himself dying in the military or in a police shootout or rescuing someone from a fire. This type of fantasy has been closely related to the "hero complex," which is one of many subsets of excitement-based fire setting.

Since little investigation work was ever done on Berkowitz's fires, it is difficult to accurately label him. There is no mention in any literature whether he preselected targets, scouted locations, drove his car, or used a delay device. He most likely did not do any of those things in his younger years. In his early years, his fires occurred at targets of opportunity in secluded areas near his home. His target selection ranged from trash, dumpsters, and vegetation to abandoned cars and buildings. It's fair to say here that his choice of abandoned building fires, while not normal for most serial arson offenders, is probably normal for the serial offenders who reside in large, dense metropolitan areas, since these are the places where they can commit their crimes unseen.

After his release from the army, Berkowitz claimed to have gone on a massive fire setting spree for the next two to three years. Those were the events he documented in great detail in his diary. By that time he was mobile and had access to a vehicle. However, it is still unknown if that was used in his fire setting. It is probably fair to say that he somewhat refined his fire setting and probably had the typical evolved MO that we see in all longtime offenders.

David Berkowitz's murder spree was also a unique event. He specifically went out "hunting" in certain areas and at certain times, but without a specific target in mind. When he found a likely target, he would observe and stalk them and then wait for the right moment at which to commit his crime. Although this shows a bit of organization, it is still classified as a disorganized event.

David Berkowitz never married and never had intercourse with a female, although he claimed to have engaged in oral sex with prostitutes. Most analysts believed him to be sexually confused and probably struggling with homosexual desires. He was described as soft, effeminate, quiet, and unassuming. He had few friends, no lovers, and bounced between low-level jobs. He, like every other arsonist on this list, was a consummate loner, who had no open disputes with anyone and was considered to be "a nice boy."

The last few weeks of his freedom were highly frenetic, and he conducted himself in an increasingly risky manner. He killed a neighbor's dog, sent messages to the police and fire departments, and then lit his final arson fire at the door of a police officer who lived in his building.

David Berkowitz, known famously as the "Son of Sam," is also quite famous on this list as he was one of the most prolific-known arsonists in United States' history. He was a disorganized offender who ignited targets of opportunity with a simple match or lighter, who quite often hung around to see the excitement he caused. He was a firefighter "wannabe," and his prime motivation was no doubt excitement.

Conservatively, he is believed to have ignited over two thousand fires, although some fire officials greatly dispute that fact. He is currently spending a life sentence in prison for his murder spree in 1977.

Robert Lee Parker: Serial Murderer/Serial Rapist/Serial Arsonist
Period of Activity: 1995-96, Seattle, Washington

Yet another denizen of the Seattle area involved in arsons, Robert Parker is a bit different from some of the other more famous serial fire setters from that region. Firstly, Parker is a black man. Secondly, his arson crimes were probably an afterthought to the brutal rape/murders he conducted.

Robert Parker was born in Arkansas in 1971. When he was six years old, his father died. Other than that fact, very little is known of his family life. Like many arsonists, Parker suffered from fairly low mental health scores. Upon his sentencing in 1999, the trial judge noted that his IQ score was above average, despite the fact that his defense attorneys argued that he was borderline mentally retarded. A court-ordered exam showed that "although he does not meet the statutory definition of mentally retarded . . . is classified as borderline intellectual functioning." Throughout the brief period in his adult life when he was not in jail, he drifted between a variety of low paying jobs as either a laborer in a warehouse or as a fast food restaurant worker.

Parker was not a native of the Seattle area. He was raised in Arkansas. He first came to the attention of authorities in 1990 when at nineteen years old he was convicted of a residential burglary. He was given a ten-year prison sentence and served less than half of that time. Upon his release from prison in 1994, Parker became a fugitive from his parole officer and relocated to the Seattle area. Almost as soon as he got there, he again appeared on the police blotter, this time for the possession of cocaine. After a short stint in jail for that violation, Parker emerged on the Seattle streets as an angry man with a cocaine problem. At some time during that year, he met a woman and fathered a son with her. They moved in together in an apartment in the Shoreline district of Seattle.

On February 24, 1995, Robert Parker forced his way into the apartment of forty-four-year-old Rene Powell, a registered nurse at Harborview Medical Center. She was a neighbor of his in Shoreline. He found Powell alone and brutally attacked her. Menacing her at knifepoint, Parker removed all of Powell's clothing except for her bra, which was forced upward to expose her breasts. He then bound her with an electrical appliance cord, gagged her with her panties, vaginally raped her, stabbed her several times in the abdomen, and then strangled her with a ligature.

In a separate but nearly identical incident, a month later on March 26, 1995, Parker forcibly entered the nearby apartment of fifty-five-year-old Barbara Walsh, who worked as a registrar at a walk-in clinic in the area. He committed a near identical attack on Ms. Walsh as he had on Rene Powell. He also left a good deal of physical evidence, including his semen at both scenes. Because of that aspect, Parker gave some thought to hiding the forensics at both scenes. Prior to fleeing each rape/murder scene, he lit each woman's apartment on fire. Both of these crimes occurred in the same Shoreline district neighborhood four weeks apart and were exact clones of each other.

Despite his efforts at crime concealment, Robert Lee Parker was identified via his DNA which was found at both scenes. He was arrested on November 5, 1996.

While he awaited trial in King's County, Washington, it was learned that he was the suspect in the shooting murder of a man who had been driving a car in the Seattle area in 1996. There was never enough physical proof to link Parker to that offense, despite witness statements placing him at that scene. Additionally, and even more sinister, Arkansas authorities considered Robert Lee Parker to be the only suspect in a near identical rape/murder/arson that had occurred in their jurisdiction shortly after his release from prison. His "relocation" to the Seattle area was deemed proof of his flight from the Arkansas authorities as they were moving in to arrest him on that crime.

On February 25, 1999, a jury convicted Robert Lee Parker of two counts of first degree murder, two counts of forcible rape, two counts of residential burglary, two counts of robbery, and two counts of arson to an inhabited dwelling. He was sentenced to life in prison without the possibility of parole. Because of this conviction, the Arkansas murder/arson case was never pursued.

———

Investigator Analysis

Robert Lee Parker was an arsonist who lit his fires out of necessity. There is little doubt that his behavior (as far as fire setting goes) was learned behavior. This twenty-five-year-old man had spent almost five years, or one-fifth of his life in state prison, learning his trade. Just prior to his release, it became national news courtesy of the O. J. Simpson case as to how DNA was an important identifier at crime scenes.

It is my opinion that Parker was a violent sexual sadist whose main motivation was sexual assault. Murder and subsequent arson were most likely means of destroying the evidence in the case. The murder was to destroy any witness testimony and the arson was of course to destroy any trace or physical evidence. There is little doubt that this young maniac learned the value of evidence destruction in the years he spent in prison. As DNA and other forensic evidence procedures will become even more accurate in the future, I believe that more and more experienced criminals will resort to arson as a means with which to destroy the evidence they leave at the scenes.

CHAPTER 4

The Mass Murderers and Spree Arsonists

A final small category combining arson and murder exists. In very rare incidents, an offender goes on a spree of violence that lasts minutes, hours, or even days. This is most often manifested (particularly in the United States) in a phenomenon known as a "mass murder." This is generally defined by almost any expert in the field as a person who plans and conducts a massive act of violence with very little expectation to survive the conclusion of that event. The event usually begins with a list of specified targets and then degrades to the offender attacking whatever target he can find until he eventually is killed by the police or just as often commits suicide. Infamous examples of mass murderers include Charles Whitman (Texas Clock Tower Sniper), James Huberty (San Ysidro Mcdonald's shooter), the Columbine Massacre, and Charles Starkweather (Nebraska murderer). These five were among the first of this type of group, but they were followed in the next few decades by dozens of similar men who "went postal" and committed mass murders at worksites, schools, and colleges. A few in this group also added arson fires to their murder sprees. While not exactly serial arsonists, this group is significant and notorious.

Mark James Robert Essex: Mass Murderer, Spree Arsonist
Period of Activity: First week of January, 1973, New Orleans

Mark Essex defies any profile that we have come to accept as a serial arsonist. Firstly, he was a black man. Secondly, he grew up in an intact,

Midwest, wholesome family with no known trauma or strife. He was well adjusted, crime free, and never saw the inside of an institution like so many in this book. He grew up free of childhood stress and in a community where race was not a serious issue. Essex had good grades and a bright outlook on life. In 1969, Mark Essex made the decision to step out of that idyllic life and join the United States Navy. The next two years of his life in the navy would become the catalyst that turned that quiet, bright Midwestern boy into an angry, hate-filled revolutionary who despised everything about the white man and his culture.

When Essex left his cloistered existence in the still-sheltered Midwest, he picked the era when whole sections of the United States were undergoing a violent social revolution. Racism, always rampant in the rural South, was something of a hidden secret in the Midwest. When Essex got stationed in San Diego on the West Coast, he learned firsthand about the overt racist views of many Americans. Essex left his boot camp with outstanding marks in all areas and was encouraged by officials to seek advanced placement in a technical field. He ended up working as a dental assistant for a navy doctor. He did extremely well and soon sought out the doctor's advice on becoming a dentist in the future. Off duty though, all was not well. Essex soon began to hear words and slurs he had never before heard spoken to him. The enlisted men's barracks was rife with open hostility between the races, and Essex was soon caught up in the dramatics. On one side was the overt racism of several white sailors who hailed from other parts of America. On the other side were a group of young, militant black sailors who spoke continuously of the Black Revolution.

Mark Essex soon learned that there were unwritten "rules" for a black man that accompanied living in the San Diego area. On a daily basis, he was stopped and searched at the base gate by white guards who knew him by face. He was ordered to seek a white sailor's permission before entering any room. He was harassed for dating a Hispanic woman, and his car was stopped frequently by local police for no apparent reason. A series of confrontations and physical altercations between Essex and some white sailors soon led to more than one court martial proceeding. Not willing to accept minor punishment from the navy for infractions he did not believe he had committed, Essex soon rebelled and went AWOL. By October 1970, Essex, unable to sleep and eat properly due to the stress of his on base issues, fled the navy and returned home to Kansas. After a month at home, his parents convinced him to return to the navy and face another court martial proceeding. The officers presiding over the court martial acknowledged that Essex was driven to his infractions by racial harassment. Nonetheless, they convicted him of the unauthorized absence and gave him a minor sentence of a month of base restriction and the forfeit of a month's pay. Two months later, Essex's commanders advised him to sign papers for a general discharge from military service due to his inability to conform to rules and regulations.

From that point on, Mark Essex stopped being the "all-American" boy and began associating with several radical black groups. He even spent some time in the Oakland area attending meetings hosted by the Black Panthers, whose notorious militant wing had openly declared war against American police officers. Essex was an easy convert to the ideology of Black Revolution and soon became obsessed with the literature. From 1970 through 1972, he was seen in Oakland and New York with various black militant group members, sometimes peddling militant newsletters on street corners. He was vaguely connected to the most radical faction of the Panthers, the New York based Eldridge Cleaver faction, which was the leading proponent of violence toward the police. A roommate would later relate that Essex became enraged at the slaughter of mostly black inmates by police in the Attica prison uprising. Essex also commented favorably on the murder of four New York police officers by black militants. Among the texts he was reading by that time were *Black Rage*, and the black urban guerilla manual *Right On*. Essex became particularly interested in a revolutionary theme regarding the "lone wolf"-type sniper who would become a catalyst for an uprising by directly targeting the police. In the wake of reading these and other books, Essex purchased the suggested revolutionary weapons: a Ruger .44 carbine and a .38 revolver.

Essex eventually settled in the New Orleans area and lived for a time with a black Muslim roommate. That roommate indoctrinated Essex into his roots and the history of black men in Africa. Essex began reading volumes on history and soon began adopting Zulu language into his speech. He even took a Swahili name. He also continued to practice regularly with his weapons. He became more and more withdrawn and radicalized. He also developed severe insomnia and migraine issues. His hatred of all things white continued to fester.

A triggering event in 1972 sent Essex's hatred beyond its boiling point. On November 16, during a campus demonstration in Baton Rouge, the local police shot and killed two black student demonstrators. As a result of this, Essex declared war on the police. In late December, he sent his declaration of war to a local television station announcing the time, date, and target of his attack. His warning went unheeded. He then sent a final letter to his parents and advised them that he was now at war with the whites. He signed it with his new African name. Knowing that he would not return alive from this mission, he gave away all his possessions to his friends.

On New Year's Eve 1972, heavily armed and carrying a gas mask and lot of ammunition, Mark Essex made good on his threat and set up a sniping position across the street from a New Orleans police jail facility. He began shooting his rifle as a young white police cadet emerged from the building. Missing that male with several shots, Essex ironically got his first kill with a shot through the heart of a young black police cadet, Al Harrell. He also wounded a lieutenant before fleeing the area. Essex did not run far as he soon triggered a burglary alarm as he shot the lock off a door at an office building several blocks from the shooting scene. He lay in wait for the officers he knew would soon respond. Unbelievably, the two officers who responded to this alarm were not even aware of the recent nearby police shooting. As they exited their squad car, Essex began firing, hitting one officer in the stomach. It took two agonizing months for that man to die of his wounds. Somehow Essex was wounded at that point, but managed to flee this building before officers could set up a cordon. A tactical team found discarded ammunition and blood where Essex had been hiding.

Essex then fled to a nearby church, but left a trail of live bullets every few yards so that police could follow him. He waited for them in yet another ambush site. A nervous police administrator, noting the rising tension levels of other blacks in the neighborhood, did not allow his men to enter the church and flush out Essex. The police were ordered to pull out of the neighborhood, and Mark Essex later walked quietly away from the church. Essex did not remain quiet for very long, nor did he "cool off" after that first wave of violence.

Just hours after the police let him escape from the church, Essex set two arson fires in warehouses near the church. Those large fires continued to burn for several days, tying up over two hundred firefighters. Essex even returned to the same church at least two more times to await the police. Officers later found live ammunition and bloodstains throughout the church.

One week later, on January 7, Essex walked into a grocery store and shot the white manager. He then carjacked a black driver on the street but advised him that he wasn't going to shoot any black people. Using the stolen car, he drove to a downtown Howard Johnson's hotel and began his final act of carnage. Carrying his rifle, he climbed a staircase and entered the eighteenth floor, passing three black workers. He told them not to worry as he wasn't there to hurt any black people. They later told the cops that Essex stated, "I want the whites." He then shot and killed the first two white people he came across, a doctor and his wife. Essex then entered their room and set it on fire. As hotel employees responded to the alarm and smoke, Essex began firing and killed a manager. He then shot another manager in the back. For the next hour, Essex worked his way down to the eighth floor, shooting people and starting fires in rooms.

The police and fire departments descended upon the building, and Essex immediately began firing at any uniform he saw. He severely injured a fire department lieutenant who was climbing a ladder. Essex continued to set fires in several rooms and began firing out of several windows. The police department surrounded the building and started firing at every sighting of Essex. Over the next several hours and into the following day, over six hundred cops from twenty-six agencies, including state, local, and federal units descended upon the scene and engaged Essex in an ongoing gun battle. They brought with them armored cars, helicopters, and any high-powered firearm they could find.

That gun battle took on grotesque, even cartoonish, proportions as the various police agencies began shooting at anything that moved in the building, including other officers, firefighters, and other hotel guests. As the scene was played out in the media, a large number of militant blacks showed up at the hotel and began protesting the actions of the police and encouraging the actions of Essex. To add to the circus-type atmosphere, a number of civilians, some in various pieces of military uniforms, began showing up to shoot at the building. Meanwhile, Essex who had a lot of experience shooting guns as a teenager was methodically picking off targets in uniform. He continued to rain down effective fire against targets of opportunity. He also specifically ignored easy targets that were not in uniform. Among the many officers who were killed or wounded was a senior ranking official. NOPD Deputy Chief Louis Sirgo attempted to lead an ad hoc SWAT team up the stairs of the hotel. They were met with well-aimed rifle fire on the sixteenth floor, and Sirgo was killed by a shot to the neck.

As the day wore on, Essex continued his mayhem and developed a method for lighting effective fires. He usually entered a room and placed a phone book under a mattress or the drapes. He then poured some lighter fluid on the phone book and ignited it, and the fire would usually ignite the much larger fuel load. This resulted in many smoky fires throughout the upper stories of the hotel.

Late in the day, Essex was eventually pushed to his final battle ground, the roof of the hotel. He found excellent cover in the concrete-covered doorways. As the then close-quarters gunfight progressed, the cops could hear Essex yelling pro-Africa and anti-police slogans at them. They in turn replied with racist taunts in an effort to draw him into the open, all the while firing hundreds of ineffective rounds in his direction.

The erratic battle continued, and Essex began shooting at a police helicopter. In response, authorities summoned a large U.S. Marine Corps CH-46 from a nearby Reserve base. This behemoth arrived in the late afternoon carrying two marine sharpshooters with scoped rifles and three police marksmen with their own carbines. In a surreal scene of darkness, fog, a searchlight, and some light rain, the military helicopter made nearly fifty strafing passes over the hotel roof. Added to that onslaught was the fact that hundreds of police officers (and some civilians) had set up on nearby rooftops with large caliber-scoped hunting rifles. This unorganized effort resulted in hundreds (if not thousands) of rounds directed into the area where Essex had taken shelter. This assault caused even more Essex supporters to arrive and conversely the arrival of even more vigilantes who wanted to assist the police.

By about nine that night, Essex had apparently had enough. As the marine helicopter swooped in for another pass, Essex stepped out of cover and openly engaged it with his rifle. The cops responded with a tornado of bullets from all angles, and Essex was literally torn apart. The volume of gunfire directed at Essex was so intense that it broke open a large water main, which flooded several police out of the stairwells.

While, due to poor tactics and deplorable command and control issues, this will go down as one of the most embarrassing American police events ever, it will also be marked as one of the deadliest. A decent shot, Essex had fired a total of about 150 rounds of ammunition. He killed nine persons and wounded ten during the hotel assault. Another dozen or more cops were wounded by "friendly fire." At his autopsy, authorities recorded nearly two hundred bullet holes in Essex's body.

A follow-up investigation revealed that Essex, while influenced by various groups, acted alone. His apartment was a treasure trove of information, and he left racial taunts for investigators he knew would surely show up after his death. He had covered his walls with African words, drawings, and hate-filled vitriol toward the white police.

Investigator's Analysis

Again, this case is not one of a true serial offender, despite evidence that Mark Essex lit upwards of twenty to twenty-five fires. The fires in this case appear to be used for tactical purposes and were designed to confuse and disorient authorities. They also may have been a means of revenge as they were set against businesses that could have represented white society.

Mark Essex, a true "spree arsonist," actually developed an effective method for lighting his fires to get maximum damage. His first two fires (warehouses) caused massive losses and kept firefighters busy for days. He no doubt used an accelerant to boost those events. His last fire event, which in reality was a couple of dozen fires in the same large structure, also was effective, efficient, and well planned. He used an effective ignition scenario which included an accelerant and the staging of flammable materials in a "ladder of fuels." By this, Essex showed some intelligence and some degree of sophistication with his fire setting.

Ernst August Wagner: Mass Murderer, Spree Arsonist
Period of Activity: September 4, 1913, Muhlhausen, Germany

Ernst Wagner and Mark Essex are linked together in history for their final frenzies of violence. The two could not have come from more different backgrounds. In stark contrast to Essex, who was a black man in America, Wagner was a white German in an area filled with persons of the same race and nationality. He, however, had the horrible childhood that has become synonymous with serial murderers and arsonists.

In *Hunting Humans,* author Elliot Leyton clearly describes the marked differences between Essex and Wagner. Ernst Wagner was born in the age of industrial Germany, before the First World War. He was from a large family of twelve children. Despite those great numbers, most of his siblings perished at a young age so that by the time Wagner committed his greatest crimes, only four siblings remained. His family was from the peasant class, and Wagner's alcoholic father died when Wagner was a baby. His mother made a meager living and soon remarried. She had numerous affairs and was soon divorced. Wagner bore the shame of his mother's promiscuity throughout his young life. From early on, Wagner suffered from suicidal thoughts and bouts of depression.

Despite Wagner's poverty, he was considered quite intelligent and soon earned grants and scholarships that would allow him to attend higher education. He excelled and became a teacher. Although teaching was his profession, Wagner's first love was writing, and he made several attempts as an adult to become a writer or a poet. His adult life was a string of failures in those endeavors, and he was forced to remain a teacher, which he thought was a poor career. Wagner also struggled with mental illness, and early in his teaching career, he was suspended for a lengthy period of time due to nervousness and irritability.

By 1901, Wagner was teaching in the small village of Muhlhausen. In that burg came the major traumatic point in his life. Suffering from the same alcoholic tendencies as his birth father, Wagner was observed to be drunk and having sex with a farm animal. In another incident, he was alleged to have been engaged in a brief homosexual affair. Immediately after those incidents, Wagner began displaying signs of paranoia as he believed that everyone in the town was mocking him behind his back. He began carrying a revolver in case he was confronted by authorities for his indecent acts. Also, at that time, Wagner met and later married the daughter of a local innkeeper. He was never happy with the marriage and felt that his wife was stupid and mocked his interest in literature. To add more misery to that same year, Wagner's mother passed away. He later told investigators that her death greatly affected his mental health. That same year, school administrators transferred Wagner out of Muhlhausen to a remote tiny village.

By the summer of 1904, the warning signs were beginning to grow. Wagner tried twice to commit suicide, both times failing. He later chided himself for being weak. Despite hating his life, Wagner stayed on as a husband, father, and schoolteacher. For the next several years, Wagner and his wife had five children, one of which subsequently died. Wagner was not interested in the children and considered them a burden on his life.

Years later, Wagner would reveal to psychiatrists and investigators that 1906 was the year when he began planning his attacks. He became increasingly paranoid in that period and began believing that the sodomy and bestiality incidents in Muhlhausen had become knowledge in his new town. Because he believed that the men of Muhlhausen had caused that rumor to spread, he began plotting revenge against the town. Over the next two years, Wagner purchased two "broom handle" Mauser semi-automatic pistols and began covertly practicing with them in remote areas. For months, he plotted a massive attack against his former town and even picked a date for the event.

In the week prior to the attacks, Wagner put his plans to paper. Those items were mailed to a major newspaper on the day of his spree. He wrote that his plan was to return to the town of his birth to murder his brother and his entire family and then burn their home to the ground. He next planned to go to the home of his birth and burn it and its occupants to death. His final dramatic act was described as him going to the Royal Castle in Ludwigsburg, killing the guards, and setting the castle afire. He then planned to commit suicide by dying in the flames or possibly jumping from the walls.

On September 4, 1913, Wagner put his plan into action. First, he attacked his sleeping wife with a blackjack (club) and dagger. He stabbed her numerous times, killing her. He then methodically went into his sons' room and clubbed and stabbed both of them while they slept. He finished them off by cutting their throats. He followed suit in his daughters' room. Within minutes, his entire family of five was dead. He later described that slaughter as a merciful act so that they would not have to live with the shame of his sins.

Following his plan, he rode to the village where his brother lived, but did not find him at home. He told his brother's wife to expect him later that night as he had errands to run. She agreed to leave the door unlocked for him.

Wagner then left his autobiography with a publisher, mailed his final letters (including one to a cousin, urging her to poison herself), and rode to Muhlhausen. He arrived in the outskirts of the village just before midnight. Within an hour, the village residents were awakened to find four fires burning throughout their village. Wagner then entered the streets of the village, partially disguised in a hat and a veil covering his face, and began shooting at any male who happened to come into his view. He quickly killed eight men and a girl and wounded a dozen others. As he paused to reload his pistols, villagers attacked him with farm implements, nearly killing him. He lay for an hour on the street severely wounded and unconscious, with the villagers thinking him dead. A passing policeman found him near death.

Wagner was arrested and immediately confessed to those killings and the earlier killings of his family. He also admitted to numerous arsons, with numerous more planned. He was very upset to learn that only nine people in the town of Muhlhausen had died. Lastly, he admitted that his attacks were based partly in shame for his sexual indiscretions that had occurred over a decade before. Finally, he was extremely upset that he had been too injured to carry out his suicide as planned.

Wagner gave lengthy interviews and confessions. He requested to immediately be put to death by decapitation. His wishes were to remain unfulfilled. A criminal psychologist gave the authorities the opinion that Ernst Wagner was quite insane, and Wagner was sentenced to life confinement in a psychiatric ward. Ernst Wagner died in the psychiatric ward twenty-five years later in 1938. Till his death he believed that he was completely sane and that the victims of his crimes deserved their fate.

Investigator Analysis

While not a serial arsonist per se, Ernst Wagner had many life experiences that were consistent with others in this book. He had a very traumatic childhood marked with intense poverty, numerous deaths of siblings, a broken family, and the shame of a promiscuous mother. He was highly intelligent as are many serial arson offenders. He indulged in at least a few homosexual (and bestial) acts, which is also a familiar theme with many serial arsonists. He harbored great resentment toward an institution, in this case the male populace of a town.

When Wagner finally lashed out, it was with years of preparation and planning and with the belief that he would not survive the event. This is the one area where he differs from most other serial arsonists. Most serial arson offenders, being complete cowards, have every intention of surviving the fire and continuing their activities.

CHAPTERS 1-4 SYNOPSIS

The fifteen arsonists described so far in this book represent some of the most infamous and prolific arsonists that have been identified. Obviously, there is little data available from the rest of the world, as those men are all from the United States and Europe. However, with this very small but important sampling, we can notice some interesting traits that are common among them. Eleven of the fifteen are white. Only three of the men used delay incendiary devices, and all three were firefighters or had firefighter training. Almost half of the men on this list were firefighters or had expressed fascination with the fire service.

Only one, John Orr, was considered to be the classic organized offender; however, at least two more were considered to be close to becoming an organized offender. Most of the men on this list showed an evolving method of operation, and their latter fires appeared much more organized than their original fires. Only two men on this list had prior arson arrests before their most famous fires.

A very surprising fact discovered by me was that at least ten of the fifteen arsonists self-reported or were diagnosed as being either homosexual or confused about their sexual orientation. Two more on the list claimed to be heterosexual, but investigators believe that they too are most likely homosexual. This is probably the most common trait that all shared. Nine of the fifteen had been institutionalized in their life prior to their final arrests. Only one, John Orr, was married at the time of his fires. Orr was married four different times.

The most glaring statistic is that this group represents about seven thousand arson fires. These case reviews showed that about two-thirds or around forty-five hundred of these fires were never recognized as arson events until after the investigation.

CHAPTER 5

The Extremists and Hate Arsonists

This next group of serial arsonists exemplifies how one's hatred for institutions, ideals, or people can consume them. It also shows that for some reason, churches of various denominations have a very visceral effect on some arsonists and have become the favored targets of many serial fire setters.

Varg Vikernes: Serial Church Arsonist, Murderer
Period of Activity: 1992-94, Bergen, Norway

Much has been made in the United States in the past twenty years regarding arson attacks on religious buildings. Indeed, some of the most heinous crimes in American history were the burnings of black Christian churches in the South during the American civil rights movement. In the 1990s after what appeared to be an onslaught of similar attacks, the Clinton administration formed the federally funded Church Arson Task Force, which is a full-time unit dedicated to the "problem" of church arsons. Although the task force has been greatly downsized in recent years, it still exists and still looks into any arson attack at houses of worship. In reality though, close examination of church fires reveals that the majority of church arsons in the past thirty years were not at all related to "hate crimes" or racial issues. The investigations reveal that the vast majority of church arsons in the United States were related to some sort of internal matter at the church or to insurance fraud. This result shows that church arsons are not a whole lot different from the average arson in the United States.

That being said, there are a small spate of church fires that are directly linked to "hatred" of that particular religion or church. One such series of fires occurred in the early 1990s to several churches in Norway. In 1994, a semi-famous "heavy metal" musician named Varg Vikernes was arrested for the murder of a bandmate. During the murder investigation, it was made public that Vikernes was also a suspect in the torching of several Christian churches in Norway. A few of these buildings had significant historical interest.

Varg Vikernes was born in 1973 in Bergen, Norway. His parents were professionals, and he had an elder brother. A very early influence in his life was his father, who was an engineer by trade. During interviews later in life, Varg would give sketchy details about his childhood. One detail that emerged was that he believed both of his parents to be very strongly minded regarding racial issues. He said his father maintained a Nazi flag in the home and his mother always voiced concern that he would bring home a girlfriend who could be "black" or "colored." It should be noted that portions of Norway were very pro-Nazi during World War II, and Varg's father grew up in that culture.

At a very early age, Varg began to read and study ancient religions and cults linked to both the Vikings and the Nazis. He was also loosely affiliated with the neo-Nazi skinhead movement that was sweeping through Europe at the time. Although his father had an affinity toward the World War II Nazis, he frequently admonished Vikernes to stay away from both the neo-Nazi and skinhead groups in the area.

His parents split up when Varg was around twelve years old. He continued to study and read about such dark topics as paganism and Satanism. Within a short time, he began listening heavily to Northern European heavy metal music. This was a much darker and twisted version of either British or American heavy metal, and its lyrics were based heavily on the occult and Satanism. By fourteen, Varg had taken up the guitar and immersed himself into the heavy metal genre. Shortly, he began writing his own music and started having success in a series of heavy metal bands. Soon his writing and music style began to adapt to an even darker genre called "death metal." By the time Varg was eighteen, he had achieved tremendous commercial success and was a well-known figure in the "death metal" music scene. From this, he began slipping into an even more obscure type of music called "black metal." He soon released four albums related to that type of music.

During that same period, Varg began delving deeper and deeper into pagan religions and Satanism. Soon he began fervently practicing many bizarre and ancient rituals of those beliefs. He developed a heavy interest into any type of weapon and loved all things German. Conversely, he began to despise all things British or American and began to openly reject their Christian-Judeo ideology. At the time, he was heavily involved in the teachings of the national socialist movement in Norway among local skinhead gangs.

During Hitler's power in Germany, German youth were taught to turn their backs on Christianity and the major Christian churches. Certain Germans, particularly those associated with the elite SS units and schools, began to study ancient religions and practices from the early Germanic tribes and their northern cousins, the Vikings of Sweden, Norway, and Denmark. Many of those practices were based on pagan rituals and beliefs. Hitler's Germany modernized and adopted some of those pagan beliefs into the Nazi "religion." Chief among those beliefs was a sense of racial superiority and the rejection of Christian religions. That belief set was often called heathenism or Odinism.

Throughout that time period, Varg openly espoused his belief in Odinism and other Aryan cult movements. In a writing by Varg, he clearly calls for the avenging of past "heathens" (like himself) by desecrating cemeteries, burning churches, and killing priests: "For each devastated graveyard, one heathen grave is avenged, for each ten churches burned to ashes, one heathen hof (hall or meeting place) is avenged, for each ten priests or freemasons assassinated, one heathen is avenged."

Apparently, he was not about making empty or idle threats. On June 6, 1992, the Fantoft Stave Church, which was an ancient historical building dating back to the twelfth century, was completely torched in an arson fire. Over the next six months, a wave of similar attacks happened throughout Norway. There was the attempted arson of Storetveit Church and the arson of Asane Church, both in the city of Bergen. Those were followed by arson attacks at the Skjold Church in Vindafjord and the Kolmenkollen Chapel in Oslo. In total, there were at least seven arson attacks on Stave churches, including a Christmas Eve fire.

In August 1993, Varg went to confront a bandmate over an unknown issue. During that confrontation, the bandmate was killed. He was found with twenty-three cut wounds to his head, neck, and back. Varg later admitted to killing the man, but insisted it was in self-defense. One report suggested that Varg killed his friend because he was sympathetic to local left leaning groups, when Varg was an ardent supporter of right wing groups. The real reason for the murder was never really clarified. Jurors would later note that Varg's actions after the killing were very suspect. He did not report the event and in fact threw his bloody clothes into a lake soon after the attack. He was soon arrested for this crime and for the church arsons. Upon his arrest, Norwegian authorities found over three hundred pounds of explosives in his home along with many weapons and three thousand rounds of ammunition. Vikernes told people that that weaponry was part of his imminent plan to attack and blow up a leftist radical enclave in Oslo. He was ideologically opposed to the group whom he considered communists, while he considered himself a fascist.

A jury trial ensued in early 1994. The jury acquitted Varg of the original church arson at Fantoft Stave church, but convicted him on four other church arsons in the spree. He was considered the prime suspect in the other church arson attacks. The motive for the attacks was described as Varg's hatred for the Christian ideology along with his promotion of a heathen ideology. Additionally, Varg was convicted of the stabbing murder of his bandmate. He was sentenced to a total of twenty-one years in prison. For some reason, Varg was granted a short furlough from prison in 2000. He did not return at the appointed time and was arrested later while driving in a stolen car and in possession of an assault rifle, pistol, knives, and military gear. He was given an additional year in prison for that incident. Under Norwegian law, only about half the sentence needs to be served. In 2009, Varg Vikernes was released from prison after serving sixteen years.

For his part, Varg has not shied away from the spotlight. He continued to make digital communications and grant interviews from prison. He never openly admitted his guilt, but obliquely conceded that all of the church arson attacks (except for one) were the work of a single person for the benefit of a belief in heathenism (Odinism). After his parole from prison, he has continued to write and speak about his belief in a religion he has refined while in prison, called nationalist heathenism, which he describes as a combination of Nazism, Norse mythology, the occult, and racism. It is all part of a wider movement known as the Heathen Front.

A side light of Varg's case is the copycat arsons it has created. In 1994, a nineteen-year-old guitarist in an Australian metal band claimed to have been heavily influenced by Varg's music when he was caught for burglarizing and torching a one-hundred-year-old church in Vale, Australia. He was convicted and sentenced to three years in a youth detention facility. In May 2006, an eighteen-year-old Finnish drummer involved with a metal band was arrested for burning a cathedral in Finland. He admitted to doing the act out of hatred of Christianity and in support of Vikernes. He was sentenced to over six years in prison for that attack. Another incident in 2006 involved three persons arrested in Manitoba, Canada, for the arson attack of the Minnedosa United Church. The million-dollar-loss fire was set on Varg Vikernes's birthday, and the three were sentenced to terms of two to three years in prison.

Investigator Analysis

Vikernes engaged in one of the most fringe motives for serial fire setting—the religious or ideological offender. Although there is not enough public information available about his fires to comment on, his case is interesting in that it will always stir up "copycats" or sympathetic, screwed-up people to commit a similar offense half a world away, which will end up leaving the local investigators scratching their head and just wondering. Because of his notoriety in a fringe music genre, Varg's influence will no doubt spur several more disenfranchised "metal heads" to commit similar acts. The difficulty in recognizing this crime will be substantial as there will appear to be no motive for the event, and it will probably occur on some sort of weird anniversary date that only the offender will know.

It should be noted that arson attacks on churches are not rare at all. There was a spree in Alabama in the late 2000s and another spree in Texas in 2009. Arrests were made in both of these sprees, but the motive for each is a bit obscure. Neither appears to be related to hate crimes.

Benjamin Matthew Williams/James Tyler Williams: Synagogue and Abortion Clinic Arsonists/Murderers Period of Activity: 1999, Sacramento, California Area

The summer months of 1999 were a watershed era in the world of hate. On June 18, three coordinated arson attacks were carried out by unknown suspects against Jewish synagogues in Sacramento, California. The resulting fires destroyed priceless artifacts and did over $1 million in damages to the structures. On July 1, an arson attack was attempted at a Sacramento medical building that housed an abortion clinic. Also on July 1, in nearby Redding, California, a gay couple was found murdered in their bed.

This orgy of violence kick started even more high-profile events. Within just a couple of days, in the states of Indiana and Illinois, an avowed racist and member of the white supremacist World Church of the Creator, Benjamin Nathaniel Smith went on a shooting spree targeting random black people he saw in the streets. A few weeks later, in the final act of what would be called "the Summer of Hate," white supremacist Buford Furrow Jr. would storm into a Jewish day care center in Los Angeles and gun down several children and adults.

At first, federal investigators believed that those were coordinated events between members of a highly organized white supremacist movement. Eventually, after all the details were fleshed out, the events were exposed for what they actually were—unplanned and poorly coordinated individual acts of hate. The only thing the perpetrators had in common was a similar system of racist-inspired religious beliefs based loosely on the teachings of several Christian Identity movements in the United States.

Gary Matson and Winfield Mowder were a gay couple from Redding, California. They had been together for fourteen years and were also partners in a nursery business. As part of that business, they had become acquainted with another business pairing of brothers in the landscaping business named Matthew and Tyler Williams. The Williams brothers, both of whom were known by their middle names, were an odd pair, but no one was aware of the danger they posed.

126

Born and raised in rural Gridley, California, both brothers grew up in a very strict fundamentalist Christian household. The family stayed away from other families in the area, and the Williams boys were homeschooled by their parents. Although both boys eventually enrolled in the local high school and became honor students, their parents forbade them from hanging out with other kids and would not let them participate in sports or other extracurricular activities. Neighbors would often recall fundamentalist sermons and music emanating from the home.

To reinforce their isolation, the family was very self-reliant and grew their own food and raised their own chickens. At some point, citing "God's orders," their fundamentalist father, Benjamin Williams, moved the family to Redding. After they left, neighbors found literature and other mail from militia groups that continued to arrive at the vacant home.

Matthew Williams, the elder son, eventually joined the navy after high school for a short stint. After the navy, he gravitated toward college in Idaho and became enamored with the various extremist Christian churches in the area. He soon became a rabid follower of the more charismatic churches and eventually moved on to throw his zeal behind white supremacist movements. He also began to display some other quirky behavior. He became interested in bizarre diets that would "purify" the body, which resulted in him training himself and his brother to have "perfect" bowel movements.

Soon Matthew became absorbed in white supremacist issues and constantly pored over anti-Semitic literature. By 1998, he was actively involved in the Montana Militia movement. He soon graduated to the even more radical Christian Identity movement. That movement was known for its avowed racism, intolerance, and strict fundamentalist interpretation of the Bible. Matthew took that strong belief system home to California with him and began indoctrinating his younger brother, Tyler. By 1999, both had become fervent believers in the movement. Part of that system was a belief that the Jewish religion was an extreme threat to Christianity and needed to be eradicated. Other tenets included a belief that being gay was a sin and that abortion was murder.

At some point after the Williams brothers met the business partners Matson and Mowder, they learned that the two were a gay couple. Incensed by that knowledge and by the fact that they considered most Christians too cowardly to actually be warriors for the movement, the Williamses set up a plan of action. The details of the plan emerged in a series of surprising newspaper interviews that Matthew Williams gave after his arrest for arson and murder. During an interview with the Sacramento Bee, Matthew, much to his attorney's chagrin and against all legal advice, happily expressed his views on race, religion, and politics and freely admitted his role in the arsons and murders that occurred in 1999.

Matthew Williams admitted that he along with several other "Christian Warriors" met in the spring of 1999 at a survival expo in Sacramento. From there, they established a coordinated attack on three different Jewish synagogues in the area. Matthew Williams admitted that he gathered some gasoline and oil in a "firebomb" mixture and brought several of those items to a mall parking lot early on the morning of June 18. They chose the targets in the state capitol to make the boldest of statements to the world. Matthew said he passed out some firebombs to other conspirators and then they all set out to start the attacks. Matthew said he broke into the synagogue Congregation B'nai Israel at about 3:00 a.m. along with two other males. They poured the gas and oil mixtures throughout and ignited the blaze. Matthew admitted to leaving the firebomb containers at the site but believed the fire would destroy the evidence. He claimed not to know any of the other attackers.

After that event, Matthew and his brother Tyler began to look at their next targets, the gay couple. On the morning of July 1, 1999, the brothers drove to Redding and broke into the home of the victims. They forced the victims to record an answering machine message and then forced them at gunpoint into their bed. At that time, the victims were shot several times each with a .22 caliber gun. Two hours after the murders, a caller ordered over $2,000 worth of ammunition from an Arizona dealer, using one of the victims' credit cards to pay for it. The ammo was to be sent to a PO box in Yuba City.

A relative found the victims' bodies and notified authorities. The victim's car was missing, and Matthew would later admit that they stole it and drove toward Yuba City. Shortly after, police in Oroville found the victim's vehicle abandoned on the road. The Williams brothers were found and arrested later that afternoon in Yuba City at the mailbox business where they had ordered the ammunition to be sent. Matthew was found to be wearing a bulletproof vest, and both were carrying handguns.

After their arrest, a search warrant was served on a storage locker that the Williamses kept, and detectives found references to the earlier synagogue arsons. They also found a "hit list" of prominent Jewish citizens from the Sacramento area. Investigators also located a large amount of white supremacist, anti-gay, and anti-abortion literature.

Shortly after their arrest, Tyler Williams admitted the murder scheme to a probation officer. He said his elder brother Matthew had selected the pair to be killed because they were homosexuals. He said that Matthew did not believe it was murder because in their belief system the two men had been "judged" by God and he was merely carrying out a judgment.

Within a few months, Matthew began his very public admissions to the Sacramento Bee. He grew an Adolf Hitler style mustache in jail and planned to use his belief system as his defense in court. He vowed to use the trial as his forum to promote anti-Semitism and his hatred for homosexuals and abortionists. He planned on wearing a Nazi uniform to court during the trial. He admitted his role in the attacks and took full blame for the events. Investigators would later discount his description of an organized group of arsonists in the synagogue attacks and attribute all three fires and the abortion clinic attempt to both of the Williams brothers.

After Matthew's much reported admissions in the media, several persons came forward and openly questioned his sexual identity. Several former friends and roommates described how they had always believed that Matthew was most likely a "closet homosexual" who was having severe issues with his own identity. They described him as "neat, prissy, and overly fastidious" and a person who became very emotional at even the discussion of homosexuality. One acquaintance reported that in early 1999 Matthew had tried to reach his closest friend from his Idaho days, only to learn that that man was now openly gay, a gay rights activist, and an HIV prevention advocate. That acquaintance later opined that that information was too much for Matthew to deal with and caused him to carry out the murders on the gay couple in Redding.

For whatever reason, the Williamses' case never went to trial. Both brothers reached plea deals in September 2001. By December, a federal judge had sentenced Matthew Williams to thirty years in prison for his synagogue and abortion clinic arsons. His younger brother, Tyler, received a twenty-one-year sentence for his role in the arson attacks.

Matthew did not go away quietly, nor was he content to wait around for the murder trial. In June 2002, Matthew's attorney paid for a newspaper ad announcing that Matthew had been ordained as a minister by the Christ Covenant Church. Four days after the ad ran in the local media, Matthew and another inmate, in an apparent escape bid, attacked a guard at the Shasta County jail with a homemade hatchet. The attack caused guard Tim Renault to suffer a skull fracture and broken jaw and left him in critical condition. The escape failed, and Williams was sent to the segregation unit of the jail after that incident. On November 17, 2002, Matthew Williams committed suicide in his jail cell by slashing his arms, legs, and throat with a jail razor. Just prior to that event, he had mailed a full confession to his brother's attorney, taking the blame for the murders of Gary Matson and Winfield Mowder.

Despite that, in March 2003, Tyler Williams pleaded guilty to the murders and received an additional twenty-nine years to life in prison on top of the twenty-one years he would serve for the arsons. By doing that, he avoided the death penalty.

Investigator Analysis

The Williams brothers were a product of their upbringing. They were openly racist throughout their adult life and were easily suspected in those hate-motivated attacks. Like in many arson cases, the target of the arson attack provided the best clue as to who the arsonist would be. If it had been only one synagogue that was attacked, then there was the possibility of an internal issue or insurance fraud. However, since the attacks appeared to be linked to each other and were similar in nature, then it would be a fairly simple thing for investigators to start looking at the anti-Semites in the area. The related attack on the abortion clinic also helped narrow the field of suspects. Based on their previous actions, the Williams brothers' names soon came up.

These events are related more toward hate crimes than to a serial arsonist, but they illustrate how much impact an arson attack has on a religious institution. The only aspect that this case has in common with serial arson cases is the allegation that Matthew Williams was believed by his close friends to be struggling with his sexual identity. This is an often recurring theme in this list of serial arson cases.

Jay Scott Ballinger "Missionary of Lucifer": Serial Church Arsonist, Murderer

Period of Activity: 1993-99, Indiana and Multiple Other States

Angela Wood: Serial Church Arsonist (Accomplice of Ballinger)

Donald A. Puckett: Serial Church Arsonist (Accomplice of Ballinger)

Sgt. Steve Hiatt of the University Police at Ball State University (Indiana) listened to his instincts. In February 1999, he heard a radio call asking for an ambulance for a man with significant burn injuries. A thirty-six-year-old white male had arrived at the Ball Memorial Hospital with major burns that were at least a few days old. His story about how he had gotten the burns was vague and inconsistent. His rationale for waiting a few days to be treated was just as oblique. Sgt. Hiatt, an eighteen-year police veteran, was well aware that a church arson had occurred in the area just a few days earlier. More importantly, he recognized the burned man in the hospital as having a sinister past with links to Satanism. Sgt. Hiatt placed a phone call to a local arson task force, and they soon arrived and placed the injured man, Jay Ballinger, into custody. Subsequent to the arrest, the task force raided the home of Ballinger and found, among other things, a gas container, numerous books on Satanism, and a significant "paper trail" of credit card receipts and journal entries that connected Ballinger to a string of church arsons.

Jay Ballinger grew up in a mobile home in Southern Indiana. Little is known about his childhood other than the fact that neighbors described him as a loner who didn't play well with other kids. He dropped out of high school and was only able to maintain very menial jobs. He was frequently unemployed. He was well known in his small town for his very vociferous affinity to Satanism. Ballinger openly proclaimed his loyalty to the devil, and he even tried to start his own "church." He just as openly proclaimed his hatred for organized Christianity. Ballinger first came to the attention of local authorities in 1993 when he was arrested for contributing to the delinquency of a minor. This crime occurred as a result of Ballinger's recruitment efforts to entice over fifty high school students in southern Indiana to "pledge their bodies and souls to Lucifer." Part of this act was to have the students sign "contracts." A typical contract read, "I promise to do all types of Evil in service to our Lord (Satan), until the end of time." He was able to convince those kids to actually sign the contracts in blood. Ballinger described himself to his underage "flock" as "an evangelical for Lucifer (Satan)." He mortified local parents by urging his young followers to wear black clothing and black lipstick and to dye their hair black. The final touch was to have them wear very pale makeup on their faces giving the appearance of death. A coincidental side note to this arrest was that about two months after his incarceration, national headlines were made as a result of the Columbine massacre in Colorado, where two disenfranchised youths dressed in a similar Gothic style murdered several of their high school classmates.

The parents in the small Indiana town were of the belief that Ballinger was more interested in exploiting the bodies of the young women than in their actual souls and basically drove him out of town with real and implied threats. Soon after, Ballinger carried his hatred for Christianity to a new level.

This incident was the first public inclination about Ballinger's very devout beliefs. It also demonstrated that Ballinger had some degree of charisma as he was able to exert influence over many young minds. This charisma would manifest itself later as he was able to convince others to join him in his church burning spree.

Shortly after his release from jail, Ballinger decided to take his love for Lucifer to the extreme and launch attacks against the enemies of Lucifer—Christian churches. He started by attacking several Indiana churches on his own. His favored method was to forcibly break into a remote, rural church late at night, deface the property with a satanic symbol, and then pour a flammable liquid mixture into the church. He used a match or lighter to ignite the blaze.

Ballinger's charisma allowed him to recruit two willing followers in this plan. The first was a twenty-four-year-old stripper named Angela Wood.

Wood met Ballinger as she traveled the exotic dancer circuit. Her parents later described her as a lost soul who was drifting aimlessly through life and had become ripe for Ballinger to exploit. He connected with her through their shared interest in Satanism, and the two had a child together. Ballinger started to follow Wood as she earned a living on the exotic dancer circuit. Their travels eventually took them to several states where the two eventually became involved in church arsons.

At some point, the pair met up with another believer named Donald Puckett. The thirty-seven-year-old Puckett accompanied Ballinger and Wood on their very first church arson. Ballinger had convinced the other two that he could create a "new world order" by attacking Christian churches. On the night of January 9, 1994, the trio broke into and vandalized the Concord Church of Christ in Lebanon, Indiana. The vandalism included painting upside down crosses inside the church and then pouring a flammable liquid inside. At some point, one of the three struck the match that set the building ablaze. This fire completely destroyed the famous old structure, which had been featured in the film *Hoosiers*.

That fire was just the beginning. Over the next three years, the group lit an additional eleven fires to rural churches in Indiana, four in Kentucky, three in Ohio, and at least one each in California, Alabama, Missouri, and Tennessee. In 1998, agents from the FBI made inquiries about Ballinger in his hometown in Indiana. At that point, he and Wood decided to leave the area to avoid talking to the feds. The trio split up, and Ballinger and Wood continued to her home in Georgia. In late 1998, the pair took their arson spree into high gear. On December 20, they drove their van into Scottsburg, Indiana, and torched a Christian church. They then drove straight to Bonnieville, Kentucky, where the very next night they torched a Baptist church. The frenetic pace continued as the duo drove the van from that scene to Manchester, Tennessee, the next night and burned another Baptist church. After driving all night from that event, they ended up in Dalton, Georgia, on December 22. Within hours of arriving, Ballinger drove to another Baptist church, broke a window, and poured gasoline inside. He then torched it with his cigarette lighter. On the twenty-third, at just past one in the morning, he attacked yet another Baptist church and burned its fellowship hall to the ground. Following that string, the pair set out for Athens, Georgia, where Wood's mother lived. Along the way, they came upon the Sardis Full Gospel church, which was hours away from its Christmas Eve services. Ballinger and Wood started a fire which destroyed that building.

Apparently Ballinger and Woods took a short Christmas break, as their next event did not occur until a week later. On New Year's Eve, 1998, at the New Salem United Methodist Church in Commerce, Georgia, Ballinger, using his preferred method of attack, broke a window with a tool and then poured a gasoline mixture into the church. He ignited the vapors and then sped away in his van. That fire had a bit different outcome than his previous attacks. The large blaze caused a rapid and large response from area firefighting agencies. One of these firefighters who responded was twenty-seven-year-old Kennon Loy Williams, who was a volunteer firefighter in Banks County. Although the fire was technically out of his district, Williams responded and eventually entered the structure with other firefighters. Tragically, the blaze weakened the roof, and it collapsed on the fire crews, severely injuring two firefighters and killing Williams. Kennon Williams was a posthumous recipient of the National Medal of Honor by the National Fire Academy.

Despite killing a firefighter, that tragic event did not seem to have an impact on Jay Ballinger. Several hours later, he attacked a Methodist church and severely damaged it with fire. Wood and Ballinger parted ways at that point, and on January 16, 1999, Ballinger drove alone back to Indiana. He left a trail of burning churches to mark his progress back home. On January 17, he torched a Baptist church in Franklin, Kentucky. Hours later he burned a Methodist church in Elkton, Kentucky, and the next night hit another Baptist church in Beaver Dam, Kentucky.

On February 7, his luck ran out, and his Satanic spree came to a merciful end when he burned himself while igniting a blaze at a Methodist church in Brookville, Ohio.

Partly as a result of the activities of this group, along with a perceived rash of church arsons across the United States at the time, the National Council of Churches put pressure on the administration of President Clinton to do something about this alleged wave of "racist attacks."*** From this, in June 1996, the Federal Church Arson Task Force was formed and remains in effect to a small extent today. A branch of this task force investigated the church arsons across lower Indiana, Kentucky, and Ohio. It was this group who the astute Sergeant Hiatt contacted with his suspicions about Ballinger.

True to his beliefs and confronted with the evidence found in his home, Ballinger gave a fairly quick confession of his activities to investigators. He stunned investigators by bragging about committing over fifty church arsons in twenty-three different states. He did not hesitate to name his two accomplices, and they were both soon arrested for arson. The awesome power of the United States government came to bear on the two accomplices, along with the threat of lifetime sentences in prison, and both soon agreed to plead guilty and to testify against their leader.

Donald Puckett pled guilty to the Concord Church arson in October of 1999 and was sentenced to twenty-seven months in federal prison. He gave a full admission as to the roles of himself and his accomplices in that spree. He said the three entered the church late at night and sprayed a flammable mixture of gasoline, kerosene, and paint thinner throughout the structure. He said that Ballinger insisted that all participate so they would be equally guilty, and he ordered his girlfriend Wood to paint the Satanic crosses on the church steps. Puckett said that Ballinger actually struck the match at that event. Puckett confirmed that he had assisted the pair in numerous church arsons in Indiana, Kentucky, and Ohio.

Angela Wood pled guilty several weeks later to an open charge of multiple church arsons. She presented evidence at her sentencing hearing that she was a victim of physical and emotional abuse by Ballinger and that she participated in the fires out of fear of him. She admitted that she had acted as the "lookout" on most of the fires but that Ballinger had forced her to strike the match at two of the events in order to "get her dirty." She complied out of her fear for her safety. The court was not impressed by that tact and eventually sentenced her to over seventeen years in federal prison for her role in the arson series.

Finally, after the convictions of his partners and faced with the prospect of being charged for all of the arsons, Jay Ballinger pled guilty in July 2000 for arson attacks on twenty-six churches in eleven states. The remaining charges were dropped, and Ballinger was sentenced to forty-two years in federal prison. At the time of his sentencing, he denied any involvement in the Georgia church arsons.

Not to be denied their justice, federal officials in Georgia indicted Ballinger for three of the Georgia church arsons and the death of a firefighter. Under the threat of a federal death penalty, Jay Ballinger eventually pled guilty in 2001 to the Georgia arsons in exchange for a life sentence on those charges. Inexplicably, for reasons only attorneys would understand, Ballinger's case was briefly overturned on an automatic appeal, but was mercifully reaffirmed by the federal court in 2005. Jay Ballinger would spend the rest of his life in prison after being convicted for burning a total of twenty-nine churches in twelve states. Church Arson Task Force Investigators are convinced that he burned over fifty churches in twenty-three states over a four-year period. He remains the most significant church arsonist ever identified.

*** Investigator's Note: The Federal Church Arson Task Force is still in existence today, albeit on a very much reduced scale. The task force was formed in a political climate in 1996, which espoused the theory that there was an ongoing wave of race-motivated attacks against black churches across the United States. Most investigators that I have spoken to, including many federal agents who refuse to be named, are of the very strong opinion that this alleged "wave of racist attacks" is yet another myth in the fire investigation world. There has been for decades a significant number of church fires. Isolated, poor, and older churches in rural areas seem to have the largest number of fires. Investigations have shown that many of these incidents are accidental in nature due to poor fire standards or conditions, and the few cases that are actually arson events are for the most part related to the same motivations that all arson fires are. Most of these arson fires have been linked to internal church issues, insurance fraud, and personal revenge issues. In the end, very few church arsons can be attributed to "racial attacks." The Church Arson Task Force was instrumental in the Ballinger case, although its conclusions were that Ballinger and company were attacking targets of opportunity with little regard to which race the parishioners belonged. The facts of the case show that while Ballinger, Wood, and Puckett were white, they attacked both predominantly white and black congregated churches. Like most church arsons, race was not a factor at all in target selection.

Investigator Analysis

The Ballinger case is yet another unique arson episode. The man's hatred for Christianity and its institutions was overt, blatant, and consistent. His arson attacks were a natural progression of his original anti-Christian beliefs. There is little doubt that had he not been captured, he would have done dozens or perhaps hundreds more attacks. The pace of his final group of attacks was staggering, and he seemed to be working himself up to bigger and faster events.

While there is bare mention of it, there is little doubt that Ballinger either recorded those attacks in a journal or kept press clippings of his events. He wanted recognition and wanted to show his "followers" his accomplishments.

The fact that he brought about his own demise by burning himself was almost predictable. Despite being a very experienced fire setter, he did not refine his ignition methods to a point where it gave him a safety or delay factor. If he used a gasoline mixture on all of his fires, there is little doubt that he had a few close calls where he was scared or got slightly burned while setting the fire.

Catching a person like Ballinger would seem a very daunting prospect. He seemed to have selected random targets that were in very remote areas. He eventually spread his attacks over several states. Predicting his attacks was impossible, and the only way to catch him was to follow him, which would be difficult if he stayed in remote areas. However, a review of his attacks showed that they were in a linear pattern (while he traveled) and attacked churches of all denominations. A profiler could infer that the subject had to be someone who had a grudge against all Christian churches.

In the end, Ballinger was an extremely disorganized offender, who while he roamed and ranged over great distances appeared to select his targets at random. He no doubt chose them for their isolated locations, construction, and ease of entry. His method of attack was somewhat juvenile as he broke

135

exterior windows and poured gasoline. His Satanic signature left at the scene was not at all clever and would surely (as it did) bring investigators to his doorstep because of his earlier overt acts.

Despite his unsophisticated manner and overt lifestyle, Jay Ballinger managed to elude suspicion for over four years while on his reign of terror.

Richard Thomas Andrews: Serial Abortion Clinic Arsonist Period of Activity: 1992-95, Northwestern United States

In 1996, the Federal Church Arson Task Force was formed under the Clinton Administration, at the direction of U.S. Attorney General Janet Reno. This was in response to a belief that there was an organized group of hate mongers attacking black churches across the South. Shortly after the Church Arson Task Force was formed, Attorney General Reno formed a second similar task force in response to a belief that there was another organized group attacking abortion clinics across the United States. Indeed, the National Abortion Federation reported in 2007 that there had been over two hundred documented bombings or arson attacks at reproduction clinics since the mid-1970s.

The Church Arson Task Force diminished in size over the next few years as investigations proved that organized church arsons were mostly a myth. The Abortion Clinic Federal Task Force learned within two years of its formation that the bombing, firebombing, and arson attacks on abortion clinics were also not part of a nationwide organized effort. However, the task force did find that there were several "lone wolf"-style arsonists whose favorite targets were abortion clinics. Most of those arsonists had links to very conservative religious groups.

In the early morning hours of a June day in 1996, alert patrolmen from Vancouver, Washington, police pulled over a car in a routine traffic stop. The vehicle was suspicious in the predawn hours and was similar in appearance to a car that had been seen leaving a recent arson attack at an abortion clinic. Officers contacted the driver and identified him as sixty-year-old Richard Andrews. The husky, heavily bearded Andrews was alone in the car that held several five gallon plastic containers of gasoline. The curious officers also noted that there was a ski mask and rubber gloves in the passenger compartment, an array of highway flares, butane lighters, and the written addresses of several abortion clinics. Additionally, the car had an active police scanner that monitored frequencies in several cities and maps of the same cities. That night the officers noted all the evidence and cited Andrews for erratic driving prior to letting him go. However, they were sharp enough to recognize the suspicious activity and immediately forwarded his information to a federal arson task force.

The task force had been mired in a wide-ranging investigation involving arson attacks on several abortion clinics in the western United States. They immediately focused their attention on Richard Andrews as a prime suspect in their case. Andrews proved to be a fairly open book. He was immediately recognized by federal agents as an ardent foe of abortion. He was well known as a very angry religious fundamentalist who spent many years openly campaigning against pornography and who also led boycotts of hospitals that provided reproductive services.

As the investigation unfolded, the background of Andrews began to emerge. He was a resident of Wenatchee, Washington, and had three children. He had worked in the insurance field, but had retired with a disability injury in 1992. Since the 1980s he had been arrested four times for his involvement in organizing anti-abortion rallies for a group called "Operation Rescue," which was the national anti-abortion organization. Andrews was well known as one of the top two leaders of the group in the state of Washington.

Police records showed that Andrews had received speeding tickets in areas very close to where abortion clinic arson attacks had occurred. A search of his home by federal agents led to the discovery of documents placing him in the cities and areas at the time when other abortion clinic arson attacks had taken place. Soon the task force began to assemble the circumstantial case against Richard Andrews. The following attacks were linked to Andrews by the evidence found within his car and home:

1. January 18, 1992: arson attack at Planned Parenthood in Helena, Montana
2. June 6, 1992: arson attack at Feminist Women's Health Center in Redding, California
3. March 29, 1993: arson attack at Blue Mountain Clinic in Missoula, Montana
4. May 27, 1993: arson attack at Women's Health Care in Boise, Idaho
5. October 9, 1994: arson attack (second time) Feminist Women's Health Center in Redding
6. October 9, 1994: arson attack at Planned Parenthood in Chico, California
7. October 11, 1994: arson attack at Armstrong Clinic in Kalispell, Montana
8. September 18, 1995: arson attack at Emerg-a-Care Clinic in Jackson, Wyoming.

On May 29, 1997, Richard Andrews was indicted in California on three counts of arson and several other charges for the attacks in Chico and Redding. The very first fire in that group in 1992 destroyed the entire clinic and collapsed the roof of the building. That caused over $100,000 in damage. The damage closed the facility for over eight months. He hit the exact same facility a second time eighteen months later. He faced nearly one hundred years in prison on these charges.

On February 10, 1998, while facing an additional indictment on the remaining charges, Andrews agreed to a plea deal with the feds. He pled guilty to all eight charged arson attacks in that series. He also admitted that his attacks amounted to over $700, 000 in property loss. On April 28, 1998, he was sentenced to seven years in federal prison for those arson attacks.

Investigator Analysis

Abortion clinic bombings and arsons are yet another of the extremist subsets of this crime. They can be vaguely linked by ideology to similar attacks on churches, government buildings, and gay bars. While not very common in occurrence, those attacks had tremendous impact on the media and the public as a whole. As the Abortion Clinic Arson Task Force quickly found out, there were very few cases in this genre that could be linked to an organized group. This, like many hate crimes, is an act perpetrated by the "lone wolf" offender. This type of suspect is usually someone who is partially organized in his behavior and who acts out his extremist and intolerant beliefs by himself. Most of the offenders in this group do belong to more mainstream groups, but their attacks are solely their own work.

Richard T. Andrews is the quintessential lone wolf-style arsonist. He is an organized offender who researched and sought out his targets. He arranged his arson equipment and employed tactics that would help him achieve the maximum damage for his efforts. He was a true believer to his cause, and his entire goal was to stop those facilities from carrying out their operations. In many cases, he was quite successful.

As an investigator, that case does not seem like a difficult one to solve. The targets are the key to the offender, and there are a small group of people who would soon appear as potential suspects once the victimology of the target is analyzed. Andrews was a well-known person in the anti-abortion movement and was well known to law enforcement. There is little doubt that federal agents already had some sort of intelligence file on him listing him as an extremist. Sooner or later, suspicion would have fallen on him.

What allowed Richard Andrews to operate successfully for such a long time period was the fact that he spread out his operations to many states, as opposed to operating in one small area. His operations occurred in the northwest of America, where there were large numbers of people who expressed similar (if less extreme) anti-government and conservative religious views. Andrews was able to carefully plan and space out his activities in such a manner that the sheer size of his attack area was enough to stymie an investigation. He was careful to operate under cover of darkness and to take anti-forensic measures (rubber gloves). He used counter police measures (scanners) and appeared to stake out his targets prior to attacking them. All in all he was a fairly organized arson offender.

Rachelle Ranae "Shelley" Shannon: Serial Abortion Clinic Arsonist, Would-be Assassin
Period of Activity: 1992-93, Pacific Northwest

On August 19, 1993, at seven in the evening, a thirty-seven-year-old woman stood in the driveway of a medical clinic in Wichita, Kansas. The clinic was a special facility and one of only six in the United States that performed a unique procedure called a "late stage" abortion. The doctor who performed those procedures, fifty-two-year-old Dr. George R. Tiller, would remain a controversial figure throughout his life. His clinic had been the site of constant picketing by anti-abortion activists over the preceding months. As it was, his life nearly ended that day as the woman began shooting a gun at Tiller the moment he emerged from a clinic. Hit twice, Dr. Tiller dropped to the ground while his assailant was seen running away. A durable sort, Tiller received gunshot wounds to both arms but returned to work the very next day.

The would-be assassin was not the most sophisticated of criminals. She was observed speeding away from the clinic in a rental car. The car was traced to a heretofore unknown Oregon housewife name Shelley Shannon. Later that same day, Shannon was arrested at an Oklahoma City airport terminal where she had gone to turn in her rental vehicle. At the time of her arrest, she was carrying a Bible and a doll that resembled a fetus.

Within hours of her arrest, authorities in Kansas asked for help from the feds and from the state police in Oregon. A search warrant was served on Shannon's home which she shared with her husband in Grant's Pass, seeking evidence linking her to the shooting. The detectives were surprised to find much more than what they had hoped for. The search revealed books on explosives making, a book entitled *The Army of God*, and the most critical item, Shannon's personal diary. The diary was critical in that it linked her to a recent wave of firebombings and arson attacks on abortion-related facilities in several states in the Pacific Northwest.

Upon learning that the cops had raided her home, the incarcerated Shannon wrote a letter to her daughter. The letter was intercepted by investigators, and in part, it said that the world would soon know of the other things Shannon had done. Regarding the attempted murder of Dr. Tiller, Shannon wrote, "I'm not denying I shot Tiller. But I deny that it was wrong. It was the most holy, most righteous thing I've ever done. I have no regrets. I hope he's not killing babies today." ***

Shelley Shannon was born and raised in rural Wisconsin. She was bright and did well in school and was active in her church. Her mother was a bit of an odd influence as she was married four times, twice to the same man. Shelley was described as artistic and also did quite well in math. A major occurrence in her young life happened when she was a junior in high school. At sixteen, Shelley became pregnant with her daughter Angi. Six months after she graduated, and with a one-year-old daughter in tow, she married her husband David Shannon. All of her friends would later say that although she was active in her church, no one would ever describe her as being religious. They were all surprised several years later in the mid-1980s when Shelley became a born-again Christian.

Shortly after her graduation, the Shannons packed up and moved to the Pacific Northwest. Shelley Shannon's husband would later tell reporters that when he met his wife, both were fairly normal, middle-of-the-road people who had faith, but were not necessarily religious freaks. She was a stay-at-home mom who homeschooled her own daughters. He said as they grew older, his wife began to lean to a much more conservative view of life and became much more ardent about her religious beliefs. At some point in the mid-1980s, Shelley and her daughter attended a film on abortion. From that point on, Shelley became an increasingly active member of the anti-abortion movement in the Northwest. She was a simple housewife, but occasionally traveled great distances out of state to attend anti-abortion rallies. Soon she began actively taking part in pickets, protests, and sit-ins. She was arrested on several occasions for trespassing, and she told her family stories of how the police abused her with excessive force. Shelley at one point told her adult daughter that she could justify the firebombing of abortion clinics after they were closed so that no one would be hurt. Eventually, she went even further in her views and expressed that she could justify the killing of one man if it would save the lives of thousands of unborn babies.

Shelley Shannon soon began to radicalize and became closely associated with a leading anti-abortion activist named John Brockhoeft, who eventually was convicted himself of several abortion clinic firebombings. She began to edit the anti-abortion newsletter "The Brockhoeft Report." By 1990, Brockhoeft had openly advocated in his newsletter the firebombings of abortion clinics. He stated that it was an act of love for babies each time he burned a clinic. Brockhoeft's actions soon landed him in federal prison in Kentucky. Shelley Shannon maintained a constant stream of letters with Brockhoeft over a three-year period.

Shannon also established a letter writing correspondence with another anti-abortion radical named Michael Griffin. This thirty-one-year-old man was then currently in jail in Florida awaiting a murder trial for gunning down another abortion doctor, Dr. David Gunn. On July 30 and August 1, 1993, Shelley Shannon made a pilgrimage to the federal prison in Kentucky to consult with John Brockhoeft. Two weeks later she attacked Dr. Tiller in Wichita.

After her incarceration, Shannon made sporadic contact with various members of the media. She was adamant that she was not a criminal but described herself as a "rescuer." She refused to talk about herself other than to say that she became a Christian in the past decade, led a normal life, never committed any other crimes, and was not abused as a child. She refused to call her movement an "anti-abortion" movement, but adamantly referred to it as a "life rescue" movement.

Meanwhile, federal agents in the Northwest were wondering about the diary they had dug up from Shelley Shannon's yard. The diary made numerous claims to her active role in the firebombings of several abortion clinics in the Northwest. The agents, realizing that those incidents were closely linked to other similar incidents throughout the country, formed the opinion that it was possible that there was a massive nationwide conspiracy afoot to target those clinics. They formed the Federal Abortion Clinic Arson Task Force in response to that perceived threat.

They also began to evaluate Shannon's diary and to compare it to known incidents. In her diary, Shannon claimed to have committed the following attacks on abortion care facilities:

1. April 11, 1992: arson attack to Catalina Medical Center, Ashland, Oregon. Broken glass jar and gasoline found at scene. $380,000 in damage.
2. August 1, 1992: arson attack to Lovejoy Surgicenter, Portland, Oregon. An incendiary device of plastic bottle with gasoline and 4 "ground bloom" fireworks found at scene.
3. August 18, 1992: arson attack to Feminist Women's Health Center, Sacramento, California. Three plastic bottles with gasoline thrown on exterior, plus one Molotov cocktail device.
4. August 18, 1992: arson attack to West End Women's Clinic, Reno, Nevada. Plastic containers of gasoline thrown at windows.
5. September 16, 1992: arson attack to Feminist Women's Health Center, Eugene, Oregon. Two plastic bottles containing gasoline found at scene.

6. September 16, 1992: noxious chemical attack to West End Women's Clinic, Reno, Nevada. Shannon entered building and injected a noxious chemical into the wall of the bathroom.
7. September 17, 1992: noxious chemical attack to Feminist Women's Health Center, Chico, California. Shannon entered building and injected noxious chemical into the wall.
8. November 28, 1992: arson attack to Pregnancy Consultation Center, Sacramento, California. Glass jar with gasoline thrown through a glass window. $175,000 damage.

The majority of those arson and chemical attacks caused little structural damage, but did cause significant emotional damage. Two of those fires grew into large events. Investigators were able to find other written documents, newspaper clippings, and other evidence at her home that confirmed the validity of the claims in the diary. Additionally, Shannon had been identified by the media months prior to those attacks as she had openly picketed many of these clinics. Lastly, witnesses at several of the scenes described a woman fitting Shannon's description just prior to or after the events.

On March 25, 1994, a federal jury convicted Shelley Shannon of attempted murder on Dr. Tiller. She was sentenced to ten years and eight months in prison.

On October 14, 1994, federal agents conducted a lengthy interview of Shelley Shannon while she was in federal prison. During that taped interview, she freely admitted to the above arson and chemical attacks and provided specific corroborating evidence to confirm her confessions. Through her notes and musings, agents were also able to identify a coconspirator who assisted Shannon by supplying materials, information, and lists of potential targets. His name was John Bell. He subsequently admitted his role in those attacks to the feds.

On June 7, 1995, Shelley Shannon pled guilty in federal court to five counts of arson and five other various counts related to the arson attacks on the clinics. On September 8 of that year, she was sentenced to an additional twenty years in federal prison.

* * *

Dr. George Tiller's escape from death in that incident only postponed the inevitable. He was continuously hounded by anti-abortion protesters for the next sixteen years. Finally, in 2009, another radicalized, lone wolf member of the movement tracked him down. On May 31, while Dr. Tiller was serving as an usher in his church in Wichita, anti-abortion activist Scott Roeder walked up to him and shot him through the eye with a pistol in full view of the shocked congregation. Roeder fled the scene and was arrested three hours later in Kansas City. He was convicted of murder in January 2010 by a jury and sentenced to life without parole for at least fifty years. The abortion issue remains to this day one of the most polarizing and controversial subjects in the United States.

Investigator's Analysis

Like Richard T. Andrews in the previous case, Shelley Shannon was a true believer and a dedicated warrior to her cause. She was not as skilled at fire setting as Andrews and lacked the sophistication to get away with her crimes. She was extremely overt in her actions and was witnessed at several crime scenes. She also used a vehicle that could be traced to her.

Despite her ineptitude as an arsonist and a criminal, Shannon was able to elude suspicion for those events for over a year. She only became a suspect when her diary was found after her arrest for the attempted murder.

While not a serial arsonist in the classical sense, she was a compelling character. She obviously used items and chose targets at the direction of other persons. She even attacked some of the exact same targets as Richard Andrews. Had a serious federal investigation taken place from the start, there is little doubt that Shannon would have been apprehended months sooner for her amateurish activities. As it was, because she hit targets in a wide variety of locations, she was able to elude the authorities for well over a year.

Shelley Shannon is a true believer in her cause, and no amount of counseling or incarceration will ever sway her from her steadfast belief that she is doing the right thing. Like many of those zealots, she is a very scary person.

Jason Robert Bourque: Serial Church Arsonist
Period of Activity: 2009-10, East Texas

Daniel George McAllister: Serial Church Arsonist
Period of Activity: 2009-10, East Texas

In late 2009 and early 2010, an alarming series of church arsons erupted across a portion of eastern Texas. Traditionally a very strong "Bible Belt" state, Texans were shocked by that attack on their houses of worship.

On December 8, 2009, unknown suspects broke into the Fletcher Emanuel Church Alive in Lumberton, Texas, and set it afire. Three weeks later on New Year's Day, 2010, a similar attack occurred at the Little Hope Baptist Church in Van Zandt County. From that point on, the frequency of the attacks increased dramatically. Arson and burglary attacks occurred at Baptist churches on January 2 and twice more on the eleventh. By that time, local authorities had summoned the ATF to establish a task force to combat those events. The ATF took the case so seriously that they withdrew agents who would normally be working at the Super Bowl and diverted them to the East Texas Church Arson Task Force.

Despite the presence of the feds, the attacks continued into the New Year. Church arsons occurred on January 16, 17, and 30. An additional arson occurred on February 4 and two more on February 8. Also during that same time frame, there were three attempted break-ins of churches in the area. All told, there were fourteen incidents at churches in eastern Texas over a six-week period.

Despite few leads, task force investigators did what came natural. They processed each scene as an individual incident. Each fire was investigated by a qualified team of fire investigators. Forensic evidence was located at many of the scenes, including trace evidence from clothing. Those items were sent to a lab for DNA analysis. Footprints from similar boots were found at several of the scenes and sent to the lab for analysis. Witnesses were interviewed, and security cameras from nearby businesses were viewed for evidence. That dogged investigative work paid off in spades for the task force.

Lab technicians were soon able to locate similar DNA extracted from items from multiple fire scenes. Two different shoe impressions were located at various fire scenes. Investigators soon realized that they had at least two suspects in that case. One was linked to a pair of size 13 or 14 Red Wing brand boots. This boot print was found on a door that had been kicked in at the February 8 fire at Dover Baptist Church. This print matched other prints found at some of the previous arson scenes and at some of the burglary scenes. A second shoe brand, Skechers, was found at multiple arson and burglary scenes.

The final fires in the series caused the biggest breaks in the case. On the same night of the Dover fire, February 8, a nearby gas station's security camera recorded two white males in the vicinity at the same time as the blaze. That same night, at the other church fire that occurred, one of the same males from the Dover fire appeared on a security camera at a business near the second church arson. Officials then had photos of at least two suspects in the case. That same night, multiple witnesses observed a dark blue four-door sedan parked near the second church fire.

The next big break in the case was one all investigators hope for. A phone tip was taken off a "hotline." The caller actually gave investigators the name of a possible arsonist in the case—nineteen-year-old Jason Robert Bourque. Investigators found his photo and compared it to the surveillance camera footage. It was a close match. They soon started a surveillance operation on the home of Jason Bourque. They noted that he drove a blue 2008 Ford sedan that was a close match to the suspicious vehicle observed at two arson scenes. On

February 11, task force agents approached Bourque at his home and engaged in consensual conversation. They were rewarded with another big break in the case when, during their interview, they noted that in his open garage were a pair of muddy Skechers shoes that matched the pattern found at several crime scenes.

The investigation team left Bourque's home and began amassing their evidence. They were soon led to Bourque's longtime friend, twenty-one-year-old Daniel George McAllister. His photo was a match for the other arson suspect seen on the surveillance tape. Subsequent interviews with family members revealed that McAllister wore size 13 Red Wing boots, which matched the footprints found at several scenes. Investigators learned that on February 10, McAllister had purchased a one-way bus ticket to San Antonio, Texas. He appeared to be fleeing the area as the investigation closed in.

After investigators left Bourque's home, they began an intensive surveillance operation on him. During the next ten days, he was continuously monitored by agents. Their surveillance paid off with the final big break in the case. On one occasion, undercover agents watched Bourque enter a bathroom at a business. After he left, they checked the bathroom and saw graffiti proclaiming "Little Hope (church) was Arson." Underneath that slogan was drawn a burning upside down cross. That was recognized as a reference to the Little Hope church arson of January 1. Also, the upside down cross was a reference to either Satanism or atheism. A computer search of Bourque revealed that he was a member of an online group that was described as a "bonfire fan club" that included hundreds of images of people watching bonfires.

On February 21, 2010, the task force dropped the hammer, and those two males were taken into custody. Found among their possessions were documents about Satanism and atheism along with some weapons.

While the investigators have not revealed much more of that case, local reporters dug into the pasts of those two suspects. It was learned that both had attended the same East Texas Baptist church when they were young. A local minister recalled that both had been involved in a church break-in about seven years prior, but he dismissed it as a youthful prank and noted that nothing had been taken or destroyed.

Jason Bourque was not your typical arsonist. He grew up fairly well off and was known to be very intellectual. He was fond of quoting philosophers and was a former high school state champion in debate. Just prior to his arrest, he was seen attending a Baptist church service at his college. His former pastor described him as outgoing and highly intelligent with a near photographic memory. He showed an early interest in Bible studies and was very inquisitive. A female acquaintance told reporters that Bourque had been kicked out of a Texas college and that he had undergone depression over the previous two years.

Daniel McAllister was described as a quiet boy who had been raised by a devoted mother who often volunteered at her Baptist church. She had homeschooled Daniel up until she died a few years ago. Friends described him as being despondent and devastated by his mother's death, and he had been unable to obtain steady employment. Neither of those two young men had any sort of criminal record.

Bourque and McAllister remained in jail on a $10 million dollar bond each. In December 2010, after months of proclaiming their innocence, both Jason Bourque and Daniel McAllister pled guilty in that case. In January 2011, they received extremely severe sentences in that religiously conservative state. Jason Bourque was sentenced to five life sentences and two twenty-year sentences for his role. McAllister, who was recognized as more of a follower than a leader in that series, nonetheless received a severe sentence also. He was given two life sentences and two twenty-year sentences for his somewhat diminished role in those events. McAllister, following his plea, gave a vague rationale for his actions. He said during the entire series he had been only assisting Bourque who had convinced him that churches were evil, corrupt, and controlling. McAllister also gave the excuse that he was under the influence of prescription drugs and marijuana during that period. Their convictions cleared up at least fourteen burglaries or arsons on churches in eastern Texas.

Investigator's Analysis

Like most serial arson cases, this case was solved not by gimmicks, gadgets, or exotic techniques, but was in fact solved by plain, old-fashioned investigative work. Arson scenes are not much different from other crime scenes (other than the large amount of damage) in that there is often a good deal of forensic evidence available if it can be located. This case appears to have been solved by the proper collection and analysis of the forensic evidence, which was then followed up by a proper surveillance operation. And an old axiom in law enforcement appears at play in this case as you are often rewarded for your hard work. In this case, a phone tip, that elusive clue that all investigators hope for but seldom get, was an instrumental part of the criminal investigation.

This is yet another case of church arsons that are not racially motivated (as is the popular notion). The main motive in this case is a deep feeling of resentment toward Christian churches by the pair. It was brought on by some unknown perceived failure by the church toward the pair. It is not uncommon for people to "lose faith" in their church or religion and attack the very institutions that they were brought up to believe in. Again, like the majority of church arsons, investigators, when looking for a motive, should first start by looking within the church itself.

Chapter 5 Synopsis

The preceding ten arsonists mark a distinct difference from the first group of fifteen. Most in this group engaged in attacks against institutions as opposed to individuals or worthless properties. The targets were all attacked at night when the arsonist knew no one would be around to get hurt. Several of these arsonists worked in teams, which defies another stereotype of the lonesome arsonist. It should be pointed out that when there were teams, at least one member took the dominant leadership role and the others assumed positions as "followers." At least four of these arsonists used some form of device (although none were time delay devices), and most if not all used an accelerant of sorts. Many of these arsonists consulted extremist literature prior to making their devices and planning their attacks. Many of these events were to preplanned targets. Of note, every one of these arsonists in this group attacked a target for a religious reason. They were either a Christian extremist or an anti-Christian extremist. Either way, their fires greatly affected a large number of people. All of the arsonists were white, and there were two females involved in this group. Another contrasting point of this group compared to the first group of arsonists is that none of those in the latter group had a criminal history or a history of being institutionalized.

Readers will note that there is a large void in this chapter. A major group of extremist arsonists who operate around the world are the animal rights arsonists. This semi-organized movement is the most prolific group of arsonists in the world. This group, along with their close cousins the earth rights or environmental arsonists, represents hundreds of preplanned and well-coordinated arson attacks. Their fires have done billions of dollars in damage, and their increasingly violent assaults have begun to target persons as well as institutions and buildings. Dozens of those people have been arrested, and hundreds of their failed devices have been recovered. That group is well known to use a standard type of delay incendiary device that has a failure rate of about 20 percent. This author had planned to include several ALF/ELF attacks in this book, but perhaps that is a slightly different subject better left to a future literary project.

CHAPTER 6

The Firebugs

Every community has its share of oddballs, weirdos, nuts, and creeps. Bigger cities seem to have one or more in just about every other neighborhood. Some are homeless, while many have some sort of slight-to-moderate mental disorder, and most have problems with alcohol or illicit drugs. If they are born or raised in the community, most are usually well known by the locals, and their odd behavior is either tolerated or ignored. Few are ever considered dangerous or sinister, and they freely amble about the neighborhood and often just blend into the background.

Many of these people have a penchant for erratic behavior, which quite often includes fire setting. Their acts seem annoying and minor and often are not reported to the local authorities. In cases where the fire or police department does respond, the officials usually resort to a stern warning and just prod the oddball to be on his way down the street. These types of people will commit dozens if not hundreds of small acts of arson and other annoyances and are seldom prosecuted for their crimes until a significant event occurs.

Sometimes, the local people sort of adopt those characters and are reluctant to assist authorities during investigations. Suffolk County (NY) Fire Marshal Brett Martinez in his book *Multiple Fire Setters* aptly describes that group of offenders as follows: "Firebugs are individuals who frequently appear in many communities. Typically they are known by names such as 'Lenny the Light,' 'Bicycle Bob,' and 'Tony the Torch.' They often achieve early release from prison, rarely get prosecuted for anything more than petty offenses, and almost always return to their old habits in the same community upon release from incarceration." While this is a very decent representation of that group, this author finds it odd that Martinez, with all his experience in the field, still differentiates between that group and the more serious group of serial arsonists. I find those firebugs every bit as dangerous and perhaps much more prolific than some of the more celebrated serial arsonists. After all, once a fire is lit, no matter how benign it may first seem, the results of that fire are totally out of the hands of the fire setter. Only the environmental condition, luck (both good and bad), and some human factors hold control over the final outcome of the event.

This author, while working in a sprawling urban environment, has personally encountered those "street people" arsonists or more colloquially "firebugs" on at least eighteen occasions. In almost every case, the firebugs had been involved in at least a dozen arson events and had been detained by fire or police agencies numerous times. The following group is but a small representation of what I believe is the most common type of serial arson offender in this country.

Christopher John Dominguez "Hollydale Arsonist": Serial Arsonist
Period of Activity: 2004-09, Paramount, California

For all of those readers out there who do not believe in fate or coincidence, this one is for you.

On August 23, 1986, in the working class suburb of Los Angeles called Paramount, a twenty-four-year-old man named Chris Dominguez, fueled up on beer and marijuana, slammed his motorcycle into another driver who was just exiting a Los Angeles County fire station. As a result of that collision, the other driver was killed, and Dominguez had to be forcibly extricated from the wreckage by several patrolmen and firefighters arriving there. For the next twenty odd years, Chris Dominguez had an endless number of contacts and interactions with the police and firefighters in his city. Of note, one of the first responding patrol officers to the scene who helped pull Dominguez from the debris was a young Los Angeles County sheriff's deputy named Michael Digby.

Deputy Digby, for the next twenty years, worked his way up the ranks of detectives in the large department, piling up awards and commendations for his tireless investigative work. Among other honors, he was named the State of California's Narcotics Officer of the Year in 1997. Eventually, due to his impressive record as an investigator, he was selected to join the sheriff's elite Arson and Bomb Squad in 1998. On his very first day with that unit, he was assigned as an assisting detective on a high-profile mass murder/arson. In that case, Sandi Nieves killed her four daughters by starting a gasoline fire in their home after she drugged them. For her efforts, Nieves was subsequently awarded the death penalty.

By 2009, Detective Digby was one of the senior arson/bomb investigators in the department. On March 25, 2009, Digby and his partner, Det. Rick Velazquez, were working the normal night duty when they were called by patrol deputies from the Paramount area. The deputies reported that they had arrested a male for the arson of a palm tree, but that he was suspected by local firefighters of several dozen more "nuisance fires" in the area. Digby and Velazquez responded and interviewed the suspect, Christopher John Dominguez. For the most part, Dominguez was a hardened convict with a belligerent and agitated attitude toward police. He barely answered questions and seemed to actively dislike the detectives. About a half an hour into the interview and after reviewing Dominguez's criminal record, Digby inquired about a large scar on Dominguez. When the suspect related the story about his major car accident, Digby immediately recognized him from that same event twenty-three years earlier. Once Dominguez realized that Detective Digby was one of his rescuers (and arresting officers) of that day, his attitude almost immediately changed. He became practically chummy. Within an hour, Chris Dominguez admitted to and described one of the more prolific arson series in Los Angeles's history.

Chris Dominguez was raised and lived in the same small tract home on Lugo Avenue in Paramount for his entire life. When he was young, the area was a primarily white, middle-class neighborhood with relatively little crime. Before his teens, the Watts riots had exploded in a black neighborhood just five miles west of Paramount, and from that point on, the "white flight" from the communities just south of Los Angeles proper commenced. The Paramount area remained a working class city, but the population began to evolve with the influx of more Hispanic families. By the mid-1980s, Paramount was about half Hispanic and half Caucasian, with a sprinkling of blacks, Asians, and Pacific Islanders. During that same period, the incredible proliferation of street gangs exploded across the entire Los Angeles basin. Chris Dominguez, while never in a street gang, became a product of the growing racial tensions and gang strife within his neighborhoods.

Chris wouldn't talk about it much, but his father would later relate that he was a fairly normal kid with very few disciplinary problems. All that apparently changed when he was about sixteen and his mother died of complications from diabetes. From that point on, Chris began a slow spiral into drugs and alcohol. Although there is no record of police contact until he was about twenty-four, Dominguez and his father admitted that he was involved in truancy, shoplifting, marijuana use, and alcohol. He dropped out of school in the ninth grade and worked occasionally at odd, menial jobs. From his teen years through his mid-twenties, he stayed in the same small area of tract homes he would later call "his neighborhood."

As a result of the fatal car accident in 1986, Dominguez received his first felony conviction for vehicular manslaughter. The records show that he received a suspended prison sentence and was placed on probation. Another result of the accident was that Chris had severe injuries to himself, including head trauma, which later resulted in some mental impairment and ongoing issues with seizures. It also caused him to walk with a limp. Another byproduct of the crash was that Chris never drove a vehicle again, but spent the next twenty-five years walking or riding a bicycle.

Within a short period of the crash, Dominguez's arrest record began to expand. He was arrested for narcotics possession in 1988 and drunkenness in public later that same year. In 1989, he was arrested for narcotics use and armed robbery. As a result, he spent the next year in state prison. One day after his release from prison in 1990, he was arrested for possession of cocaine. He was sent back to prison for another year for that crime. Again, within a month of being released from prison, he was arrested again, this time for petty theft and possessing cocaine. He was again sent back to prison. A year later, shortly after his release from prison, he was rearrested for burglary and sent back to prison yet again. This pattern of arrest, imprisonment, release, and rearrest within a short time continued every year from 1988 until 1995. At that time, even the overburdened Los Angeles courts system had enough and sent Dominguez to prison for a nine-year stretch. It is obvious after reviewing that record that Chris Dominguez was struggling with a heavy narcotics use problem and was doing high-risk crimes (burglaries) to facilitate his drug habit.

Because of that lengthy prison record, Dominguez stayed off the arrest sheet until 2003, when he was again picked up for narcotics use. This time he had switched to an even more addictive drug, methamphetamine. He was released after a short jail stay. On October 5, 2003, Dominguez was observed setting fire to some trash behind a Hispanic bar. He was caught at the scene by patrons, and he told the arresting officers that he set the fire to "clean up the area." At the time of that event, he was riding a bike and carrying a butane cigarette lighter and matches. That same night of his arrest, a police officer in the neighboring city of South Gate drove up to the arresting sheriff deputies and remarked that they had had a series of four or five similar fires in their city the same night. Those fires occurred behind some businesses less than six blocks from where Dominguez was arrested. For reasons that baffle reviewers of this case, no detectives were informed of those fires and no agency investigated the link between the two events. Dominguez was later released on that arson charge when the Hispanic witnesses of the bar fire failed to show up in court.

Shortly after Dominguez's release from custody, patrol deputies began to notice a large number of small "nuisance" fires in the alleys and streets near his home in Paramount. The target of those fires was usually trash, brush, or vegetation. On January 14, 2004, someone placed a box of trash against the door of a business and ignited it. Responding firefighters saw Dominguez on his bike watching them put out the fire. Two days later, Dominguez was again spotted by firefighters as he watched from his bike while they extinguished a vegetation fire near his home. Three days after that fire, a man in the area saw Dominguez lighting brush and trash on fire in a field under some power lines. He was arrested nearby by responding deputies and was found to have a lighter in his pocket. He told the arresting officers that he had been just burning the trash because "it was ugly." Sheriff's arson investigators inquired with nearby Southgate, and they advised that they had at least two unsolved arsons to trash bins behind businesses in their area over the same time period.

Other than his admissions to the patrol deputies, Dominguez refused to speak to any of the three sheriff's arson investigators on that case. He was subsequently charged with and later pled guilty to seven arson events. He was convicted and sent back to state prison for a three-year sentence in 2004.

Within a year of the latest prison sentence, prison officials recognized Dominguez as being a "mentally disordered" inmate. He spent the final two years of his sentence in state prison psychiatric ward in Atascadero, where he was questioned by doctors about his fire setting behavior. He was released back in Paramount in 2007. Shortly after his release from prison, Dominguez reverted to his old ways and was arrested again on a narcotics charge. Despite his many years that he had already spent in prison for several convictions, court officials placed him on probation and released him from custody within a few short weeks. By 2009, Chris Dominguez had six felony convictions on his record and had done at least five different stints in the state prison system.

On March 25, 2009, Dominguez was observed by witnesses riding a bike away from a burning palm tree a few blocks from his home. When he was stopped by deputies a short time later it was found that he had a butane lighter in his pocket. He subsequently told investigators that he burned things that were "ugly," like trash, debris, and palm fronds.

Later that night, Dominguez was reunited with Det. Mike Digby.

During the lengthy interview, Digby noticed that Dominguez did not appear to like Digby's partner at all. He frequently looked at Det. Rick Velazquez with hate and inquired if he was "a wetback," which is a derogatory term for Mexicans who have entered the United States illegally. During the questioning, the two detectives who had also reviewed numerous previous reports from that case noted that on almost all of his police contacts, Dominguez had made negative references to Mexicans and "wetbacks." He also used the term "nigger" frequently in front of the investigators. Finally, the detectives asked him why he used those terms when he was of Hispanic heritage himself. Surprisingly, Dominguez insisted he was white and that his family had been in the country for decades. Dominguez then went into a long rant about how all the "wetbacks and niggers" had destroyed his neighborhood and had made everything dirty, untidy, and ugly. He explained that while he was in prison he was constantly attacked by both black and Hispanic gang members and had developed a deep hatred for both. Dominguez showed several deep scars where he was repeatedly "shanked" in prison and had his throat cut.

Dominguez also explained that one of the reasons he refused to speak to earlier sheriff's detectives on that case was because they were "all wetbacks." Indeed, all three of the previous arson detectives who had interviewed Dominguez had Spanish surnames.

At the time of his 2009 arrest, Chris Dominguez had never been married, didn't have a job, skill, or any sort of work career, had several physical and mental disabilities, and lived with his elder brother and elderly father. On a daily basis, he smoked cigarettes and marijuana and drank beer. He claimed to be not addicted to harder drugs, but his arrest record told a different story. He was forty-seven years old.

Finally, the detectives got a detailed account of Dominguez's fires. Over a series of in-depth interviews, he revealed that he "set impulse fires." He said he could not sleep at night, had frequent seizures, and waited for his dad to go to bed so he could go out riding around on his bike. He then made a startling admission. He said that after being released from prison from his previous arson charge, he had gone down to the county registrar's office to register as an arson offender as required by his parole officer. Within minutes of registering as an arsonist, Dominguez left that building, walked six blocks to the nearest shopping center, and then lit two separate fires outside of a McDonald's.

Dominguez said that over the next two-plus-year period, he lit several fires each week in the industrial and commercial areas near his home. He said his purpose was not to hurt people, but to just clean up "my neighborhood." He expressed true rage that blacks and Mexicans had not kept his neighborhood up to grooming standards. He said he usually rode around on his bike until he spotted something untidy or unsightly and then just lit it on fire with his lighter. He said some nights he lit five to seven of those fires in a spree, then he would go a few days before lighting any more. He then began to detail exact areas and locations where he lit his fires. His most common targets were untrimmed vegetation, palm trees with dried or hanging fronds, overflowing trash dumpsters, old, unpainted fences, and items stored or stacked around businesses. Dominguez lit the majority of his fires at night, but he admitted that when he had the strong impulse, he would ignite some items in the daytime.

In his most surprising revelation, Dominguez said that he had been stopped and chastised by firefighters several times for his activities. He said that a local fire captain had even come to his father's home and advised him that his son was setting lots of fires in the area. Dominguez said he frequently stayed around the area after he lit his fires so that he could watch the firefighters arrive and go about their duties. He had also been yelled at several times by neighbors for his fire setting activities. He did not ever believe that he had burned a structure and said that he had never hurt anyone with his fires. Eventually, Dominguez gave written descriptions of his scenes and pointed out other fires on a map of the area.

After an initial pair of interviews, the detectives began to research some of Dominguez's claims. Because his area of operations was at the border of three jurisdictions, a lot of legwork was needed to confirm some of those incidents. Soon the detectives found some really interesting evidence. Neighboring South Gate Police had video evidence of at least three recent fires. A review of some of that evidence showed clear images of Chris Dominguez walking through a strip mall lot at night and lighting several small items on fire with his lighter. One of those items was a curtain that was hanging out of the front door of a business. That particular fire extended into the business and caused a structure fire. Other evidence showed Dominguez on a bike igniting an overflowing trash dumpster. The resulting fire extended to a large business, causing major structural damage. Just down the street, video images captured Dominguez sticking a lighter into a mail slot on a dental office door, igniting plastic blinds on the interior. A nearly identical event by Dominguez was observed by surveillance cameras a night later and just a few doors down from the dental office.

Other than that evidence, the detectives found several unsolved brush, trash, and palm tree fires in the immediate area of Dominguez's home going back two years. Among those unsolved events was an arson fire at the property directly next to Dominguez's home. That fire occurred on a sofa in the yard at about one in the morning. When confronted with that fire, Dominguez said the Samoan family next to him had left a sofa out on their yard. He said he burned it because it was an eyesore. What he failed to disclose was that the fire from the sofa also destroyed a car in the driveway, a fence, and then did some moderate damage to the home.

After they had reviewed the files from three local agencies, investigators were able to locate thirty-seven unsolved arson events in the very small geographic area surrounding Dominguez's home. Those events were nearly identical in that they all occurred after midnight and all involved an open flame to vegetation, trash, brush, or items surrounding a business. The investigators spent the next few weeks driving through the area and noted dozen more small burn spots that had never been reported to the police. Many of those items were not found in fire department records, and one could assume that they self-extinguished or were put out by citizens.

Soon detectives had generated maps of all the fires in that area over a two-year span. The results were startling. By plotting those events on a map overlay, it was clear that there was an extraordinary number of fire calls in a small Paramount neighborhood called Hollydale. Dominguez's family home sat directly in the middle of that neighborhood. The fires from that area emanated out over all the major avenues and boulevards. All of those main streets were lined with businesses, strip malls, and some commercial buildings. The vast majority of those fires were handled by the local fire captains, with very few of them ever being referred to arson investigators. Most were classified as "trash" or "nuisance" fires, and there was no follow-up investigation.

The detectives soon began visiting all of the local fire stations, and it was soon clear that many of the fire captains and battalion chiefs were quite aware of the fire setting activities of Chris Dominguez. Many knew that he was a convicted arsonist and arson registrant, and at least one had confronted his father about Chris's arson activity. At some point, a local chief even mailed Dominguez's name, driver's license number, and photo to his department's arson investigation section. Yet, Dominguez was never contacted by investigators from the fire department, and local sheriff's deputies failed to bring him to the attention of their own arson investigators.

After a review of Dominguez's statements, a review of the unsolved arson events in the area, and a review of all of the unrecorded fire events in the area, investigators tallied up a list of fires committed by Dominguez. The number was over two thousand fires by the most conservative estimate and up to three thousand fires by another. Dominguez himself did not dispute those numbers. He freely admitted that he usually set multiple fires a day when he had the "urge" and sometimes set up to seven to ten fires a night and would go on long fire setting binges.

Christopher John Dominguez pled guilty in a hearing in Los Angeles to thirty-eight deliberate acts of arson committed from January 26, 2007, until March 25, 2009. Under California's "3 Strikes Law" (arson being considered a serious and violent felony and worthy of one strike for each fire), he should have been held for life imprisonment on his original arson convictions from 2004. Even with all of these additional fires, he was sentenced on June 25, 2009, to only thirteen years in state prison. Because of his lengthy criminal record, he could not get early release as he had so many times before, but was required to serve a minimum of 85 percent of his time or eleven years of real time.

Investigator Analysis

This case was included in this writing as it best illustrates the biggest hurdle in capturing serial arsonists. Fire and police agencies are doing a deplorable job at even recognizing when they have a serial fire setter in their area. By reviewing all of the serial arsonists in this writing, the reader can see that this phenomenon is not unique to California or even the United States. Worldwide, this seems to be consistent behavior by police and fire agencies. There is little documentation of trash or nuisance types of fires, and those seemingly minor events are seldom tracked, nor are they often referred by firefighters to the arson investigation units. Additionally, your writer is greatly aware and concerned that the vast majority of police and fire agencies in the United States do not investigate vehicle fires, as many chiefs believe they are not worth the time and money spent. It is this writer's very strong opinion that the vast majority of vehicle fires these days are incendiary acts related to insurance fraud. Without including trash, vegetation, dumpster, and vehicle fires in investigative statistics, there is no way at all that police and fire agencies can maintain accurate arson statistics. Without this accuracy then, there is no way that investigative agencies can track arson trends, series, and sprees.

What makes this an even more glaring problem is that Chris Dominguez was not a sophisticated and cunning arsonist, nor was he transient or a "drifter" as in some of the aforementioned cases. He was a drug—and alcohol-addled career criminal who was well known by many persons around him (including some local police and firefighters) as a problem fire setter. He lived in the same house for decades, committed almost all of his crimes in a very small geographic area, and was a registered serial arsonist for the majority of his fire setting spree. His crimes were committed in a high-density population area that was patrolled by massive and modern police and fire agencies. Like many arsonists, he was literally hiding in plain sight.

The explanations for his ability to run wild for over two years are fairly simple. It is endemic in the fire service to discount minor nuisance fires, particularly in a large urban area. Those events are seldom referred to as "arsons" or criminal acts, but are written off as "trash, juvenile-related, or nuisance" fires. Most are seldom referred to the arson investigation section of large departments and are considered minor local problems.

Another explanation is that firefighters (and some naive fire investigators) by nature tend to believe that fire setters are just being mischievous and that many of these events are merely "pranks and horseplay." This is particularly true with attitudes toward juvenile fire setters. It is this writer's learned opinion that the majority of the fire captains, upon confronting a juvenile or transient fire setter, believe that a stern lecture and warning would suffice in making the young lad stop that sort of activity. Often, if an offender shows remorse, the fire captains seldom document the event and verbally refer the offender and his parents to a "juvenile fire setter program." All too often, those programs fall way too short of what those offenders actually need, which is tracking, trained psychological counseling, and intense follow-up visits. In many cases, the offender is just given a tour of the local fire station and admonished about how fires they set can endanger firefighters. That wayward youth is then sent home and told to offend no more. The biggest failure in this is that the offender is not "treated" for his issues, and his fire setting activity is seldom officially recorded. This system allows "at risk" fire setting juveniles to set dozens if not hundreds of fires over the course of their teen years and go virtually undetected.

Chris Dominguez also appears to be a very representative example of the most common serial arsonist that investigators encounter. He had a lengthy criminal history, had a long history of drug and alcohol abuse, no visible means of support, had limited mobility in that he traveled on foot or bicycle, and used an extremely simple means of ignition. Despite hundreds, if not thousands of fires, his MO did not change or evolve, and he almost always applied an open flame via a butane cigarette lighter to any available combustible material. He then always carried his lighter away with him as opposed to throwing it away. He was a very simple and unsophisticated offender, who should have been identified and arrested for arson at least dozens of times before.

Dominguez, like most offenders, had a mixed motive. His stated motive may be true in that he did not like things that were untidy and messy. Surely a psychologist would have a more clinical opinion as to why that was, but for my part, I have noted that several arsonists I have arrested and interviewed also expressed a high amount of interest in fastidiousness. Perhaps that has something to do with an obsessive/compulsive disorder, or as I have heard experts opine, fire setting can be a "cleansing" behavior to some serial offenders.

Dominguez also comes across as a very angry person, and another motive for his fires could well be revenge. He could have wanted revenge against society for his messed-up life or revenge against minorities for his perceived decay of his neighborhood. While Dominguez has expressed racist views of whole classes of people, there is no evidence that he targeted a specific property due to the owner's race. Additionally, he was never aligned with any hate group.

What else is notable about this case is the work of the investigating officers. Several of these famous arson cases have been solved by fantastic interviews of the suspects. Detective Superintendent Sagar developed a tremendous rapport with Bruce George Peter Lee, thereby causing him to admit to twenty-six arson murders for which he was never even suspected. ATF agents and a local investigator were able to develop the same level of communication with DC Arsonist Thomas Sweatt, thereby causing him to fully confess his involvement in hundreds of fires. A similar situation developed between Seattle serial arsonist Paul Keller and investigators in that area. In the Dominguez case, the interviewing skills of the final two investigators who were able to overcome a very hostile and agitated offender caused the successful prosecution of this massive arson case.

Christopher Dominguez is an excellent example of a disorganized offender serial arsonist who randomly selected targets and ignited them by placing an open flame to the materials found near the fire scene. He currently has two separate arson convictions for two separate arson series. The first series was for seven fires and the second series was for thirty-eight fires. He is suspected of having lit over two thousand arson fires, the vast majority being small, unreported events.

Chris Dominguez will be eligible for parole in 2018. He will be fifty-seven years old, and there is little doubt that he will continue his fire setting behavior.

Robert Bruce Driscoll "Skidroad Avenger": Serial Arsonist Period of Activity: Early 1930s, Seattle, Washington

One of the often cited motives for serial arson activity is the revenge motive against an institution. That motive may account for many fires at churches and schools for some perceived wrong inflicted on the arsonist by that institution. An offshoot of that motive is the "revenge against society in general" motive. An old arson case history that depicts that motive quite well is the case of Robert Driscoll, who was also known at the time as the "Skidroad Avenger." (Readers will note that "skidroad" is an old logging term for the rough roads created by the skidding or dragging of logs. It soon became synonymous with any rough and bawdy street with saloons, flophouses, and whorehouses that seemed to spring up in every logging town. Seattle, being the heart of the American logging industry, no doubt at the time had the most notorious skidroad. Since that era, the term "skidroad" seems to have morphed into the more well-known "skid row." Like its earlier meaning, it is designated to that seedy area in every city that seems to have cheap saloons, the homeless and countless other denizens of the streets who, for whatever reason, have found themselves "on the skids.")

The West Coast seems to have an inordinate number of serial offenders. Seattle in particular seems to have a few more cases than are documented in most major cities. This writer won't speculate on why this is so, but suffice it to say that something about the Seattle area seems to produce some real oddballs.

In the 1930s, Seattle, like the rest of the United States, was in the depths of the Great Depression. Jobs were hard to come by, and the unemployed filled the streets of that city. Seattle could have been a destination for many homeless men of the time as it was a seaport and the western terminus of a major railroad. It was also home to a formerly thriving timber industry and a similar fishing and shipping industry. That could have been a place where desperate men went seeking jobs. One of those men was Robert Driscoll.

A *Time* magazine article written in 1935 later described Driscoll as a derelict having a "short, diabetic body." He was malnourished and weak from years of little or poor food and had spent the past five years as a hobo, riding the rails and getting by on whatever he could find.

During that painful period, Driscoll developed a deep-seated hatred for all of those persons who ran the large railroads, lumber mills, and manufacturing in general. He had a particular grudge against the railroads as he had spent many a cold night curled up in a freezing boxcar, only to be forcefully ejected from that meager shelter by the train yard "bulls" and other thugs hired by the railroad barons.

The Depression highlighted the massive chasm between the "haves" and the "have nots" in the United States. The rich at the turn of the century had accumulated immense wealth and property with little oversight and few scruples and were so obscenely rich that they literally lived like royalty and thus earned the titles of "robber barons." That was years before government regulations and the influence of labor unions. The wealthy business owners, including shipping and railroad magnates, manufacturers along with mining and timber barons, operated with as much power as the state and federal governments. Working conditions were generally poor, and pay was generally meager. In those days, if you had a complaint you kept it to yourself or lost your job. Most manufacturers kept a private "army" of enforcers, including local policemen on their payroll, to dissuade unrest in the workplace and to forcibly eject malcontents. This environment bred great fear and resentment in the average unskilled worker of the day. He was quite literally at the whim and mercy of the industrialist.

After a long time in that miserable lifestyle, Robert Driscoll found himself yet again sleeping in a freight car on a freezing night. His thoughts turned to revenge, and he found a way where he could strike back at the "enemy." In a Seattle rail yard in 1931, Driscoll assembled some available materials including waste oil from a rail car and struck a match. His fire burned several rail cars in the yard.

A few weeks after that fire, a massive blaze destroyed the Albers Milling Company plant. That loss totaled over $300,000 in 1930's dollars. Soon many factory and business owners began receiving odd notes. The notes were handwritten ramblings that threatened future fires to the businesses.

Six months later, on the Fourth of July, 1932, there was a minor league baseball game followed by a large fireworks show at Dugdale Park, a large sports field in Seattle. Sometime after the show, the massive wooden bleachers caught fire and burned to the ground. At the time, the blaze was blamed to be a result of the fireworks activity. Other officials believed the cause could have been arson. The question would remain for another three years.

Soon, arson fires struck numerous factories. Large fires consumed stacked lumber that was set to be sold at the market. Fires continued at train yards. This time the arsonist did not target empty boxcars. Soon freight cars containing valuable goods and materials were torched. One particular fire destroyed boxcars filled with automobiles. So many arson fires erupted in the next three years in Seattle that the average cost of fire losses tripled.

The spree gained the attention of the local press who printed lurid headlines about the man they now dubbed the "Skidroad Avenger." His notes and threatening letters spelled out his hatred for society in general and the rich industrialists in particular.

That arson spree topped one hundred unsolved fires and went unabated until May 3, 1935. Patrons of a restaurant in the Russian community of Seattle saw a man setting fire to their Russian Orthodox Church on Lakeview Boulevard. They ran out and apprehended the disheveled man and held him for police and fire officials. Investigators noted that that arson was attempted by the use of simple and handy materials. Driscoll had placed papers and kindling he found on the street under the corner of the wooden structure and then ignited them with a match. There ended the arson spree of Robert Driscoll.

Upon his arrest, Driscoll received considerable attention from fire officials, police executives, and the district attorney. They induced him to write sentences on papers so that they could compare his writing to the notes received by factory owners during the arson spree. After some consideration, they were convinced that the writing was a match.

Soon, after being confronted with the handwriting samples and the fact, he was caught in the act of setting an arson fire, Robert Driscoll began to talk. He spent the next four days confessing to his acts of arson. He even drove around with officials and pointed out the factories and plants he had burned. In particular, he told them how he had set the fire at the baseball stadium on the July 4, 1932. In the end, authorities closed the books on the 115 arson fires committed at the hands of Driscoll. His rationale for starting the fires was simple. He was mad at being destitute and "sore at the world in general."

Time magazine would later opine that Driscoll, after spending so many months being hungry and poor, was spurred on by the street corner orators who seemed to haunt "skid road." They stood on soapboxes near breadlines, soup kitchens, and any other place where the destitute congregated and extolled the masses to rise up against the capitalists, industrialists, and big businesses who had caused all those men to suffer so much. Driscoll, on his part, was able to "even the playing field" and cause over $1 million in losses with just a match and some kindling.

Investigator's Analysis

Robert Driscoll is typical of the more common type of arsonists wandering the streets of any major city in the United States. His life had not turned out as planned, and he obviously blamed the industrialists and "big business" for his plight. He could not fight them or their enforcers, so he did the next best thing he could. He attacked their livelihood. He attacked their buildings, properties, plants, and wares. He attacked inanimate objects that could offer no resistance and would have the maximum amount of impact for the minimum amount of effort.

What makes Driscoll different from the exact same type of arsonist in modern times is that in this day and age he would not have been able to achieve such dramatic results. In the 1930s, the building materials were extremely vulnerable to attack by fire. There were little to no fire protection materials or systems within the structures to prevent the spread of fire, and the smallest flame could soon become a massive conflagration. An arsonist prior to the 1940s really did not need to use any form of liquid accelerant. Just a flame, with maybe a little paper and wood as kindling, would start the desired blaze. In modern times, with all of the fire prevention measures, construction standards, and fire resistant materials, many of Driscoll's acts would be extremely minor events. He would have to resort to burning trash, cars, and vegetation like the street arsonists of today as his fires would have little effect on modern buildings.

Robert Driscoll was a disorganized offender who vented his rage against "the man" by torching his most valuable assets. He had no money but was able to achieve fantastic results with his fires by employing the simple and crude materials he found on the scene. He is not unlike any of the following offenders on this list. It would have been near impossible to locate him in his day as the streets of his city were awash with hundreds of similar people.

Rickey Jimenez "Tri Valley Arsonist": Serial Arsonist Period of Activity: 1979-2007, San Fernando Valley, Rural Northern Los Angeles County

For a two-week period from October 12 until October 26, 2007, the Santa Ana winds had been blowing in Southern California. That condition causes dry, hot, gale force winds to blow in off the deserts creating temperatures over hundred degrees, humidity as low as 5 percent, and wind speeds often over sixty miles per hour. Those hot desert winds are in direct contrast to the cool, moist coastal breezes that usually blow on shore along the California coast. The areas most affected by those winds are the low coastal mountains that contain heavy growths of brush, grasses, and trees. For the past fifty years, the urban sprawl of cities has slowly encroached into those brushy mountains, and tens of thousands of homes now sit among the brush-covered foothills.

In those conditions, even routine small fires have the potential to explode into massive catastrophic events. As so often happens when the Santa Ana blows, the wildfires erupt across the Southland. During that same two-week period in 2007, five major wildfires and about a dozen smaller ones raged in and around Los Angeles County. Hundreds of homes had already been destroyed, and tens of thousands of people had been evacuated. By October 25, the "devil winds" began to abate, and many of the fires were finally contained by the thousands of firefighters swarming the area. That activity was broadcast on all local television stations twenty-four hours a day for the entire event, and everybody who lived in any areas near the brush land maintained one eye on the news at all times.

One person who had been closely monitoring the fires on his television was Rickey Jimenez. Rickey was a fifty-two-year-old man who lived in a ramshackle camper trailer at the back of a small ranch in a rural canyon about fifty-five miles north of Los Angeles. That canyon, known as the Lake Hughes area, had been Rickey's home for the past twenty years. Rickey was a local character in the close-knit community and eked out a living doing brush clearance, odd maintenance jobs, and working occasionally at a nearby church camp.

Lake Hughes was just a small junction on a rural roadway. Further east about five miles was its sister town, Lake Elizabeth. Another ten miles east of Lake Elizabeth was the very small rural canyon called Leona Valley. All three of those "towns" were merely road junctions, each with a gas station, grocery, bar, and a few churches sprinkled in. Those towns all serviced the "hobby ranches" in the area, which were mostly owned by people who had fled the sprawl and tract neighborhoods of Los Angeles. The isolated valleys were a collection of small ranches and fruit and nut orchards. Many of the occupants knew each other, and all tried to avoid the massive city of Los Angeles looming beyond the low mountains. Rickey was one of the many in the valley who had fled Los Angeles decades ago.

Like every other resident of the rural communities, Rickey was greatly concerned about the wildfire threat. That area had been plagued by grass and brushfires for most of the twenty years that Rickey had lived there. It was an area of low mountains that were covered with heavy brush and a few trees. The brush grew up to twenty feet tall and comprised heavy growths of very oily *manzanita*. That type of bush, when dried out, was extremely explosive and spread fire very rapidly. Because of the threat every summer and fall of wildfire, Rickey always found work clearing brush and downed trees at the edges of local rancher's properties.

On October 26, Rickey was feeling depressed. A lifelong "recovering alcoholic," he knew he was making a big mistake when he drove his car up to the only tavern in town, the Crossroads Bar. Even the bartenders knew that Rickey had a drinking problem and took notice when he sat down at the bar. For the next several hours, Rickey sat on a stool, drinking beer and watching the television coverage of the brushfires in the area. It looked like the valleys had been spared the firestorm for that season as the winds were dying and the temperature was dropping.

About 10:00 p.m. that night, the door to the bar opened, and Rickey's boss from the church camp walked in. Rickey visibly cringed as he was the same person who had been counseling him on and off for years about his struggles with alcohol. Someone at the bar had called the church leader and told him about Rickey. Several patrons watched while Rickey sat quietly at the bar and was sternly admonished by his boss for this lapse in judgment. After the church leader left, Rickey sat quietly for several minutes, then abruptly got up and left the bar. What the patrons and bartender didn't see was that Rickey had reached into a glass bowl at the end of the bar and pulled out three white books of matches.

Twenty minutes later, Rickey was seen buying beers at the only bar in nearby Lake Elizabeth. He was then seen driving away in his car. Within the next half hour, a motorist called in a brushfire to the local fire station, just a mile away from the Crossroads Bar. While driving toward that fire, firefighters saw two other small fires in the brush along the roadside. While they were extinguishing the original large brushfire, they were notified that another large fire was burning three miles away at the opposite end of the valley. Over the next hour, eight separate fires were found burning in the brush along the roads in the canyon. The last two fires were found burning about hundred yards away from Rickey's camper. Another fire was found burning on the slope just below the home of the church leader who had confronted Rickey about his drinking.

Unknown to Rickey at the time, his closest neighbor next door was a fruit and nut rancher named Larry. What Rickey did not know was that Larry was also an arson investigator for the Los Angeles Sheriff's Department. Another thing that Rickey did not know was that Larry was fully aware at the time of that event that Rickey Jimenez was a registered arsonist with convictions dating back over twenty years.

Larry, who would later become the lead investigator in that case, immediately distanced himself from Rickey and called four other investigators from his unit and the U.S. Forest Service to assist him in the arson spree. Your author was one of these investigators and was later tasked with first interviewing Rickey Jimenez. First, however, the team of investigators had to investigate each separate fire. Over the next twelve hours, the team scoured the roadsides and heavy brush of each fire scene. Luckily, just hours before the start of each fire, the weather in the area had changed drastically, and the moisture levels in the air had skyrocketed from around 5 percent humidity to well over 25 percent. The winds had died almost completely, and the fires did not spread beyond a few dozen acres each. Investigators later determined that had these fires been lit just eight hours prior, the fires would have exploded into the hills across the tri-valley area and would have endangered dozens of rural ranch properties. As it was, only brush and trees were burned in that event.

The eight fire scenes were processed, and investigators were able to locate two white matchbooks and a total of twelve paper matches from the scenes. All of the fires were lit in the exact same manner with a paper match being placed against very dry grass and brush. There were no incendiary devices located and no other forms of ignition. A later follow-up investigation would reveal that those match books were an exact match to the ones provided free to the customers at the Crossroads Bar. Interviews with several witnesses showed that Rickey Jimenez was seen speeding back and forth across the small valley during the one-hour period when the fires were reported. He drove a very distinctive car and was one of the few drivers out on the road at that late hour. When the fire engines passed the Crossroads Bar in the middle of that event, a firefighter saw Rickey sitting in his car parked in the bar parking lot facing the street, apparently watching them.

A time line was drawn up of when the fires had occurred, and it was determined that the two fires furthest from the town center occurred first, and the final six fires were ignited closer and closer to the town center and to Rickey's trailer. The final two fires were lit on the roadside just hundred yards away from and in full view of Rickey's trailer.

Because it was a potentially catastrophic event that could have impacted the entire town, numerous people stopped by to speak to the investigators as they were processing the scenes. Many reported Rickey's odd behavior to the investigators. Most notably, many people were shocked that Rickey never came out of his trailer to observe the investigators or engage them in conversation as he was known as a bit of a "busybody" who was always doing such things. Nobody in the valley had any idea that Rickey was a registered arsonist, but they just thought of him as a "reformed drunk" who occasionally fell off the wagon.

The investigators formed a plan, and after processing the fire scenes, they decided to try and interview Rickey Jimenez. He opened his door and agreed to speak with the detectives. Rickey was polite, compliant, and even appeared meek and a bit mild. The detectives noted that despite his many old street gang tattoos, Rickey did not appear to be threatening in anyway. He did, however, appear to look completely guilty as he hung his head and refused to look the investigators in the eyes. His answers were very vague, and he was quiet and docile. He denied setting any fires, but he admitted that he had "screwed up" last night. He admitted that he was a registered arsonist and that he had been to prison several times for various offenses. He said all his problems were related to alcohol addiction. Rickey admitted that he had been very embarrassed and upset that his boss at the church camp had chastised him at the bar. During that same interview Rickey told detectives that he was "dumb" and not very intelligent. He said that his entire life he had been considered "stupid." He denied being mentally retarded and denied having a drug addiction. He said he had only been diagnosed in the past with depression and anxiety. He said he had no psychiatric issues.

The investigators were unable to find any physical evidence linking Rickey to the fires. They did find matches in his car but of a different brand than those found at the fire scene. They also found pill bottles for prescription drugs related to depression and anxiety. Before the detectives left the home, Rickey promised he would attend a polygraph examination (lie detector test) that was to be scheduled the next week.

For the whole of the following week, the detectives researched Rickey Jimenez's background a bit deeper. They found that Rickey had been arrested twice before for arson and that one of the arrests was for an arson series. No police reports were available, but detectives found some of the original investigators on his previous arson series who were able to describe the events. Rickey was born in 1955 and grew up in Panorama City. Rickey was a member of an old street gang in the San Fernando Valley of Los Angeles in the 1970s. Most of his tattoos were from that era. His first major arrest was in 1975 for burglary. He was convicted of that crime and received probation. While on probation, he was arrested for drunken driving, grand theft auto, and another burglary. He served about a half year in jail for those crimes.

By 1979, he stepped up his activities and was arrested for possessing illegal firearms and burglary. Later that same year, he was convicted again for burglary and for the arson of a vehicle. He was sent to state prison for the first time for a three-year stint. He would later tell investigators that he had another arson arrest for starting a fire in the forest, but that does not show up on his local criminal record.

After his release from prison, he had a series of convictions for prostitution and for alcohol-related offenses. Based on those old records, it appears that Rickey may have been acting as a homosexual prostitute, although there was no clarification in the file. By 1982, he had been convicted for burglary again and was sent back to prison for four years. Upon his release, he had more alcohol and prostitution arrests until about 1988.

During 1988, a series of odd burglaries and fires was occurring in a small area of the San Fernando Valley. During that time, an offender was burglarizing beauty salons and, after stealing items, was setting the businesses on fire. All of those events occurred in a relatively small area during the nighttime hours. At some point, Rickey Jimenez was identified as a possible suspect. The Los Angeles Police Department assigned their famous SIS surveillance squad to tail Jimenez. On January 19, 1988, they followed on foot and watched Rickey Jimenez break into a beauty salon. He stole some minor items and then attempted to set fire to the building. The fire failed, and the detectives followed Rickey as he walked to a nearby liquor store, purchased beer and a couple of books of matches, and then returned to the beauty salon. The detectives watched as he then set fire to the business. They immediately arrested him and extinguished the fire. They noted that he had been drinking during that event. He then admitted to the sixteen other similar burglaries/arsons of beauty salons in the area over the previous months. As part of a plea bargain, Rickey was convicted of four of the seventeen arsons and sentenced to eleven years in state prison for his second arson conviction.

By the late 1990s, Rickey was out of prison and had ended up in the remote Lake Hughes area. He continued to struggle with alcohol and had convictions in 2003 and 2006 for drunken driving. He had no other fire events recorded against him since 1988.

Rickey Jimenez had never been married. He was a loner and had no family to rely upon. His jobs had been mostly menial labor jobs such as construction, painter, laborer, and landscaper.

About a week after leaving Rickey's home, investigators learned from a local reporter that Rickey had attempted suicide just hours after the investigators had left his home. He took a series of pills and alcohol in this attempt. After being released from the hospital the next day, he immediately checked himself into an alcohol addiction center and told them that he had made "a huge mistake" over the weekend. Three days later, he checked himself out of the center against the advice of the caregivers.

Three weeks later, the detectives again found Rickey and asked him to come in for a polygraph exam. He showed up on his own and was found "deceptive" during the exam. When confronted with that, he admitted that he had set five of the eight fires on October 27. He admitted that he had set them because he had been drunk and angry with his boss. He said he used the matches he took from the bar and drove around setting the fires. He also said that when none of them got big, he got frustrated and set the fires in front of his own home. Rickey was arrested on the spot and searched. During the search, detectives found a razor blade hidden in his clothing. He told the detectives that he had planned to commit suicide if they were going to arrest him.

Several weeks later, Rickey Jimenez pled guilty in court to eight counts of arson to forest land, his second conviction for a series of fires. He was sentenced to fourteen years in state prison for this offense. He will have to do twelve years before he is eligible for parole.

The case of Rickey Jimenez is far from over. Since about 1998, the rural tri-valley area where Rickey had lived has been plagued every year by a rash of suspicious brushfires that have occurred directly alongside the main rural canyon road that runs through that area. Investigators have formed the opinion that most of those suspicious fires were set in the exact same manner as the latest eight fires set by Rickey Jimenez. The statistics show that this ongoing series of fires was noticed about the time that Rickey Jimenez was released from prison and moved to that area in the late 1990s. All of those fires are unsolved events, and detectives believe that they total about eighty fires. Efforts will be made in the future to conduct a detailed interview of Rickey Jimenez in his prison cell with the hopes of solving many other fires. Additionally, analysis will be made of the number of fires in that area over the next five-year period while Jimenez was in custody compared to the number which occurred when he lived in the area.

Investigator Analysis

Rickey Jimenez is a very similar case to the previous case of Chris Dominguez. Both are Hispanic males in the midlife age group with lengthy criminal histories. Both show lifelong problems with drugs, alcohol, prescription medications, or a combination of all of the above. Again, this case was included in this writing for the lessons learned from it and for illustrating what is probably the most common group of serial arson offenders.

Rickey's known arson activities span nearly forty years. Serial arsonist research, as little as has been done, suggests that these offenders commit a large number of fires in their youth years and tend to stop or slow their activities in their twenties through forties. For some unknown reason, the studies suggest that the arsonists tend to get more active again later in life. Perhaps, as Rickey suggested to investigators, they are upset about how their life has turned out.

Rickey was an easy person to arrest in this case as his actions were blatant and impulsive and were an immediate response to the stress applied to him when confronted by his boss. He committed his crimes within minutes of several witnesses observing the events leading up to the fires. His actions were reckless and possibly suicidal in nature as a major brushfire would surely have destroyed his own property and could have trapped him in the valley as well.

The fire scenes in this case closely profile the actual offender. They were unsophisticated scenes and were set in the closest and most accessible fuel available—the dry brush on the roadside. The manner of ignition was equally unsophisticated as it was the use of a paper match applied to the dry brush. There was no elaborate target selection and no use of a sophisticated delay device. Even though Rickey was an experienced fire setter, he was clearly disorganized

168

in his actions as he used an excessive number of matches (several were found at each scene) and left the obvious evidence in plain view (matchbooks) at each fire that no doubt carried his fingerprints and DNA. His target selection on his final three fires clearly shows his rage as he set one on the slope just below his boss's home with the obvious intent of starting a fire to burn upslope to the house.

Rickey's mobility was mixed as he drove to his first five fire scenes and probably walked to the last three, which were all near his home. It should be noted here that an unsolved arson fire burned a barn directly in front of Rickey's home right about the time he moved to the valley. Additionally, an "undetermined" fire destroyed a large building at the church camp where Rickey worked just ten months prior to this series. Spatial studies show that most arsonists set fires very close to where they live and work.

When confronted, he showed a clear consciousness of guilt by his clumsy suicide attempts and his statements to several people that "I made a big mistake" on the night of the fires.

Like most offenders, Rickey had a mixed motive. The obvious motive was revenge for the humiliation he felt at being chastised in public by his boss. A second motivation was most likely excitement as he was seen observing the firefighting activity. The last two fires were set in clear view of his home, and he could monitor the events from his sofa.

Less is known about Rickey's reasons for his early fire setting activity. His prostitution arrests suggest he may have some sort of problem dealing with latent homosexuality, but that is just conjecture as apparently nobody has ever documented the interviews with him. The fire series in the beauty parlors is really interesting and may suggest some sort of fetish. This investigator is still hoping to contact Rickey in prison and interview him about all of those events.

Rickey Jimenez is a disorganized serial arsonist who used unsophisticated means to set at least twenty-seven fires that we can confirm. His three separate arson convictions span four decades of activity with at least two major series among them. At this time, he is considered a person of interest in another eighty suspicious fires in the rural valley areas. Based on the number of years between his first recorded arson event and his latest, it is probably safe to speculate that Rickey has set hundreds more fires.

Andre Paul Labrecque: Serial Arsonist
Period of Activity: 2006-09, Kitchener, Ontario, Canada

Another painful reality that occurs in a majority of serial arson cases is the leniency that is heaped upon the offender by the courts, press, and in some cases by the prosecutors themselves. Even more baffling in this investigator's experience is the large number of fire chiefs who actively campaign for leniency and counseling on the behalf of arsonists on a routine basis. Obviously, this is not just an American phenomenon as the below case of Canada illustrates.

What little is known about Andre Labrecque is provided by fragmented newspaper accounts and input from his girlfriend, Debbie Gould. Labrecque and Gould lived in a very inexpensive apartment in the Canadian city of Kitchener. All of his adult life, the fifty-year-old man had struggled with mental health issues. He had been diagnosed at some point in the past with a bipolar disorder and had been taking psychiatric medications for many years. His girlfriend also suffered from the same mental health issue. His mental health condition was so serious that in 2003 he was hospitalized in an institution for those problems. Over the years, he had been diagnosed with anxiety, depression, and schizophrenia. Despite those issues, Gould and Labrecque had a son together in 2006, and both the adults received income from disability pensions.

Labrecque's childhood obviously influenced his later life. He grew up a ward of the Crown (state) and lived in a series of foster homes. It came out at his later trial that when he was very young, he was physically and sexually abused and removed from his parents by the authorities. When he was seven years old, the foster home he lived in exploded into flames, and firefighters pulled him and his foster parents from the burning building. Since that time, his girlfriend said he expressed utter terror of fire. As an adult, he was not employed due to his mental health issues and spent many hours on a daily basis just roaming the neighborhood talking to people. He was described as a friendly sort with numerous acquaintances. He was often seen with a beer and cigarette in his hands. He later admitted to being a longtime alcoholic. A slight man, he was easily recognizable by his disheveled appearance and long, gray hair.

In 2006, Kitchener authorities began recognizing a pattern of suspicious fires. These fires were occurring in vacant buildings, sheds, garages, decks, and porches. Most were ignited by someone with an open flame that was placed against the available materials at the scenes. The fires continued sporadically over a three-year period. Some of those fires occurred at occupied structures, and there were occasions when the residents barely made it out. By 2009, investigators had identified Labrecque as a possible suspect. He lived directly in the middle of a cluster of fires and was often seen at or near the various fire scenes, both before and after the fires. One of the larger fires had occurred in a building next to where he lived. The building's owners said that they had a recent dispute with Labrecque, and he was very upset with them. That fire started shortly after the dispute on April 27. The arsonist had broken into the basement of a four-unit apartment building and had ignited some cardboard that had been left lying around. The fire caused nearly $400,000 in damage and resulted in the building being torn down. Shortly after that large fire, another fire was started on May 15 in a detached garage in the same area. Lebrecque had been seen in the area of that event.

Andre Lebrecque soon moved to the top of the suspect list. Immediately after the cops developed him as a suspect, they began a loose surveillance on Lebrecque. They did not have long to wait for his next fire. Three days after the detached garage fire, surveillance detectives were monitoring Lebrecque as he shuffled through the streets. They saw him enter another garage in the same area. He soon emerged from the garage, and minutes later, smoke and fire was seen emitting from that structure. Police extinguished the blaze and arrested Lebrecque in a nearby alley.

A police interview following the arrest resulted in Lebrecque admitting to the three latest fires, including the large burglary/arson in April. He was charged with those fires and additional twenty-four arson events in the area over the previous three years.

The pretrial phase of the case had several illuminating aspects. Lebrecque's horrific childhood and extensive mental health issues were brought to light by both the defense and the prosecution. A psychiatrist testified that Lebrecque's fires were not set for money or to cover up a crime. The doctor opined that Lebrecque lit the fires to "burn away" feelings stemming from an abusive childhood. His defense attorney admitted that those fires were a result of Lebrecque "lashing out . . . because of all the hurt and pain he's experienced in his life." Even the prosecutor seemed sympathetic to Lebrecque's cause. Crown Prosecutor Mike Murdoch agreed that Lebrecque should not be sent to a federal penitentiary, but would be better served in a treatment facility. Lebrecque agreed to plead guilty to the three most recent fires. The court, agreeing with all sides, sentenced Lebrecque to a minimal term in a treatment facility where his extensive issues with addiction, emotional, and mental health could be treated. He received an approximate four-year sentence. The remaining twenty-five or so arson counts were not charged.

Investigator Analysis

Andre Lebrecque's case is consistent with so many other serial arson offenders. He, like many of the others in this book, is the product of an extremely brutal childhood. Looking back, a premonition of things to come was probably in that large house fire that occurred when he was seven. While there are no records to suggest that, it is an easy assumption to make that it is very likely that Lebrecque lit that fire. Based on the histories of all of the other arsonists in this book, there are likely hundreds of other fires that Lebrecque lit throughout his life that were never attributed to him. He did not just start lighting things on fire at the age of forty-eight. He likely had sprees of arson activity, followed by weeks, months, or years of cooling off. At some point, a triggering event would most likely start the fires burning again. This has been the case in many of these investigations.

As an investigator, this author feels that it is his sole duty to serve the victims and the public. It shouldn't really matter what causes the suspect to do his acts, but we need to understand him in order to catch him. However, at that point, a sober assessment of his danger level should be made. In this case, while Lebrecque was indeed a pathetic and tragic character, it did not mitigate his danger level. He attacked several occupied structures with a potential to murder people with his fires. This was not a man who targeted benign items like dumpsters, wood piles, or trees. His fires impacted occupied dwellings, and by that fact alone, he needs to be separated from society for a lengthy period of time. Of course, treatment is a great idea here, but let's face it, the chances of this man re-offending when he has a bad day are extremely high. The courts in every jurisdiction need to focus on the potential of an act and not just the fact that the acts may have failed or were extinguished prior to anyone getting hurt. I am still baffled by how many legal authorities including some prosecutors and even fire chiefs fail to acknowledge the danger level of many of those serial arsonists.

Andre Lebrecque is a disorganized serial arsonist who appeared to operate in arson sprees with substantial cooling-off periods between them. He used crude materials found at the fire scenes and ignited targets of opportunity. His fires began taking on an even more dangerous level when he actually started to enter the buildings he was burning. He has been positively linked to over twenty-five arsons and likely set hundreds more. He will be released sometime in 2012 and will likely re-offend within just a year or two.

Kevin Todd Swalwell "Greenwood Serial Arsonist": Serial Arsonist
Period of Activity: 1983-2009 Seattle, Washington

For some unknown reason, certain geographic areas tend to spawn a higher number of serial arson cases than other areas. For instance, the foothill regions throughout California seem to spawn an amazing number of serial fire setters. Perhaps that's because of the explosive nature of the fires in those areas and the excitement they cause. Another area that has recurring serial arson problems is the greater Seattle area. Like everybody has always said about the Pacific Northwest, maybe it's the weather. This case comes from that region.

In the early morning hours of Friday, November 12, 2009, an alert police officer saw a familiar figure shuffling down the sidewalk in the Shoreline area of Seattle. He recognized the man as a transient who was wanted for questioning in several recent arson fires in the area. In the hour prior to that man being seen, a vacant retail store had erupted into flames. The patrolman noted that that transient, Kevin Swalwell, was within a few blocks of the still burning building.

On June 19, 2009, an arson fire broke out in the "OK Corral Barbeque" building on North Greenwood Avenue. That would be the first of fourteen arson attacks that would rock the northern Seattle "Greenwood" neighborhood over the next five months. All but one would be centered on a very small cluster of businesses that surround Greenwood Avenue. In the June 19 fire, the arsonist lit a stack of cardboard boxes in the basement of the empty structure. The damage was minimal in that event, but was a harbinger of future events.

Seven weeks passed before the next arson event was noted. On August 12, the arsonist stuffed a *Seattle Weekly* newspaper under the rear door of a vacant home. Again the damage was very minor as a neighbor noticed the smoke and extinguished the flames with a garden hose.

Later that same night, the arsonist struck again, when he ignited a piece of cardboard and shoved it through a mail slot of a commercial building. Hours later, another fire was started with the use of lighter fluid. The arsonist had sprayed the fluid on a residential property late at night and ignited it. The fire was a near fatal incident as within the home a sixty-eight-year-old man slept. He barely escaped the blaze with significant injuries over his entire body. The structure sustained over $170,000 in loss. The first major break in the serial arson case came from that scene as the Seattle police located a lighter fluid container at the scene. Sometime later, forensics experts were able to lift a usable palm print off the container.

After that event, a local arson task force was mobilized to track down and identify all arson offenders in the area. The task force comprised Seattle police and fire department investigators along with some ATF agents. The task force felt immediate and intense media pressure during that time, as the exact same area had suffered a similar reign of terror in 1992 at the hands of the notorious serial arsonist Paul Keller. That highly publicized case was still fresh in many people's minds.

On October 23, at 4:00 a.m., a burglar broke a rear window at the "Green Bean Coffee House." He gained entry into the office area and broke open a safe. After taking items of value, the burglar set fire to the office using cardboard and paper found within to start the blaze. This fire grew out of control and eventually consumed the coffee house and three adjacent restaurants. The financial total for this event was in excess of $2 million.

This large fire may have inspired the arsonist as soon the pace of his activities accelerated. On November 5, he lit two fires. A pile of cardboard was ignited under the porch of one structure, and the second fire was caused by the arsonist dragging some clothes from a donation box to the fire scene. The fire caused over $20,000 in damage to a commercial building.

On November 8, the second major break in the case occurred. The arsonist set fire to the rear of a building housing a photo shop. A K-9 officer on patrol in the area identified Kevin Swalwell as he walked just a few blocks away from that event. At that time, Swalwell gave the officer a fake name and the officer noted it, but couldn't link him to the fire. The fake name was of Swalwell's cousin and did not match any of the known arsonists in the area. A day after the fire, the arson task force in the area descended on the neighborhood. They did not at that time identify Swalwell, who was actually loitering about and watching their activities. While the task force did not take note of Swalwell, they were able to secure video footage from some businesses in the area. They received quite a surprise when they later reviewed the video.

Unknown at that time a very small fire occurred within just a few hours after the photo shop fire. A male transient (later identified as Swalwell) was observed removing combustible items, including paper and cardboard from a dumpster behind a nearby restaurant. The video captured the man actually igniting the materials on fire with a butane lighter.

Despite the overt police presence in the area, Swalwell kept up his attacks. Hours later, the arsonist brought copies of a free local newspaper to a secluded area behind a convenience store and ignited them with a lighter.

An alert corrections officer then provided an additional clue for the arson task force. After those two recent events were highly publicized, he called the task force and gave them the name of a serial arsonist he was aware of named Kevin Swalwell. The corrections officer said that he knew that Swalwell was still in the Greenwood area as he had recently dealt with him on some narcotics charges. By that time, the task force had already confirmed that Swalwell's palm print was on the lighter fluid can from the August 13 fire. They distributed his name and began an all-out search for the elusive transient.

Three nights later, forty-six-year-old Kevin Swalwell ignited what would be his last fire. He took a bus from his Greenwood area to downtown Seattle. From there, he took a second bus out to the Shoreline district. After wandering around a bit and scrounging some coffee and cigarettes, he went to a dumpster and found some cardboard material. He took that to the rear of a vacant building and placed it among some other cardboard items. He then ended his thirty-year arson string by igniting the cardboard with his lighter. Like he had done many other times, Swalwell walked off into the night.

After his arrest that night by the patrolman, task force investigators focused on the life of Kevin Swalwell. First they did a detailed search and found that he had a history of fire events going back at least twenty-five years.

At age nineteen, Swalwell had been arrested for arson and burglary. He had broken into a home, stolen a coin collection, and lit a fire. Swalwell was an acquaintance of that victim and was contacted by the police immediately after the event. He soon admitted his role in the theft and fire. He said he was aware that the homeowner had been on vacation. Swalwell was sentenced to prison for that incident. He was sentenced to ten years, but like many arsonists was released in 1987 after serving just half of his sentence.

From that point on, Swalwell was a habitual problem for law enforcement, although he was not identified in any fire setting incidents again until 1995. A series of four arson fires occurred in an apartment complex in which Swalwell was living in North Seattle with his grandmother. Prior to one of the fires in a vacant unit, police found a threatening note that was later linked to Swalwell. The note gave a dire warning, "You're going to die in a fire tonight." The fire started hours later, and at least four occupants were injured as a result of those arson attacks. Upon his arrest for that series, investigators also linked Swalwell to a fire in a home where the residents were on vacation. Swalwell pleaded guilty to those fires and was again sentenced to a ten-year stretch in the state pen. This time he would serve seven of the ten years. Task force investigators in 2009 noted with interest that in at least one of those 1995 fires, a local newspaper was utilized to start the blaze. That was consistent with some of the 2009 fires.

After that series and prison term, Swalwell returned to the streets of North Seattle and was afflicted for years with drug addiction and homelessness. He was also diagnosed with a form of mental illness. He was a familiar figure in his neighborhood, and all of the local cops were aware of his odd activities.

The 2009 arson task force began to build their case. The burglary arson in August was consistent with at least two of the cases in Swalwell's past for which he had been convicted. In this latest spree, he had been spotted at or near four of the arson scenes just before or just after the fire. On the night of his arrest, Swalwell was wearing the exact same clothing as seen on the surveillance video when he lit the trash on fire just a few days before. His palm print matched the August fire. The manner of ignition of most of the recent fires, which was flame to cardboard or a newspaper, was identical to some of the fires Swalwell had been convicted of in the past. The task force analyzed that with their arson experts and determined that Kevin Swalwell was the Greenwood arsonist.

They confronted Swalwell in an interview with that information. He quickly admitted to setting eleven of the fires in that spree, while denying six more the task force believed he was responsible for. Swalwell described to them in detail how he had lit each fire. He told them that he just wandered about and saw a secluded target that caught his eye. He then found papers, cardboard, or other materials nearby and arranged them in a fashion to start the fire. Swalwell told investigators that he was supposed to be on anti-psychotic medications, but had not been taking them during his fire setting spree.

In April 2010, Swalwell pled guilty to eleven counts of arson in relation to the Greenwood Arson spree. At the time, he apologized to the victims and promised to continue to take his psychiatric medications.

The Seattle prosecutors took the bold step in this case to implore the sentencing judge to take into account the history of Swalwell and the fairly lenient sentences he had been given in the past. They stressed that his fires, which started out in vacant buildings and to inexpensive items, soon grew into blazes at occupied structures in the dead of night, where there was a high chance of serious injury or death for the occupants. In the media and in the court, the district attorney appropriately labeled Swalwell as an "incorrigible serial arsonist." The prosecutors asked the judge to deviate from the sentencing norms in this case and to give Swalwell an extraordinary sentence to suit his risk category. Surprisingly, the judge obliged and in April 2010 sentenced the thrice-convicted serial arsonist Kevin Swalwell to a thirty-year prison term.

Of his known fires, Kevin Swalwell lit seventeen fires, fifteen of which were to structures, five of which being occupied structures. His fires caused injuries and near death to at least five persons. He is suspected of an additional half a dozen known fires.

Investigator Analysis

Stop me if you've heard this one before. The Swalwell case is a carbon copy of several cases already cited here. He defines what I believe is the most common and prolific serial arsonist type in the United States. It is my contention that there are hundreds of these types of serial offenders currently on the streets of this country. The numbers are easy to justify since every city in this country has a significant number of homeless and other persons with some sort of mental health issues just wandering the streets. If every city has at least one of these types of fire setters, then the numbers are into the hundreds. It is probably very safe to speculate that there are several hundred to a few thousand of these fire bugs loose in this country at any one time. They may wander the streets for months if not years without setting fires, but then for some unknown reason a triggering event occurs, and they began their fire setting activity. Many of these offenders will set multiple fires in a single night and basically burn anything that they note as a target of opportunity. It is not a significant stretch of credulity to believe that each of these offenders has lit anywhere from fifty to five hundred fires of varying sizes in their lifetime. If these numbers are even half true, then it would be easy to estimate that this type of offender is responsible for hundreds of thousands of fires in this country.

The nice thing about these types of offenders is that the majority of their fires are minor, nuisance-type events that cause very little damage and generally do not cause injuries. Another positive note in these cases is that by their lack of sophistication, overt actions, and the fact they remain in the same areas year after year, these offenders are the easiest arsonists to identify and catch. Sadly, for reasons that have been discussed at great length, these types of offenders don't even get looked at until one of their fires does some sort of significant damage. To continue with the ongoing theme of this book, we in the fire and police service who investigate arsons seldom even recognize, note, or monitor these "nuisance" fires, and this low-level arsonist can get away with dozens or hundreds of them for years before he gets our attention.

This case, like many of those other successful adjudications, also shows that it was facilitated by damn good police work at the street level. Patrol officers took steps to identify all persons in the area of the fire scenes, thereby linking Swalwell to four scenes. Evidence was located and held for analysis, which forensically linked Swalwell to one scene. The task force used the media blitz to their advantage, and an astute corrections official, after reading about the events, was quickly able to steer the task force toward Swalwell. Finally, great research and a patient interview caused Swalwell to not only admit his crimes, but to also describe in great detail the manner and methods he used. Again, as has been shown many times, most of these cases are made by deliberate and detailed detective work. The task force did an exceptional job in this case.

Swalwell differs a little from those other offenders in that at some point he began to target houses and occupied dwellings. Since in his case he was not charged with the crime of attempted murder, it would seem a safe bet that there was no proof that he was aware that any of the structures were occupied.

Another aspect of Swalwell is that he, like most fire bugs, had significant mental health issues. It seems his fire setting activities diminished if he took his medications and increased if he deviated from that regimen. That too is extremely common in these cases. Another common aspect is that arsonists of nearly every ilk seldom serve significant time in prison for their criminal offenses. By the time Swalwell set his second grouping of fires in 1995, he should have been recognized as a multiple fire setter with mental health and narcotics issues and should have been deemed an extremely high risk to re-offend. He should have been given a much more severe sentence than the seven years he received.

Luckily, in the end he received a proper sentence. Perhaps it was because the Seattle Fire Department has a long memory and had already been scarred by significant past serial arson cases, or perhaps the district attorney finally saw that man for what he really was and not just the typical goofy fire bug who meant no one harm.

Kevin Swalwell is an extremely disorganized offender who used items found at the fire scene to attack targets of opportunity. He maintained his uncomplicated ignition scenario for the twenty-five known years he was involved in fire setting. He is believed to have set at least twenty-five and probably over fifty fires during his time on the street.

Chapter 6 Synopsis

These five arsonists define to me the classic serial arsonist who is most prevalent on the streets of America and no doubt in other modern countries. This type of offender is so common in this business that my unit has handled six of these cases in the last two years alone. A brief Internet search of the term "serial arsonist" will give the reader a fresh news story about every other week of an offender from this group. Major metropolitan areas have several of these types of guys operating at any one time.

These offenders are the easiest to catch and the easiest to prosecute. Almost all of them operate on impulse with no planning whatsoever, and most commit their acts with little regard for getting caught. They are usually unsophisticated and have a lengthy history of mental health issues, along with many years of prescription drugs, narcotics, or alcohol abuse. Almost all have been institutionalized in their lives at least once before their major arrest. Many live on the streets, and most are very well known in the areas where they light their fires.

The biggest problem with this group is that they commit their crimes right under our noses, and we give them very little consideration during our manhunts. They light dozens if not hundreds of smaller fires before one of theirs causes harm or serious damage and thus are seldom brought to the attention of an arson investigator.

When these types of offenders are finally caught, it is difficult to link them to all their arson events due to poor documentation of minor fires and an ongoing failure of fire agencies to maintain records of older cases. Many of these offenders, when they do cooperate, are unable to recall exactly how many fires they have lit. Additionally, these people are so pathetic in appearance that the courts and even the prosecutors almost always minimize their crimes and fail to take into account their true danger level. Most of these denizens of the street are soon out of jail or the psych ward and begin lighting fires as soon as the pressure gets to them.

This group of offenders does not use incendiary devices and does not plan the event. Their demographics reflect the communities where they operate, and you will find them in every ethnic group and in both sexes. It is not uncommon to find members of this group ranging in ages from fifteen to seventy-five years old.

CHAPTER 7

Female Serial Arsonists

The few past studies in this field strongly suggest that a female serial offender is an extremely rare person. I have conducted a detailed search and has come up with very little documentation of female serial fire setting. This is not to suggest that it does not occur, but maybe it occurs with much less frequency than male fire setting. Another factor is that maybe, like so many other things in the arson investigation business, female serial arsonists just are not identified and caught. Noted FBI Profiler John Douglas, in his book *The Anatomy of Motive*, briefly discusses female fire setters. He believes that females do engage in fire setting activities, but with some differing characteristics than males. Douglas states that while both sexes engage in serial arson behavior, the males will tend to set fires at night away from their home and in some sort of identifiable pattern. He believes that this sort of activity is directly related to the predatory nature of male offenders, which causes them to lash out and attack other people or institutions. In contrast, the female fire setters are more self-punishing and self-destructive and will often set their fires during daylight hours in or near their own homes. The female fires tend to be less dramatic in size and scope and will usually cause much less damage than male-set fires. The following examples are from the few known serial arson cases involving females. Sadly, there is precious little documentation of the crimes themselves and very little useful material for the investigator to study.

Shirley Baron Winters: Serial Arsonist/Serial Murderer
Period of Activity: 1979-2007, Upstate New York

Few people in this world have had as many traumatic events happen to them as occurred in the life of Shirley Winters. Born Shirley Baron in 1958, unspeakable tragedy occurred to those around her on a near annual basis. By the time she was seven years old, she had three siblings: eleven-year-old Peter, ten-year-old Joyce, and four-year-old Lita. On a cold January day in 1966, while Shirley was away visiting her grandmother, a strange accident occurred in her home. Investigators would later attribute a damaged furnace exhaust vent in the home to asphyxiating the three young children with carbon monoxide. Miraculously, Shirley's mother was rendered unconscious, but survived.

When Shirley was eighteen, she and her soon-to-be husband Ronald Winters Jr. hung around with another high school friend. That woman died in a car accident. Friends of Shirley would later say that both these events greatly impacted her life. Soon after, in 1977, Shirley married Ron Winters, and the two moved briefly to California. Upon her return, Shirley told a friend that while on the West Coast, she had been kidnapped and beaten up. The story was never really believed or verified by anyone at the time and was just chalked up as an odd tale.

Shirley and Ron had three children together. On September 11, 1979, a fire fifty miles from the Winters' home killed the three young children of a close friend of Shirley. The very next day, a suspicious fire broke out in Shirley's home while her husband was at work and she was watching TV. That fire killed two of her young children who were asleep in a bedroom. Shirley would tell investigators that she became aware of the smell of smoke coming from the bedroom and tried in vain to enter it to save her children. Although that fire was eventually blamed on faulty electrical wiring, something was just not right within that family. Ron left Shirley shortly after the event.

At the time they split up, Shirley was pregnant with their third child, Ronald III. After he was born, she moved them both to a trailer home in Otisco, New York. On November, 21, 1980, a little more than a year after the fire deaths and on the birthday of Shirley's mother, young five-month-old Ronald suddenly died. His death was ruled as sudden infant death syndrome (SIDS).

Six weeks later, on January 3, 1981, two small fires broke out in Shirley's trailer. One started on a sofa, the other in a bedroom. Both could be classified as arson. Five weeks later, two more fires erupted in her trailer. Again, one started on the sofa. The second small fire started in a box of clothing. This time local authorities arrested and charged Shirley Winters with arson. While she was out on bail on that case, another fire broke out in the trailer of Shirley

Winters. A new arson charge was added to the ongoing original arson case. Shirley Winters in a plea bargain pled guilty to "criminal mischief" in lieu of arson charges and was ordered to undergo counseling.

After that fifth known arson fire, authorities reopened the case from 1979, wherein her two children had died in a fire. That case was then reclassified as "suspicious." They also contacted the mother of the three children who had died in a fire the day before Shirley's children died in a similar fire. She told investigators that Shirley had been to her home prior to the fire, but she did not believe at all that Shirley had anything to do with the fire. That fire was never investigated by an arson investigator and remains classified to this day as "suspicious in nature."

By 1985 Shirley had two new babies, both girls. In 1986, Shirley was living in an apartment complex in Marcellus, New York. On November 12, a fire of unknown origin broke out and destroyed the structure.

In 1987, Shirley gave birth to a son. With her three young children, she moved back to the Syracuse area. She took up residence in the second floor of an apartment building on Willis Avenue. On November 12, 1989, a fire erupted in the basement of Shirley's apartment building. That large fire was ruled arson by local investigators. Shirley was seen leading two of her kids from the burning building. She claimed that she "lost" daughter Joy in the smoke. Four-year-old Joy was later found outside as she had made it to safety by herself. Investigators would later note that that event occurred three years to the day after the Marcellus apartment building fire. Neighbors would later comment about some odd things that occurred surrounding that event. Immediately after the fire, neighbors had witnessed Shirley Winters laughing. When asked if she had cried at the time, some longtime acquaintances said that they had never seen her cry. Additionally, neighbors reported that just prior to that fire, Shirley had inquired with them if they had smoke detectors.

After the Willis Avenue fire, local children's services agents opened a neglect investigation in regards to Shirley Winters. They learned that there had been many odd incidents surrounding that woman. In one recent case, her young son Clayton had fallen down the cellar stairs in his walker. A male friend had found the boy unconscious, and Shirley had made a strange comment to the man that seeing Clayton face down had reminded her of another kid who'd died. She didn't elaborate, but the friend noticed that Shirley kept a picture of Clayton's battered face on her refrigerator after the event.

After the Willis Avenue fire, and while the neglect investigation was continuing, Shirley moved with her kids to a home on Split Rock Road. On January 6, 1990, just seven weeks after the apartment fire, another fire broke out at Shirley's new residence. That fire was ruled an arson by local authorities. Almost immediately, a prudent Family Court judge removed the three small children from Shirley. Her mother then reported that after that event Shirley Waters checked herself into a nearby psychiatric center for a few days.

When she emerged from the psych ward, events shifted into high gear. On March 18, fire broke out at Winter's new apartment on Lakeview Avenue. Winters escaped that blaze. Another family downstairs, a couple with their twenty-two-month-old baby, also narrowly escaped. Investigators noted that that blaze, like the Willis Avenue blaze, originated from within the basement.

On April 10, 1990, Shirley was indicted on arson charges and willful neglect for the Willis Avenue fire. Shortly she began two jury trials in that case. The first trial deadlocked, and a second trial was scheduled. As she awaited the second trial, fires occurred at two different houses where Shirley was living. The first, on September 21, occurred in an attached garage at the home of Shirley's aunt. On October 5, a second fire occurred in the exact same garage, destroying both the garage and her aunt's home. The day after the second fire, Shirley was arrested and charged with making harassing phone calls. At the time of her arrest, she was combative and assaulted a police officer. She also damaged a patrol car.

All the while, the second Willis Avenue arson trial was just beginning. Frustrated prosecutors and investigators would later lament that they could bring none of Shirley Water's history or current activities into the courtroom. Further, they had to prove a case with little physical evidence and no witnesses. Not surprisingly, the second trial went in her favor, and she was acquitted of the arson charge on Willis Avenue.

Neighbors on both Willis Avenue and Griffin Road (the scene of both arson fires at Shirley's aunt's home) held community meetings and expressed fear of the out-of-control woman. Incredibly, a victim of the last two fires, Shirley's own aunt, Mrs. Floyd Sanford would refuse to believe that Shirley would ever have started the fires. She, along with Shirley's mother and the childhood friend whose three children had died in the 1979 fire, all steadfastly refused to believe that Shirley had any problems. They claimed that she had been a loyal and loving friend, daughter, and niece all her life who just had bad luck and was being persecuted by a "lynch mob" for her misfortunes. The women complained that Shirley had been fighting those accusations for years and that "someone was trying to discredit her" or set her up.

On November 14, of 1990, Shirley was charged with the arson of a bowling alley in the town of Camillus. That would be the fourth different arson charge of her life. As a result of this latest series of events, Shirley was charged with several crimes. She was convicted and pled guilty to the assault on a police officer. The fire charges were dropped, and she spent a short time in prison for that event.

The very people who stood by Shirley Winters for many years would eventually be rewarded in a very macabre manner for their loyalty. In 1997, Shirley Winters set fire to her own mother's home. Upon arrest, she admitted that she knew a cousin was inside at the time of the fire. Winters received an eight-year prison sentence for the arson/attempt to murder. In keeping with all of the other tragic events of her life, Shirley Winters's mother, loyal to her to the end, died in a car accident two months before Shirley began serving her prison sentence.

In 2004, Shirley was briefly released and then rearrested for carrying a lighter in violation of the terms of her parole. She finally made parole in 2005. While still on parole, the circle of friends and relatives who had been so loyal to her for forty-plus years continued to give her chances. In 2006, she stayed with the Rivers family in Pierrepont, New York. Those people had longtime connections to Shirley, and coincidentally were cousins to the three children who had died in the fire back in 1979. On November 28, 2006, the twenty-three-month-old son of the Rivers, Ryan Rivers, drowned in a bathtub in the home. The event came immediately under investigation when local officials realized that Shirley Winters was visiting in the home at the time.

That event prompted the reexamination of the earlier deaths of Shirley Winters' children. In early 2007, the bodies of her daughters who had died in the fire in 1979 were exhumed. The body of her son who had died due to SIDS was also exhumed and examined. The results of those examinations showed that the two girls had died of blunt force trauma before the fire. Her son had died of suffocation as opposed to a medical condition.

On March 16, 2007, Shirley Winters attempted suicide and was hospitalized for her efforts. On March 28, she was indicted for the murder of her son Ronald Winters III, which occurred in 1980. Later that summer, she was indicted for the drowning murder of young Ryan Rivers in 2006.

On April 21, 2008, Shirley Winters pled guilty to manslaughter in the Ryan Rivers "drowning" case. She also pled guilty to first degree manslaughter in the death of her own son Ronald Winters III in 1980. She received sentences of twenty years in one case and twenty-five years in the second. As part of the plea bargain in those matters, she avoided prosecution in the deaths of her daughters in 1979. Additionally, she can serve both sentences concurrently and be eligible for parole after just seventeen years.

These shockingly lenient sentences were awarded to a woman who is linked to seventeen arson fires and the deaths of four children and the probable attempted murders of at least four more children and several other adults.

Investigator's Analysis

The case of Shirley Winters is the only one where this author will attempt to ham-handedly delve into a bit of amateurish psychology. There are very few recorded female serial arson offenders. However, there have been many cases where women have killed their own children for a variety of reasons. This act, known as filicide, is the main reason for several women to be currently residing on death row in this country. When it involves fire, filicide occurs in the form of a preplanned murder or possibly a preplanned murder-suicide, where for whatever reason the suicide portion of the plan fails or is not carried out. This author has attended at least two of those types of events wherein multiple children perished. Shirley Winter's case may fall under those categories. Her fires may be related to failed murder-suicide attempts.

However, there is another aspect of her fires that bears consideration. A psychological problem known as "Munchausen's syndrome" can cause certain people to create or portray themselves in countless situations as "victims." There are many aspects to Munchausen's, but one aspect is where a grossly inordinate number of unfortunate events occur in a person's life. A review of those events will show that many are either made up or staged by the "victim." Such may be the case for the bizarre claim of being kidnapped that Shirley related to friends. A related disorder is Munchausen's by proxy. In this form, usually a mother reports an inordinate amount of bad luck, misfortune, rare diseases, accidents, or other trauma to one or more of her children.

These Munchausen's issues have been cited in numerous high-profile murders and "kidnapping" cases where the mother is eventually arrested and charged with staging the event. Most psychologists will give laymen's explanations of each case, which generally boil down to the mother's deep-seated need for attention and sympathy.

In all cases like this, there is usually a total disregard for the safety or welfare of the children, and any survivors are in grave danger for future events. This narcissistic behavior is akin to similar behavior by most arsonists, who have little regard for the danger they are causing, but are just fixated on their own needs and desires.

Shirley Winters set her fires for two reasons. One was to cover up the abuse she inflicted upon her children. The second reason was to achieve an outpouring of sympathy and attention from family and friends. She was successful enough at that latter ploy to fool many people for over forty years who stood by her despite a mountain of evidence against her.

There is little doubt to anyone that the tragic death of Shirley's three siblings at the age of seven was the major factor in all of the following tragedies. However, another speculation is that possibly Shirley's mother also had Munchausen's syndrome as this event was so eerily like the following ones in Shirley's life. Again, there is just not enough credible information on many of those events to make a legitimate opinion on them.

A study of the few known details in this case will show that her fires followed a general pattern. If, and it's a big if in this case, the fire that killed the three children of her childhood friend in 1979 was indeed an accident, then it would be safe to assume that the fire set the next day that killed Shirley's children was done because Shirley desired the same sympathy and attention that her friend was getting. It's amazing in hindsight how two similar but extremely rare events could affect two friends within twenty-four hours of each other and that no family members or authorities at the time would think that that was suspicious.

Another glaring red flag in this case is the two near identical fire events that occurred on the same day of the year, three years apart, on November 12, 1986 and 1989. Additional to these is that on November 14, 1990, she was charged with a different arson event. Some studies involving serial arsonists suggest that they offend for various reasons in sprees surrounding "anniversary dates" of some significant day in their life. In 2004, while prosecuting a serial arson case, this author met with Dr. Dian Williams, a nationally recognized expert on fire setting behavior. In that conversation, Dr. Williams discussed that certain fire setters have a surge of events leading up to an anniversary day in their life. Those events are usually a spree of fire setting or other illicit activity that intensifies as the date approaches and then usually diminishes shortly after the anniversary date. A review of the offender's fires and other acts will show clusters of activity surrounding certain dates. Usually, only the offender will understand the significance of a particular date. It may be when they had set their most significant fire, a date of personal trauma in their life, a death date of a significant person in their life, or any other event that has some meaning to them (Williams, personal communication, August, 2004). Several incidents occurred during the months of October and November for this woman, including several fires and the "drowning" death of the Rivers child for which she was later convicted of manslaughter.

Another small cluster of significant dates to Shirley Winters was in mid-March. On March 18, 1990, an arson fire occurred at her home on Split Rock Road. As a result of that, the court removed her children from her custody. On March 16, 2007, she attempted suicide.

Another trend with this woman was that nearly all her events involved the victimization of young children, either hers, a relative's, or a neighbor's. Being a young child anywhere near Shirley Winters was indeed a dangerous prospect.

In the end, Shirley Winters will go down as a serial arsonist and serial child murderer. Many of her fire events appear to be additional attempts to murder her three surviving children, her mother, her aunt, and possibly the children of her neighbors. Her fire scenes were not at all sophisticated and were usually done with an open flame, usually a lighter applied to whatever combustible material was in the area. However, due to the lack of qualified investigators at the time, the inability of law enforcement to connect her to multiple events, and the ongoing disbelief in many person's minds (that still exists) that a mother would never do that to her children, Shirley Winters, as unsophisticated an offender as she was, continually defied the odds and routinely beat the justice system over and over.

She is an extremely disorganized offender. She is specifically linked to seventeen arsons of occupied structures and has been held accountable for the criminal deaths of at least four young children. There is little doubt that there were probably numerous other events or attempts to harm other children. A testament to how prolific this woman was in her fire setting is that by 1990 she knew personally all of the local arson investigators in her area. She will be eligible for parole by the year 2024.

** Author's Note

In 2002, this author adjudicated a case of another suspected serial arson offender in Southern California. That offender, a mid-thirties white male, who worked as a tow truck driver, came to the investigators' attention after he "discovered" over a dozen brushfires in a two-month period. Soon thirty-two brush and vehicle fires were linked to that suspect. In a plea deal, he eventually pled guilty to arson for staging a fire at his home. That offender had posed as a firefighter, police detective, and accident investigator for over a decade and had a true "hero complex." A side light to this case was that his in-laws advised investigators that he had a bad case of "Munchausen's syndrome" as well. In a very short three-year time period, he was linked to over fifty automobile accidents where he was almost always listed as a "victim." He was the "victim" of three accidental vehicle fires, all in cars he had rented. In at least two of those incidents, he told the rental company that he had barely "escaped with his life" as their vehicles had burst into flames for no reason. Additionally, he "happened upon" several crimes in progress and reported himself and his family as "victims" in assaults and threats by unknown parties. Most alarmingly in all of this, the suspect had claimed on several occasions that his young children had been injured in bizarre accidents, always involving a large retail business. He had sued several stores where his kids were "injured" when the automatic doors closed on them or when shelves had fallen on them. None of those injuries were ever serious, and the incidents always ended with the arsonist receiving a check from the retail store. After his arson conviction and those other suspicious activities were made known to the courts, they miraculously stopped occurring.

Belle Gunness "Lady Bluebeard": Serial Murderer/Serial Arsonist
Period of Activity: 1896-1908, Chicago and Indiana

"Belle" was the Americanized name this Norwegian immigrant settled on when she arrived in the United States in 1881. Three years later, at age twenty-five she was married in Chicago to another Norse named Sorenson. Belle was not necessarily a classic beauty and on her best days could be described as fairly stout. She grew in girth as she grew in years.

Sorenson attempted to make something of his life, and eventually the pair opened a candy store in Chicago in 1896. Less than a year later, a turning point occurred in the lives of Sorenson and his wife. A fire occurred within the business when Belle claimed that a kerosene lamp exploded. The blaze destroyed the small business. A subsequent insurance investigation revealed that there was no such lamp in the debris. Despite that anomaly, the insurance company paid out handsomely to the couple. That insurance money went to good use, and Belle and Sorenson purchased their first home. That watershed event gave Belle a taste for insurance money, which she never lost for the rest of her life.

Shortly after moving into their new home, a fire leveled the property, and Belle and her husband received yet another substantial insurance settlement. That money was used to buy an even bigger home. Astonishingly, that second home also burned, and yet another property was purchased with yet another large insurance check. That event was the third major fire in just a few years for the young couple.

Questionable fires were not the only maladies to plague Belle and her husband. In 1896, their first daughter died, followed two years later by the death of their first son. Both died of "acute colitis," which has similar symptoms to certain poisonings. Two years after that, Belle's husband Mads Sorenson died while at home under her care. His symptoms were consistent with strychnine poisoning, but the doctor refused to conduct an autopsy since Sorenson had an ongoing heart condition.

After collecting a life insurance check for over $8,000 from Sorenson's death, Belle finally quit Chicago and relocated to a colorful farm near LaPorte, Indiana. The forty-eight-acre farm had been a former upscale whorehouse, and Belle established herself as the well-to-do Widow Sorenson. She brought along with her the two surviving daughters from her marriage and a younger adopted daughter.

Not the prettiest woman in the world, Belle however was extremely strong. She was always a large woman and her weight varied between 230 and 280 pounds. She was a hard worker and was particularly skilled as a butcher. She turned the basement of her home into a butcher's shop and personally handled the killing, dissection, and butchering of beef on a daily basis. She was able to make a decent living selling her meat to local markets.

By April 1902, Belle had married another Norwegian immigrant named Peter Gunness, who was also a farmer in the area. He too soon learned about the tragic luck that seemed to follow Belle as he died just eight months later in a rather bizarre "accident." Belle reported that apparently a heavy meat grinder fell from a shelf and crushed his skull. Later reports attribute his death to being murdered by a meat cleaver. Belle's own child told a classmate that her mother had murdered Peter with a cleaver. Although the local coroner and the sheriff had their doubts about the veracity of Belle's story, the matter was dropped out of pity for the twice-widowed woman. Belle also profited from that death as she received a $4,000 life insurance payout. Before the second husband died, he and Belle had conceived a male child. Suspiciously, within a couple of years of that event, the adopted daughter, Jennie, disappeared from the farm and was never seen again. When questioned about the young girl, Belle gave vague answers about her attending school in California.

Because she was a single mother trying to run a farm, Belle hired a succession of drifting men to assist her with chores. Most of those men were only seen for a few days and seemed to "move on." None were ever heard from again. Belle also started penning "lonely hearts" letters in Norwegian newspapers throughout the Midwest. She boasted that she was a widow of financial means who wanted to start a relationship with a single male of similar financial means. She required that if men were to visit her that they bring money as proof of their financial standing. Apparently, she was quite gifted as a writer as numerous males responded to her letters, and many of them arrived at her farm with large amounts of money upon them. For the next few years, many men showed up at Belle's door, stayed for a day or two, and then "moved on" as she told neighbors. Most were never seen alive again.

The most dramatic chapter in Belle's sordid life came to pass on April 28, 1908, when neighbors spotted a large fire consuming her rural home. By the time sufficient crews could get to the scene, the brick farmhouse was completely destroyed by fire. A search over the next few days revealed the headless corpse of a woman, along with the bodies of Belle's three young children, all heavily burned by fire in the basement of the home.

The local sheriff, Albert Smutzer, recollecting the odd and bizarre events that seemed to surround that woman and her home did an extraordinary crime scene investigation of the fire. After a very detailed arson and coroner's investigation, which included the use of a local miner and his water sluice to "sift" the crime scene, it was concluded that the event was arson and that the deaths were murders. Many witnesses, however, pointed out that the woman's corpse in the basement appeared much smaller in stature than the rather robust (280 lb) Belle. Indeed, even the coroner, sheriff, and fire investigators believed that the headless woman seemed much smaller than Belle, even after taking into account the effects of the massive fire. However, the sluicing operation revealed a partial bridge denture next to the body, which was positively identified by a dentist as belonging to Belle Gunness. Despite many protests to the contrary, the coroner eventually ruled that the body was of Belle Gunness.

Responding persons and fire crews later reported to the sheriff that during the middle of the blaze, they saw Belle's former handyman, Ray Lamphere, waiting on a roadway near her home. Lamphere had worked for and lived with Belle Gunness for several years. He was the only male who seemed to stay around her. Even though he was considered mentally "slow," Lamphere often came to town, got drunk, and bragged about sleeping with his employer, the widow Gunness. Apparently the two had had a parting of the ways in the past few months as Belle had fired him and hired a new handyman. The day prior to the fire, Gunness complained to Sheriff Smutzer that Lamphere was harassing her and she was in fear of him. Specifically she told the lawman, "Ray told me he would burn the house down around my ears." She claimed he was in love with her and angry with her at the same time. Immediately following her visit to the sheriff, Gunness had gone to a local attorney and drawn up her will "in case something happens." Within the next twelve hours, it apparently did happen.

Lamphere seemed a likely suspect in that arson murder. He was arrested, and Sheriff Smutzer found several items on him which appeared to have belonged to some of the missing suitors.

The arson murder investigation continued for some days. Sheriff's deputies continued to dig at the farm looking for the severed head of the female corpse. Relatives of missing men who had come to suit Belle showed up and joined in the effort. Eventually, watches, clothing, and other personal effects of several missing men were located. Soon, in the hog's pen, four men's bodies were located. The bodies were wrapped in a cloth and all had been dissected. The discovery made national news, and more relatives descended on the farm to help in the digging. Eventually, the bodies or portions of bodies from fourteen different men were located on the grounds. All were eventually identified as lonely men of financial means who had answered personal ads from the widow Gunness. All had arrived at the farm with substantial amounts of money and had disappeared within just a few days. Tests revealed that most showed signs of poisoning.

Many theories were spawned after those events, including the prevailing notion that Belle Gunness had staged that final arson act and had fled the area after killing her children. In fact, one of the bodies recovered from a shallow grave at the home was identified as the adopted daughter Jennie, who Belle had stated had gone to California. Indeed, the sheriff later tallied up a total of $30,000 that Belle had made during her "lonely hearts" scheme. He would later find out that Belle herself had withdrawn substantial amounts of cash from area banks in the days leading up to the fire.

Despite that evidence, the sheriff and local prosecutors charged hapless Ray Lamphere with the arson and murders of the children. After all, he did have in his possession some of the items stolen from the dead men who had come to court Belle. Soon Lamphere began to talk and asserted that Belle was alive and living elsewhere and that she had arranged the murders and staged arson. The authorities actually believed most of the story but were convinced that Lamphere had an active role and that he in fact had killed Belle. Oddly, Lamphere was acquitted of any murders, but was convicted of the arson to the home. He was sentenced to twenty-one years in the state penitentiary. Soon he contracted tuberculosis in prison. As his death approached, Lamphere gave a full confession to a cellmate. He admitted to helping Belle lure and murder dozens of men for their money at her farm. In most cases, the men were poisoned as they ate or drank, and then Belle would often hit their heads with a meat cleaver. She routinely cut up the bodies much like a butcher and then sometimes fed them to her hogs. The majority were buried by Lamphere in the yard. Lamphere admitted that the female corpse found at the fire scene was in fact a derelict woman from Chicago who was lured to the farm. She was poisoned upon her arrival, her head severed to prevent identification, and her body placed in the basement with Belle's poisoned and strangled children. Belle started the fire, and she was supposed to meet Lamphere on the road near her home where he waited to make their getaway. In the end, she left him stranded to be accused and arrested as she left the property by some other means.

Although there were rumors of Belle Gunness sightings over the next few decades, she was never positively identified. The most promising story came in 1931 when a Los Angeles prosecutor wrote a letter to the LaPorte sheriff asking for him to come to California to identify a female murder defendant named Esther Carlson. Carlson was awaiting trial for allegedly poisoning eighty-one-year-old August Lindstrom for his insurance money. The DA said that Carlson carried photographs of three children that resembled the deceased trio of kids of Belle Gunness and that Carlson was a Norwegian immigrant and physically resembled Gunness. Due to financial issues during the Great

Depression, the LaPorte sheriff was unable to go to Los Angeles, and the female suspect (Carlson) died of illness before her trial.

Belle Gunness's legend (and apparently her beauty—she was often described as looking, acting, and dressing like a large man) has grown to mythical proportions, and she is considered one of the most infamous of all female serial killers. She has been positively linked to sixteen murders, all via poison. Additionally, she is the suspect in at least four arsons of structures and the possible murders of at least two husbands. She also appears to have murdered all six of her children by poison and fire. Lamphere asserted that he watched her kill forty-nine "lonely hearts" or drifters over the years.

Investigator's Analysis

Like many of the older cases, the author is reliant upon accounts and stories passed down over the decades. This one is a truly fascinating tale of greed and cold-blooded murder. Although Belle is listed as a serial arsonist due to her (at least) four structure fires, it appears that arson was just another tool in her scheme of murder and insurance fraud.

Like more than a few arsonists and specifically women arsonists, another weapon that she wielded was poison. Both of the weapons (poison and fire) are indirect weapons that can easily be explained away as accidents, particularly in the early 1900s' time frame. Like several of the women in this book, Belle took on the role of "nurse" for her husbands and others and was able to control their lives and administer poison in that capacity. Like most of the other women listed here, Belle lit her fires at home or at work, which is typical of nearly all female fire setters.

Belle's main motivation for her crimes seems to be financial gain. Her crimes were preplanned, and she took great pains to hide the identities and bodies of her victims. She is an organized serial offender who dedicated her life to her schemes.

Virginia Rearden: Multiple Murderer/Serial Arsonist
Period of Activity: 1953-87, New York, Kentucky, California

On April 2, 1987, twenty-year-old Deanna Wild, taking pictures while wearing unstable high heels, fell off a four-hundred-foot cliff to her death in picturesque Big Sur, California. At least that's what her two traveling companions told the local sheriff's office and coroner. The death was considered vaguely suspicious, but Monterey County officials were never able to classify it as a murder. The traveling companions of the dead girl were Billie

Joe McGinnis and his fifty-year-old wife, Virginia Rearden, who claimed to be her future in-laws.

That was not a noteworthy death and would have likely been forgotten had not an insurance carrier in another state refused to a pay a meager $3,500 death benefit to the deceased girl's mother. Frustrated with dealing with a reticent insurance carrier, the dead girl's mother sought advice from the only lawyer she knew. She approached a successful corporate attorney in her Louisville, Kentucky church, Steve Keeney. Keeney, a very affluent partner in a large corporate law firm, had no experience whatsoever in criminal law, insurance issues, or in dealing with human clients. His client list included massive companies, shipping firms, railroads, and the like. Recovering the $3,500 death benefit hardly seemed worth his time since he made that sort of money on a daily basis. Nonetheless, Keeney took pity on the bereaved mother and offered to help her recover the money on a *pro bono* basis. At the time, Keeney felt that a strongly worded letter from a high-powered attorney would probably settle the matter. Five years later and after thousands of free hours of investigation and legal wrangling, Keeney and the girl's mother finally settled the matter.

The informal investigation Keeney launched with a simple phone call to the coroner's office in Monterey County, California, unraveled a thirty-year web of poison, death, fraud, and fire. The center of this case would eventually fall around the "future mother-in-law" of the dead girl, Virginia Rearden.

Virginia Rearden was born on a dairy farm in rural Ithaca, New York, in 1937. Her father, a former marine, was a drunkard and pretty much a failure in life due to his slovenly habits and bizarre behavior. He had dabbled as a security guard and as a cop in New York City. He moved to the small farm in upstate New York, but was known as a bad neighbor and a poor farmer. At one point, he was accused of fraudulently diluting the milk he sold to the local creamery. Virginia's family was not a warm and friendly bunch, and their house was routinely described as a pigsty. Young Virginia was used by her father as just another farmhand, and she grew up dirty, poor, and angry. She was known to have been beaten and whipped on numerous occasions by her father, and a relative would later admit that her own elder brother had often sexually abused her in the family's barn. That same brother as an adult was later implicated in the sexual molestation of a young boy in the area. Clearly, Virginia's family embodied the term "dysfunctional." Something was definitely wrong with that clan.

When she began to hit puberty, Virginia's father accused her openly of being a slut. Indeed, schoolmates would describe that when Virginia was around eleven years old, a local neighbor would act as the "bus driver," and in his station wagon, he drove several kids to school every day. The man would always invite Virginia to sit next to him in the car, and he would routinely fondle her crotch area as he drove the kids to school. Classmates recalled that Virginia never seemed to mind that assault. Other friends would later reveal that throughout her teen years, Virginia who was larger than all the other girls was a mean bully, who liked to hit people and frequently engaged in sex. On one occasion she was seen having sex with two boys at once. She was described as being extremely cold, non-emotional, and someone who almost never smiled.

Two major events highlighted Virginia's sixteenth year of life. On a fall day in 1953, the family's barn burst into flame and burned to the ground. The cause of the fire was never identified, but Virginia's brother (the same one who had molested her in that very barn) later told several people that Virginia lit the fire. A significant result of that fire was that an insurance man arrived and quickly paid Virginia's father a large amount of money for the burned barn. An odd incident occurred as the barn was burning to the ground. Because the fire took several hours to burn the large structure, a crowd of neighbors had gathered. One would later describe that Virginia seemed somehow excited by the event and even left with a neighbor boy to have sex while the fire was still burning.

The second major event in Virginia's life that year was that her father shot her horse. For no particular reason whatsoever, Virginia's father decided that the horse ate too much and took up too much space, so he decided to shoot it and sell its carcass to a glue factory. Virginia came home to find her horse dead and being winched onto a truck. Her father seemed to take glee in her shock. That horse was the only creature toward which Virginia had ever shown affection.

Within a few months of that event, seventeen-year-old Virginia, rebelling against her father, got pregnant by and then married a nineteen-year-old neighbor boy named Dick Coates. Years later, Dick Coates would reveal the dark history of Virginia Rearden. He said that while he was dating her she told him that her father had beat her so much that she was unable to get pregnant, so it was okay to have sex. Coates was surprised when she soon told him that she was in fact pregnant. After they married, the young pair moved in with Coate's family. Trouble started almost immediately. Coates and his parents soon found new tools, purses, and other property around the home. Virginia claimed that she had "found" the items or that a passing truck had dropped them. Soon neighbors, shopkeepers, and others arrived at the home and accused Virginia of stealing those items from them. Virginia never ever admitted to thefts, but would often return the items. Soon rumors arose that Virginia was forging documents and passing bad checks in nearby towns. There were allegations that she had affairs with numerous men. She often showed up at home with unexplained amounts of money or goods that her family knew she couldn't legally possess. She started amassing a large collection of exotic lingerie and jewelry despite not having any sort of income. That went on for months until literally everybody in their community knew that Virginia was a kleptomaniac who stole or swindled on a daily basis. Coate's parents threw them out of their home, and the two were forced to move back in with Virginia's family.

In 1955, Coates finally saw the true mean and greedy side of Virginia. He had neglected to bring his paycheck home after a job one day, and Virginia confronted him about it. When he told her he'd bring the money the next day, she seemed incensed. Later, as Coates drifted off for a nap, he heard someone running toward him. He opened his eyes in time to see a very pregnant Virginia lunging at his stomach with a large butcher knife. She made several attempts to stab and hack at him with the knife. The next day, she acted like nothing had happened at all. Coates would later recall that Virginia seemed obsessed with having money, power, and possessions.

When Virginia and Coates moved into their own home and had their second child, her behavior seemed to calm a little. However, Coates was well aware that Virginia liked to seduce men. She was fond of dressing up and wearing lingerie, and there was a lot of evidence that she frequently had affairs with some of Dick Coates's own friends. Coates would later say that infidelity had run in her family because soon after the two were married Virginia's own mother had tried to have sex with him (Coates).

By 1958, Virginia and Coates had two young sons and a small home. Her spree of thefts continued, and she seemed to take a delight in stealing something and then later revealing it to the very victim she stole it from. She stole a pair of expensive boots from a shop and then later walked into the very same shop wearing the stolen boots. On another occasion, she invited her landlady to tea and served snacks on a china service that she had stolen from the very same landlady. When confronted with these facts, Virginia would stare down her accusers and boldly deny their claims. She was a large and imposing person who frequently faced down many accusers with a ruthless and cold stare. She dressed and wore expensive jewelry well beyond her means and seemed to carry an air of wealth and power around her despite having a very meager income and a rundown home.

One night in 1958, Dick Coates and Virginia were sleeping with their kids. Coates awoke to find Virginia gone, but the ceiling of the room was on fire. He grabbed the two kids and ran outside to find Virginia fully dressed and standing there watching the home burn. She never warned him or tried to wake him or the kids. The fire was ruled an accident related to the stove, but Coates was aware that it had started on the opposite side of the room from the stove. Virginia never discussed her actions (or non-actions) with Coates.

Coates was a fairly slow-witted man, but by 1959, even he realized what type of woman he had married. That year, Virginia was arrested in a nearby town for passing several stolen and forged checks. She was using several aliases at the time, and even Coates realized that she had developed some level of sophistication. She was subsequently convicted of multiple counts of fraud and grand theft. She was placed on two years' probation for those crimes.

Despite being on probation, Virginia continued to steal on a near daily basis. She also started to become extremely physically aggressive toward her husband, and the two frequently argued and fought. Their two sons were seldom cared for and grew into little trouble causers. In 1961, another fire occurred in their home in the middle of the night. Dick Coates and a guest awoke in the early morning hours to smell fire coming from the basement. He was able to put it out before serious damage occurred. He and his friend searched the basement and found that someone had set fire to the electrical insulation with several matches that were found at the scene. Virginia was the only other person present, but made no comment about the fire.

By 1966, Virginia and Dick Coate's fights had escalated to the level that the two came close to killing each other. Virginia left Coates on Christmas Eve of that year. Coates only saw her once after that night. He read in a newspaper a year later that Virginia and their sons had escaped another four in the morning house fire. Coates later learned that Virginia received an insurance settlement for that fire. A few weeks later, he learned that Virginia had been staying back at her parents' home after her most recent fire and that their barn burned down the second time. Coates learned of those two fires because Virginia had purchased insurance policies for both of those properties and placed them in Dick Coates's name without his knowledge. Not wanting to be involved with that evil woman any longer, he signed both insurance checks and gave them to Virginia upon her demand. Coates was shocked when she showed up to get the checks driving a new Ford Mustang. After he gave her the insurance checks, Coates said that Virginia tried to run him down with the Mustang as she sped out of his yard. Although he never saw her again, she left him with one more parting gift. Throughout the last several years of their marriage, Virginia had run up massive bills at stores and businesses and refused to pay them. Dick Coates was hounded by her creditors for the next several years. In the brief thirteen years that Dick Coates was associated with Virginia Rearden, he was aware of at least five suspicious structure fires that occurred when she was present. Virginia received insurance settlement checks on at least four of those events.

There are no details available about Virginia for the next several years. By 1971, she had relocated with her mother who worked at a veteran's hospital in the Port Hueneme area just north of Los Angeles. Virginia soon got a job working as a "home nurse" for elderly people. At that time, she met and married her second husband, Bud Rearden, who was a career navy man. Like Virginia's previous husband, Bud liked his alcohol. The two and their combined family soon moved to Louisville, Kentucky. Kentucky neighbors would later report that Virginia was a large intimidating woman who always dressed expensively, was very well groomed, and portrayed an image of wealth and power, despite having little or no income. She had several expensive antique items in her very modest home, which just didn't seem to fit. She often told neighbors that those items were left to her in a will by an elderly patient she cared for in California. Virginia also was not shy to admit that the elderly woman's heirs had believed that Virginia had somehow stolen or swindled the items from the sickly patient.

A neighbor of the Reardens who also happened to be a local cop reported that there were numerous odd things about the clan. He said that Virginia often bragged about being a "practical nurse," but never seemed to have a job. Bud Rearden soon became stricken with cancer and was bedridden for the next year. As soon as Bud Rearden became bedridden, Virginia forbade anyone but her to care for him. She soon drove Bud's two adult sons out from the home and moved her own two adult sons in with them. Virginia's sons by that time had become complete hell raisers and were involved in drug use and sales, assaults, and endless bouts of drinking.

The year 1972 became a deadly year for the Reardens. Virginia had a three-year-old daughter named Cynthia Coates. (When asked about the girl years later, Dick Coates said that he never knew he had a daughter as he had stopped all contact with Virginia at least three years prior to the girl being born.) That year, Cynthia's body was found hanging from a cord in the family barn, although Virginia was just several feet away. The death was ruled an "accidental hanging," as the coroner believed the little girl accidentally slipped off a tractor on which she had been playing. Police and neighbors all noticed that the only person not upset by that horrific event was Virginia. Within a day or two, she nonchalantly appeared at a neighbor's door with all of the little girl's clothes and toys to give away. The neighbors were too shocked and horrified to respond. Visitors after the death noticed that the little girl's picture in the home had been turned face down within a few days of the "accident."

Shortly after Cynthia died, neighbors learned that Virginia had collected on an insurance policy for the little girl. Everyone thought it odd that someone would have insurance on a young child.

Within a few short months of that death, Bud Rearden's health began to fail faster than anyone had predicted. Again, Virginia, acting as his "home nurse," controlled all of his medications and care. One night in a fairly casual manner, she advised Bud's youngest son to go say good-bye to him as he would soon die. The son did not think that Bud's death was imminent at the time. Later that same day, Virginia gave her own sons some money and told them to take Bud's son out "for a long drive." It was an odd request since neither of those people liked each other. When they returned hours later, Virginia announced coldly that Bud had died. She refused to let the son near the body. Virginia and her mother spent several hours cleaning the body and room before calling the authorities. She also staged a brief funeral for Bud without even notifying the rest of his family that he had died. Virginia waived the autopsy in this case. Immediately after the death, Virginia ordered Bud's sixteen-year-old son to leave the home and never return. She then submitted life insurance policies on his behalf and even sent paperwork to the military seeking death benefits and other pension-related items. Military authorities recognized that many of the documents had oddities and irregularities that in effect gave Virginia all of Bud's estate with none of it going to his children. Doctor's records would later reveal that Virginia had changed the dosage in Bud's medicines contrary to what his doctor had ordered. Nobody at the time seemed concerned that Virginia was acting as a "nurse" in life and death situations despite having no education beyond the tenth grade.

Just weeks after Bud's death, yet another late night fire struck the Reardens' home in Louisville, burning the roof. Local firefighters responded in time and stopped the blaze before it could destroy the home. Virginia was the only person present during that event. Immediately following that fire, Virginia filed her usual insurance claim and was reported to be upset when the insurance carrier offered her a settlement that wasn't as large as she expected. Just a few weeks later, the neighbors watched as she and her two sons loaded up a truck with the contents of their burned home. Amazingly, shortly after that, again in the middle of the night while Virginia was home, the house caught fire again, this time burning completely to the ground. After filing a much larger insurance claim, Virginia and sons fled the state for good to return to California. By 1973, Virginia had been the "victim" of seven structure fires and two deaths within her family, all while she was present. All but one of those events resulted in an insurance settlement for her.

By the 1980s, Virginia and her mother had purchased a home in Palo Alto, California. In the same time frame, Virginia married her third husband, B. J. McGinnis. This was a very odd choice as BJ was known to be homosexual. He also had a fairly lengthy history of criminal involvement in thefts, scams, and con jobs. In 1985, a nighttime fire occurred in Virginia's Palo Alto home. Investigators found a two-gallon gas can at the origin of the blaze. State Farm Insurance offered $85,000 to rebuild the home instead of paying the claim. A week after that fire, a neighbor found all of Virginia's dogs poisoned. That same neighbor reported that Virginia's sons showed up and began emptying the home of its contents. Almost as soon as they finished and had driven off, a second nighttime fire occurred at the home. Again, a can of gas was found in the debris. Investigators called the fire an "incendiary act," but did not investigate it beyond that point. That second fire burned the home to the ground, and State Farm paid Virginia $127,000 for the loss. With the proceeds from that fire, Virginia and her mother bought a home in San Diego.

State Farm investigators would later show that Virginia and BJ soon submitted several insurance claims in the San Diego area. In early 1986, they claimed their home had been damaged in a windstorm and received over $1,100. By October of that year, they claimed a nearly $10,000 loss due to a burglary. During that event, the "burglars" had stolen an old Datsun pickup from the home and had torched it several miles away without removing any items of value. This was highly inconsistent with what car thieves normally do. Two days after that claim, they made an additional $900 claim for a water loss in the home.

While all of that was going on, Virginia's two sons had evolved into fully grown hard-core criminals. Both had become drug addicts and convicted felons several times over. Both received prison time for their roles in homicides. By the 1980s, both had been in and out of California jails and prisons on numerous occasions.

By late 1986, her mother had died (while under Virginia's nursing care), and a life insurance claim was paid out on that death to Virginia.

Virginia's final scam was her most notorious. In 1987, she approached her insurance agent and made an inquiry about purchasing life insurance for her new prospective daughter-in-law, Deanna Wild. The agent thought it an odd request and demanded to see the girl in person. A week later, Virginia showed up with Deanna at the insurance agent's office, and Virginia filled out and paid for a life insurance policy on the girl for $35,000. The beneficiary of the policy was Virginia's son who was in prison at the time of that event. Virginia explained that she had "power of attorney" for her son on all legal and financial matters. Over the next few days, Virginia frequently called the agent, demanding to know when the policy became effective. On April 1, 1987, the agent confirmed to Virginia that the policy was now in effect and that he had received final payment from Virginia. Her last question for him was to ask if the policy paid out double on accidental deaths.

The very next day after the policy became valid, Deanna Wild, while in the company of Virginia Rearden and B. J. McGinnis, "falls" off a four-hundred-foot cliff to her death. Virginia told the Monterey coroner's office that she was unaware if the deceased girl had life insurance (despite Virginia having purchased it the day before). The case was listed as an accident, despite there being some very suspicious circumstances. One week later, Virginia Rearden made a claim for the girl's death. In a letter to her son in prison, she asked about his health, his needs, and as an afterthought mentions that his "fiancé" died in a fall. She then added that the dog was doing okay.

Corporate Attorney Steve Keeney's four-year investigation into that death as a favor to a fellow parishioner dredged up Virginia Rearden's sinister past, and he eventually sued Rearden and McGinnis for wrongful death in civil court. He won the case and received a judgment. As soon as the case was recorded, Virginia "gifted" all her assets to another party to prevent them from being taken. Finally, after years of trying, Keeney convinced the San Diego district attorney to file murder charges against Rearden and McGinnis. They agreed, and the pair was arrested four years after the death.

Even in custody, death seemed to shadow Virginia Rearden. Her third husband, BJ McGinnis, on the eve of his murder trial died in custody due to complications of the AIDS virus. Some acquaintances would later suggest that Virginia had purposely infected him with the virus via a dirty needle a few years earlier. Dick Coates, Virginia's first husband, committed suicide while she was awaiting trial. Finally, the sheriff's deputy who recovered Deanna Wild's body from the base of the cliff at Big Sur also committed suicide in the months surrounding Virginia's trial.

In 1992, a San Diego jury convicted Virginia Rearden on a charge of murder for profit, a special circumstance conviction in the death of twenty-year-old Deanna Wild. The trial judge would later sentence her to life, without the possibility of parole. Within months of her conviction, a Kentucky coroner exhumed and reexamined the body of Virginia's three-year-old daughter who died of an "accidental hanging" in 1972. After weeks of reviewing the case and examining the remains, he changed the cause of death from accident to homicide. Virginia herself also acknowledged that the child's death was a homicide, but denied any involvement, despite the fact that she was present when the death occurred. Still later, an elderly Kentucky jeweler came forward with evidence that she had appraised tens of thousands of dollars worth of jewelry for Virginia Rearden during the 1980s. Those were the years when Virginia was purported to be working as a "practical nurse" for several elderly patients, some of whom died in her care.

Virginia Rearden's final known total was ten suspicious or incendiary fires and five deaths of persons under her care, including her own daughter, husband, mother, and the murder of a future daughter-in-law. At least two of those deaths were classified as murders.

Investigator's Analysis

Two female fire setters/murderers that we have already studied, Belle Gunness and Shirley Winters, have seemingly similar case histories. Both killed their own children and both were involved in numerous fires of their own homes. A deeper analysis will show that both cases are decidedly different. Shirley Winters was probably not the same schemer, plotter, and organized offender that Belle Gunness became. Gunness, at an early age, got a taste for insurance money, and that seemed to be a major factor in all of her fires and murders. She was an unemotional, cold, and heartless killer who used murder and arson as a means to profit. Winters, while no less evil, showed little interest in financial gain for her crimes; she seemed to be seeking some sort of emotional gain.

Bridging the gap between those two murdering arsonists is Virginia Rearden. Her case history is a mixture of evil, greed, cunning, unmitigated gall, and just pure brass balls. Her case is strikingly similar to Belle Gunness in that she posed as a nurse, and the people in her care, including a husband, child, and other parties, died while she was administering medicines to them. Both women were large, masculine figures who appeared to prey on foolish, naive, or otherwise hapless men. Both appeared to use drugs, poison, and fire as tools in their schemes to acquire wealth. Both were able to convince doctors, coroners, and police that the deaths in their care were purely natural events. When each was confronted with allegations of their suspicious activities, both audaciously faced down scrutiny by authorities. Both also developed an unquenchable thirst for insurance money.

This author has investigated hundreds of insurance fraud-related arson events. After studying many of those cases in depth, one can find that in many cases, insurance fraud and arson are both learned behaviors. It is extremely common to find that the person involved in insurance fraud-related arson has one or more prior insurance claims. In fact, I have noted in dozens of insurance fraud arson cases that the "victim" had numerous small insurance events that predated a large structure fire. By studying the insurance claim history of persons involved in that, an investigator can often find insurance claims for wind damage, water loss, vandalism, and burglary/theft. Each of those claims tends to get larger in size and scope, and the "victim" almost always seems to have some sort of convenient alibi story as to where they were during that event.

The overriding motivation for that sort of criminal activity is the monstrously large payouts and settlements that insurance carriers seem to provide with very little investigation. In recent years, a typical fire loss in a suburban home in California easily exceeds $100,000, even for fairly small fires. There is an entire cottage industry surrounding the fire loss field that includes board-up companies, clean-up companies, fire rebuild companies, and public insurance adjusters. I have arrested several members of these types of companies for fraud, theft, and numerous staged arson events. All are motivated by the huge checks and guaranteed income stemming from a fire loss.

There is no doubt that like most of her peers in the serial arson world Virginia Rearden lived a very troubled and abusive childhood. The hardening of her soul was probably the biggest single factor for her later despicable behavior. She learned in her teen years the wondrous "magic" of insurance settlement money.

Predictably, her youth was highlighted by sexual abuse, sexual promiscuity, compulsive theft, and violence. As Virginia grew older, she became more sophisticated and less blatant in her theft schemes and through sheer numbers became very experienced in the ways of insurance fraud. She seemed to choose men she could exploit and use. Her husbands were weak, prone to drugs and alcohol, and were not very intelligent. There is no doubt she attempted to kill her first husband, probably did aid in the death of her second husband, and would likely have done harm to her third husband had she been able to get an insurance policy on him (she tried).

Rearden was a predator on the highest order and was extremely similar in nature to the notorious Belle Gunness and Nurse Jane Toppan. She sought out and victimized the feeble, sick, weakest, and dumbest persons she could find. She isolated her victims from others and carried out her schemes with very few witnesses.

Virginia Rearden is an organized arson offender whose crimes were well planned, thought out, and carried out in the dead of night. She was able to manipulate crime scenes before and after an event and had the nerve to face down any inquisitors. She was also savvy enough to obfuscate issues by frequently changing her name and often moving from the area immediately following a major event. To Rearden, arson was just a tool with which to commit massive fraud. She is also unique in that she seemed to revel in the fact that people knew what she did, but just couldn't or wouldn't do anything about it. In many cases, she bragged about or threw her crimes into the faces of her victims or their families.

The majority of the information about this monster comes from an excellent book about the case written by David Heilbroner, called *Death Benefit*. Heilbroner describes attorney Steve Keeney's monumental inquiry into the life of Virginia Rearden. Despite the research of that highly skilled attorney and several police and insurance investigators, there are several large blocks of years within Rearden's life that are unaccounted for. Based on her overall lifestyle and method of operation, there is little doubt in this author's mind that there are likely several additional arsons and probably some unknown poisoning deaths that can be attributed to Virginia Rearden. However, Keeney's work is still laudable, and this author, a working law enforcement detective, is compelled to tip my hat to an attorney (cringe) for outstanding work.

Jane Toppan: Serial Murderer/Serial Poisoner/Serial Arsonist
Period of Activity: 1880-1900, Massachusetts

In 1863, a widower showed up at the Boston Female Asylum with his two young daughters in tow. The father, a downtrodden Irish immigrant and drunkard named Peter Kelley, begged the asylum to take custody of his daughters as he was unable to care for them any longer. The asylum had been in existence for over fifty years caring for and educating female orphans and young women with severe mental health and family problems. The main purpose of the asylum was to give the girls a meager education and moral upbringing and to prepare them for a life as domestic servants. The girls were routinely "sold" as indentured servants to wealthy Boston families upon reaching the age of twelve.

The entry records for the sisters noted that both appeared to have been raised in extremely miserable circumstances, even by 1863 standards. Brought to the asylum that day was eight-year-old Delia Kelley. Her four-year stay at the asylum did not achieve the desired results as she lived a wretched life as first an indentured servant and then spent the remainder of her days as a drunk and a prostitute before dying at a young age in a filthy slum.

Delia's six-year-old sister, Honora led a much more colorful, if not notorious, life. She stayed but two years at the asylum and was then "bonded" over to a Boston family at the age of eight. With them, she changed her first name to something less ethnic and adopted the family's surname. She would become infamous in her day as Jane Toppan.

Jane Toppan lived with the Toppans for the next twenty-two years. A social outcast in the White Anglo-Saxon Protestant world of upper crust New England, she was constantly reminded of her lowly Irish "Paddy" heritage. She grew up taking great pains to hide her heritage and was known to openly voice hate and disdain toward the Irish Catholic throngs that would be arriving in Boston on a near daily basis. Because she was of Irish descent, she was never formally adopted by the Toppan family like so many other young girls in her position. There is little doubt that she grew up bitter and full of revenge toward society in general for her life's circumstances.

Jane grew up alongside the Toppan family's daughter Elizabeth who had everything Jane craved: money, prestige, beauty, and many interested suitors. Jane was known to be extremely jealous of her "sister" Elizabeth as she (Jane) had never garnered much interest from men. By her early twenties, Jane had expanded in weight to a very plump 170 pounds. However, she was known as a very outgoing girl, who got into a lot of minor trouble at school, who was a very accomplished storyteller, and who seemed to be able to mix quite well with people. Later, her friends would report that her many stories were in fact obvious lies that Jane told to try and impress people about her life. Everyone remarked that she was a very skilled liar.

In her mid-twenties, Jane's "adopted mother" died, and to Jane's dismay, she left her entire wealthy estate to her own natural daughter Elizabeth. Jane was bitter that not only had she never been adopted, but she had also been left exactly nothing in the will. After working briefly as a housekeeper for her "sister," Jane decided to leave and embark on a new career. In 1887, at the age of thirty, she chose one of the few careers available to women of the day—nursing.

The Victorian era of nursing in the 1880s was as close to military training as possible. Trainees were on strict schedules with grueling work routines and lengthy fourteen-hour days, seven days a week, with only two weeks off each year. They were treated as "boots" in any military camp, and along with handling workloads of fifty patients, they were also required to study, prepare meals, clean and scrub their wards, wash laundry, and stoke the furnace. They had strict moral codes and were rewarded for their efforts with a crisp uniform and cap along with a meager paycheck as their prize for the two years of exhausting training. By all accounts, Jane was extremely popular with her superiors and patients, who referred to her as "Jolly Jane." This was due to both her gregarious manner and her ever-expanding girth.

Conversely, Jane was not at all popular with her peers. She was known as a malicious gossip whose stories frequently got other women in trouble. She seemed gleeful when her false rumors actually got at least two student nurses fired. She was known as a pathological liar whose stories got more fanciful by the day. Of a more sinister nature, she was also suspected by many of being a habitual thief who skillfully stole all manner of items and monies and was extremely clever in her abilities. All those who suspected her were amazed at the very skilled level at which she was able to conceal her activities. Throughout her career as a nurse, she was described by many persons as "cunning and manipulative."

The first hint that something was seriously wrong with Jane came when it was learned that she had taken steps to prolong the hospital stays of some of her patients. Jane was very popular with some patients, and she in turn was fond of many of them. Because of that, she began to lie on their medical records to deceive doctors into keeping them longer, or even at some point, she began to administer excessive medications in order to worsen their condition somewhat so they would not be discharged. Jane was also open in her views toward the elderly patients in her care. She was heard at least once making statements that she wished some of the elderly died. Indeed, during her training years an inordinate number of elderly patients seemed to die under her care. Later, during her famous confessions, Jane Toppan admitted killing several people during that time period, but even she was unsure of the number. She later stated that it was at least a dozen.

Jane was also an extremely interested student in medicines and poisons. She was known to study those areas more than any other, and the notes in her medical books reflected her obsession with that subject matter. In those days, the use of certain poisons in medical treatment was commonplace. Jane was also fascinated with opiates. In later years, Nurse Jane Toppan would admit to beginning her secret medical experiments on patients with various opiates and poisons.

Jane Toppan would, years later, confess to the most unbelievable of crimes with her patients. She admitted that she would experiment with helpless patients and inject them with morphine. Sometimes she would cause them to die, other times she would take steps just prior to death to "save" them. She did that so often that she became somewhat of an expert on the symptoms of the narcotic. She then began similar experiments with another drug called atropine. This drug caused near opposite reactions to what morphine caused. After she became skilled in its symptoms, Jane learned that she could fool many doctors by administering various combinations of the two drugs, which would then give very confused sets of symptoms in the patients. She later shockingly admitted that she became obsessed with that sort of power, and it actually became somewhat of a sexual thrill for her to play with life and death like that.

Jane said she also took "voluptuous delight" and "delirious enjoyment" at the idea of "saving" her patients from her own experiments. She took many patients to the edge of death by administering drugs and then tested her medical skills by bringing them back to health. In this manner, she confessed, it gave her a great deal of satisfaction and notoriety with the other staff.

Like a true organized offender, Jane was so sophisticated that she was able to hide her evil side from everyone. When she finished her nursing training at Cambridge Hospital, she sought employment at the very prestigious Massachusetts General Hospital. She received glowing recommendations from her former superiors and was hired despite the dislike and overt bigotry of her new head nurse, who was not fond of the lowly Irish. She was so proficient in her duties that she not only quickly passed her probationary period, she was actually assigned to fill in for the head nurse when she was away. Soon, as before, she alienated most of her peers and was known as a self-promoting liar. She was accused of fabricating charts, tampering with medical records, and was named in an ongoing pattern of thefts. None of them realized, of course, that she was continuing her depraved medical experiments on her patients. In later years, investigators would try without success to determine how many patients died at her hands at that facility.

One startling story from a survivor of that era did emerge years later. After Jane was exposed and an intense investigation had begun, a Mrs. Amelia Phinney came forward and offered an amazing tale. Phinney had been a patient in the Massachusetts General Hospital because of a severe stomach ailment. She awoke late one night to find jovial Nurse Toppan leaning over her and staring intently into her eyes. Nurse Toppan then gave her a strange, bitter drink that almost immediately caused her entire body to become numb. Then Mrs. Phinney, while unable to move, was shocked to feel Nurse Toppan climb into bed with her and begin to caress, kiss, and fondle all over her. Several times the nurse stopped to peer deeply into Mrs. Phinney's eyes. Finally, Nurse Toppan tried to give Mrs. Phinney some more of the bitter liquid, but Mrs. Phinney was able to resist long enough for someone else to come to the ward. Nurse Toppan quickly hopped off the bed and fled the room before another nurse could arrive. The next morning, Mrs. Phinney was unsure if that had been a hallucination or a real event. She kept it to herself for several years.

Because she was not a popular person among her peers, Jane Toppan made a grave mistake in her formal nursing career. Within days of her final certification and licensing, she uncharacteristically left her patients alone one night. Other nurses quickly reported her, and the hospital staff used that as an excuse to fire the odd nurse just days short of being licensed. A doctor on staff would state later that he always was suspicious of Jane's behavior with her patients and used that event as an excuse to prevent her from obtaining her professional nursing license. Years later, investigators would estimate that at least two dozen persons died under her care at that hospital.

Hardly deterred, Jane immediately embarked on a more lucrative career as a full-time private nurse. From 1892 to 1900, she was one of the more highly regarded and successful private nurses in the Boston area. A long line of reputable physicians kept recommending her to all of the best families in the area. Her reputation as a nurse not withstanding, she also continued to be known for her quirks. Her lies and stories became even more unbelievable. Most people attributed that to her Celtic roots as the Irish were always known as wild storytellers. She was also a constant suspect in many minor thefts from her employers. One egregious act was of note when she was suspected in the theft of a diamond ring from one of her deceased patients.

Jane also continued her dislike of elderly people. In 1895, she poisoned her seventy-year-old landlord, Mr. Israel Dunham. Two years later, she poisoned his wife. The deaths of these two people seemed to propel her into high gear. In 1899, she was hired as a nurse for the elderly Mrs. Mary McNear, who was nursing a cold. One day after being hired, she reported to McNear's family doctor that the old lady was dying of severe stomach problems. Immediately after the funeral, the family noticed that many of the deceased women's clothes were missing. They immediately suspected the new nurse, but the doctor who had recommended her adamantly vouched for her reputation as one of the finest nurses in the area.

In 1899, while in the midst of her successful private nursing career, Jane decided to settle some old very personal grudges. She invited her "foster sister" Elizabeth, with whom she had remained in contact, to stay at a summer cottage in Cape Cod. The pair enjoyed a picnic, but by the next morning, the otherwise healthy Elizabeth became deathly ill. By the time her husband arrived to assist her, she was in a deep coma and died shortly thereafter. Upon her death, her husband found a good deal of cash missing from her purse. Jane gave no explanation for the cash, but was quick to tell the husband that it had been Elizabeth's dying wish for her, Jane, to keep her expensive gold necklace. It was later learned that Jane had pawned the jewelry for cash almost immediately. Years later, Jane would give explicit detail of that event during her written confessions. She described that she had hated Elizabeth for years and had been planning revenge for over a decade. She wanted Elizabeth to suffer more than any of her other patients, so she watered the poison down a bit to make the suffering all the more intense. While Elizabeth lay in her death bed in utter agony, Jane took the sadistically perverse pleasure of climbing into bed with her and hugging her so she could feel the agony and the life leaving Elizabeth's body.

A year later, Jane did the exact same thing to another long-time friend. She had been jealous of another nurse named Myra Conners, who had a job in a large school. Jane had long coveted that esteemed job, despite the fact that Myra was one of her few friends. In February 1900, Jane, upon learning of a recent illness to Myra, showed up to offer her services as a nurse. Four days after taking the job, Jane was on hand when Myra died of completely different symptoms from what was noted in her original illness. She had died in such agony that it had displaced her limbs. The doctor at the time was baffled by the change and noted that the death bore the resemblance of strychnine poisoning. However, he did not seriously consider that foul play had been a factor. Jane soon went to her friend's work and was shortly awarded her job. That was the one career where she did not do well, and within a few short months, she was fired for incompetence and suspected theft.

In the summer of 1901, an extraordinary and ironic event occurred. Leading up to that, Jane had been living with her new landlords in Cambridge. In the previous months, she had poisoned both of them and their housekeeper, but she had only used enough morphia to make them miserable and to control them. She graciously allowed the three to live, blissfully unaware that she controlled their very lives. At that time, Jane was visited by the owner of her beach cottage, Mrs. Mattie Davis, who came to collect a substantial debt that Jane owed on the cottage. Jane almost immediately poisoned her to prevent paying the debt. As Jane was sitting with the severely ill woman, a local doctor was summoned. That poor man would later represent the ultimate in irony.

Dr. John Nichols had gained a large amount of infamy about fifteen years earlier when he had misdiagnosed a stomach ailment in a patient. In fact, that patient had been poisoned by the last female serial killer to plague the New England area, a home nurse named Sarah Jane Robinson. Dr. Nichol's misdiagnosis would be exposed years later, but only after Sarah Jane Robinson had murdered a dozen of her patients, including three of her own husbands and ten of her own or adopted children. Robinson was later convicted of the murders by poison (arsenic) and sentenced to death. Dr. Nichols swore at her trial never to be fooled again.

Sadly, the hapless Dr. Nichols would remain forever impossibly linked to two rare, but nearly identical female serial murderers. As had occurred fifteen years earlier, Dr. Nichols was fooled again by a sinister, poison-wielding nurse. Sensing that she was much more clever than the doctor, Nurse Toppan began a seven-day torture of the patient and her family completely under the nose of Dr. Nichols. She would later admit to injecting varying drugs to alternately taking the patient close to death and then bringing her back to a seeming recovery. This alternated back and forth to the point that the family was in utter anguish. Finally, Jane Toppan allowed that woman to die of a fatal dose of morphine. It was later believed that she sadistically dragged out that death to punish Mattie Davis and her family for daring to demand from Jane their back rent on the summer cottage. Apparently not satisfied with that one death, Jane attended the woman's funeral, and according to her later confession, while there she planned to wipe out the entire Davis family because they had offended her.

The story of Jane Toppan is documented in the book *Fatal: The Poisonous Life of a Female Serial Killer* by Harold Schechter. In the midst of describing her murderous exploits, Schechter spends an entire chapter on her fire setting behavior. In his book, he calls serial fire setting by her and other noted serial killers like David Berkowitz and Ottis Toole *pyromania*. Schechter states that it is likely that Toppan had been engaged in pyromaniac activities for as long as she had been killing patients and perhaps back in her miserable childhood. This author would agree with that statement, but of course does not agree with the term *pyromania*. Based on her deliberate and well-planned murders and the fact that she was able to get away with them for so many years, it is likely that Jane Toppan was involved in just as many fires earlier in life. Sadly for us in the fire investigation field, the murder cases against that woman were so outrageous that nobody did more than a perfunctory inquiry into her serial fire setting behavior.

What is recorded in history is that Jane Toppan was at the scene of several fires within her victim's home. After murdering Mattie Davis (the owner of her beach cottage), she was offered a job to stay with the Davis family and care for them in that hour of crisis following their matriarch's death. Apparently, the valiant (staged) efforts that Jane showed when trying to "save" Mattie convinced the family that she was a godsend. In the summer of 1901, Jane Toppan moved into the Davis family mansion in Cape Cod.

Jane would later admit that within days of arriving, she waited one night for the entire family to fall asleep. She then started a fire inside a closet in the parlor with some available paper. She giddily ran to her room to wait for the fire to spread, hoping the entire house would burn down and kill the family. The father, who couldn't sleep, smelled the smoke and immediately extinguished the flames. Jane, to avoid suspicion, rushed to his side and assisted in putting out the fire.

A few days later, Jane lit a fire in the pantry and then walked casually to a neighbor to establish an alibi. The neighbor soon noticed the smoke, and the two rushed back to the Davis house and put out the fire before serious damage or injury could occur. One week later, Jane set another fire in the home, which was extinguished by the father. As she had learned to do so many times before when engaged in theft or murder, she quickly deflected suspicion from herself and reported a "suspicious man" whom she had seen lurking about the area. The local village soon broke into hysteria about the "firebug" despite the fact that he only seemed to be attacking one home.

Before any serious inquiry could be made into the mysterious firebug, the small beach town was soon preoccupied with a wave of tragic events. First, the youngest daughter of the Davis family, thirty-one-year-old Genevieve, while deep in mourning for her dear departed mother, suddenly and violently took ill. Jane would later recall that she had to do a bit of planning and staging to pull off that murder, as the victim was in excellent health. One day, Jane pulled the eldest sister aside and told her that she believed that Genevieve was so distraught that she might be planning to kill herself with poison. Jane told the elder sister that she had seen Genevieve reading the label on some arsenic-based insecticide. Despite the warning, Genevieve grew violently ill two days later and died. A syringe of poison was found near her body. Jane later admitted to injecting the poison into the woman and then planting the syringe at the bedside to stage the event as a suicide.

Two days later, Jane was again attending the funeral of one more Davis family member and gleefully planning the murder of the next one. She didn't wait long. Two weeks after the funeral, she poisoned Alden Davis, the elderly head of the family. His death was ruled a cerebral hemorrhage, brought on by the stress of losing two family members. Jane's tempo was increasing, and she only waited four days to murder the final sister. Deviating from her occasional bizarre routine of climbing into the bed with a dying victim, Jane took that sadism to the highest level, and while the woman was in her final agonizing death throes, Jane would later relate that she climbed into the bed of the ten-year-old son of the victim and hugged and fondled him while his mother died nearby. Amazingly, Jane Toppan was able to skillfully pull off those poisonings while her victims were directly under the care of a doctor. She admitted that she used three different means to administer the poison: by injection, dissolved into a liquid form, and taken orally, or if a doctor was really suspicious, she came in late at night and administered the poisons via enema.

In a five-week span, Jane Toppan was able to start three arson fires and commit four poisoning murders within the same small family group, in a small, close-knit town, while never once being considered a suspect. In fact, as a token of gratitude for her valiant efforts in attempting to save the victims, she was given a hearty recommendation by the doctors and was presented with a gold coin by some relatives. Nobody cast her so much as a suspicious glance as she left town immediately following the final murder. Well, actually, a rich and powerful family relative began to suspect that something was not right.

Shifting into high gear, Jane rushed back to Cambridge where she had some unfinished old business. She had long wanted to marry her former "sister" Elizabeth's widowed husband, Oramel. When she got to his home, she saw that two other women were in her way. Oramel had a sister living with him and a female housekeeper. Two days after Jane arrived she poisoned the sister, who died the next day. She also poisoned the housekeeper. After those events, she tried to coax Oramel into marrying her or at least letting her live there as his nurse. He refused and ordered Jane out of his home. Within hours, he fell violently ill, and Jane stayed for several days to nurse him back to health. Little did Oramel realize that Jane had poisoned him. However, as soon as he was well, he kicked her out of his home. This rejection caused Jane to attempt suicide by poison twice in a week. Oddly, she was unable to kill herself despite being so proficient at the art of poisoning.

Jane left town and moved in with another couple. She later admitted that she soon began planning their murder. What she didn't know was that as soon as she had left the scene of the Davis family massacre, a group of well-to-do men (not doctors) began to believe that something evil had happened. They applied pressure on the local district attorney to open an inquiry. The district attorney began building a case and soon focused on Jane Toppan. He assigned a detective to watch her full time. The DA also got court orders to exhume the Davis family. The disinterred bodies all revealed the effects of poisoning. Two more of Jane's patients were dragged from their graves for examination, and that too produced similar results.

On October 29, detectives formally arrested Jane Toppan for the Davis family murders. To their surprise, she was not at all upset, but only complained about their rude manners.

While her arrest was overshadowed by the assassination of President McKinley by an anarchist in nearby Buffalo, New York, the trial of Nurse Jane Toppan was decidedly the second-most talked about event in New England. Every manner of pseudo expert and medical quack came forth with his opinion on that woman. The most agreed upon theory was that no sane person, let alone a woman, was capable of such heinous deeds. The fact that she was a professional nurse made the case all that more unbelievable. She was judged by the public as either insane or addicted to opiates. In that era, opiates were commonly purchased over the counter and were used to treat all manner of symptoms from pain to depression. They were thought to be quite safe, although a few people had become addicted to them. It was a not so well-kept secret that many medical professionals of the era, both doctors and nurses, were addicted to morphine or other opiates.

The question of her sanity received much attention. It was revealed at that time that her birth father had been known as "Kelley the crack" and was believed to have been fully insane at the time of his death. An elder natural sister had been in a mental institution her entire life and had died in an insane asylum. A few childhood friends revealed that Jane had indulged in erratic behavior most of her life and many believed her to be a lunatic.

During the ongoing police investigation, it was revealed that a possible motive for many of those poison murders was financial gain. Searches revealed a startling amount of jewelry, pawn tickets, clothing, and other items in the possession of Jane that had belonged to many of her victims. In each case, she assured investigators that those had been gifts or payment for her nursing duties. Other testimonies came up at the trial from grieving relatives that, following the deaths of their family members, certain sums of cash seemed to have gone missing. That included a $500 payment that Jane had made to the Davis family to settle her debt with them. It was last seen in the possession of the patriarch, Alden Davis, hours before he died in the care of Jane Toppan. Another witness revealed that the day before her death, Genevieve was asked by Jane to sign a paper forgiving Jane of her debts to the family. Genevieve died just hours after she refused to sign the document.

Jane's thieving history caught up with her at that time when past employers and peers provided testimony that she was a habitual thief and that she was known to be inappropriately interested in the private lives and financial affairs of many of her patients. She had been lectured on those issues by many past doctors and supervisors.

As the investigators delved further backward into Jane's previous patients, there turned up more suspicious deaths. Soon they found another suspicious fire. Jane had been the only person in the home of a patient in 1898 when a fire broke out.

The prosecution was dealt a setback during their investigation when they found that their original theory of arsenic poisoning was not holding up. There was no record of Jane ever having purchased arsenic. Some experts deemed her too clever to use such an obvious drug since it was easily identifiable by treating physicians. The autopsies were skewed because arsenic was used during the embalming process. However, at some point, a lay person, not a doctor, came up with the theory that Jane probably used a form of morphine or atropine to conduct her poisonings. Indeed there were witnesses that would testify that Jane had ordered and purchased those drugs on occasion. In December 1901, a grand jury, citing the probable use of morphine and atropine, released an indictment against Jane Toppan for the Davis family murders. She pled not guilty to all the charges.

A panel of psychiatrists soon found that Jane Toppan was insane. The prosecution then brought an additional panel of three noted psychiatrists to examine Jane at the jail. After initial denials, Jane soon began calmly admitting to a life of "pyromania and murder." The stunned psychiatrists heard Jane admit to four arsons and eleven murders of close friends. She never showed signs of remorse and seemed to take pleasure in describing the last agonizing moments of her victim's lives. She shocked the doctors when she told them that being with a dying person was sexually stimulating to her. She then described her bizarre ritual of climbing into bed with her dying patients and kissing and fondling them while they died. She said she was quite sane but didn't understand why she felt no remorse from the incidents. She also said she took great pleasure in fooling all of the doctors who had attended the victims. Jane Toppan told the panel that she could have gone on killing patients for years as she knew she had already fooled some of the best medical doctors in New England. She acknowledged that her mistake was to kill so many family members in such a short time period (the Davis family). The court soon took the advice of the panel and ruled that Jane was not guilty by reason of insanity. She was sentenced to a full life term in a "lunatic asylum."

Immediately after her sentencing and transfer to the asylum, the real bombshell dropped. Jane's attorney revealed that she had admitted to a total of thirty-one poison murders to him. She also admitted to a lifetime of fire setting and other poisonings that did not result in death. At a later date, she gave the names of some but not all of her poison victims. While she was in the asylum, the Hearst newspapers printed her full, lengthy confessions and attributed her death total to near hundred persons. There seems to be little factual basis in that high number. In that printing, Jane further admitted that there had been many more murders by poison of some of her earlier hospital patients, but she could not recall their names.

Jane Toppan entered The State Lunatic Hospital at Taunton in 1902. She believed that she would get released in just a few years. This was not to be as she ended up dying in the asylum in 1938 at the age of eighty-one.

Investigator's Analysis

In 2010, this author as part of his investigative duties met Beatrice Yorker, a Dean at California State University, Los Angeles. She was presenting a talk on her extensive research into the subject of health care professionals (nurses, generally) who are serial murderers of their patients. At some point, we talked and realized that more than a few of the subjects in her studies also show a history of fire setting behavior. Again, a history of fire setting behavior in any serial murderer is not uncommon. The case of Nurse Jane Toppan is probably the best example of this link between serial fire setting and health care providers who murder their patients. Dean Yorker found the parallels of nurse/murderers and firefighter/arsonists to be quite significant. This author, after briefly examining the phenomenon of nurse/murders, concurs wholeheartedly.

Jane Toppan, in her day, was considered the most deadly person ever in America. What made her case so unique and newsworthy in her era is that her crimes of depravity and cunning are something that the American public only attributed to men up to that point. The detectives, court, and esteemed medical and psychiatric experts involved in her case had an extremely difficult time dealing with the fact that those heinous acts were perpetrated by not only a benign appearing woman, but in fact a highly regarded nurse or "Angel of Mercy." In review of that case, there is only one other case in this book that even compares in shocking the conscience, that of esteemed arson investigator/ serial arsonist John Orr.

The comparisons of the two offenders are highly interesting. Both were well regarded as efficient and professional in their chosen fields. Both were very well respected by the public and their supervisors, but treated with suspicion by their peers. Both developed massive egos and had the audacity to pull of their most daring crimes directly under the noses of other trained professionals. Toppan conducted all of her poisonings with patients directly under the care of a doctor. John Orr pulled off dozens of fires while conducting surveillances with other arson investigators. Both seemed to revel in bedeviling the best minds in their respective fields. Indeed, both studied their weapons (poison and fire) quite in depth and were probably more versed in them than any other persons around. Both pulled off extremely sophisticated crimes with detailed planning, cunning, and preassembled devices or concoctions. Both were involved in heavy staging of crime scenes, and both were involved in the initial investigations of the events and were able to throw "red herrings" into the scenes to skew the investigation. Both painted themselves as "heroes" on dozens of occasions as they seemed to save people and solve arsons that other peers simply weren't able to do. Both were highly manipulative, unapologetic, and had never expressed one ounce of remorse for their actions. Both seemed to thrive on the events and seemed to speed up their tempo of activity as time went on. Both will go down in history as the single most notorious people in their respective fields. Both are considered to be highly organized serial offenders.

In the realm of serial fire setting, the known history of Jane Toppan is not nearly as impressive as others. However, many profilers recognize a distinct link between some types of serial arsonists and poisoners. It can reasonably be concluded that prior to her knowledge of poisons at the age of thirty, Jane Toppan no doubt used the weapon of fire on a routine basis. She readily admits to a life of "pyromania," but no one in her day seemed interested in that subject, so there are no quantifications to use here.

The four fires that are detailed in the only known book about Jane Toppan are not at all different from other female fire setters. The fires were set in the home or work area, which is the hallmark of female fire setting. While she used poisons that were obtained and prepared ahead of time, the fires appeared to be set at times of her choosing with very little preparation. It is interesting to note that she was clever enough to appear to be helping to put out her fires in an effort to throw suspicion off her. She also planted a "red herring" by casting blame on a "suspicious person" in the area.

Jane is also very similar in nature to David Berkowitz in that she routinely pulled off many small crimes under people's noses while always carrying on with a very sunny nature. She had a lifetime of thefts which is also consistent with other serial arson offenders.

Jane's motives appear to have been mixed or at least evolving. Her fires appear to be motivated by a need to seek revenge against the Davis family and were attempts at murdering an entire family. Her other crimes are a mixture of excitement-based events, recognition or hero events, monetary gain events, and revenge-motivated events. She does have an admitted degree of sexual stimulation within her crimes, but her main thrill seems to be from the power she derived from controlling life and death and from manipulating and fooling other medical professionals.

Jane was never married but confided that she did have a male lover who jilted her at a young age. She demonstrated sexual behavior toward both male and female victims, and Schechter's book describes her in an illicit sexual relationship with another female inmate at her asylum.

Jane Toppan is one of the few organized offenders on this list. Her fire setting activity was not documented well, so we can only speculate on it at this point. However, her skill, planning, and cunning involved in her poison murders were extraordinary, and she can be considered among the most dangerous offenders in this book. She is a serial murderer who also engaged in serial arson.

Sarah Wheaton: Serial Brushfire Arsonist
Period of Activity: 1993-(?), Coastal California

In 1993, a nineteen-year-old female college freshman was forced into a secure mental health treatment facility in California. The reason cited was that she was a suspect in five minor arson events on her college campus. None of those fires succeeded in creating significant damage, nor did any persons get hurt. At some point, her roommates and the college authorities recognized that bizarre and dangerous behavior and summoned the police. The police, as they handle many similar cases, assumed the woman was having a mental health breakdown and arrested her under the 5150 section of the Welfare and Institutions Code. That "arrest" seldom goes into a criminal record and is more often recorded as a "mental health hold" or detention for a seventy-two-hour period. Persons brought to psychiatric care facilities under this code are held for a minimum of three days and can be extended for up to fourteen days if they are deemed a danger to themselves or to others. Under California law, most if not all are released after the fourteen-day confinement, with little or no mandated psychological follow-up treatment.

That woman, later identified under her pseudonym "Sarah Wheaton," was brought in for a seventy-two-hour hold and soon escaped from her confinement. She was shortly rearrested by police and brought back to the facility where she made a weak attempt at suicide by cutting herself with plastic and glass. She was deemed a danger to herself, and her stay was extended for the full fourteen-day period.

The hospital compiled a brief background on the patient. She was a very bright college student who maintained a full class schedule and held full-time employment at a pizza shop. She had a past history with the police for calling them and threatening suicide. The staff noted that she was highly unpredictable with wild swings in her behavior. She was bright, charming, and endearing in one instant and then self-destructive in the next.

She reported that her mother was an alcoholic and bipolar and that her father and she had attended family therapy together. She was the victim of sexual abuse at the hands of an elder stepbrother for a two-year period starting when she was nine years old. Her counselors noted that after a few days she started to calm down and talk about herself. She tended to run from issues, to try and help others and not herself, and to not look at her own problems. She was released from that hospital with no further treatment.

In 2001, Sarah Wheaton (pseudonym) penned a case history of herself in support of her master's thesis in psychology. That case history was published in the journal *Psychiatric Services*. In that writing, she described in detail her past eight years of compulsive fire setting behavior. The writing omitted the locations, dates, and other details that could identify the criminal act, but gave a fantastic if clinical account of the arsonist's thoughts and feelings surrounding the fire event and fire in general.

Sarah described that she anxiously anticipated the "fire season" as it is known on the West Coast, when the days are hot and dry and the winds began to rise. That time of year usually starts in late July and extends deep into October in California. She set all her fires by herself and took measures to ensure that she was not followed. She said she never planned her fires, but routinely scouted the area for a time period before the event.

Sarah wrote that the fire event was preceded by feelings of loneliness, neglect, or even boredom, which then manifested itself into anxiety and emotional arousal. She then felt physiological changes, including severe headaches, rapid heartbeat, uncontrollable movements, and tingling in the arms.

When she entered a target area, she ensured that it was secluded and that she had identified potential escape routes. She moved via vehicle or foot and watched or drove through the area for a significant period of time before the event.

Sarah took steps not to leave a pattern or use any sort of signature. She acquired her ignition materials at convenience stores and gas stations and used matches, cigarettes, and small amounts of gasoline. She never set fires in the same spot twice and favored secluded target areas, including roadsides, canyons, cul-de-sacs, and parking lots. Surprisingly, she claimed she set many of her fires after nightfall to avoid detection. She said she forced herself to drive slowly and normally when she left an area to avoid suspicion and had often passed responding fire engines. She also stated that she liked to watch the fire scene from a distant vantage point so that she could enjoy the excitement and observe firefighting operations. At the time of the event, she would often call authorities on the phone to report the fire or monitor the radio.

Depending on her mood, Sarah lit several small fires in a spree or one large fire. She claimed that the moment of ignition was when she experienced a tension release or emotional response that could include excitement or even panic.

After the fire was out, Sarah described feelings of sadness and anguish, along with a desire to set another fire. She usually revisited the fire scene within twenty-four hours, and her feelings vacillated between remorse, anger, and rage at herself.

Sarah stated that she enjoyed following her fires in the media, particularly the fire investigation. She read the papers and followed the news to learn of the investigator's speculation about the origin, cause, motive, etc. She was fascinated by the notoriety of the unknown fire setter and loved to see depictions of the damage on television or on a map.

Outside of her own fires, Sarah described herself as having an inordinate fascination with arson in general. She voraciously read literature about arsons, arsonists, pyromania, and everything related to suspicious fires and fire setting. She said she actively studied arson investigation techniques and detection methods and had frequently contacted agencies involved in arson investigation. She watched movies, read books, and listened to music associated with fires and arson. She said she dreamed about fires on a routine basis.

Not surprisingly, Sarah Wheaton made the assertion that she was glad that her fires had never harmed any persons.

Among her other related behaviors, she claimed a past history of threatened or attempted suicides, making phony 9-1-1 calls to fraudulently report fires, calling to confess to fires she had not set, and pulling fire alarms.

Sarah claimed she visited fire scenes on the anniversary of the event, including fires that other persons had set. She also had a fascination about other arsonists and would follow jealously the exploits of another arsonist in her area. She said that she enjoyed the excitement of other person's fires, but it usually fueled her to compete with that subject by setting larger fires. She also expressed an interest in that other person's motives and reasons for lighting his fires.

In Sarah's writing, she admitted that recidivism rates for arsonists were extremely high, and they needed continuous support to avoid the need for setting a fire. She said that fire setting could be such a big part of the arsonist's life that they simply could not give it up.

What was implied in that writing was that Sarah Wheaton was undergoing continuing counseling for her fire setting behavior. She listed her latest prognosis (as of 2001) by her psychiatrist as "very guarded given the severity of her condition."

Her diagnosis was listed as "major depressive disorder, . . . with psychosis . . . obsessive compulsive personality disorder, history of pyromania; borderline personality disorder." It also noted that she had had thirty-three hospitalizations after her initial seventy-two-hour evaluation.

In her final paragraph in 2001, Sarah Wheaton stated that she was undergoing a new drug treatment with favorable results and had been fire free for eight months.

Investigator Analysis

This is one of the cases where we as investigators are forced to take the information at face value. The name "Sarah Wheaton" is an alias contrived by the writer to cover up his/her identity. This may have been done to conceal criminal activity or, to be skeptical like all investigators strive to be, it may have been done to create a person who really didn't exist. For the purpose of this book, this author will assume that "Sarah Wheaton" does exist in the context presented.

Given that, Sarah is a fascinating study. Her background and writing show that she is educated and bright. She is also completely consumed in her thoughts and work by fires, fire investigations, and arsonists. There is no doubt that this woman has been a regular visitor to fire houses or to fire scenes, and if enough California arson investigators read her story, someone will be able to figure out her real name, as she will undoubtedly be known in investigation circles.

She pointed out some things that this author has noticed in his very few cases involving women serial fire setters. All report some form of sexual abuse as a child, all at the hands of an older male relative. All report heavy use of prescription medications, usually related to moods, depression, or anxiety. To be fair, most of the male serial arsonists this writer has encountered also report the heavy use of prescription medications. Like some of her male counterparts, Sarah reported physiological symptoms related to fire setting activity, including headaches and tingling of extremities. This information also matches several persons in this author's case files and some of the persons cited in this book. For example, George Peter Lee (Hull, England, serial arsonist/murderer) reported tingling in his arms and fingers just prior to fire setting.

The most important physiological impact that Sarah reported was a general feeling of release at the time she actually started the fire. This is by far the most common reaction that I have noted among serial fire setters. Most have reported a general buildup of pressure and excitement leading up to the actual ignition event and then an immediate dump or release of pressure just after the flame is lit. This is followed by a general euphoria, increased excitement, and then eventually a depression and guilt of some sort. Many investigators will note that these symptoms are almost identical to those experienced during illicit sexual activity and during illegal narcotics use. Indeed, fire setting as described by Sarah seemed to be her addiction.

Of particular note in the analysis of Sarah's writing is her assertion that no one had ever been injured during any of her fires. This is a very consistent theme with serial fire setters as they tend to disassociate massive damage and injuries or death from the small fires they initially set. If we are to believe Sarah in that she set many fires in brush or wild land areas during the California fire season, then you would have to expect that many of those small fires grew into massive blazes due to the terrain, dry fuels, and strong winds. In most of those fires, traumatic losses in property, livestock, and pets are frequently reported. Injuries to firefighters and civilians and deaths to the elderly due to shock, stress, or heart attack are frequent outcomes in many wild land fires. For Sarah to maintain that her fires never injured anyone is bordering on the absurd, but is in keeping with similar claims by narcissistic arsonists.

On the investigative side of the equation, there is little wonder why Sarah has presumably never been arrested or connected to those fires. Finding a serial arsonist is difficult enough, but very few fire investigators would even contemplate looking at a female offender. The fact that she took great care in target selection, "staked out" target areas before starting the fire in order to plan escape routes and avoid detection, used a vehicle, and took great pains not to leave a "signature" made this woman a tremendously elusive subject for investigators. The only acts she did that could bring her to the attention of investigators were the high-risk acts of reporting the fires or making calls to falsely report fires. In the modern era, a motivated investigator would be able to track and trace cell phone calls. Another factor which increased her exposure to getting caught was her inordinate interest in the fire service. There is little doubt that someone in the fire service has found this woman to be odd or suspicious at some time in the past.

If Sarah Wheaton is indeed real and her exploits are factual, then this author believes her to be a truly unique individual who probably lit hundreds of arson fires in her life. Further, this author believes that Sarah undoubtedly has continued to set fires since 2001, particularly during times of stress or trauma in her life. A search for the identity of this woman would be a very interesting prospect. She is most likely white, single, and there is a history or fires around her home, schools, and job sites. She is a frequent user of prescription medications.

Sarah Wheaton is a semi-organized arson offender, who used simple tools combined with detailed planning to commit her arsons and avoid being caught. She most likely sets fires during specific times of the year and probably has lengthy cooling-off periods between fire sprees.

Helen Judith White: Bushfire Serial Arsonist
Period of Activity: 2006-07, South Australia

Like the Western United States, Australia has vast expanses of grasslands and brush areas known locally as the "bush." In the months of December and January, which are generally considered the height of the Australian summer, the bush is tinder dry and the temperatures routinely exceed hundred degrees. Not surprisingly, more than any other country outside of the United States, the bushlands of Australia are plagued annually with massive wildfires. In recent years, with the ever-encroaching urban interface into the bush, those fires have become increasingly catastrophic events, resulting in the loss of many lives and the total destruction of entire villages.

Australian fire authorities have arrested dozens of persons for intentionally igniting some of these fires, including sadly several Australian firefighters. In the early 2000s, Australian fire and police authorities deemed the ongoing arson problem so prevalent that they formed a task force to conduct ongoing, aggressive investigations into this phenomenon. The task force operated under the name "Operation Nomad." In 2007, part of this task force in the Adelaide region recognized an ongoing trend of small arson fires. The Adelaide Hills region is the coastal foothills just east of the city of Adelaide in South Australia. The region is known for its small suburban ranches, upscale horse farms, and wine making. The Harrogate area is an upper-scale semi-rural enclave within the Adelaide Hills and is known primarily as a horse farm area. In the summer months of 2006 and 2007, a series of over forty small fires were set in the dry hillsides surrounding the area. The majority of the fires were within several hundred yards of ranches and farms. Luckily, most of the fires stayed fairly small in size and caused very little damage, save for a few hundred feet of fencing.

Authorities knew the fires could be attributed to a single serial arsonist, as they routinely found similar ignition devices and matches at most of the scenes. The ignition devices were designed by affixing the matches to commercial mosquito coils that had been left in the dry bush. A mosquito coil is a chemical substance in a solid form that when burned gives off an odor adverse to a mosquito. The typical coil is a glowing source of ignition similar to incense and can burn up to eight hours. If matches are affixed anywhere on the coil, it makes a time delay incendiary device. When the glowing coil burns down to the matches, they ignite and start an open flame which is generally what is required to cause the ignition of dry vegetation. Depending on where the matches are affixed to the coil is how long the time delay is for open flame ignition. This device is little more than an enhancement of the standard cigarette and matchbook delay device, which is somewhat common in brushfires areas in the United States.

Australian authorities, like their British counterparts, are very keen in their use of forensic evidence and do so in arson cases quite regularly. In this arson series, the investigators routinely submitted all evidence for forensic analysis. In reward for their efforts, they were able to identify the fingerprints from the same suspect on devices from several of the scenes. The fingerprints in question did not, however, relate to any known arsonists or criminals.

The local authorities also noted a peculiarity with this series of fires. The arsonist would set many fires in a short period of time and then "cool off" for a significant number of weeks or even months. The fires occurred sometimes as many as five to ten times in a single day. In keeping with a solid investigation, over the twelve months of the events, authorities began an aggressive patrol of the areas in question. As part of that, they stopped and identified any and all suspicious persons in the fire setting area. One of those persons was the forty-four-year-old wife of a local farmer. She was stopped and questioned by authorities on a "red flag" day while alone in the rural area. A major crime detective detained Helen Judith White and questioned her intently about her suspicious actions. At the time, she denied any involvement in fires and professed that she was actually out helping spot the arsonist. She maintained that she was volunteering to watch a neighbor's property. The detective released her after several minutes but noted to his superiors that she was acting odd and that he considered her a person of interest in the case.

His suspicions seemed to be well founded as within hours of her release, Helen White lit up to nine brushfires. After being questioned, Helen White's fingerprints were compared with those found on the incendiary delay devices. They were a match. In December 2007, Helen White was arrested and charged with setting forty-seven bushfires in the hills surrounding Adelaide in the previous year. Upon her arrest, White told investigators, "I didn't set them all." She then gave a partial admission to several of the fires. Part of the statement included the revelation that White set up to thirteen fires in one night and nine in another night.

Prosecutors asserted that White was an extreme danger to the community, and much argument was made to keep her in jail pending her trial. Immediately, her case made headlines across the continent as she differed entirely from the person the general public believed was setting the fires—a young white male. Slowly, her attorneys revealed some aspects of her life.

Helen White had, within the past five years, married a local farmer from a well-known family and had moved into the area. She and her husband Darren had produced two young daughters, and she appeared to have lived a relatively uneventful life. However, as her case wound through the judicial process, her attorneys conceded that Helen had severe psychiatric issues that influenced her behavior. A slew of psychiatrists and defense experts weighed in that White felt an enormous sense of "powerlessness, anger, and depression" in her life, which caused her to act out in that manner. The prosecution countered that the arson fires were not a cry for help from White and noted that when first questioned by detectives, she came up with a well-constructed "fanciful" tale. Additionally, the prosecution pointed out that White's fires utilized a good deal of forethought, planning, and premeditation. They said she lit her fires during days of high fire threat, used devices she had to purchase and assemble, and took pains to go to secluded locations to carry out her crime. In the prosecution's mind, she was not some raving psychiatric patient who uncontrollably lit fires, but was in fact a cold and calculating serial arsonist who intended injury to her neighbor's properties. On January 17, 2008, a judge ordered that Helen White answer the allegations against her and remanded her to custody pending the trial.

After much debate and analyzing, the defense recognized the evidence against them was fairly overwhelming. On November 10, 2008, Helen White agreed to a plea deal in this case and pled guilty to twenty-one arson fires to bushland. Again, the defense and prosecution geared up for the sentencing hearing by enlisting an army of analysts and therapists. Presiding Judge Michael Boylan heard defense arguments that White was not a danger to society and that in fact society owed her a treatment for her illness. They cited her lack of criminal record and the small amount of physical damage done by her fires as mitigating circumstances. They promoted the fact that she was a mother of two young girls. The prosecution maintained its original mantra that Helen White was an extreme danger to society and had planned and carried out her arson attacks in a cold and calculating manner. The court, noting that White was "not a typical arsonist," accepted that she had a psychiatric condition that caused her to feel powerless and angry. However, he also believed that persons who started bushfires needed to be severely punished as a deterrent to others. On April 7, 2009, Judge Boylan imposed a fairly severe eighteen-year sentence on Helen White, with a mandatory nine years in prison before she would be eligible for parole. News reports described White as "shocked" as the unexpected harsh sentence was read.

Almost immediately, an appellate court heard arguments from White's lawyers about her "manifestly excessive" prison sentence. Not surprising in most arson cases, and particularly in one involving a female offender, the higher court agreed with the defense and reduced her sentence to thirteen years total, with a mandatory prison term reduction to six and a half years. Chief Justice John Doyle noted that her original sentence was "a very heavy one." He further opined that White had a good prospect for "recovery" and also noted her previous good criminal record. Helen White will be eligible for release as early as 2013.

Investigator Analysis

Helen Judith White is truly an anomaly. She is one of the rare women serial arson offenders who actually used a delay incendiary device. This seems to be a trait reserved for the male brushfire arsonists.

This case is noteworthy in many ways, but for discussion's sake, it clearly points out that women will commit the exact same crimes as men in some cases. The difference is that women are seldom prosecuted the same as men. The court, while handing down its original sentence, referred to the fact that White had a sickness or disease that compelled her to light fires. While this author applauds the court for its sentencing, I find the judge to be in error on his assessment of Helen White. So many people, including judges, some prosecutors, many public agency officials, and even some investigators, are quick to conclude that serial arson is a sickness that can be treated. Those same people would never dare to take that same stance with a pedophile or a rapist.

In this case, the prosecution is correct in their assertion that Helen White is a cold and calculating arsonist who took steps to plan out her crimes, gather resources, and pick a time and place of her choosing. She no doubt researched her delay incendiary device and conducted some limited experiments with it, as surely her male counterparts do. There is no doubt that she derived great pleasure and power in her ability to cause a potentially massive wildfire.

On an investigative note, this case also highlights another aspect lacking in the investigation of arson crimes. Many arson investigators are not skilled or lack the training to effectively utilize forensics in arson investigations. Many of the dozens of experienced arson investigators this author is personally familiar with have never sought out fingerprints or DNA evidence at their arson scenes. This is a result of poor funding, poor training, and a lack of knowledge on their parts. By now it should be obvious that many of the more dramatic cases in this book were solved by forensics. The White case does highlight another effective tactic in serial arson investigation. The proper use of law enforcement to stop and identify every suspicious or unexplained person in an "at risk" area is paramount to a successful arson investigation.

Helen Judith White is a significant serial arson offender who is suspected of lighting over forty-seven bushfires with a delay incendiary device. She is currently in prison after having been convicted of twenty-one of those fires.

Elizabeth Lee Sanford Drezek: Serial Arsonist
Period of Activity: 1990-2007, Los Angeles

The arsonists that should be the easiest to identify and arrest are the least sophisticated offenders who live and operate in a small area in a large urban city. However, as we note in some of the above cases, a few inexplicably slip through the cracks and are allowed to offend for years. Elizabeth Drezek fits this offender type perfectly. The only thing that prevented her from earlier identification and arrest was that she was one of the very few female serial arson offenders we were aware of. Chances are that if we have an arson problem in a given area, we would be more apt to start looking at suspicious males instead of the females.

There is not a lot of background information on this woman as she had no local relatives and was generally in a fairly incoherent state when arrested. Her criminal history tells a story of a woman who came to the attention of law enforcement for the first time in 1990 in the very affluent city of Beverly Hills, California. For the next eighteen years, this homeless woman drifted back and forth across three different jurisdictions which are fairly close together—Beverly Hills, Hollywood, and West Hollywood. All were patrolled by different large and modern police agencies and all had different large and modern fire departments. These factors also influenced how Drezek was able to avoid arson scrutiny for so many years.

Another huge factor is that Drezek was a long-time homeless woman with severe mental health issues. She lived and moved about in an area rife with similar types of men and women, so in essence, she had been hiding in plain sight for almost two decades.

Born in 1947, Drezek, was first arrested at the age of forty-three in Beverly Hills for vandalism. After that conviction and release, she was rearrested in the same area a month later for trespassing. Somehow, there were no new arrests until ten years later when she was arrested for "squatting" in a vacant home in Beverly Hills. Squatting is basically moving into a vacant home that isn't yours. This was followed a few months later by another vandalism arrest and an arrest for causing a fight. In 2003, she was again arrested for "squatting" and vandalism to a vacant property and for harassing and annoying business owners.

By 2006, she had additional arrests for vandalism and later that year received her first arson arrest. That case was dropped when the victim refused to testify, but five months later, she was rearrested on another arson case. Again, for an unknown reason, that second arson case was also dropped. In 2008, Drezek had an arrest for petty theft. In almost all of those above cases, Drezek did little more than a few days in jail and pled guilty at her first court appearance.

In the early months of 2007, LAFD arson investigators were aware that they had about thirty to forty "nuisance"-type fires in a small neighborhood in Hollywood. A check with the LAPD officers in the area brought Elizabeth Drezek to their attention. Many neighborhood business owners, transients, and citizens had already identified her as a person who had set dozens of small fires in the area. There were complaints that she was seen lighting other transients' shopping carts full of property, trash, and boxes outside of businesses, dumpsters, vegetation, and even an abandoned car or two. Her method was simple and her actions were blatant and obvious. She just shuffled down alleys and side streets, sometimes in daylight and sometimes after dark, and lit whatever she saw on fire with a butane cigarette lighter.

When the LAFD investigators went out to find her, they literally tracked her by all the burned items in the areas where she stayed. Eventually, she was arrested and convicted for lighting a car and vacant structure on fire. In their attempts to interview her, they found her nearly incoherent.

Finally, after so many years of obvious mental health issues, the arson investigators brought to the attention of the courts and district attorney her dangerous activities. As part of the punishment, the court wisely remanded Elizabeth Drezek to a state prison mental health facility for intense treatment. While in Patton State Psychiatric Hospital in 2009, Drezek was declared "mentally incompetent."

Investigator's Analysis

Elizabeth Drezek is but a typical example of the arsonists who slip through the cracks in every major city. Her arson activities tended to be minor in scope, and the few times she was arrested, the victims did not want to be involved. This behavior can be typical among certain homeless people, and they go on to set hundreds of minor "nuisance" fires for months or years until they set one big enough to gain an investigator's attention. Additionally, homeless people, drug addicts, and transients set many "unintended arson" fires, when in a negligent manner they start a fire to heat food, warm themselves, illuminate an area, or use drugs. This author has been to well over hundred of these types of fire scenes, and while they don't rise to the level of a criminal arson, they are illegal acts and can have devastating results. Some transient fires have resulted in large fires in vacant buildings where other homeless people have died or in massive wild land fires. A recent massive wild land fire in the Los Angeles area burned over 100,000 acres and resulted in the deaths of two firefighters. A homeless man who had been detained twice for illegal fires in the past was the sole suspect in that event.

To combat this problem, if an investigator notes a trend of minor fires in an area, he can "profile" them and determine if they are related to juvenile activity, transient activity, or a serial arson offender. The next logical step would be to contact the local patrol officers, business owners, or anyone else who is in the neighborhood on a daily basis. Most of those people will know exactly the cause of those events and will point you in the right direction.

Nicole Martinez
Period of Activity: 1995-98, Los Angeles Area

*This case is an investigation involving me. It is told in the first person format.

Nicole was pissed again. She knew she had already smoked her afternoon cigarette, but she wanted another, and the staff had refused her request. She didn't like this place. They were too strict. She was used to getting her way with just a little threat. This place was new. They hadn't seen the results of her threats. They thought she was just a "pretend suicidal." They would soon learn that she was deadly serious about getting what she wanted.

Nicole walked into her room and removed the matches from the pillowcase. She knew from past experience that beds and sheets were tough to light. She didn't know why, but assumed the cloth was somehow fireproof. She'd learned to add a page or two from the newspaper to get a larger flame. She didn't like it when the bedding material just shrank away from the flames and got black and hard. She wanted to see the flames. As she had learned before, Nicole started on the edge of the bed at the foot. She was able to get a decent flame with only two matches and the newspaper. There wasn't much smoke yet . . . but she knew it would come. She watched the short flames proceed in both directions. Soon the blanket edges began to smolder and burn and the flames started to build. The newspaper started, and the flames got several inches higher. Never looking back, Nicole walked out of her room and wondered if it would be much more interesting in county jail. She had never been to county jail, but everyone said the conditions were better than the psych hospitals. She thought that maybe she would actually die this time. Nicole walked down the hall and sat in the day room. She began watching the news. She never even glanced back at the room burning twenty feet behind her. Within a few minutes, she heard the sound of the smoke alarm. She heard people yelling and running. Nicole continued to stare impassively at the television.

This author was in his first week as an arson investigator. On a cold evening in mid-December, 1997, I was assigned my very first arson case. My partner and I drove to a secure psychiatric hospital in Temple City, California, where an inmate had set fire to her room. There were several psychiatric-related facilities in that area of the San Gabriel Valley. Some held higher security inmates, and others were more like "board and care" homes. That particular facility was a contract hospital for the county court system and was a "secure" facility. That meant that it would be a violation of probation if the "patient" left the locked facility.

My partner prepped me about his experience with psychiatric facilities. Most were not cooperative with sharing information to law enforcement. They seldom disclosed any psychiatric patient information and sometimes didn't even let the investigators interview the patient. The exception would be if a patient/inmate had attacked a staff member. We were to soon learn that apparently another exception to the rule was the crime of arson.

We were given a briefing by the head nurse who then walked us into a small room. The nurse left, and we found the inmate/patient's case file sitting on a table. The patient, Nicole Martinez, was just nineteen years old, but a quick look at her file showed she had been quite a handful over the past few years. She had spent the better part of the past fifteen years in any manner of youth homes, psych hospitals, board and care facilities, and juvenile halls. Eighteen months earlier, she had been tossed out of a Van Nuys group home for attempting suicide and threatening to burn the place to the ground. Two weeks later, she actually lit a bed on fire in a second group home after being upset about switching counselors. Six months ago, she lit a bed on fire in that very hospital and was transferred out. She came back a month ago, and within a week, she attempted suicide here. Then the day before this final fire, she complained of hallucinations and again attempted suicide. While we were going through the file, a male psych nurse stepped into the room. He told us that he was personally aware of two similar mattress fires that Nicole had started in that very facility two years ago. He explained (off the record of course) that there had been no police or fire response and the hospital had covered up both incidents due to liability issues. He said that if they were to record those incidents, they would not be able to transfer Nicole to any other facility, as "no one wants firebugs."

In all, we were able to find five arson events related to Nicole, along with three instances of attempted suicide, theft within a facility, and assaultive behavior toward staff. There was a brief mention of her personal history in the file. Additional information was learned over the course of several legal proceedings. Nicole was born in 1978 and had severe psychological issues since a very early age. There was documentation describing the fact that she had been sexually assaulted at a very early age by an older male relative. She had been taking one form or another of prescription medications related to anxiety, depression, or psychological issues for years. She had a lengthy history of living in foster homes, "board and care" facilities, juvenile hall, and other psychiatric facilities for the past several years. She had been kicked out of or released from several facilities due to violent or disruptive behavior on numerous occasions. There were several mentions of "arson threats" or attempts in her case file.

After reviewing the file, we looked at Nicole's room. A hospital-type bed had been ignited from one corner. The mattress was barely burned, but the blankets and sheets showed much more damage. We found torn, burned newspaper and at least two paper matches on the floor. The fire damage was not that severe and had not actually burned anything other than the bed.

We were surprised when the nursing supervisor offered to let us interview Nicole. We found her sitting in the television room in her pajamas. She was extremely obese for such a young girl, and it was difficult to get her to stop watching television long enough to answer questions. Nicole was bored. She kept drifting back to the TV and couldn't focus on the questions. She abruptly admitted she lit the fire and hoped we would just send her to county jail as she was tired of psychiatric hospitals. She told us that she usually was allowed to smoke one cigarette each afternoon in that facility and was provided with matches for that purpose. She had decided to smoke a second cigarette, but the staff stopped her. She said she got mad and went to her room and lit the edge of the bed on fire with two matches. She said she had done that several times in the past and knew that she would eventually get what she wanted. She finally focused on us and said, "Look, I just want to go to county jail. If you guys don't get me there, then I'll burn this place down next time." From that point on, Nicole went into great details about her suicide attempts and fire setting in an attempt to finally get transferred out. She told us that she had lit beds on fire in secure living facilities on at least six occasions. She said that she knew the hospitals lied to each other just to get rid of her as a patient. She promised to us that if we sent her to the women's jail, she'd stop lighting fires. We honored her request and sent her to the psychiatric portion of the women's jail. We labeled her as an extreme-risk inmate for both arson and suicide. Nicole seemed pleased that she was able to manipulate the system.

I saw Nicole several more times again over the next few months as she was in court for various hearings. Each time she had the dull, listless look of someone who had either given up on life or was heavily medicated. She usually just sat and stared forward and seldom said anything. I was called at one point to give testimony in that case. The testimony was to determine how much of a future risk Nicole would pose to herself or others. I had done much reading on the subject by that time and believed that Nicole was an extreme risk to herself and other persons living or working in any facility in which she was housed. My opinion is that jail and institution fires are extremely dangerous as persons are unable to flee the toxic smoke or deadly flames. A single bed fire can produce sufficient heat to burn down a structure or enough smoke to asphyxiate other occupants. I considered that troubled girl to be a significant fire risk.

After much discussion by mental health "experts," they agreed to extend her probation only and to reassign her to yet another secure mental health center. She did however receive her first conviction for arson and was then listed as an "arson registrant" for life.

I got a phone call in 1999 from a detective in the San Gabriel Valley asking if I remembered Nicole. The detective told me that Nicole had been arrested for setting fire to several beds in another hospital in the area in which she was a patient. The detective was contemplating recommending counseling only for her as she had mental health issues. After that event, the district attorney finally dropped the hammer on Nicole and sent her to state prison for the two arson fires.

Ten years after my first contact with Nicole, I found her file in my drawer of serial arson offenders. I ran her updated history and found that she had remained all that time in various state prisons, hospitals, and mental institutions. She had been charged with the San Gabriel Valley hospital arson in 1999, and the courts had combined our original case and the San Gabriel case together for a five-year prison sentence. That was the start of Nicole's incarceration. Her prison record showed that she had been charged three separate times while in prison for assault on other inmates and staff. She was eventually declared insane in 2005 and remains in Patton State Prison Hospital. She is a lifetime arson registrant. I tallied up her arsons and found evidence of eight separate fire incidents, all fires to mattresses by that girl. Apparently no one has died . . . yet.

Investigator Analysis

Nicole Martinez is a sad example of a child who was subjected to so much emotional and physical trauma at a young age that there was little hope for her to be anything other than who she ended up being. My partner at the time, a thirty-year-veteran detective, told me, "This poor kid's gone. She's never had a chance," after we had spent an hour looking into her blank, emotionless nineteen-year-old eyes.

Her type of fire setting activity was a cry for help and the only power she could wield in an otherwise devastated life. Her crimes were blatant and not at all sophisticated and would surely have resulted in her death or the death of others if she had continued. Years down the road from that case, we believe that she probably had had other arson events while in prison, but like a lot of things in institutions, they had been hidden in one way or another.

Although serial fire setting in females is fairly rare (that we know of), it's safe to say that any female fire setter is most likely to report some sort of childhood sexual or emotional abuse.

Gina Ann Gray: Serial Arsonist
Period of Activity: 1996-2008, Hamilton, Ohio

At forty-one years of age, Gina Gray was dealing with a lot of issues. She had mental health and prescription drug problems. She was losing what few looks she had left and was gaining a lot of weight. Those problems were not helping her obtain work in her chosen profession, which was as a prostitute. To make matters worse, Gina was mad. She was livid at her plight in life and furious about how people had treated her. That included people within her own family. As a relatively powerless woman, she sought out and used the only power she could muster. She had used it before and was well aware of its effects and power. Gina began to light fires to terrorize and destroy her enemies. By the fall of 2008, the Hamilton, Ohio, police and fire investigators realized that they had a series of up to a dozen structure arsons in their "Fourth Ward" area. That was the same area frequented by Gina Gray.

Hamilton is a city midway between Dayton and Cincinnati. It was the long-time hometown of Gina Gray. Up until the age of forty-one, Gina had become extremely familiar with the streets of that town. The streets and the local police were very familiar with Gina. Over the past twenty years, Gina had racked up over a hundred arrests and detentions by the local police. The vast majority of those arrests involved her chosen profession—prostitution. As far as prostitutes go, Gina was on the bottom rung of the ladder. She was a lowly street corner prostitute. With her diminishing looks, she was forced to ply her trade at the most dangerous levels of the profession. As such, she was the frequent target of robberies, beatings by johns, theft, and drug abuse. As part of that dangerous lifestyle, Gina began to develop a sense of street cunningness and survival that kept her alive.

While she was cunning enough to avoid being killed in this dangerous life, Gina was not as sly when it came to being arrested. She amassed an incredible number of arrests. The vast majority were for crimes associated with prostitution, including loitering, trespassing, theft, and solicitation. She was a frequent sight along Hamilton's streets at night as she waved down potential customers.

By 2007, Gina had somehow taken stock of her miserable life on the street, and her anger began to fester and grow. For some unknown period of time,

Gina had begun lighting fires. She admitted to a detective in 2008 that most of her fires were lit out of frustration and anger. She was quick to point out that she only torched items of little value and did not hurt anyone. Her criminal history told a different story. Although the actual facts have been lost in the passage of time, her criminal history showed a significant event that stood out among her dozens of misdemeanor arrests. In 1996, Gina was arrested and convicted for aggravated arson. This serious charge usually denotes an arson attack on an occupied dwelling.

Her mother would later try and explain her actions to a sentencing judge. The mother told the court that Gina was a product of her environment. She had mental health and psychiatric issues going back to when she was sexually assaulted as a child. Her mother admitted that she and Gina had kept that information secret for over thirty years. It was not known exactly who the purported suspect of Gina's childhood abuse was, but maybe a clue emerged in one of Gina's more dramatic fires. In 2008, an arson fire occurred at the occupied home of one of Gina's uncles. That was among three arson attacks in the same area against homes. That fire occurred while five persons were within the home. The investigation of that event led detectives to Gina. Witnesses and emergency personnel described seeing Gina Gray in the vicinity of at least four fires in the arson spree.

Once her name came up, detectives quickly realized that she had a current arrest warrant out for trespassing. In February 2009, they picked her up on that warrant and used the opportunity to interview her about the fires. Hamilton Det. Steve Rogers developed a rapport with Gina, and she soon admitted to him that she had lit a few small fires. She was quick to minimize her actions and to stress that she had never done any of the large fires he was asking about. After the interview, Gina apparently had a change of heart. She asked to speak to the detective again. This time she came clean.

Gina Gray admitted to Detective Rogers that she had lit as many as eleven fires. She said she was very angry with some people in her life for the wrongs that they had done to her, and she set the fires out of anger and vengeance. Some of the victims were known to her. Others, she told the detective, were just random targets of opportunity. Gina told investigators that she never used any form of accelerant, but would find something at the scene to start the fire. She said she usually found some paper or trash at the scene and would ignite it with her lighter. After she ignited the blaze, she would stand at a distance and watch the fire grow. On at least two incidents, she returned to the scene after her initial ignition attempt did not grow and re-lit the fire. That detailed interview with Gina cleared up a dozen arson attacks on homes and garages in the area. Three of those were to occupied homes. Other items she targeted were at least one car and some trash bins.

In May 2009, Gina Gray pled guilty in the court to ten counts of arson. As part of that plea, any other arson charges and pending investigations were dropped. Noting her repeat arson offender status and the high probability that she would re-offend, the court sentenced her to a term of fifteen years in state prison.

Investigator's Analysis

Gina Gray is typical of the "firebug" or street person type of arsonist. Her case history is fairly common to this type of offender as she alludes to having been sexually abused in her past and has continuing mental health and drug addiction problems. All of these traits are common among female serial arsonists and to some degree even among male serial arsonists.

This case again demonstrates extremely solid detective work and fantastic interviewing skills, which brought this series to a successful conclusion. These are the hallmarks of any successful serial arson investigation.

Gina Gray is a disorganized serial arson offender who accessed her targets via walking. She used only a lighter and whatever combustible materials she could gather at the fire scene to ignite the blazes. She had a mixed motive and chose some targets out of a personal connection and anger toward that party, while other targets were just items that she came across. By her own admissions, she sometimes lingered at the scene to monitor the results. She was not careful, sly, or clever as she was spotted by witnesses at four different fire scenes.

There is a large gap in her known fire setting behavior from 1996 to 2007. It would be a safe bet to speculate that she set dozens of other fires during that time period during times of depression or anger, which were never attributed to her. Her known fires total about fifteen, but a number exceeding fifty is more likely.

Lee Jo van Haaren: Serial Arsonist
Period of Activity: February-May, 2005, Kaitaia, New Zealand

In January 2005, Kaitaia, New Zealand, authorities were alerted to the possibility of a child living in substandard conditions. The police and child welfare personnel were directed to a squalid trailer (or caravan) in a semi-rural transient encampment under a bridge. There they found a young girl in the care of her forty-four-year-old grandmother, Lee Jo van Haaren. Noting that the child was indeed staying in very substandard conditions, the authorities dutifully removed the young girl from her grandmother and placed her into a state-run home.

This "triggering event" launched a three-month-long wave of revenge-motivated arsons that terrified the town and even cast suspicion on members of the local fire brigade. Kaitaia is a small beach town with about five thousand residents on the far northern coast of New Zealand. It has very little crime and thrives on tourism, logging, and farming.

The fires lit during that arson wave were different from almost all described in this book. All of those fires occurred to buildings owned by the township or related to the schools in the area. On February 14, 2005, an arsonist broke into and set fire to a ninety-nine-year-old villa where the community art center was housed. The fire caused the destruction of the irreplaceable historical property and its contents. On February 24, there was a failed attempt to set fire to the District Council (County Council) building. On April 16, 2005, an arsonist set fire to the Kaitaia Primary School, causing over $235,000 in damages. In the next few weeks, similar fires were set at two township council offices, a local church, and a public building that housed the children's welfare services. A smaller attempted arson occurred outside of a home where a primary schoolteacher lived. The total damage of these events was nearly $600,000.

From mid-February to mid-May, the arson attacks continued in the late night to early morning hours. By May, twenty-one arson events were attributed to the same offender. Most of the targets were public buildings or schools owned by the entire community. Only two of the attacks caused significant damage.

That arson spree emotionally devastated the local town that enjoyed a relatively crime-free lifestyle. Rumors began to circulate that the serial arson offender could be one of the many volunteers at the local fire brigade who was just looking for some excitement. The authorities had no witnesses and very few clues to the offender until they learned from citizens that Lee Jo van Haaren had been talking frequently about the fires and that she had information which would allow her to collect a reward.

A check of van Haaren showed that she was a transient woman who had only resided in the area for about the past three years. She maintained a dilapidated trailer and kept to makeshift camps in the areas surrounding the town. She had a history of narcotics use and even had a minor warrant out for her arrest for narcotics. Authorities soon approached and arrested her for the minor narcotics violation. After a thorough interview with van Haaren, detectives were able to get her to confess to three of the arson events. They later searched her trailer and saw that she had a detailed collection of press clippings about all the fire events. Further interviews with acquaintances showed that she had expressed extreme rage in recent months toward the township, the school district, and a particular teacher whom she believed had caused the authorities to remove her grandchild from her care.

Lee Jo van Haaren was arrested and charged with twenty arson events related to the three-month-long series. She was ordered to undergo psychiatric evaluation by the trial judge. It was learned that she was fit for trial and that she was extremely upset with the schools, township, and teacher for the removal of her granddaughter.

On August 23, 2006, after a ten-day trial, a jury convicted Lee Jo van Haaren for eight of the most serious arson counts against her. She was acquitted of three minor arson offences. During sentencing, the trial judge agreed with the prosecution that the motive for these offenses was the extreme rage the suspect felt against the various institutions she believed had taken her granddaughter away from her. One month later, the court sentenced van Haaren to over seven years in prison.

Investigator's Analysis

This case is included to show that these types of serial offenders probably occur in nearly every portion of the globe. In this case, the offender is a female with mental health and narcotics issues who chose a transient lifestyle. When the authorities removed her only granddaughter, she struck back against those institutions in the only manner she could. She purposely set out to destroy the most cherished symbols of the community that had "wronged" her: the church, art building, and community center. Again, the key to this successful investigation was to examine the targets of the attack and ask, "Who would want to do this?" There are no doubt thousands of men and women in the world who are in similar circumstances as van Haaren and who are at risk to be multiple fire setters.

Chapter 7 Synopsis

The ten women named in this section are but a representation of the probable dozens if not hundreds of female serial arson offenders. Like their male counterparts, they range in degree from serial murderers/arsonists to the more typical "firebug" type of street offender. All but one listed here are white, but there is little doubt to this writer that there are similar women serial arsonists who come from every race.

The common denominator that these women share is that most reported a history of physical or sexual abuse in their life. Other commonalities in female serial arson cases are that most of their fires are set within their home or at their work site, and many have attempted suicide at least once in their life. Their choice of targets is the one fact that is totally different from male serial fire setters. Most fires set by females are set in the daytime periods, and few women use devices of any sort. Unlike male serial arsonists, most of these women were married at some point in their life and about half had children. Two of the women set their fires as a tool with which to commit insurance fraud.

Besides these more famous cases, this author is aware anecdotally of many other cases of women involved in multiple fires. Discussions with other investigators by this author have revealed many cases of "street transient" women involved in multiple fire setting. These cases are seldom prosecuted, and the woman is usually referred to a mental health facility. Further, with the proliferation of methamphetamine addiction in large portions of this country, this author is aware of multiple fire events related to both male and female meth addicts. Lastly, a subject that arises frequently among arson investigators is the phenomenon of multiple fire events related to "average housewives" who have a history of prescription drug use. Most of these types of fires are in or around the home and most are classified as "accidents." There is very little documentation about these types of fire as they tend to be minor in scope, and many do not get reported to a qualified investigator. However, many investigators this author is in contact with agree that "pill popping moms" have an inordinate number of fire events in their life.

CHAPTER 8

The Hero Serial Arsonists

Security Guards

Over the years, there have been numerous anecdotal cases of fires set by persons entrusted with the security of a structure or an area. The persons apprehended in those events are generally not in the "serial fire setter" category as they are often caught after just one or two events. They tend to be extremely disorganized persons who do not plan the event well and leave many clues about their involvement.

Not all but a substantial number of persons employed in security work are those who have been rejected for professional law enforcement employment. Many have alcohol or minor drug issues, criminal records, or have shown the inability to either work with people or maintain employment. Some are overly officious in their duties (ala John Orr), and quite a few manifest the overly macho "wannabe cop" attributes that they have copied from movie screen cops such as *Dirty Harry*. Added to this is that in their everyday duties, security guards deal with bad hours, loneliness, low pay, and a great deal of disrespect by the persons they come across. They seldom receive recognition or respect from their clients and are considered to be a necessary evil by the very companies who hire their services. Often they come in contact with the local police and are considered to be oddballs and amateurs by the officers they deal with. From those difficult employment conditions arises a group of people who are striving for action, recognition, compensation, and respect. They sometimes do desperately silly things to achieve those goals.

A case that highlights this desperation borne out of frustration is a singular act by security guard Richard Glenn. Glenn, who was thirty-nine years old at the time of his crime, was a personal security guard for legendary singer James Brown. On April 28, 2000, an arson fire tore through the office at "James Brown Enterprises" in Georgia. That fire destroyed several priceless mementos from the singer's career, along with the original master tapes of some of his most famous works. Several months later, after following a poorly concealed paper trail, investigators arrested Brown's friend and security guard Glenn. Glenn had stolen several things from Brown's office, including a check for $75,000 to the singer from "Pepsi." The fire was then staged to cover up that theft. The check later ended up deposited in an account controlled by Glenn. Richard Glenn was subsequently convicted of the theft and aggravated vandalism in lieu of arson and received a fifteen-year prison sentence. While not a serial arson case, this event does showcase the type of "staging" that security guard arsonists will do.

Another singular act by a security guard was done not out of profit but out of revenge. In 2008, in the Hainan Province of China, a forty-one-year-old security guard known as "Zhou" became dissatisfied with his employer. Zhou had an ongoing dispute with a large tobacco firm and had voiced his displeasure over pay and work conditions on numerous occasions. He eventually left the company, but not without revenge on his mind. At 3:30 a.m. on a summer night, Zhou entered his former workplace. In preparation for his attack, he had purchased forty bottles of medicine from a pharmacy and had dumped out the liquid medicine. He replaced the liquid with gasoline and brought the "medicine" and a cigarette lighter with him on his late-night mission. He poured the gasoline over the main factory floor and lit the vapors. The resulting fire was immediate and fast moving. Soon three hundred firefighters were involved in fighting the large blaze. The fire did almost $2 million (US) in damage and caused injuries to a factory worker and a Chinese firefighter. Feeling immediate guilt, Zhou turned himself in to authorities before the fire was even extinguished.

Security guards, loss prevention agents, bodyguards, ambulance drivers, parking and code enforcement officers, low-level park rangers and game wardens, and all other manner of part-time security, rescue, EMTs, volunteer, or safety work have shown a history of creating events and incidents where they can become heroes.

Michael J. Huston—Universal Studios Security Guard: Serial Arsonist
1990, North Hollywood, California

In the late summer and fall of 1990, Universal Studios was having a small problem with fires. Fires are not unique phenomena at movie studios and back lots. The equipment and special effects in use at these locations often produce accidents and unintended fires. Most studios even have their own fire department. Universal Studios is perhaps the largest and most famous studios in the Los Angeles area and has its own fire department—the legendary "Engine 51" of the 1970s TV show *Emergency*. This is an actual fire station that employs full-time firefighters during the daytime hours or when there is active filming.

Universal Studios on a given day has thousands of employees and tens of thousands of guests and tourists in their public areas. The back lot and television and movie filming areas have another several thousand employees. The entire operation is massive in scale and is literally its own city. Like any other city, Universal Studios has its share of internal issues that include crime and fire. To combat the crime, the studio has various levels of security starting with a full-time station staffed with over thirty-five Los Angeles sheriff's deputies and detectives. This sheriff's station is augmented with a large number of persons employed by Universal as corporate security and investigators. Finally, within the various productions at the facility, dozens of security guards work for various contract firms. This three-layer blanket of police and security is generally a well-oiled machine that does a decent job of providing protection to the location, employees, and guests. One of the people in 1990 tasked with this protection was Michael Huston, a forty-year-old man from the nearby town of Tujunga.

Michael Huston had only been employed for about two months by the contractor "Burn's Security," but he had already come to the attention of his supervisors. He seemed to be a highly motivated employee who was constantly on the lookout for theft and safety violations. His post was in the back lot near the old movie sets of *Dick Tracy* and *The Sting*. This 1930s' style cityscape set was then currently (in 1990) being used to film a new Sylvester Stallone movie. The only thing that bothered his employers was that Huston seemed a bit odd. He claimed to be an army veteran, and his coworkers said that he acted like a "dinged-out Vietnam Vet." However, his employers would later note that he was not that different from any of the dozens of other guards they routinely employed.

Huston had one significant difference. He seemed to have a knack for spotting trouble. There had been about a half dozen small but suspicious fires on the back lot in the previous few weeks. Many had been found in trash cans or in small piles of construction materials or debris. All had been attributed to carelessly discarded smoking materials or minor electrical problems. None of those fires had grown beyond their original size of about a few feet, and all had been noticed by alert employees. Michael Huston had spotted at least two of those fires himself and had extinguished both with a fire extinguisher. For his actions, his employers had given him at least one written commendation.

The company was quick to laud Huston as the studios was deathly afraid of fires. Movie sets for the most part are empty facades that have no fire protection systems within them. Their construction is usually without the normal fire safety design found in modern homes and buildings. A fire in one of those facades can spread quickly and do massive damage in a short period of time. Universal was very concerned about fires as they were worried about the potential loss of many historic sets and pieces of equipment. The history of the studios is marked with several massive fires over the years. It seemed that a major fire strikes Universal Studios about every twenty years. Nearby Warner Brothers Studios in Burbank had been attacked just a few years earlier in a large fire suspected of having been ignited by serial arsonist/fire investigator John Orr.

On November 6, 1990, at about 7:00 p.m., Huston was on duty at the New York Street Lot. The lot was closed after a day of filming. At 7:15 p.m., Huston called a supervisor to report a small fire burning in a paint shed. He said he was going to extinguish it himself. A few minutes later, he called back and said that he tried to put it out, but it grew too quickly. Like many fall nights in Southern California, the winds were blowing fairly strong at sundown. That fire quickly whipped up in the winds and soon spread to other nearby facades. Before it was extinguished several hours later, it destroyed at least 20 percent of the Universal Studios 420-acre back lot and caused about $25 million in damage. It took six months to rebuild the area.

Arson investigators from the Los Angeles Sheriff's and County Fire Department began an immediate coordinated investigation. They quickly ruled out accidental ignition sources and concluded that the fire was set with an open flame. They were also told of Huston's past "discoveries" of fires and realized that this was the third similar fire he had "discovered" in just a few weeks. The investigation soon centered on him. Over a several-hour period, Huston was interviewed by Det. Ron Ablott and Det. Wally Scheurell of the Sheriff's and Investigator Dave Westfield of the County Fire Department. All three men were highly experienced arson investigators with many years of investigations between them. Originally, Huston maintained his initial story about just happening upon the fire during his normal duties. Each time he told the story, however, it began to change. Confronted with his ever-changing story, Huston eventually began to crack. At one point, he told Investigator Westfield that he had chased a raccoon into the paint room and had discarded his cigarette into a paint can. When the sheriff's detectives went to verify that version, Huston saw the writing on the wall and eventually confessed to Westfield that he had lit the fire with his butane lighter. The investigators then focused on the previous events. Huston would later admit to starting at least half a dozen small fires. He claimed that he had a split personality and that his other half lit the fires.

During the trial of Huston, his family made an emotional appeal to the press and to the court. They described him as a former Viet Nam vet who was suffering from exposure to Agent Orange, a toxic defoliant used heavily in the latter stages of the war. The family also said that Huston had been suffering from a severe electrical shock he received during an accident about three years before the arson spree. The Veterans' Administration would only acknowledge that Huston had been a patient, but would provide no details as to his mental condition.

The jury convicted Huston for the arson fire, and the judge sentenced him to several years in prison. Since his release, Huston has taken up residence (sort of) in nearby Burbank, where he can still see the Universal Studios from the vehicle in which he now resides.

Investigator's Analysis

Most of the records of this case have been destroyed, but the author gleaned most of this account from direct conversations with some of the investigators who worked on this case. Dave Westfield worked alongside this author for about four years at the end of his thirty-plus years of service to the Los Angeles County Fire Department. Sheriff's Arson Detectives Ablott and Rich Edwards (who also assisted on this case) are long-time partners and personal acquaintances of me and two of the more distinguished investigators in the recent history of the Los Angeles basin. Edwards and Wally Scheurell were two of the team of lead investigators on the massive John Orr serial arson case.

All involved describe Huston as a fairly pathetic individual who had obvious mental health issues in his life. He was a prototypical "hero"-type arsonist who lit his fires for the purpose of "discovering" them and putting them out in order to gain attention from his bosses. The investigators believe he may have lit up to a dozen or more small fires in and around the Burbank area over the years. His method of attack was a simple "hot set" via a cigarette lighter, and he often was in the area when the fire department arrived. He was completely unsophisticated, and the suspicion was already upon him within minutes of what would be his most dramatic blaze.

Michael Huston's name came up briefly again in 2008 when yet again another massive fire erupted on the Universal back lot, destroying almost half of the movie sets and doing nearly $100 million in damage. This author was the lead investigator during that recent event, and initially suspicion was pointed at the odd actions of yet another recently hired security guard. The guard's odd actions were never really explained, but within hours, it was 100 percent clear that the fire was an accidental event due to a roofing operation.

Bryan Yeager: Security Guard/Firefighter Arsonist 2007-08, Bluffton, South Carolina

Twenty-one-year-old Bryan Yeager was a young man with two careers. He had worked as a paid firefighter for the Lady's Island/St. Helena's (South Carolina) fire department since about 2006. His record with that agency is unremarkable with no notable incidents. In late 2006, he started a second career of working part-time as a security guard at a housing development called the Palmetto Bluff Plantation.

While Yeager's fire service was fairly unremarkable, his security work seemed exciting in comparison. On the night of January 20, 2007, someone set fire to a dump truck parked near the entrance of the development. That case went unsolved with no suspects. The housing development remained quiet for several months until a fire was discovered in a trash bin at a golf course in the area on November 25. Soon the fires increased in their frequency. On December 16, the woods in a park in the area were set on fire by an unknown suspect. A month later on January 10, 2008, an arsonist set fire to a wooded area on a home lot. Just two days after that, the arsonist struck again, this time ramping up his activities and attacking a home under construction within the development.

The local police investigation found no similarities in those attacks with the exception being that they had all occurred within the Palmetto Bluff Plantation housing tract. However, upon further analysis, they did discover that there was one other significant factor common to each event. On the night of every fire, security guard and firefighter Bryan Yeager was on duty alone. This was significant since Yeager was a part-time employee and did not work that many shifts.

As soon as suspicions focused on Yeager, the local police asked for the assistance of the State Law Enforcement Division. This unit began a "surveillance" of sorts on Yeager as they had the capabilities of monitoring a GPS tracking system that had been installed in his security patrol vehicle.

Within four days of the final arson attack, police officials from multiple agencies arrested and charged Bryan Yeager for four counts of arson. The tracking system "hits" led them to charge Yeager on January 17, 2008, with a fifth fire in that series. A review of that system showed Yeager's patrol vehicle present at five different arson scenes at the time of each event. Police officials stated that Yeager was now a person of interest in several other suspicious fires in the area.

On August 23, 2010, on the eve of a jury trial for that arson series, Bryan Yeager accepted a plea bargain deal and pled guilty to five arson fires. He was sentenced to five years in state prison for those fires.

Investigator Analysis

Bryan Yeager hits the suspicion meter on two levels. He is a young man in two fields of endeavor that have a history of arson incidents. He is a recent hire of a small town fire department and is also a recent hire at a low-paying private security job. Both jobs offer long hours of boredom and idle time. Those have always been hazardous conditions for action-minded young men.

An analysis of Yeager's brief arson series shows that it is classic in its growth. The arson attacks grew more frequent and to more serious targets as the series increased. By the end of the series, the attacks were just days apart and a structure had been targeted. There is little doubt that Bryan Yeager was in the infant stages of what probably would have been a spectacular arson series with the next logical targets being commercial or occupied structures. There is currently little information available about this case, and I am unaware of the method of attack and the ignition sequence of any of these fires. It is unknown if a device was used or the fires were "hot set." What is clear is that Yeager was on the upswing of an increasingly dangerous series that did not bode well for the local population.

Like most serial arson cases, Yeager's arrest and conviction was brought about by solid detective work and an insightful analysis of the fire patterns and targets. This work caused the investigators to quickly focus on Yeager, and the use of electronic surveillance techniques soon solidified the case.

Aaron Lee Speed: Security Guard
December 6, 2004, Indian Head, Maryland

Large construction sites are the favored targets of vandals and thieves. It is too expensive and time-consuming for companies to move or lock up equipment each night, so they routinely hire security guards to watch over their equipment for the duration of a project. Those guards are very necessary as in many urban areas there are organized groups of thieves who use trucks and vans to move into a major site and take hundreds of thousands of dollars worth of equipment in just a few minutes.

Other than the organized gangs of thieves, large construction sites are often targeted by environmental groups and even established neighbors who are opposed to new construction or the ever-growing urban sprawl. Additionally, the sites are dangerous playgrounds for curious and mischievous youths and teens who may use those areas to vandalize or play in.

Any fire in a partially completed construction site has an immense chance to grow rapidly and spread because all of the fire-resistant materials are not yet in place. In 2000, this author assisted another arson investigator in a case where fourteen partially completed homes burned to the ground in a matter of minutes at a new housing tract, on a hot and windy day in Southern California. All of the usual factors were examined such as union troubles, irate neighbors, and eco-terrorism groups, but within a day it was found that the culprits were a pair of nine-year-old boys who lived next to the large site. They found the partially built homes to be fantastic places to play in and were quick to discover that some plumbers had left matches and "blue glue" (used for connecting PVC piping) in the homes. The boys also learned that "blue glue" burned quite nicely and began pouring it on the wood floors and igniting it. As could be expected, the fire quickly got out of hand and ignited the home that was little more than wood framing at that point. Once one home started, the bare wood frames burned almost explosively and led to one home after another exploding into flame from the radiated heat of the burning home next door. Those fourteen homes burned to the ground in under twenty minutes and greatly threatened nearby neighborhoods. That particular site did not have security or fencing around it.

From its inception, the Hunter's Brooke subdivision was a topic of controversy. The proposed subdivision in Indian Head, Maryland, was yet another affluent community in the greater Washington D.C. area. When it was initially proposed prior to 2003, the 319 unit subdivision was indeed grand in scale and design. Each unit was a one-fourth acre parcel upon which sat a home valued at about $400,000-$500,000 The controversy about this sprawling tract surrounded the fact that environmental groups were highly upset that it was infringing upon fragile wetlands in the area. Additionally, a "Sierra Club" report on the development labeled it the "quintessential sprawl" that also impinged upon historical sites in the local Chesapeake Bay area.

From the moment ground was first broken, the developers of that massive project were aware of the controversies surrounding it and took pains to hire full-time security at the site to inhibit theft, vandalism, and any attacks by eco-terrorists. One of the security guards on site was a twenty-one-year-old man named Aaron Speed.

In the first week of December 2004, the DC area had been soaked by a steady rain that spanned several days. This factor and the fact that the homes on the construction site were widely spread out made this area a fairly low risk for fire spread.

At five in the morning of December 6, a large number of fires were found burning in several homes at the property. The fires were unconnected to each other and did not impact more than one home site each. By the time firefighters from several jurisdictions arrived, they found twenty-six separate fires burning in twenty-six separate homes. Ten of those fires self-extinguished and caused minimal damage, while the remaining sixteen caused total destruction. Additionally, investigators found evidence that an additional ten arson attacks failed to ignite properly. It was clear from the volume of targets alone that it was a highly organized and well-planned arson attack. Almost immediately, federal officials suspected the involvement of eco-terrorists, and dozens of federal investigators joined the growing arson task force that had been formed to investigate that event.

Soon media leaks began to skew the investigation. There were leaks from undisclosed federal sources "close to the investigation" that this was indeed the work of eco-terrorists. Oddly though, the usual graffiti that eco-warriors almost always leave at their burn sites was not present. A review of the normal web sites that espouse those types of eco-attacks was also notable for the lack of any group claiming to have committed that assault. The anomalies in the case persisted, and investigators soon discovered some even more sinister information. Graffiti had indeed been found at or near that site, but it was not eco-terror group graffiti. The slogans found in the area were racist in nature and were directed at the black families who were thought to be the future residents of that community. Soon the original eco-terror hysteria faded, and as the real investigation ground on, the specter of it being a hate crime actually began to unfold.

The fire scenes themselves also did not fit the exact MO of environmental terrorists. The usual delay incendiary devices found at eco-terror attack scenes were not present. The scenes did yield, however, a substantial amount of physical evidence in the form of large buckets that had held flammable liquids, rubber gloves for anti-forensics, one and three gallon containers, road flares, matches, and even a propane torch. Whether or not eco-terrorists were involved in that event, the fire scene investigators were fairly sure that that attack was a well-planned operation that had to have involved several persons. They based that on the sheer volume of arson incidents and noted that the fires were sporadic in nature and did not hit thirty-six homes in a row but jumped around. Investigators were aware that that fact alone meant that the assailants needed vehicles to move around and also needed to spend a great deal of time at the site. Investigators also found a great deal of flammable materials at each fire set and determined that those items either had to be carried into the area en masse or secreted in pieces before the attacks. Either way, the investigators were suspicious because the site employed a full-time security guard, and surely that person would have noted that large amount of activity.

With that, some of the task force investigators descended upon the on duty security guard. He quickly told them that he had left the site just before the incident. Under questioning, the guard admitted that he had been convinced to leave the site by another guard named Aaron Speed. Speed, who was off duty, approached the on duty guard and convinced him to leave. The task force rapidly redirected its efforts toward Aaron Speed. Speed adamantly denied any involvement, but did agree to attend a polygraph exam, which he gloriously failed. Soon after being confronted with his less than honest answers, Speed began to talk. He soon revealed a long-planned conspiracy by at least five male whites to attack that housing development.

As the conspiracy unfolded, so did the motivations of Aaron Speed. To suggest that he was a disgruntled employee would be a gross understatement. Aaron Speed and his young wife Tamara suffered a tragic loss when their infant son died in the spring of 2004. For the remainder of that summer and into fall, Speed grew increasingly upset with his employer Security Services of America for what he perceived was their lack of empathy toward him and his family's needs during that time period. Speed told investigators that his boss refused to allow him bereavement leave following the loss of his son. By late fall, Tamara was pregnant again, and Speed was still upset with his employer.

In that time frame, Aaron Speed came into contact with a twenty-one-year-old male named Patrick Walsh of Fort Washington, Maryland. Walsh was the pseudo leader of a small group of white males who were upset with the prospect of a large number of African Americans moving into their area via the new housing tract. After Speed spoke to Walsh at length, he too became disillusioned with his lot in life and began to form animosity toward the people who would be moving into the new posh homes he was guarding on a nightly basis. Soon Walsh and Speed began to concoct a plan to exact revenge on the future homeowners and on Speed's employer as well.

On the night of December 3, 2004, Aaron Speed was on duty at the Hunter's Brooke site. During that night, he helped arrange for a large amount of flammable liquids and materials to be stolen and secreted at the construction site. The materials were placed inside innocuous-looking five-gallon buckets used for painting and drywall at the site. They were hidden in plain view for the next two days. Also during that time, Speed provided hand-held radios, rubber gloves to hide fingerprint evidence, a propane torch to be used as an ignition device, and a hand-drawn map on how best to enter and leave the construction site. Walsh would gather the remainder of the materials and would enlist the aid of three followers: twenty-one-year-old Jeremy Parady, twenty-one-year-old Michael McIntosh, and twenty-three-year-old Roy Thomas McCann, all residents of the local Maryland suburbs.

Sometime in the very early morning of December 6, Aaron Speed approached his coworker on duty and convinced him to leave the site. The coconspirators moved in, and with Speed's direct help, they began pouring flammable liquids on the unfinished homes within the project. Aaron Speed was careful to point out to the arsonists the one home in the entire tract to avoid as people were already residing in it. By 5:00 a.m., thirty-six fires had been lit with twenty-six fully burning, and all of the coconspirators had fled the scene.

As the media swarmed in on that event and the facts began to emerge that it was more a hate crime than a crime of eco-terrorism, the full weight of the federal government began to crush the resolve of the coconspirators. Following Speed's arrest and admission on December 16, the others were soon identified and rounded up. They soon were arrested, and all began to talk and accuse each other. Jeremy Parady was the first to reach a deal with federal officials. He admitted that the attack was partially racially motivated, and he pled guilty in April 2005. He accepted a prison sentence of about eight years. By June 2005, Aaron Speed who had admitted to being one of the leaders of that conspiracy pled guilty in the federal court. He eventually received a sentence of about ten years in prison. Roy McCann and Michael Everhart both pled guilty in January 2007 to conspiracy to commit arson charges. Each received sentences in the range of four to five years in federal prison.

The ring leader of that band of misfits was Patrick Walsh. He was the only person to take his case to a federal jury trial. A witness and another conspirator, Parady had already given statements that Walsh was an avowed racist who had long talked about burning homes to prevent blacks from moving into the area. Investigators revealed that both Parady and Aaron Speed had made racist comments to them during earlier interviews. The other coconspirators had also revealed that it was Walsh who planned the assault, provided the expertise and most of the flammable materials, and had recruited the other members. In the months before his trial, a search of his cell revealed a large number of handwritten documents about Walsh's plan to establish an organized criminal band called "The Unseen Brotherhood Coalition." The plans detailed future criminal scams, including stock fraud, investment schemes, check fraud, and phony fund raising efforts.

Walsh's efforts in court were unsuccessful. He was convicted by a federal jury in September 2005 and eventually sentenced to twenty years in federal prison. Despite the racial overtones of the case, federal prosecutors never charged any persons with "hate crimes." They later expressed that the attacks were likely made more out of economic envy than out of racial hatred.

The Hunter's Brooke arson spree was the largest ever arson attack in Maryland's history and a task force of over one hundred local, state, and federal investigators formed to solve it in relatively short order. Thirty-six homes were targeted with at least sixteen being totally destroyed by fire and with significant damage to an additional ten. The damage to the partially completed homes was around $4 million.

Investigator's Analysis

While this case is not an actual arson series, it is too noteworthy of a spree to ignore. The security guard in this case was not motivated by heroism, but was in fact motivated by a combination of envy, hate, and revenge. The attacks were fairly well planned and designed but with somewhat low level results as the bulk of their fires did not reach their potential. This was most likely due to the youth and inexperience of the fire setters and the fact that they set their fires to the exterior entryways of homes rather than inside.

Aaron Speed does not have a noteworthy criminal record before this event. His planning was not at all sophisticated as his actions were sure to lead investigators to his doorstep in a short period of time, as did occur. His odds of getting away with this event were minimal, and he goes down as a significant disorganized arson offender.

Thomas Jerry Sexton: Hospital Security Guard August 2, 2009, Clarkesville, Tennessee

In 2009, the Gateway Hospital in Clarksville, Tennessee, had been relocated to a new modern facility. The old hospital building had been slated for demolition and had remained vacant over the past few months. In order to keep out the curious and prevent vandalism, security guards were hired to monitor the property.

One of those guards was a young man named Thomas Jerry Sexton. Nineteen-year-old Sexton seemed like an ideal candidate for the job as he had high aspirations and a seemingly bright future in front of him. Sexton had been a police explorer with the Clarksville Police Department and had recently gone through an internship to be a police investigator. He had also enrolled in and had been accepted to join the air force. While waiting to get into the military, Sexton had spent the summer working long, lonely twelve-hour shifts around the vacated hospital grounds. Like all young men with high aspirations in the police, fire or military, Sexton was raring to go and looking for some action and excitement. He pursued his security duties with zest and zeal.

On the night of August 2, 2009, his keen police observation skills came into play. While on his routine patrol, he noticed a shattered door on one of the vacant buildings. While he should have alerted the local police to come investigate, Sexton took matters into his own hands and entered the structure. He soon located dense black smoke and a smoldering fire in the building. He retreated and called for backup. Firefighters and arson investigators soon discovered that an arson fire had been lit along about 160 feet of hallways. They additionally located between thirty and forty other small spots where a suspect had attempted to light fires. The investigators noted that it was a serious attempt to burn down the building and couldn't think of why anyone would want to do that.

However, the arsonist was not that clever and had left critical evidence behind. Two containers of Kroger brand charcoal fluid had been left behind at the scene. The crime lab matched those to the accelerant poured throughout the building. Investigators, following the most basic of investigation steps, went to a nearby Kroger's store to track down the containers. Upon reviewing store security cameras, the investigators quickly picked out security guard Sexton purchasing the containers during his security shift. They quickly arrested the guard, and within hours the young man confessed to his actions.

Sexton would later plead guilty in court, and his lawyer said the late, lonely hours on duty for the young man had caused too much stress, which in turn caused this aberrant behavior. Not impressed, the court sentenced Sexton on July 6, 2010, to four years in prison. He was granted a bit of mercy and over three years was suspended, while he served at least six months in jail. Of course, the air force is no longer interested in his services.

Investigator Analysis

Like the firefighting field, law enforcement is also filled with its share of "wannabes" and "posers." Most law enforcement agencies avoid hiring people like Sexton as they are often screened out by psychological testing and the polygraph. This method worked well when both the Los Angeles Sheriff's and LAPD denied John Orr's employment for "abnormalities" noted on his psychiatric evaluation. Still, more than a handful of applicants are able to beat some police vetting processes.

It is debatable whether Sexton would have ever been hired as a police officer, but at the time, he was trying to immerse himself into the culture via the "explorer" program offered by his local agency. That type of program, somehow affiliated with the Boy Scouts and police and fire agencies, is very common among hundreds of agencies. Quite a few explorers go on to be successful police officers and firefighters. However, anecdotally, there are countless stories similar to Sexton's where explorers are involved in theft, crime, gang activity, and other inappropriate behavior. There is very little vetting process at the explorer level, and sometimes parents put their "at risk" kids into these systems as an effort to "straighten them out" for the risky behavior they are already involved in.

As an experienced arson investigator, my suspicions are always on high alert when a case involves a volunteer, explorer, security guard, or any other person who is dabbling in the law enforcement or firefighting field. There are just too many case histories to ignore this factor in a case.

Sexton is a classic police officer and hero "wannabe," and his actions were clumsy and disorganized like most members of this sub-type. Like most other suspects in this group, the chances of being caught are extremely high due to the obviousness and unsophisticated method of the crime. Although Thomas Sexton is not a "serial offender," this spree is a classic example that is too big to ignore.

Jackie Morales: Hotel Security Guard
1981, New York City

The Harley Hotel was a forty-story tower of opulence, which cost over $75 million to build in 1980. All through its construction, it was beset with a myriad of problems, none more alarming than the six suspicious fires that occurred during the last few months of construction. All of those problems seemed to have been in the past as the owners proudly opened the gleaming hotel on February 18, 1981. The historic day was marked by several dignitaries attending the grand opening, including New York Governor Carey and New York City Mayor Koch. The two co-opened the hotel in the early evening, stayed for an obligatory cocktail, and were then whisked away by their staffs to other social functions.

Within minutes after the two esteemed guests departed, a fire broke out in the hotel. The fire, although small in size, created a great deal of smoke and panic. Guests fled the ballroom, and the entire hotel was forced to evacuate into the cold February night. All told, thirty-six guests suffered smoke inhalation and hotel managers suffered extreme embarrassment due to that event.

The next day, New York City Fire Department investigators classified that event as an arson attack. The case went unsolved for about a month until a second arson fire occurred in a closet at the same hotel. During that second event, investigators quickly identified a security guard who extinguished that fire and was also present at the discovery of the first fire in February.

Nineteen-year-old security guard Jackie Morales had "discovered" the second fire and told a breathtaking and lurid tale of how he fought the flames.

Investigators immediately recognized him as a "wannabe" firefighter and a hero worshiper. They focused their questions upon him and his actions, and soon the "hero" admitted to them that he had started that fire in the closet because he wanted recognition from his bosses. Gradually, after further inquiry, the "hero" also admitted to setting the fire on the opening night for the hotel. Morales was extremely excited to be viewed as a hero and wanted his employers to recognize his efforts. He was arrested and subsequently convicted for his actions. He was a suspect in several of the other fires at the hotel, but never charged.

The spring of 1981 also yielded an almost identical incident at another high-profile hotel in New York City. Just weeks after the arrest and publicity in the Harley Hotel fire, a fire broke out in the Vista International Hotel within the World Trade Center. Soon investigators classified that event as arson and quickly arrested a hotel security guard for the crime. The twenty-year-old guard also quickly confessed to setting that blaze after being extremely angry over an argument with his wife. The two incidents were uncannily similar in occurrence and took place just a few weeks and a few miles apart.

Investigator's Analysis

Like many others in this category, Jackie Morales was a very obvious suspect from the very beginning. He was young, extremely immature, and obviously excited about his role as a "hero." Just as predictable, he soon gave a full confession to his activities. He was a disorganized offender who set his fires for the purpose of recognition. He had a very high likelihood of getting caught from the very beginning.

Jonathan R. Safe: Ambulance Driver, EMT, Volunteer Firefighter
Lyndsey Sgro: Ambulance Driver, EMT
2009, Buffalo, New York

On May 3, 2009, in Buffalo, New York, a fire broke out in a vacant seven-story building at about 11:30 p.m. Among the many people who responded to that scene were private ambulance drivers Jonathon Safe, twenty years old, and his partner Lyndsey Sgro, a twenty-one-year-old female. Both were qualified EMTs employed by Rural/Metro Medical Services. The fire was ruled arson with no suspect information. The fire was ignited by an open flame to some combustible trash within the building.

Just nine days later, at 4:15 a.m., another fire broke out in a vacant home in the area. The same couple was also on duty. The circumstances of those two fires were consistent with several other fires in the area in recent weeks.

Investigators looking for similarities in the events noted that the same pair of ambulance drivers was on duty and present at most if not all of those fire scenes. Interviews with neighbors actually showed that the ambulance pair made contact with people before the events and brought attention to themselves as "heroes" in some of the fires. Witnesses were clear in indicating that the pair had tried to take credit for heroic deeds during some of those fires.

Similar to police officers, it is common practice for ambulance drivers to "stay in the field" and patrol around or park in their assigned duty area so that they are nearby when a call for service arises. The calls can be few and far between and can lead, like police and firefighting work, to long and boring shifts with plenty of idle time. So seems to be the case with that youthful pair.

Because of their odd behavior, that couple soon appeared on the radar of an arson task force that was investigating the vacant building fires. A month after the second fire, task force investigators raided the home of Jonathon Safe. Coincidentally, in addition to being an ambulance driver, Safe was also recently hired as a volunteer firefighter with a small agency in the area. Subsequent to the search of his home, Safe was arrested for the last two arson fires in the series. He and Sgro were both charged with two counts each of arson.

A grand jury was convened in the case, and in December 2009, on the eve of the grand jury, both defendants reached a plea deal and pled guilty to arson charges. The couple was believed to be involved in several other fires, all for the purpose of recognition.

Chapter 8 Synopsis

This section was given very little space as the few cases presented represent a very small slice of the serial arson world. However, I ask the reader to conduct a very short Internet search using the words arson and security guard. The search will produce a near endless number of accounts describing this phenomenon. Since most of the offenders are either very young or not very bright, most commit these crimes with so little sophistication that they are quickly identified and arrested before their serial activity gets too significant. Very few of them can amass the dramatic numbers of fires we see in other sub groups.

Like many other arson cases, the target of the arson attack is the key to the offender. Many of the "heroes" were identified as they were the only persons who could have or would have wanted to burn a piece of property.

CHAPTER 9

The Firefighter Serial Arsonists

The mere mention of the phrase "firefighter arsonist" in fire investigation circles usually causes immediate tension in the air. Many seasoned investigators sadly shake their heads and acknowledge that it is an ongoing serious phenomenon. Other investigators (generally those new to the job) still maintain their unshaken faith that it is just a gross exaggeration of the three or four cases out there that continue to haunt the fire service. Still others believe that this problem only exists with part-time or volunteer firefighters. But in all cases, this phrase causes immediate debate and conflict.

John Orr, who is mentioned throughout this book, is of course the most glaring example of firefighter arson. He was one of the top five most prolific-known arsonists in the United States and one of the most cunning and skilled offenders ever identified. He sets the bar for all others. However, a mere search of the phrase "firefighter arsonist" on any Internet search engine will spew out dozens, if not hundreds, of accounts of firefighters arrested for fire setting activity. A review of many of the articles will show that the arrested firefighter is a suspect in multiple fires and will come from virtually every type of agency and every level of employment. Cases cited will show arson arrests involving fire investigators, fire chiefs, arson investigators, volunteers, "call firefighters," seasonal firefighters, full-time firefighters, probationary firefighters, reserve firefighters, and auxiliary firefighters. The age and experience of the firefighter arsonists span from eighteen-year-old rookies to thirty-year veterans who are in their fifties. Some will give weak rationale for their fire setting, such as "maintaining training levels or destroying eyesores or dangerous buildings." Others will simply admit that they have no idea why they set fires. The suspects

255

will come from small, rural agencies, large cities, state agencies, and federal agencies. Most set their fires alone, but there are several cases of groups of firefighters setting fires.

Recent firefighter arson arrests are documented in Spain, Greece, Corsica, Canada, Portugal, and Australia. The readers will note that these countries, along with the United States, have massive wild land areas where, during the dry season, explosive brushfires are common. There are anecdotal stories of firefighter arsonists dating back continuously for nearly one hundred years in this country. There have been books, case studies, documentaries, and films all related to firefighter arsonists, again dating back several decades. A former ranking member of the IAAI currently maintains an online blog that frequently highlights firefighter arson cases. Many agencies now include a bloc of "firefighter arsonist" training within their academies.

Firefighter arson is not a new or emerging problem. Case histories show evidence dating back many decades. This author recently interviewed a retired arson investigator named John Graham. Mr. Graham was an arson/bomb investigator for the Los Angeles Sheriff's Department from 1958 until 1962. During his short stint in that capacity, he arrested three firefighters and a fire chief for differing arson events. Each event was different in scope and in motive. One event involved a fire chief for the City of Palos Verdes, who along with his crew burned a famous horse stable with the intent of drumming up funding for his department. The department was disbanded shortly thereafter. A second event was a "seasonal wild land" firefighter who lit brushfires for the pay. A third event involved a federal firefighter who lit seventy-two brushfires with a delay device out of boredom. The final event was a forest service firefighter who ignited a massive wildfire in 1959 because he was upset at a change in his work schedule. Sadly, that event, known as the Woodwardia fire, resulted in the deaths of two Zuni Indian firefighters and the death of a water bomber pilot. That final event was all the more tragic as the firefighter arrested could only be charged with causing a brushfire, which resulted in a minimal fine and one year in jail, despite the three deaths. Retired Investigator Graham also told me another story that has been a shadowy rumor for several decades. During the late 1950s and early 1960s in the Los Angeles Basin, two very experienced arson investigators from a major agency spent months following one another as each was convinced that the other was a serial arsonist. Neither was ever arrested or charged with any fires, but one eventually left the profession over the accusations. That occurred over twenty-five years prior to John Orr's escapades in the same region.

The scope of the firefighter arsonist problem has never really been quantified. However, it has become such a problem that the United States Fire Administration commissioned a study in 1997, which concluded that there is a "problem" and it is "egregious." The report called for a more detailed and formal investigation into that phenomenon on a national scale. It also noted that in 1994 alone, forty-seven firefighters from the state of South Carolina were arrested for arson. In January 2003, the USFA released a more detailed study entitled "Special Report: Firefighter Arson." It conceded that there were not accurate nationwide statistics that would better define the problem, but did note that firefighter arson spanned all ages and all of the classifications of firefighters and fire agencies. Its main recommendation was in pre-hiring screening efforts. The study implored fire agencies to conduct background investigations into all firefighter applicants. The report also outlined numerous case studies of firefighter arsonists.

Another scholar began an in-depth study of firefighter arsonists several years ago, which led him to some very uncomfortable situations. Doctoral Researcher Matt Hinds-Aldrich, in 2008, offered a presentation to the British Fire Service College. He entitled his presentation, "In the Hot Seat: An Uncomfortable Take on the Firefighter Arson Issue." In this discourse, Hinds-Aldrich covered many related subjects, including some history on the subject, past studies, and his own disdain for "profiling" in that area. One of the more compelling facts of this presentation was that Hinds-Aldrich had documented in excess of one thousand different cases of firefighter arson, spanning eighteen countries and going back to as early as 1833. In 2010, in a personal communication with me, Hinds-Aldrich revealed that he now had over thirteen hundred cases in his database. He also admitted that he had stopped his research in this subject due to several factors, not the least of which was the reactions he had received from many peers for this very unpopular field of research. One of his least popular assertions (with which this author agrees) is that the overall lifestyle and work environment of the fire service may actually create that type of activity. The academy preparation and exciting stories that new hires get inundated with are quickly lost in the more realistic and tedious world of daily firehouse chores, endless mundane training, and fewer and fewer actual firefighting calls. This is in opposition to the more conventional thinking that the fire service lures arsonists to its ranks. The sheer boredom and lack of action brings up the old phrase that "idle hands are the devil's workshop." Hinds-Aldrich makes the salient point that the attributes and social characteristics that make one the "firefighter of the year" may also be the same characteristics that make one the next case of "firefighter arsonist."

This author find a lot of credibility in Hinds-Aldrich's research. This author, in a much less intensive search, was easily able to amass over 150 cases of firefighter arson within just a few weeks of scanning the Internet. A sampling of the more prolific cases is included in this chapter. The below listed cases of firefighter arson include many young men who were considered "model firefighters" and people who were well regarded as aggressive and highly motivated leaders within their departments. Many of the below listed arsonists had received special awards for leadership and heroism from their agencies. A few actually were named as the "Firefighter of the Year" in the very same time frame they were lighting fires.

This book will not attempt to rehash the tired debates of "Why do firefighters set fires?" or "Was he an arsonist who became a firefighter or was he a firefighter who got too close to the beast and became an arsonist?" Those questions are left for the psychologists and psychiatrists who love to dabble in that sort of debate. This portion of the book will not spend much time analyzing each case as the suspects themselves are probably the only ones who know why they set the fires. After reading some of those cases, the reader will most likely conclude that the most common motives cited for firefighter arsons are boredom and heroism. The reader will also note that many offenders will cite depression, prescription drug use, alcohol use, relationship problems, and financial troubles as instigating factors. This portion of the book will just tell the stories of some of the more prolific or interesting firefighter arsonists.

Jeffrey "Matches" Boyle: Chicago Fire Department, Lieutenant
Period of Activity: 1998-2005, Chicago

Even the largest and most prestigious fire departments are not immune to the potential of firefighter arson activity. In 2005, Chicago Fire Department Lt. Jeff Boyle was undergoing a lot of stress. His personal life was crumbling as his girlfriend had just left him. He was gambling a lot and losing most of the time. His brother, John, a political appointee to the City of Chicago, was under federal indictment for illegally soliciting payoffs and thousands of dollars in campaign funs. To add to Jeff's misery, John was already infamous in the local press and known as "Quarters Boyle" for a previous scheme where he was convicted for stealing $4 million in quarters from a transportation program. Lastly, like in many of these cases, Lt. Jeff Boyle was drinking massive amounts of alcohol to help him cope with all his problems.

That turbulent year came to a crashing end when Boyle was arrested for the arson of a school and an occupied dwelling in a nearby suburb. Subsequent to his arrest, Lieutenant Boyle admitted that he had set several other arson fires over the years. He said he had a hard time dealing with the stress, and when it got too much at times, he just drove around looking for something to burn.

The Boyle family had obvious political connections as noted in numerous press accounts. John "Quarters" Boyle was given a well-paying, politically appointed city job immediately after getting out of prison for his quarters scandal. Lt. Jeff Boyle, who had always got very mediocre scores on promotional exams, was promoted over two hundred other people who achieved higher scores. The political clout seemed to stay with Jeff Boyle even after his arrest, as he was sentenced twice for fires during that arson spree, each at a much lower term than the prosecutor had demanded. Tragically, in the end, Jeff Boyle served only one year and nine months after admitting to eight structure arsons, including an occupied home and a Catholic school. The normal sentence for something like that in most areas would be over fifteen years in prison.

Even more galling was the fact that, a few months after his release from prison, in a highly publicized case, Jeff Boyle demanded and received his full firefighter's pension. This serial arsonist will receive over $50,000 per year in firefighter's pension benefits for the rest of his life.

Forever known after this case in the local media as Jeff "Matches" Boyle, this twenty-five-year veteran of the professional fire service is linked to at least fourteen structure arsons over an eight-year period. It's probably safe to assume that there were many other incidents over the years.

Robert Eric Eason "Fire Marshal Bob": Capay Fire Protection District Volunteer Firefighter/Captain Period of Activity: 1988-2006, Yolo County, California

* Much of the material in this case comes from personal conversations between the author and retired Cal Fire Investigator Chris Vallerga and Supervising Investigator Joe Konefal.

On September 21, 2006, a large wild land fire erupted during a "Santa Ana" wind condition in the rural foothill region near Zamora, California. Arson investigators already had been looking at a suspect in the area, and evidence found at that fire confirmed the involvement of their suspect. Remnants of a delay incendiary device were located within the area of the origin of this blaze. That fire grew to a large size and destroyed over one thousand acres of wild land and ranch property. Numerous structures were threatened, and hundreds of sheep belonging to area ranchers were killed.

By October 2006, arson investigators from the California Department of Forestry (CDF) (now Cal Fire) served a search warrant at a home in the small town of Guinda, California. Among the many items of evidence seized at the home on that day was a container found hidden in a bin full of soiled diapers. This container was filled with the components of several incendiary delay devices, to include wooden kitchen matches, cigarettes, and mosquito coils. Those premade devices were nearly identical to several located during an arson spree in that rural valley that had lasted nearly two decades. Additionally, two unique delay devices fashioned out of matches, monofilament fishing line, and a mosquito coil were also found in the residence. That was the most compelling evidence yet linking the resident of the home, Robert Eason, to dozens of unsolved arson fires in the area. The investigators, who would normally be jubilant at such a rare discovery, later described their feelings as "miserable." Robert Eason was one of their own—a firefighter.

Cal Fire Investigator Chris Vallerga would later describe this monumental investigation to me. Prior to 1988, the foothill region that surrounded rural California Highway 16, as it wove its way north and west out of Sacramento, had its normal share of wild land fires. A few were caused by lightning, while the vast majority occurred during the harvest seasons of hay and grain. These blazes were fairly normal and mostly related to farm machinery operating on dry, hot days. Another type of fire that occurred with some regularity was the so called "range improvement" fires that seemed to spring up just prior to the first predicted rains of the winter season. These were usually attributed to farmers and ranchers who used fire as a means to clean up their range and fields. While illegal, these fires were not done with a malicious intent and were not considered a huge problem by state investigators.

Looking back years later, investigators would pinpoint 1988 as the year when the amount and type of fires in the region began to dramatically change. During that year and nearly every year that followed, the Highway 16 corridor would have a large number of roadside fires. Investigators consulted records as far back as 1945 to see if this was a natural pattern. It was not. Almost all of the roadside fires would be classified as either "arson" or "suspicious" in nature. No clues arose, and no evidence was located until a decade into this series. The amount of fires varied each year, and there were no particular patterns, except for the fact that all the fires started within a thirty mile long corridor along Highway 16.

Investigator Vallerga, his partner Randy Sanders, and the investigators who followed them began and maintained a detailed investigation. In keeping with basic police investigative work, they constructed an overlay chart on the arson fires in that region. They chose to mark each unsolved arson fire in the region with a red push pin. Each season, they made a new overlay in hopes of identifying a pattern or cluster. In 1999, they got their first break. An investigator found a small remnant of a mosquito coil in the ash of a roadside arson fire. The Cal Fire investigators recognized this as a component of a very unique incendiary delay device. Now they knew what to look for and knew that their quarry had some degree of sophistication.

Meanwhile, the investigators had their own suspicions. Among the people who began to emerge as potential suspects was a long time volunteer fire fighter in the area named Robert Eason. Robert Eason had joined the small Capay

Fire Protection District as a volunteer firefighter in 1988. At the time the area was interspersed with forests, grassland, brush and foothills. Small sheep and cattle ranches dotted the rural area.

Eason, who made his living as a part time rancher and security guard at a local casino, was well respected as a fire fighter and emergency medical technician. He had been promoted to captain in his district, was married and was the father of three children. Eason had held a variety of other jobs to include having been a salesman for ambulances and potato chips. Robert Eason's father was a long time fire chief in Contra Costa County.

Shortly after Eason joined the fire district, the series of suspicious grass fires began occurring along Highway 16. Eason came to the investigator's attention for a couple of reasons. After a few years, they realized that Robert Eason had reported more than a few of these fires. Additionally, on more than one occasion, he approached investigators at the scene who were looking for the area of origin, an extremely difficult task in brush and grass fires, and pointed to a specific spot, even though he had no training as an investigator.

Still, the investigator's had no good leads or useful forensic evidence. In the summer of 2005, the fires seemed to pick up in tempo. On a single day, five arson fires were reported along the Highway 16 corridor. At one of these scenes Cal Fire found another piece of evidence. They found a piece of mosquito coil with a half inch paper match affixed to it with fishing line. This was the second such device in the same area over the past six years. Investigators began testing this type of device and were able to reach some conclusions. They learned that a device of this sophistication would give any arsonist from five minutes to one hour of a separation time before a fire would start. The device was fairly reliable and would ignite even after thrown violently from a moving vehicle.

Another fact emerged in 2005. Investigators added all their several years worth of push pin overlay maps together and recognized three large clusters of activity. They would later place surveillance assets within these clusters. These cameras would give some positive results in the future.

Investigators also began to suspect that a device of this nature may be related to a firefighter who would be one of the few people that was even aware of how something like this might work. Again their thoughts turned back to Robert Eason. They realized now that Eason had reported several of the fires and that he in fact lived at the very north end of the fire pattern, and would have to pass most of the fire areas on a routine basis if he was going to a job. Other fire fighters told investigators that on some of the arson fires in their district, Robert Eason was already dressed in his gear even before the first report of the fire came in. Investigators quietly checked on him and found that he had an arrest as a juvenile in Contra Costa County, but were unable to find the particulars of that event. They noted that he had a "Facebook" page where he posed in full fire fighter gear and called himself "Fire Marshal Bob", even though he was not actually a fire marshal.

A couple of times in 2005 and 2006, investigators casually interviewed Robert Eason after fire events. They noted a very odd behavior that he displayed to them. Despite being a strong, burly sort of guy, and extremely macho in demeanor, when they asked him about various arson fires in the area, they saw that he had the odd habit of sucking his thumb! At first they didn't think much of it, but after a few more interviews realized that under a little bit of pressure, Eason always resorted to sucking his thumb.

This author learned from California Department of Forestry (CDF) Senior Arson Investigator Joe Konefal, that for several months, attempts were made to track the activities of Robert Eason. By 2005, arson investigators had installed pole cameras in certain areas and had placed Eason under video surveillance. Additionally, a satellite tracking device (aka "bird dog") was covertly installed onto Eason's vehicle. After a major wild land fire in 2006, these tracking devices showed Eason in the direct vicinity of the fire before it occurred.

After the September 2006 fire placed Eason at the scene, a tactical plan was devised for his arrest and the search of his home. Some investigators would later admit that a small tactical error was made during this as they tried to confront Eason about his fire setting activity in the minutes prior to searching his home. He refused to admit to anything and it wasn't until after the interview that the investigators on the search warrant located the delay incendiary devices. Another fantastic piece of evidence was located in Eason's blue Ford Tempo. The search warrant on that vehicle showed burn marks on the seats that were an exact match to the coils of the mosquito devices. This proved that Eason had lit the delay devices in his car and had driven around with them burning as he sought out a target of opportunity.

Eason was arrested in October of 2006, and since then has adamantly maintained his innocence. After a jury trial, he was convicted of 12 arson fires, the use of delay devices, and the possession of incendiary devices.

During the hearings, Cal Fire investigators would relate that Eason was a suspect in 143 fires dating back eighteen years, or literally to right after he was hired. Cal Fire Law Enforcement Chief Allan Carlson called it one of the most complex cases ever investigated by his agency. It was solved through the use of mapping, satellite tracking, pole cameras and mobile surveillance. Carlson also testified in court that "nationwide, about 30 percent of arson fires are set by fire fighters". In November of 2008, Robert Eason was sentenced to the maximum term for his fires. He was given a 40 year sentence in state prison. He and his father, also a retired fire fighter, are appealing this conviction and sentencing.

Investigator's Analysis

Robert Eason is a classic example of the "hero" fire fighter arsonist. He used sophisticated time delay incendiary devices on many occasions and was highly mobile, setting them by using a vehicle. He was involved in the reporting and fighting of these fires for recognition, accolades and hero status. He was highly prolific and is the main suspect on over 140 unsolved arsons.

Benjamin B. Christensen: White's Crossing Volunteer Fire Department Firefighter
Period of Activity: 2007-08, Pennsylvania

In a presentencing statement in 2009, a Pennsylvania county judge called twenty-six-year-old Ben Christensen both a "perpetrator and a victim." The defense had argued that Christensen had a life of utter emotional trauma and upheaval, which eventually led him to fire setting behavior. He was adopted at a very young age, and the family who adopted him soon recognized him as a "very damaged child." He would go on to spend many years in state-run juvenile homes.

Despite that very troubled childhood, Christensen was able to become a volunteer firefighter with the White's Crossing Volunteer Fire Department. That fact also added to his issues, since to remain as a firefighter, Christensen had to meet certain weight requirements. Medications he had taken since a young age controlled his emotional issues, but a side effect was that they caused him to gain weight. His defense attorney would later argue that he had to stop his use of those medications to reduce his weight in order to remain a firefighter. Christensen's attorney told the court that his one lifelong desire was to become a firefighter.

In 2007 and 2008, state police investigators were in the midst of a fourteen-month hunt for the arsonist of several buildings in the Lackawana County area. Two of those structures were priceless historical buildings. Others were commercial businesses. On March 31, 2008, arson to a commercial business, Fiorelli Plaza, caused another volunteer firefighter working on the scene to have a severe heart attack. The firefighter, fifty-one-year-old William Saxe, suffered permanent damage and was forced to stop fighting fires.

The task force had few leads until April 2008, when firefighter Ben Christensen was arrested for the statutory rape of a fifteen-year-old girl. During his interrogation of that incident, investigators learned that he was involved in the arson spree in the area. Subsequently, Christensen admitted to setting seven structures on fire. On many of those events, he acted along with

263

a partner named Robert Woolaver. Woolaver subsequently pleaded guilty and is serving a four-to-sixteen-year sentence.

During his confession, Christensen described a typical fire he set. On one occasion, he walked away from his part-time job at a gas station and started a massive fire in a large shopping complex. He then walked back to work, changed into his firefighting gear, and waited to get called to fight the fire. In other cases, he drove around aimlessly looking for a closed or vacant structure to burn. Investigators believe there are numerous other arson fires that Christensen had committed during his spree. In 2009, Ben Christensen was sentenced to a ten-to-twenty-year sentence in state prison for his fire setting.

Investigator's Analysis

Like many other arson cases, the suspect had issues or addictions related to prescription drug use/abuse. Further, again like in many of these cases, a more thorough background screening, including a psychological profile, may have precluded this troubled man from entering the fire service.

Shane Michael Manner: Brunswick Volunteer Fire Company Firefighter
Period of Activity: 1999-2001, Maryland and West Virginia

For such a young man, Shane Manner had a fairly long history of criminal conduct. In 1992, Manner was convicted of assault, battery, assault with a deadly weapon, vandalism, and theft. Two years later in a separate incident, he added a conviction for breaking and entering (burglary) a commercial property to his rap sheet. Two years after that, in 1996, he received yet another conviction, this time for stalking, assault, and vandalism. It was also fairly well known that he had a serious drinking problem. Any one of these incidents would normally have been enough to preclude Manner from obtaining any sort of trusted employment. Despite all of that, Manner was able to join the Brunswick, Maryland, volunteer fire company in 1999.

On May 1, 2000, a small series of fires destroyed recycling containers within Brunswick. On May 31, an arson fire destroyed a garage owned by the president of the Brunswick Fire Company, Chief Charles Leopold. That case remained unsolved. By July of that year, there was an arson fire to trash containers behind a supermarket. Initially, there were no suspects in any of these cases.

In the early part of 2001, due to his energy and dedication, Shane Manner received a special award from the chief of his agency for his efforts in training the other firefighters. That was the only highlight in his brief firefighting career.

Within a few months of getting that award, state fire marshals targeted him as a serial arsonist and the Brunswick Fire Company dropped him from their rolls. That action did not stop Shane Manner. He moved to a nearby town in West Virginia and immediately became the prime suspect in up to fifteen vegetation fires. His spree came to an abrupt end on November 30, 2001, when he was arrested for drunken driving and for falsely reporting a fire. Subsequent to that, officials in two states charged him with setting over twenty-four arson fires in a two-year period. Manner was subsequently convicted of setting a garage on fire and received a three-year prison sentence.

Investigator Analysis

Shane Manner's case is an excellent example of the one problem that volunteer fire departments have yet to rectify. His case illustrates the extraordinarily poor back ground checks or hiring practices that tend to plague some agencies. A simple police background check of this man should have immediately excluded him from any public agency work. He had a long documented history of violent, stalking, and erratic behavior. There were plenty of indications that he had severe problems with alcohol abuse. While many cases of firefighter arson cannot be predicted, this one seems inevitable in hindsight.

Stark T. Liedtke: Alton Fire Department, Call Firefighter Period of Activity: 2006-10, New Hampshire

On Friday, March 19, 2010, a resident in rural New Hampshire called the police to report a prowler in the area. A perimeter was set up by local and state police. One local police sergeant entered a supermarket within the perimeter and noticed a man he knew as a local firefighter. The man, Stark Liedtke, was acting somewhat suspiciously and was covered in dirt and mud, which was similar to the area where the prowler had been seen. Liedtke gave a vague answer to the officer about what he was doing. He then gave conflicting statements as to where he had parked his vehicle. Police noted a strong odor of gasoline on Liedtke and the fact that he matched the description of the prowler. He was detained for investigation. Upon searching him, officers found a large box of matches, a headlamp, knife, and a fire department pager. His vehicle was found parked in a hidden area near some public property. A state fire marshal's dog was called to the scene and tracked puddles in the area to a cache of plastic bottles filled with gasoline. They determined that Liedtke was in the area to set fire to a vacant residence by crawling under it and placing the bottles of gasoline in the crawl space. He was arrested at that point.

During the interrogation, investigators obtained a confession to that plot by Liedtke, along with his admission of setting eleven previous fires in the area. He mostly targeted vacant buildings. He crawled under some of them to place his incendiary materials. He said he set the fires over the previous four-year period because he was bored.

The next week, Liedtke was formally charged by Alton police for setting four arson fires. Among the items burned were three occupied homes in 2006. A month later, the neighboring city of New Durham charged him in an additional three arson cases for fires set to unoccupied homes. As of the spring of 2010, Stark Liedtke was also suspected in several wildland fires and arson attacks to piles of tires. Forty-four-year-old Liedtke had been a call firefighter for the Alton Fire Department for over twenty-two years. He had attained the rank of lieutenant at the time of his arrest. He was dismissed from the fire service three days after his arrest. In November 2010, Stark Liedtke accepted a plea deal and was convicted of nine arson fires in two different counties. He was sentenced to a minimum of three years in state prison and ordered to pay over a half million dollars in restitution. He was also ordered to undergo psychiatric counseling.

Investigator Analysis

This case is too new to know all the investigative details. However, the fact that some of his fires in 2006 were to occupied homes makes this man an extremely dangerous person. There is no evidence at this point about why he attacked occupied homes, but it is probably safe to say that he had some sort of personal connection to the victims. This is outside the norm of most serial offenders, who rarely attack occupied structures. It is also safe to say that Liedtke probably set many more fires over the years than what he has admitted to. Trial records revealed that he admitted to setting many fires since his teens, but he could not accurately remember how many.

Brendan Hokin: Rural Fire Service Volunteer Firefighter
Peter Cameron Burgess: Rural Fire Service Volunteer Firefighter
Period of Activity: 2001-03, New South Wales, Australia

In January 2001, a young, handsome firefighter, named Brendan Hokin, was photographed as he sat exhausted and sooty, while he poured water over himself during the middle of a massive "bushfire" (wildland) firefighting effort in New South Wales, Australia. That striking photo made him instantly famous and the face of the volunteer Rural Fire Service after it appeared on the front page of the major newspapers in the region. By 2002, however, Hokin was arrested for starting that very same string of brushfires. His only explanation to the court was "I have got a problem . . . I don't know why. I just did it." His attorney would later claim that he suffered from unemployment, relationship issues, and severe depression.

The 9/11 terror attacks on the United States and the subsequent glorification of America's firefighters spurred young Peter Burgess to volunteer as a firefighter with the Rural Fire Service in NSW. The young loner had told many people that he wanted to be a hero like the American firefighters who died in the World Trade Center. Two years later, he was arrested for setting at least three series of massive bushfires in the coastal region of NSW.

These two young men are not alone in their actions. In 2003, a special task force charged ten other volunteer and full-time firefighters in several bushfire arsons. The 2003 year was quite horrific for Australia as bushfires destroyed more than six hundred homes that season. That country has always been plagued with catastrophic wildland fires and retains a seventy-thousand-member fire service, most of which are volunteers. In 2006, State Bushfire Chief Phil Koperberg told Reuters reporters that his commanders were monitoring at least thirty firefighters as possible arsonists. He also acknowledged that his agency was forced to spy on its own workers as "up to one in five fires are lit by firefighters."

Brendan Sokaluk: Churchill Brigade, Country Fire Authority Volunteer Firefighter
Period of Activity: 2009, Churchill, Australia

In February 2009, Australia was again beset with a series of massive bushfires. This firestorm was the most deadly in Australia's recent history as over 181 people perished in the blazes. One particular fire, in the Latrobe Valley just east of Melbourne, destroyed thirty-nine thousand hectares and killed twenty-one persons. By mid-February, police announced an arrest in the Latrobe Valley arson fire. The suspect, Brendan Sokaluk, was a thirty-nine-year-old former volunteer firefighter. He was arrested after getting caught lighting a fire in a timber reserve.

A check showed he had volunteered back in the 1980s before any background investigations had taken place on applicants. He left the fire service and twice more tried to reapply, but was turned down both times after background checks revealed problems in his past. At the time of his arson arrest in 2009, he was also in possession of child pornography. His lawyer cited his rage at a failed relationship for his irrational behavior. He is currently in jail and facing twenty-five years in prison.

———

Investigator's Note

As of this writing, Sokaluk has not been convicted of any crime. Additionally, while this book centers on serial arson offenders, this is the only arson event linked to that person at that time. It should be noted that there were several similar unsolved arson events in the same area that day. The fact that twenty-one persons died as the result of this particular fire make this case worthy of mention in this writing. His actions and brief background that we are aware of are consistent with serial arson behavior.

Caleb Lacey: Lawrence-Cedarhurst Fire Department Volunteer Firefighter
Period of Activity: 2009, Nassau County, New York

In October 2008, nineteen-year-old Caleb Lacey was still a high school senior on Long Island, New York, when he joined the Lawrence-Cedarhurst Fire Department as a volunteer. Soon, however, his immaturity showed as he displayed frustration to his boss about dealing with over ninety emergency calls, none of which were fires.

On the evening of February 18, 2009, Lacey was attending a department bowling event with the rest of his crew. His captain noted that Lacey seemed edgy and distracted, and he told Lacey to go home if he wasn't feeling well. At five forty the next morning, a fire broke out in a laundry at the base of an apartment building, just hundred feet from where Caleb Lacey lived. Security footage from the fire station showed Lacey running into the station and getting dressed in his bunker gear two minutes *before* the station was notified of the fire. When the engine arrived at the scene, the fast spreading fire grew large and trapped a family in the apartment above. During the firefighting effort, other firefighters noted that Lacey was acting odd and had removed his firefighting pants. He left them at the scene as he was unable to continue his fire suppression duties. When the fire was put out, firefighters found a mother and her three children, all acquaintances of Caleb Lacey, dead from the flames.

An arson dog alerted on the odor of gasoline at the base of the fire and also on the odor of gasoline found on Caleb Lacey's discarded bunker pants. A month later, arson investigators confronted Lacey about that incident. In a videotaped admission, he told investigators that he had poured gasoline and lit the blaze knowing full well that people lived above the laundry. He said he wanted to perform a rescue and get recognized as a hero for his actions.

A year after that event, Caleb Lacey was convicted for the arson and four murders. He was sentenced to twenty-five years for life in prison for what the judge called a "juvenile act." In handing down the sentence, the judge also admonished him, saying, "I don't know what the motivation was. Heroes don't create danger. They confront it."

Investigator's Note

As in the Australian case, this is the only known fire event associated with Caleb Lacey. However, since he had done such a horrendous and dramatic event just months after being hired, it can be safe to conclude that this would have been the first in a long string of staged fires if he hadn't gotten caught.

This case also emphatically illustrates the perception of firefighting duties versus the reality. Many non-firefighters believe that fire service personnel are actively fighting structure fires on a daily basis. There is a tremendous amount of training and drilling that precedes being named a firefighter, and the perception is that the new recruit will be immediately put to the test, "facing down the beast." The reality is that in our modern society, structure fires are becoming less common every day. This is due to a combination of many factors, including the use of modern fire-resistant materials, smoke alarms, and sprinkler systems and the fact that fewer and fewer people use open flame sources in their homes. Less people smoke indoors, and people are becoming more safety conscious when it comes to candles and cooking. Most modern appliances have multiple built-in safety features and cause fewer fires.

All of this combines to create an environment with fewer fires each year. New, highly energized fire recruits soon learn that the bulk of their time is devoted to endless drilling, equipment maintenance, and cleaning of vehicles and quarters. Thrown in with this are the countless public events, parades, school demonstrations, fund raisers, toy drives, and other community service projects that firefighters are tasked with. Since many people in urban areas use the fire department as their personal doctor or problem solver, firefighters are called to handle a myriad of calls, most having nothing to do with fire. They handle animal rescue, floods, rescues, car accidents, and basically any other problem that nobody else knows what to do with. There are recent studies that show that in the major urban areas, the average firefighter is attending less than two structure fires per year. Most of their fire calls tend to be trash, vegetation, and vehicle fires. It is not exactly the face-to-face battle with "the beast" that they had expected. The more immature firefighters soon start to chafe at the bit, hoping for the chance to dash into a burning building to confront the flames and carry out a dramatic rescue. This mind-set in its extreme form creates events like the one staged by Caleb Lacey.

Conroe D. Vernon: Wilson, Oklahoma Volunteer Firefighter
Period of Activity: 2007, Oklahoma

In a brief but prolific crime spree in the summer of 2007, nineteen-year-old Conroe Vernon and two young friends started five arson fires, along with an additional series of vandalisms and burglaries. In a plea deal later that year, he pled guilty to four counts of arson and was sentenced to a six-month boot camp for young offenders.

Mark E. Morgan: U.S. Bureau of Land Management Firefighter
Period of Activity: 2005, Reno, Nevada Area

In a ten-day period in August 2005, thirty-four-year-old BLM firefighter Mark Morgan, who got paid for being a seasonal firefighter, set three separate fires in the tinder dry national forest west of Reno, Nevada. He was arrested, and he admitted to setting two of the fires with a lighter and a third with a flare gun. Morgan later told a federal judge at sentencing that he lit the fires out of boredom and a need for income. His fires burned no property, but several hundred acres of wildland.

Investigator's Note

Due to his confession and lack of prior criminal history, the federal judge gave Morgan a slap on the wrist by sentencing him to just a few months of house arrest and a fine. This type of leniency is quite common in firefighter arson cases across the United States.

Coatesville, Pennsylvania, Arson Series: 2008-09
Robert Tracey Jr.: Coatesville Fire Department, Captain
Robert Bruce Tribbett: Pomeroy Volunteer Fire Company Firefighter
James Samuels: Pomeroy Volunteer Fire Company (Unknown Capacity)

Coatesville, Pennsylvania, was once a thriving steel mill city. As in many other rust belt cities, its heyday came to an end in the 1970s, and the city slowly eroded into a failing collection of aging neighborhoods filled with vacant buildings. By 2008, investigators noted an alarming increase in arson fires throughout the city. This increase was reported in the local media, and amazingly, the fires increased in number and in scope. Over the next fourteen months, there were over fifty unsolved arson fires in Coatesville. Some of those were to occupied dwellings and resulted in injuries and at least one death. Federal investigators from the ATF were called in to help form a large local task force to investigate that arson spree.

By 2009, some progress had been made, and seven suspects had been arrested for several of the arsons. The perplexed investigators noted that there was very little connection between the suspects, and the motives all seemed to vary. More alarming was the fact that two of the suspects were Coatesville area firefighters, while two others were somewhat affiliated with the fire departments in the area.

Early in the case, volunteer firefighter Robert Tribbett, twenty-five years old, was arrested in August 2008 in connection with attempting to start a fire on the deck of the home of one of his neighbors. He was identified after his DNA appeared on a delay incendiary device made of matches and a cigarette, which was found on the porch of a home. Tribbett, after his arrest, cited issues with relationships and alcohol abuse as his reasons for starting fires. He was on probation for a drunken driving conviction at the time of that incident. Task force officials said he was a person of interest in at least twenty other fires in the region.

Another male, James Samuels, twenty-two years old, was arrested on September 3, 2008, for setting a structure fire. He was identified as being "affiliated" with the same Pomeroy volunteer fire company as Robert Tribbett.

In December 2008, a seventeen-year-old "junior firefighter" with an area agency was arrested after he set fire to an unoccupied garage in the area. He was not identified due to his age.

After these and other arrests, the fires continued. One of the arson fires burned down the residence of the elderly mother of Capt. Robert Tracey, an assistant chief of the Coatesville Fire Department. In March 2009, area residents were shocked when task force members arrested Captain Tracey for two other structure arsons within blocks of his home. Tracey had just been hired as a full-time paid fire captain after several years as an assistant chief, volunteer firefighter.

After the arrest of Tracey, the city gained national notoriety, and local politicians and fire scholars labeled "the fire-plagued city a case study in arson."

Investigator's Analysis

This is one of those cases where the number of arsons in the area, while most likely unrelated to each other at first, gained so much notoriety and attention that it enticed two or three firefighters in the area who were at risk.

By the time that each was arrested, the well-publicized arson spree was into its twelfth month. Obviously, this is just speculation, but the firefighter's arson events may have been seen as their opportunity to take advantage of the ongoing arson problem.

Taken as a whole, the arson problem seemed to be at relatively normal levels, but garnered a lot of media attention. This type of problem is consistent with cities that are eroding or declining. The media hype may well have whetted the appetites of the firefighters for their chance at fame and glory.

An interesting note on this case is the use of delay incendiary devices by firefighter Rob Tribbett. An attentive reader of this book will note that the use of delay incendiary devices is not at all common, and in the few cases where they are used, they are predominantly used by firefighters or other persons with an interest in the fire service who are involved in wildland arsons. The only other groups of fire setters that use devices on a regular basis are the professional torch for financial gain and some internal extremist groups, including animal rights organizations, earth/eco terror groups, and abortion clinic arsonists/bombers.

Chapter 9 Synopsis

Firefighter arson has been and continues to be a problem within the fire service. Although the actual numbers are quite small in comparison to the large number of firefighters in the world, there are still a consistent number of cases that seem to arise on an almost monthly basis. These cases bring great embarrassment to the profession as a whole and create a sense of mistrust within the public.

As long as human beings are hired to fight fires, there will always be some flawed individuals who manage to slip through even the best background investigations and become firefighter arsonists. While this probably can't be totally eliminated, agencies can certainly make more efforts to identify and "weed out" at-risk candidates. This will be a difficult and costly process in the beginning. With many public agencies experiencing horrific financial issues in recent years, the ability to conduct in-depth background checks on applicants is greatly diminished. However, it is not too costly or unrealistic to mandate that all firefighter applicants submit to criminal background checks, fingerprint runs, and a preemployment polygraph examination. While these are not perfect, they are certainly used on a daily basis to screen law enforcement applicants. These methods will screen out at least the most obvious applicants who have a history of substance or alcohol abuse, mental health issues, erratic behavior, severe financial problems, and shoddy work histories.

The second remedy is for fire agencies to provide intense education, training, and oversight with their employees. Many firefighter arsonists have blamed boredom and a lack of excitement for their fire setting behavior. Proper supervision, a strong training plan, ongoing physical fitness and educational programs, and close personnel monitoring by administrators may help to prevent some additional cases from occurring. Too much idle time within the firehouse often leads to pranks, hazing, shenanigans, theft, and possibly more serious criminal behavior.

Lastly, the great leniency shown by the courts, prosecutors, and some investigators toward firefighter arsonists needs to stop. These people have betrayed their profession and the public they served and need to be prosecuted for their crimes the same as any other arson offender. It's not a sickness; it's a crime.

CHAPTER 10

The Final Analysis

The Omitted Serial Arsonists

Most investigators will note that I have omitted several types of significant serial arsonists from this book. Most notable is the long list of *extremist arsonists*, including eco-terror and animal rights "warriors" who have lit dozens of fires. There are many of these "crusaders" who have participated in from one to twenty or more arson attacks. These people are important, and I give them brief mention, but they are arsonists for a cause and differ quite a bit from the main topic of this book. I also briefly mention one or two cases of abortion clinic arsonists, while there are dozens more similar cases. These are similar in nature (but differing in ideology) from the previously mentioned extremists. Other groups who have engaged in significant arson activity are racial/hate groups, anti-gay groups, and anti-government/anti-tax groups. Additionally, I have left out a couple of cases of professional, paid "torch" arsonists who have lit dozens of fires for insurance fraud. Again, that is an entirely different topic.

Street Gangs

From the time I started in this business, I was told in endless arson training courses that criminal street gangs routinely use arson as an initiation tool for new members. In reality, I have never heard, even anecdotally, over the past sixteen years of even one case of this. It appears to be yet another myth in the arson world that is still perpetuated among many of my peers. I am aware and have investigated several cases where street gang members will use arson as a tool with which to destroy evidence, commit fraud, extortion, or to settle an old score, but I can think of no serial arson cases related to active gang members. By their very description, serial arsonists are loners and would never be affiliated with a group or gang.

Juveniles

This group remains a topic of much debate. I agree strongly with Dr. Dian Williams who believes that juveniles set about half the arson fires. This is mostly true in my region. However, some of my peers will not arrest or forward arson charges against juvenile offenders, no matter how many fires the child has set or what was the intent of the fire. If charged at all, the juveniles are often charged with "malicious mischief" rather than arson. I am aware of several juvenile fire setters who have set upward of a dozen fires and yet have seldom been introduced to the justice system. Many professionals in the field won't label those kids as "arsonists" but prefer the more innocent term "juvenile fire setter."

For legal reasons, I cannot provide the names of serial juvenile arsonists in this book, but suffice to say that a few I have come into contact with continued their fire setting activity into adulthood.

The Profile?

So after reviewing each of the above cases, albeit some of them had very little information that remains, can we really develop a profile of a serial arsonist? The old "profile" was the standard white male, a loner with relationship problems, issues with alcohol, and a sense of inadequacy about his life and himself. Does this very general profile hold true or is it just too general, and would it not describe a whole slew of criminal sub types? Here is a synopsis of the cases highlighted in this book:

Race and Gender

Most past studies indicate that the serial arsonist is most often a white male.

The overwhelming majority of the serial arsonists that we have identified in this book have in fact been white males. However, as the reader will note, with the inclusion of some recent cases in my area (Greater Los Angeles), the most recent offenders have almost all been Hispanic. In fact, during 2009-11 in the Los Angeles area, this author has taken part in the investigation of twelve serial arsonists, with nine of them having been male Hispanics. This, of course, reflects the high percentage of Hispanics in this region's population. One of the top three most significant serial arsonists of all time, Thomas Sweatt was black. The author is currently involved in the court case of another serial arsonist in the Los Angeles area who is being charged with five murders, sexual assaults, and at least three arson events. He defies all arson profiling in that he is a very young black male. In a last anecdotal account, I am currently working on a case with eight fires, all with the use of exotic time delay ignition devices, where the suspect is an Asian.

This author has strong opinions of why those earlier "profiles" may be wrong. One strong belief is that "nuisance"-type fires, the hallmark of most serial offenders, occur more frequently in blighted areas, "skid rows," and other inner city areas that have traditionally been made up of predominantly black or Hispanic peoples. As has been asserted *ad nauseam* in this book, fire agencies routinely do not investigate these types of fires, particularly in inner city areas. So if a minority serial arsonist is lighting dozens or hundreds of small fires in an inner city setting, there is a higher likelihood that he will escape detection for a longer period of time than a similar offender in a suburban setting. A simple comparison is to equate these types of minor fire events with graffiti crimes. Graffiti attacks are so common in urban areas that they have become simply an accepted part of the landscape, along with stripped and abandoned vehicles, vacant properties, and broken windows on buildings. That same graffiti crime in an upscale suburban neighborhood will draw the immediate attention of civil authorities and will result in most cases in the attacks being investigated by the police. Such is the case also with nuisance-type fires.

While the numbers continue to reflect a heavy representation of white males as serial offenders, it is my belief that as we get more skilled at identification, we will find a number of minority serial arsonists who may actually reflect the per capita makeup of an area. It is my belief that race is probably not a reliable factor in serial arson "profiling."

Women Offenders

The reader will note the inclusion of a dozen female serial arsonists in this reading. There is also a good deal of online information suggesting that female serial offenders are actually not that uncommon. Despite the growing number of "at risk" females on the street or suffering from mental health issues that may lead to serial fire setting, the identified number of women offenders remains fairly low. Serial arson activity still remains a male-dominated field.

Most of the female offenders were described as being large or obese, somewhat masculine in appearance, and unmarried at the time of their crimes.

Almost none had jobs or a profession, other than the nurse arsonists. The biggest difference in female serial arsons from their male counterparts is their choice of targets and time of fires. As stated, female serial arsonists tend to set fires within their homes or workplaces and quite often during the daylight hours.

Age

Most past studies identified serial arsonists as being between seventeen and twenty-six years old.

The studies are fairly accurate with that fact. Most of the serial arsonists documented tend to be close to that age group. However, there are still reporting issues in this area because many agencies still refuse to classify juvenile serial fire setters as "arsonists." Many juvenile offenders set dozens of minor fires before they are caught. They are seldom held accountable for many of the fires.

An interesting theory was posed to me recently by another very experienced arson investigator. There have been a surprisingly high number of serial arson cases involving men in the "mid-life" years from forty-five to sixty years old. On the other hand, there have been very few cases involving men serial arsonists in the thirty-to-forty age group. My colleague's theory behind this is definitely "armchair psychology" at its best, but it did pique my interest. His theory is that young men from their teens to their late twenties are in an extremely aggravated and stressful stage of their lives filled with hormones and life-changing decisions. Many break with their families in their teens and do not find firm emotional support such as a wife and children until nearly a decade later. He believes that this group with the least amount of emotional support is highly susceptible for excessive drinking and poor decision-making, which would include fire setting behavior. The theory continues that by their late twenties through their thirties and early forties, these same males are engaged in family activities and career building and are in a fairly well-supported environment that generally keeps them away from destructive behavior. The theory concludes that by the time these men hit their mid—to late forties, they have run into family strife, failed marriages, stalled careers, and the general grind of life. Once these pressures begin to build, the male finds himself again in a highly destructive frame of mind with very little infrastructure to emotionally support him. He then again goes back to the same destructive behavior of alcohol and fire setting that marked his early years. When this author first heard this theory, I couldn't help but think of people like Pat Russ, Thomas Sweatt, David Berkowitz, and Paul Keller, who seemed to take significant breaks in their fire setting behavior while engaged in relationships and careers. They fell back into their fire setting ways shortly after one of those things fell apart.

While recently re-reading FBI Profiler John Douglas's book *The Anatomy of Motive*, this author was surprised to read that Douglas also talks about this very same theory. In addressing a study of the behavior of mass murderers and assassins, Douglas also points out that many of these offenders are men who are in their forties who have encountered great frustration with their marriage, family, and job, and this perceived failure at this emotionally critical time in their life becomes their "trigger" to violent or unhealthy activity.

Nonaggressive Personality

The vast majority of all serial arson offenders have been routinely classified as cowards or persons unwilling or unable to deal with others in a direct manner.

On reading this list of stories, this description is true almost 100 percent of the time. Almost every single serial arsonist on this list, with just one or two exceptions, was extremely non-confrontational. The majority of their criminal activity was undertaken in retaliation for a perceived offense, but was done in a covert manner, sometimes days, weeks, or even months after the perceived offense. These people truly are cowards, and most have admitted to an inability to deal with others on an interpersonal basis.

Another related common trait among serial arson offenders is their physical or mental limitations. An overwhelming number of the arsonists in this writing had some physical disability, including birth defects, small stature, speech impediments, persistent health problems, and mental health issues. Many of these physical limitations caused the arsonists to be ridiculed, bullied, and harassed at an early age or to be victimized by more physically fit persons throughout their life. The mental health issues that also include "modern" maladies such as ADD, ADHD, obsessive-compulsive disorder, depression, and migraines have caused many of these offenders to be long-term users of prescription medications. They have also produced limited achievement in academic settings.

Method of Ignition

For the investigator, the method of ignition and the motive have always been the two most important subjects of the study of serial arsonists. This author has attended dozens of formal classes related to arson from local agencies, colleges, fire marshals, professional organizations, including the

National Fire Academy, the FBI's Hazardous Devices School, and the ATF's Advanced Arson School. At nearly every one of these training classes, I was told by "experts" that arsonists commonly use delay incendiary devices and that these items are frequently found at fire scenes.

In truth, the author has personally investigated over 1,600 fire scenes and has researched through his agency another thirty thousand fire scenes and arson cases. Delay incendiary devices were found in less than fifty of these cases (0.2 percent). About forty to forty-five of these cases were found to be insurance fraud-related fires. Only a few devices were found in fires other than insurance-related fires. Significantly, these delay devices (other than insurance cases) were found in mainly wild land arson scenarios or in cases involving either firefighter arsonists or arsonists who have some background or training in wild land fires. The author has spoken about this very subject to many other peers in the field on the West Coast. They too have confirmed that they only find devices (if ever) in some insurance fraud cases or in some wild land cases where the suspect usually turns out to be related to the fire service or has had past training by the fire or forest service. Like a few other things in the arson field, the myth of delay incendiary devices continues.

This author's strong opinion at this point is that delay incendiary devices, while they have been used time and again, are actually quite uncommon in arson events. They do tend to be mainly relegated to wild land fires and insurance fraud fires. It is not common at all to find them in fire scenes. Most cases adjudicated in court show that the most common ignition scenario is an open flame (most often these days a butane lighter) applied to whatever materials are found at the scene. The serial arson cases in this book do in fact reflect that same theory, as very few of these people used a delay incendiary device to commit their arsons. Of the sixty-two serial arsonists that are discussed in this book, only seven of them show the use of a delay incendiary device. Not surprisingly, six of the seven were firefighter arsonists or "firefighter wannabe" arsonists. Most notable among the people in the use of devices is of course a firefighter—John Orr. This author submits that John Orr used delay incendiary devices because he, being a firefighter, was trained that it was common for arsonists to use such items. His ignition system was in fact a learned behavior.

As a follow-up to this paragraph, the author has also attended countless arson training sessions where the instructor deemed it very important for students to actually learn how to assemble and use exotic delay incendiary devices. Many arson classes devote significant hours to teaching firefighters, fire science students, forest rangers, etc. in the art of making delay incendiary devices in the name of "professional education." This is absolutely insane and is akin to teaching police cadets and security guards how to murder someone. We in the fire investigation field have to stop teaching these things at our training classes. A mere mention of devices and a few photos of what to look for at a scene would suffice.

Motive

A review of all of the cases in this book shows that many past studies into the realm of serial arson have it correctly. The most prevailing motive for serial arson appears to be the "spite/revenge" motive, wherein the arsonist uses the only means he or she has at their disposal to get back at a perceived wrong. Like many of the "experts" have stated, arson is indeed a crime of the weak, small, cowardly, and introverted. It is a simple crime that anyone, even persons with severe mental and physical handicaps, can accomplish with little chance of getting caught.

Some arson motives do vary within the sub groups. The main motive for security guard and firefighter arson appears to be the "hero" motive or the need for recognition. Most of these offenders will blame boredom for their crimes, but it is most likely related to the need for attention.

While the "sexual gratification" motive has been highly touted in past studies, there is almost no documentation to prove that this is a common motive. There is no doubt, however, that the "excitement" aspect is a significant part or sub motive for many of these offenders.

Targets

This one is fairly simple and straightforward. The majority of cases here show that the serial fire setter most often targeted items of little to no value. Most often the targets were trash receptacles, discarded furniture, cardboard boxes, pallets, wood and debris piles, and vegetation. Almost every one of these offenders started out attacking these targets, with the more serious arsonists eventually graduating to unoccupied structures, including outbuildings, sheds, barns, garages, vacant homes, and businesses. The most serious offenders then increased the danger level by eventually targeting occupied structures such as homes, apartments, and businesses that were open. The worst of the worst (including both Paul Keller and George Peter Dinsdale a.k.a. Bruce Lee) eventually graduated to the most devastating of targets, the multi-occupancy structure, such as hotels, apartment buildings, and elder care facilities. A study of the serial arsonist's target selections will be a good guide toward determining how long his fire setting behavior has been occurring. In reality though, it is obvious that the bulk of serial offenders seldom targeted automobiles and most seldom attacked occupied structures.

Targeting Firefighters

Another motive that I have heard during many arson training classes is that the arsonist will often start a fire with the intention of harming firefighters. In practice, many fire investigators and their chiefs believe that if the danger to firefighters was shown to the arsonist, it would cause them to cease their fire setting activity. The reality is that, after interviewing a couple of hundred fire setters, the last thought in their minds is what happens after the fire starts. The majority of arsonists have shown no ill will toward firefighters and do not even think of them when they light the fire. They are only focused on their own selfish need to start the fire. This belief seems to be a somewhat self-centered myth by some members of the fire service. In reality, the arsonist probably never even thinks of the firefighters before, during, or after the fire. Anecdotally, one arsonist told me that he liked firefighters and was only giving them something to do, which he thought they would appreciate.

On a related topic, I recently read a book of fiction about a serial arsonist operating in Southern California. The book centered around a fire captain/ investigator chasing a highly skilled serial arsonist who used hyper exotic time delay incendiary devices. While the book is obviously pure Hollywood style fiction, it was interesting to note that the author portrayed both the fire investigator and the arsonist as being excited about "matching wits" with one another. It brings up another myth in the investigation field that some investigators still believe to be true. More than one investigator within the past year has told me how he "knows" a particular arsonist set up a scene "to screw with us". If you have ever sat across a table from a recently arrested arsonist or serial arsonist, you will find that most are either drunk, stoned out of their mind on prescription meds, or are absolutely crazy. They barely know that arson investigators exist and the thought of them playing mind games with us is ludicrous. Most don't even know what day it is. Only one or two of the worst offenders have even mentioned being aware of the investigation around them. Again, their fire setting is for their own self-centered reasons, and we are not even a factor in the event.

Sexual Issues

I don't want to dabble in this issue much as I have no qualifications other than my street experience and as in most of these cases there was precious little documentation of proper mental health evaluations on the offenders. However, anecdotally at least, it appears that there are a large inordinate number of serial arson offenders who are believed to have some form of sexual identity issues. I don't know why, but a review of many of these cases of the male offenders show that many have had homosexual relationships or activity. Still others, significantly John Orr and David Berkowitz, were both believed by analysts to have gender identification issues. This is an issue that I was totally unaware of until I read all the case histories of this group of offenders. The group of sixty-two serial arsonists in this book has a reported number of nearly 30 percent of them having engaged in homosexual activity. This appears to be significantly higher than a recent Gallup poll estimate of about 10 percent of the US population having engaged in homosexual activity. Of the serial arsonists who also committed murder in these case histories, 66 percent were categorized as either gender confused or homosexual. I can only compare this list to my own casework in this field (about twenty cases) and realize that it holds true. The majority of the serial arson cases I have personally been involved with have some connection to homosexual activity. I have no explanation whatsoever for this, and I hope that this topic is professionally researched in the future.

Post-Fire Behavior

The popular myth that has prevailed for decades is that arsonists usually stick around and watch their handiwork. Indeed, nearly every arson class I have ever attended reinforces the investigative trick of photographing the crowd in hopes of finding the arsonist. Many investigators and analysts firmly believe that it is likely that a thorough search will turn up an arsonist actually masturbating at the fire scene. All of the major "profilers" in this field have suggested this as a practical investigative technique.

The truth of the matter is that the "profilers" are partially correct but for the wrong reasons. The first person to suggest that an arsonist would obtain sexual gratification from the fire was the father of modern psychology, Sigmund Freud. He made this great leap by studying only a handful of persons associated with fire. His theory was perpetuated by a famous study undertaken in the 1950s by researchers Lewis and Yarnell. Their study, published in the initial psychiatric "Bible" *Diagnostic and Statistical Manual* in 1952, was the result of their analysis of over eleven hundred prison records of offenders. This study seemed to be the sole cited material for the next forty years and is probably the main reason why arson is currently believed to be a sexual deviant crime. By 1995, more complete research had begun into the subject, and since that date, the Lewis and Yarnell research has been widely considered to be invalid. In fact, Dr. Dian Williams in her assessment of several arsonist studies has found no evidence whatsoever that anyone has masturbated at a fire scene. FBI Profiler John Douglas recounts that serial arsonist and serial murderer David Berkowitz admitted to him personally that he (Berkowitz) routinely masturbated at his fire scenes. Berkowitz's psychologist however notes that Berkowitz was a self-admitted compulsive masturbator all his life, who frequently ejaculated several times a day, even when he wasn't lighting fires. At this juncture, Douglas is the only person in this field who has reported such an event. In his own unabashed confessions, DC Serial Arsonist Thomas Sweatt admitted to a lifelong obsession with masturbation rivaling David Berkowitz. However, he too often masturbated several times a day even when he didn't light a fire. When Sweatt did cause an arson event, he was careful to leave the scene and most often relived the excitement by masturbating in his own home. There is just no data, factual or anecdotal, that supports the theory that an arsonist will stand at a fire scene to masturbate.

On the other hand, nearly every modern study shows that persons who set fires very often leave the scene at the time of the event, but then return to the site within about a forty-eight-hour period. This is supported by hundreds of interviews with convicted arsonists. Some return out of guilt, while others return to admire their work. With this information at hand, a shrewd investigator will usually assign a surveillance team to monitor a burn site for up to seventy-two hours after the event. Of course, the downside of that is that after nearly all major fires, hundreds if not thousands of people drive by in the following days to see the carnage.

Environmental Conditions

If you have read all of the case studies for the sixty-two or so serial arson offenders in this book, you will note that almost all had one thing in common. With one or two exceptions, the arsonists in this book had extraordinarily traumatic childhoods. That appears to be the main causal factor for all deviant behavior. As a barometer for these arson cases, it seems the offenders with the worst childhoods committed the worst crimes. At the least, all of these serial arson offenders suffered from neglect or from mental health issues. At the worst, a few suffered some of the most appalling childhoods imaginable.

Another common theme throughout was issues with alcohol, narcotics, or prescription medications. These were the most common issues cited with "hero"-type arsonists.

Marital Status

Very few offenders in this book were married or in a relationship at the time of their crimes. Almost none of the male offenders was married or in a relationship during their fire setting periods. Most of the female offenders were married at some time in their lives, but not necessarily during their fire setting periods.

Wild land and Firefighter Arsonists

These groups differed from the other groups of arson offenders. These all tended to be men with jobs and careers, were highly mobile, and usually used a vehicle. These two groups were the most likely to use a delay device of sorts. These two groups were more likely to set fires during daylight hours than any other serial offender. These groups were slightly more organized and were more difficult to catch.

The NCAVC Study

As I have previously stated, my own observations of the sixty-two serial arsonists in this book are merely from a detective's perspective. I have noted that my analyses in the preceding pages are actually quite close to the only serious study I have read regarding serial arsonists. As I have previously talked about, the NCAVC study was conducted in the 1990s by members of the FBI Behavioral Analysis Unit. It was a small but detailed academic research study, involving only eighty-three subjects from three different prisons. The members of that panel included some of the most well known in the study of arson behavior: Dr. Allen Sapp, Timothy Huff, Dr. David Icove, and Gordon Gary.

After comparing my analyses of the case histories with the NCAVC study, I found them both to complement each other. Among the many findings was that both studies agreed that the majority of serial arsonists were white males in the seventeen-to-thirty age group. Both studies showed significant childhood trauma in most offenders. Both studies showed that most of the serial arsonists had criminal backgrounds for offenses, including theft, trespassing, burglary, etc. Most offenders targeted items of little value, but some, as they grew older, began attacking larger and more dramatic targets. Almost none of the subjects in either study used an incendiary delay device, preferring to use an open flame and whatever materials were found near the fire scene. Both studies reflected that the arsonists suffered from an inordinate number of physical or neurological problems. Lastly, both studies agreed that that there was an inordinate amount of homosexual activity reported by the serial arsonists (25 percent by the NCVAC study, 30 percent from the cases in this book).

As a working investigator, it is my hope that some national entity in the fire investigation field, whether it's the National Fire Academy, ATF, or the FBI, would sponsor and maintain an ongoing database and archive system to track and maintain records, documents, photos, etc. of serial arsonists and unsolved arson series. A detailed archive containing accurate reports of firefighter arsonists could be included in the database, since almost every firefighter arsonist is also a serial arsonist. At present, there is no legitimate system in place. The ATF currently has the BATS program (Bomb Arson Tracking System), but this system is not consistently used by fire and law enforcement agencies, and there is no law or incentive that compels agencies to input information to this system.

CHAPTER 11

Catching the Serial Arsonist

The attentive reader will note that I did not use "Preventing the Serial Arsonist" as the title of this section. As a professional investigator for over twenty years and as a continuing student of the investigative process, I pride myself in knowing my business fairly well. I am convinced that you cannot "prevent arson" any more than you can prevent murders, rapes, and other crimes of rage, passion, and violence. These crimes are done at the whim of the attacker, at a place and time of his choosing and in conditions that would prohibit detection. I will admit that I am prone to rolling my eyes and giving a heavy sigh each time I see the phrases "national arson prevention week" or "arson awareness month." These are merely "feel good" phrases spewed out by fire chiefs, police administrators, and politicians in an attempt to gain support and funding for some pet project. Additionally, it baffles me why agencies waste vehicles, radios, and resources in such entities as "Arson Watch" or "Arson Patrol" units. What exactly are these mostly untrained civilian volunteers actually looking for? Since I've shown that arsonists assume every type of description and profile, then how are these people to identify arson activity? In days long past, a "fire patrol" was probably a necessary item, particularly in a wild land setting. In the modern era where everyone has a cell phone and civilians eagerly report traffic accidents and fires, even the fire patrol is an outmoded entity.

No credible investigator I have ever spoken to believes that you can actually prevent arson from occurring, short of locking up a serial offender and at least preventing him from committing future crimes. The best we can do is to thoroughly investigate every fire that occurs and, if it is deemed an incendiary act, attempt to link it to a suspect.

As an illustration, if the reader has paid attention throughout this writing, he will have learned that there are certain things that serial arson offenders seem to target. Vegetation, dumpsters, abandoned furniture, and outbuildings seem to top the list of favored targets for the majority of the offenders in this book. We cannot at all ban any of these items, nor can we post a policeman in every alley or every field. The best we can do as a society is to eliminate a few of the targets such as abandoned buildings, abandoned cars, and abandoned furniture. This will of course provide a few less targets, but the arsonist merely has to walk another block or two to find some other suitable material to ignite.

Surveillance Operations

One of the most popular tools and methods that seem to be employed in nearly every multiple arson case is the surveillance operation. I am a firm believer in the use of a surveillance operation to catch a serial arsonist if one of two things is known. If the subject has been identified, then I absolutely would bring in a professional team of surveillance operatives (not off duty firemen) to monitor the subject and hopefully catch him in the act. The only other time I would use a surveillance operation would be if I had a known target that has been hit repeatedly or at least a very finite area of incidents. When I say finite, I mean something the size of an apartment complex or no more than two or three city blocks. Obviously, the use of modern surveillance equipment is an excellent option. These would include high resolution cameras and possibly GPS tracking equipment on the subject's vehicle. Remember, the whole purpose of this surveillance operation is to positively link the subject to an arson or attempted arson event so that information can be used in the all-critical post-arrest interview. After all, we want him to confess to and clear up an entire series of fires.

While these above are the optimum use of a surveillance team, I have sadly noted in the majority of serial cases I have been privy to that most task forces comprise very enthusiastic but not necessarily skilled firefighters and investigators who have almost no training or experience in surveillance operations and whose appearance, vehicles, and communications equipment are actually counterproductive to the investigation. Let me repeat, surveillance operations are one of the final tactics used in a serial arson investigation, and if the case is of high enough importance, then professional surveillance specialists from police department's narcotics and major crimes squads should be brought in to conduct this delicate operation. This is not a job for amateurs.

The reasons that these surveillance operations continue to be carried out by non-professionals with poor training, improper equipment, and at the wrong juncture during a case are many. The number one reason is that the fire administrators in most jurisdictions have no idea how to run a criminal investigation. They often believe that by flooding the alleys and streets of an area with off duty firemen and other volunteers would solve all their problems. The truth is that most firefighters have no experience in contacting subjects in the field, have no powers of arrest, and have no means by which to either identify or apprehend a subject.

A second reason that surveillances are run in an improper manner is that the members of the task force or team conducting the surveillance are quite often there only for the overtime pay that habitually accompanies that sort of event. Their interest in the actual case is minimal, and their quality of work may be lacking.

Another argument involving surveillance operations is their actual value. Following basic criminal investigation techniques, one simply has to ask the question, "When was the last time a serial murderer was caught in the act by homicide detectives on a stakeout?" The answer is probably never. The odds of this are astronomical, and all homicide investigations are solved via interviews, eyewitnesses, and the proper collection and analysis of forensic evidence. So why would we conduct an arson investigation any differently?

Fire Investigator Qualifications

An additional problem with apprehending a serial arsonist is one that is touched on dozens of times throughout this book. Many serial arsonists set dozens if not hundreds of fires before anyone even recognizes there is a problem. This highlights the number one problem in all of arson investigations in the United States. Qualified fire investigators do not examine all of the fires that occur in their areas. Many fire administrators will lament that they do not have the time or funding to send an investigator to all of the fires in the area, particularly the "nuisance fires." They will claim that any experienced fire officer can certainly make the call on most of those small or obvious fires. However, this book has exposed exactly the opposite information. Most fire officers (captains and lieutenants in charge of a fire engine) have almost no credible fire investigation training and are wrong on their assessments of fire scenes as many times as they are correct. Their expertise lies in fire suppression and rescue duties, not usually in arson investigation. In my own area (Greater Los Angeles), there are dozens of large, modern fire agencies. Our own records indicate that the engine captains are wrong on the "origin and cause" investigation on 50 percent of the fires, and some agencies are wrong upward of 80 percent of the time.

Every fire investigation manual in print, including the much heralded NFPA-921, strongly advises that fires should be examined by "qualified investigators" in a thorough manner. That simply is not the norm across the United States. It is this author's personal experience that many of the professional investigators do not maintain current training and certification. As budget problems continue, I see no end to this disturbing trend.

Statistics

Another issue of great concern is crime reporting and statistical analysis. Fire agencies have traditionally been poor record keepers when it comes to their fire investigations. In addition to that is the seemingly random or haphazard manner in which agencies classify a fire event. As an example, if a dumpster behind a market is burning in the middle of the night, an agency may classify that incident in any of the following manners: "accident," "suspicious," "arson," "rubbish fire," "unknown cause," "vandalism," "mischief," "juvenile event," or as a "nuisance fire." A crime analyst for that agency often will only place fires listed as "suspicious" or "arson" in their computer. When attempting to identify a trend in the area, another investigator may only do a computer search of "arson" and may or may not identify that fire if it is listed in a different category. Some agencies, in an effort to appease a local city council and minimize the numbers of "part one crimes" in their jurisdiction, will only list confirmed arson fires in their reports and will not even report other suspicious fire incidents.

Related to this is the disturbing fact that the vast majority of fire agencies will not even send an investigator to vehicle fires, assuming (erroneously) that they are related to either product liability issues or insurance fraud. In my area, vehicle fires account for nearly half of the fires my agency investigates, with the overwhelming majority of the vehicle arsons being insurance fraud cases. Because few other agencies even investigate this, the arson statistics nationwide have serious credibility issues. Ignoring a major factor in the motive behind arsons is no way to identify the scope of the problem.

Juveniles

A last issue of great debate in the arson field is the reluctance of many agencies and investigators to conduct a thorough investigation involving a juvenile fire setter. Many investigators in this field have a preconceived notion about what an arsonist is or should look like, and they have a very difficult time dealing with the fact that a large portion (over 50 percent) of fire setters are kids from eight to sixteen years of age. I have run across dozens of kids like this who have set several fires each and yet are seldom officially logged into the criminal justice system. An age-old way of dealing with juvenile fire setters (even habitual ones) seems to include a stern warning by a well-meaning fire chief and maybe a trip down to the fire station to meet the men and look at the equipment. Way too many arson officials are extremely reluctant to charge juvenile fire setters or at the very least to log an official entry into a tracking system. Arson investigators have a hard enough time doing their jobs as it is, so I find it ludicrous that they want to spend so much time and effort being a "big brother" or conducting counseling to those at-risk kids. Let's face it. We all wish we could help those kids, but we have no training or skills whatsoever in the field of child psychology. The best thing we can do is start an official tracking of every juvenile identified as a problem fire setter or at risk youth. By entering that child into the criminal justice system, you can compel him and his parents through the courts to attend professional psychological counseling. While this seems like a reasonable process, I am still perplexed at the large number of my peers who are reluctant to track a juvenile fire setter.

Solutions and Strategies

Homicide investigators are usually considered to be the most competent and thorough detectives in the world. Yet, I have never heard of one of them catching a murderer in the act. Those detectives usually make their cases through a combination of proper crime scene management, excellent interviewing techniques, and the proper exploitation of forensic evidence. Oh yeah, and relentless hard work. With this time proven method as an example, why do a large number of arson investigators tend to do things in almost exactly the opposite manner? The arson field believes that "arsonists" are different from other criminals, and the preferred method of capture is to do "stakeouts" in order to catch an arsonist in the act. This is probably the least productive and most costly and time consuming method of investigation. We as a profession need to constantly mimic our comrades in homicide investigations and conduct sound criminal investigations to link our suspects to the arson scenes.

Some arson organizations which have an overly amount of influence from the private sector have adopted within their "code of ethics" a phrase that reads in part, "we are truth seekers and not case makers". While I would agree that the worse thing any investigator can do is to charge the wrong person for a crime, we still need to *make cases*! They don't make themselves, and the crook doesn't voluntarily jump into the back seat of your car with a confession in hand. Arsonists are only caught if the investigator is properly trained and equipped, and he follows time tested investigation methods.

Since I have outlined the major issues within the arson investigation field, I don't want to be known as just a critic and whiner. The following is my list of solutions toward professionalizing the arson investigation field, which will then lead to the earlier detection and apprehension of multiple fire setters or serial arsonists.

1. Every fire in every jurisdiction needs to be investigated by a qualified/certified fire investigator, no matter how small or how seemingly obvious in nature.

2. Each investigation should follow the systematic process and should include photos, diagrams, and a well-written narrative report. Reports with check-off boxes and numeric codes were designed by chair-warming bureaucrats. They have little value in any investigation as they are not able to give the true flavor of the case. Please stop using those forms. All fire investigation reports and photos need to be maintained and accessible for at least five years. Any report related to a significant event or serial fire setter should be maintained indefinitely.

3. Every fire should be logged into an analysis computer program for later retrieval. That includes fires that have been classified as "accidental" or "undetermined." As an arson investigator reviewing incidents, I want to know about every fire in an area. It can reasonably be expected that some of those incidents were classified wrongly.

4. Every person suspected or arrested for fire setting needs to be photographed, and a background check needs to be made. Those photos need to be maintained for at least five years in a unit file that is retrievable.

5. Following an arrest, every effort in the world needs to be made to develop a rapport with an arsonist and attempt to discuss with him his motives and reasons for starting fires. It is amazing how many of those subjects will actually talk to you about their behavior. Be very careful not to prejudge or lecture an arsonist . . . He will close down and not share valuable information with you. Get as much historical and background information as possible on the subject dating back to his earliest memories. If possible, interview people from the subject's childhood to get a clearer picture of him.

6. Attempt to "profile" each fire scene and determine a motive for each event. Usually the target and ignition scenario will help the most in determining the motive.

7. All arson investigators need to go for continuous professional training throughout their career, including at least one formal week each year from as many different sources as possible.

8. It takes hundreds of hours of training and dozens of fire scenes as an investigator to be a competent arson investigator. With that in mind, agencies need to make the job a permanent spot with sufficient pay and incentives so that skilled investigators would not want to rotate or promote out of the spot. Many agencies in my area rotate investigators in for a two-year stint and then promote or rotate them out. In my opinion, it takes three to five years to even become a competent fire investigator.

9. Allow the experienced investigator to run his case without interference from above. Most if not all fire chiefs have no skills whatsoever in running investigations, and they should leave that to the people they've trained and paid to do the job. All too often in high-profile cases, fire and police administrators come out of the woodwork and insert themselves into the case. Again, leave it to the professionals.

10. Maintain case security and integrity. The number one failure I have noted in every task force is the lack of information security. Nothing will compromise an investigation or court case quicker than the press getting a hold of your most sensitive information. Keep all the "heroes," "wannabes," and overzealous volunteers off your task force. Do not allow untrained persons to conduct surveillance operations, and do not give any information to the press that does not directly benefit the investigation.

11. Mandate the use of all possible forensics in every arson case. Investigators should utilize every bit of forensic technology at their disposal to solve these crimes, including, but not limited to, fingerprints, DNA, serology, crime lab chemical analysis, questioned documents, etc.

12. Educate prosecutors at all levels on the dangers of multiple fire setters and arsonists in general. Too often, prosecutors have an extraordinarily poor understanding of the crime and of the motivations behind it. They frequently look at the size of the fire when deciding on the appropriate crime to charge as opposed to the intent of the fire setter. I have explained time and again to prosecutors that the size of the fire event has very little to do with the intent of the suspect. Dozens of

wild land fires have been fairly small events, and the prosecutors tend to minimize their efforts according to the damage. With this policy, many persons who I believe are serial arsonists or display "at risk" characteristics of a multiple fire setter are given enormous leniency in courts because of the small size of their fire events.

13. In a bizarrely opposite position, some prosecutors "overcharge" a fire event if it becomes a large fire or newsworthy incident. To illustrate, the vast number of brushfires that occur in California are actually non-criminal events related to equipment failure, automobiles, or possibly negligent activity. Because these acts fall in the realm of criminal negligence and because many agencies are now pursuing cost recovery civil actions against negligent parties, many prosecutors are following suit and are fervently going after these "negligent arsonists," especially if the fire is a large event. What few people take into consideration is that all fires start out the same size, about the size of a match flame, and only the weather conditions and fuel arrangement make the event a large or small fire.

14. Fire investigators need to educate their prosecutors and advise them on the intent or motive of the fire setter so that they do not minimize or overcharge the act. That is why it is a good idea to do in-depth interviews with the fire setter and give a proper evaluation of his danger level and risk of re-offending.

15. Another ethical consideration is to stop blaming every fire in an area on an identified serial arsonist. I have seen some less than honest investigators who once they arrest an arsonist blame him for every fire in the area and clear all of them, whether he can be linked to them or not. Arson fires happen in all areas for many reasons. Serial arsonists are only part of the arson problem.

16. I have a strong suggestion to give to the many police and fire administrators and investigators who have the mind-set that more equipment is needed to fight the arson problem. In actuality, the majority of arson cases are not solved by equipment or technology with the exception of forensics. The majority of arson cases are solved by hard-working and dedicated investigators who employ time-tested investigative steps and measures. More money needs to be spent on training and personnel than needs to be spent on luxury items such as accelerant K-9's, volatile liquid detectors, surveillance systems,

firearms, or even infrared monitors. These are all "nice to have" items that look great at public displays and "dog and pony shows," but in reality they seldom have anything to do with actually catching a serial arson offender. Serial arsons are solved by people, not toys. Put your money into up-to-date training. Try and make it a varied amount of training from state and federal schools and make sure the training is repeated on at least a yearly basis.

17. A final suggestion to my brethren in the investigative field. Investigators have the positive duty to solve the crime, prosecute the case, and remove the offender from society for as long as they possibly can. Investigators need to stop pretending to be counselors, advisors, or therapists to serial fire setters and their ilk. We as a profession are having a difficult enough time as it is just doing our assigned job. Leave the advising and "soul saving" to licensed therapists and psychologists. Take the time to study and learn how the offender thinks and acts so that you can properly do your job. The public safety demands that you take those serial offenders and lock them up for as long as you legally can . . . plain and simple.

SELECTED BIBLIOGRAPHY

ABC News (2010) "Authorities Charge 2 Men in Texas Church Fire," February 21, 2010, Retrieved from: http://abcnews.go.com

Abrahamsen, D. (1985) *Confessions of Son of Sam,* New York: Columbia University Press.

Adams, R. (1984) *Case File #084-00103-2610-011* (Ole's Four Fatality Fire Investigation, 10-10-1984), Los Angeles: Los Angeles County Sheriff's Department.

American Arsonists (2010) Memphis, TN: Books, LLC.

Bradshaw, W. and Huff, T. (1985) *Arsonists in California and New York: A Tentative Look,* Research Note PSW-372, Berkeley, CA: Pacific Southwest Forest and Range Experiment Station, Forest Service, U.S. Department of Agriculture.

Brice, R. (2009) "Arsonist Shocked by 13-Year Jail Term," ABC News, April 7, 2009. Retrieved from: http://www.abc.net.au/news/stories/2009/04/07/2536984.htm

Caldwell, B. (2010) "Serial Arsonist Pleads Guilty to Setting Kitchener Fires," *The Record,* April 21, 2010, Kitchener, Ontario, Canada.

Case, R. (1990) "11 Fires in 11 Years of Her Life," *Syracuse Herald American,* November 25, 1990, Syracuse, New York.

Casey, J. (2009) "Praying with Fire: The Genesis of Shelley Shannon," *The Oregonian,* June 1, 2009. Retrieved from Oregon.com Live on November 14, 2010.

Castandeda, R. (2006) "Last Hunters Brooke Arson Defendant Pleads Guilty," *The Washington Post,* August 12, 2006, Washington, D.C.

Department of the Treasury, Bureau of Alcohol, Tobacco and Firearms (1996) *Arson Case Briefs 1996,* U.S. Government Printing Office, Washington, D.C.

Digby, M. and Velazquez, E. (2009) *Case File #409-00098-3310-999*, Los Angeles: Los Angeles County Sheriff's Department.

Dixon, S. (2010) "Arson Suspects Grew Up Together in Texas Church," Yahoo News.com, March 1, 2010, Retrieved from: http://news.yahoo.com/s/ap/200100301/ap_on_re_us_texas_church_fires.

Douglas, J. and Olshaker, M. (1999) *The Anatomy of Motive*, New York: Pocket Books.

Dunn, S. (2005) *Metal: A Headbanger's Journey* (Television documentary), Aired on MTV Network, November, 2009.

Dupras, M. (2007) "Timeline: The Life of Shirley Winters," *The Post Standard* (Electronic version), October 5, 2008, Syracuse, New York.

Eltman, F. (2010) *Caleb Lacey, Fireman, Sentenced to 25 Years to Life for Arson Murders*, Retrieved from: www.huffingtonpost.com/2010/04/09/caleb-lacey-fireman-sente_n_531909.html

Fewster, S. (2007) Arson Accused Can't be Left for Five Minutes, Court Hears, *Adelaide Now*, December 17, 2007, Retrieved from: http://www.adelaidenow.com.au/news/south-australia.htm

Gaddis, T. and Long, J. (1970) *Panzram: A Journal of Murder*, New York: Macmillan Company.

Gee, T. (2005) "Woman Faces Kaitaia Arson Charges," Thursday, June 9, 2005, Retrieved from nzherald.co.nz http://www.nzherald.co.nz/kaitaia/news/article.cfm?l_id=221&objectid=10329792.

Gee, T. (2006) "Police Happy Serial Arsonist off Streets," Thursday, August 24, 2006, Retrieved from nzherald.co.nz (http://www.nzherald.co.nz/crime/news/article.cfm?c_id=30&objectid=10397824)

Gekoski, A., "Colin Ireland—The Story," *Crime Library on truTV.com*, Retrieved on March 10, 2011, http://www.trutv.com/library/crime/serial_killers/predators/ireland/story_1.html

Green, S.J. (2009) "Incorrigible Serial Arsonist; 36-Year Sentence Sought in Greenwood Fires," *Seattle Times* (electronic version), November 18, 2009.

Green, T. (2010), "Clarksville Hospital Security Guard Arsonist Gets 4-Year Sentence," *The Leaf Chronicle.com*, Retrieved on July 7, 2010.

Gribben, M. (2006) "Hell Fire and Damnation, 2/8/2006," *The Malefactor's Register*, Retrieved on June 30, 2010, http://markgribben.com/?p=195.

Grigg, W.N. (2000) "The Burning Truth: The Role of Satanism in the Church Arson Epidemic," *TNA*, Vol. 16, No. 17, pp. 14-18, August 14, 2000.

Haas, H. (2010) "Alton Firefighter Charged with Arson: Accused of Setting Multiple Blazes There and in New Durham," *GJ News_20100323*, Retrieved from http://www.fosters.com/apps/pbcs.dll/article

Heilbroner, D. (1993) *Death Benefit. A Lawyer Uncovers a Twenty-Year Pattern of Seduction, Arson, and Murder*, New York: Harmony Books.

Herlinger, C. (2000) "Missionary of Lucifer Pleads Guilty to Church Burnings," *Chistianity Today* (online version), January 12, 2000, Retrieved from: http://www.christianitytoday.com/ct/2000/decemberweb-only/35.0html

Hidalgo, M. (2008) *Michael McNeill Case Summary*, Los Angeles: United States Department of Justice, Bureau of Alcohol, Tobacco and Firearms, Los Angeles Field Division.

Hinds-Aldrich, M. (2008) *In the Hot Seat: An Uncomfortable Take on the Firefighter Arson Issue*, November 12, 2008, Paper presented at British Fire Service College: Fire Related Research and Developments Conference.

Israel, C. (2011) "Texas Church Arsonist asks God's Forgiveness, *CBN News*, Retrieved from CBN.com, February 15, 2011, http://www.cbn.com/cbnnews/us/2011/Feb/15.html.

Jamieson, D. (2007) "Why Thomas Sweatt Set Washington on Fire," *Washington City Paper*. June 8, 2007.

Johnson, T. (2007) "Did Arsonist Kill Monte Wright's Grandparents?" March 5, 2007, Retrieved from http://www.seattlepi.com/local/306097_arson05.html.

Kass, J. (2008) "Editorial: Chicago Firefighter Arsonist Free Too Soon," *The Chicago Tribune* (electronic version), January 25, 2008.

Keller, P. (speaker), (1993) *Portrait of a Serial Arsonist—The Paul Keller Story* (videotape recording), Brian Halquist and Associates, Global Net Productions, Camano Island, Washington.

Kihss, P. (1981) "Guard at Harley Hotel Charged with Starting Two Blazes There," *The New York Times*, March 17, 1981, New York.

King's County Superior Court (1999) *Report of the Trial Judge: Cause No. 96-1-07511-2 SEA, State versus Robert Lee Parker*, 8-10-99, King's County, Seattle, Washington, D.C.

Larkin, S. (2009) "Helen White Lit 21 Bushfires in Adelaide Hills, But is Not a Danger," *The Australian*, March 24, 2009, Retrieved from: http://www.theaustralian.com.au/news/breaking-news.htm

Lewis, L. (2007) *Case File #407-00273-3310-999*, Los Angeles: Los Angeles County Sheriff's Department.

Leyton, E. (1986) *Hunting Humans: Inside the Minds of Mass Murderers*, New York: Pocket Books.

Los Angeles Times Archives (1923-Current File), John Orr-Glendale-Arson, ProQuest Historical Newspapers, Los Angeles Times, Los Angeles.

Lynne, T. (1995) The Riddle of Belle Gunness, *Headquarters Detective*, Vol. 51, No. 1, January 1995, Globe Communications Corp, New York.

Malkin, B. (2009), "Australian Bush Fire Arsonist Suspect Was Volunteer Fireman," February 16, 2009, Retrieved from: www.telegraph.co.uk/news/worldnews/australiaandthepacific/australia

McDonald, J. (2009) "Arsonist Firefighter Sentenced 10 to 20 Years in Prison," *The Times Tribune* (electronic version), November 18, 2009, Scranton, Pennsylvania.

McNerthney, C. (2009) "Police: Greenwood Arson Suspect Gave Three Lengthy Confessions," *Seattle PI* (electronic version), November 18, 2009, Seattle.

Miller, J. (2009) "Coatesville Firefighter Charged in Latest Arson Cases," *The Delaware County Daily Times* (electronic version), March 24, 2009, Pennsylvania.

Moynihan, M. and Soderlind, D. (1998) *Lords of Chaos: The Bloody Rise of the Satanic Metal Underground,* Feral House, ISBN 0-922915-48-2.

National Abortion Federation (2008) *Clinic Violence: Arsons and Bombings,* Retrieved from: https://www.prochoice.org/about_abortion/violence/arsons.asp

National Center for the Analysis of Violent Crime (1998) *Essential Findings From a Study of Serial Arsonists,* Quantico, VA: FBI Academy.

Norberg, B.J. (2008), "Bryan Yeager Facing another Arson Charge," *Bluffton Police Department News Release, 1-17-2008,* Bluffton, South Carolina.

Nordskog, E. & Powell, D. (1997) *Case File #497-20353-0530-271,* Los Angeles: Los Angeles County Sheriff's Department.

Orr, J.L., et al., speakers (1986) *Interview with Serial Arsonist Dale Frey* (Video Recording), Evidence video from the Glendale Fire Department.

Orr, J.L. (1991) *Points of Origin . . . Playing With Fire,* Haverford, PA: Infinity Publishing.

Orr., J.L., et al., speakers (1995) *Hunt for the Serial Arsonist* (Video Recording), Nova-Adventures in Science, WGBH Video, South Burlington, Vermount.

Pack, L. (2009), "Police: Accused Arsonist Would Sometimes Watch her Handiwork," *Oxford Press,* February 12, 2009, Retrieved from: http://www.oxfordpress.com/news/content/oh/story/news/local/2009/02/12

Reichert, D. (2004) *Chasing the Devil: My Twenty Year Quest to Capture the Green River Killer,* New York: Little, Brown and Company.

Russ, P. (speaker), (1982) *An Arsonist Talks—About Juvenile Firesetters* (Video Recording), Film Communicators, North Hollywood, California.

Sagar, R. (1999), *Hull, Hell and Fire: The Extraordinary Story of Bruce Lee,* Beverly, England: Highgate Publications (Beverly) Limited.

Saunders, G.J. (2010) "Ex-Firefighter Gets 5 Years," *Bluffton Today,* August 23, 2010, Retrieved from: http://www.blufftontoday.com/news/2010-08-23/yeager-faces-trial-arson-charges

Schechter, H. (2003) *Fatal: The Poisonous Life of a Female Serial Killer,* New York: Pocket Star Books.

Serial Killer Central (2010), Belle Gunness, Retrieved on July 12, 2010 from www.SKCentral.com

Slavin, R. (2002) "Award Winning Brunswick Firefighter Charged in Arson" (electronic version), *Gazette.Net, Maryland Community Newspapers Online*, January 10, 2002.

Sonner, S. (2006) Arsonist Gets House Arrest (electronic version), *Casper Star Tribune 2006/10/30*.

Stanton, S. and Delshon, G. (2000) *Indictments Issued in Sacramento Synagogue arsons*, March 18, 2000, Retrieved from: www.salon.com

Swanbrow, D. (1987) "Firestarters: The Compulsion of Wildland Arsonists and the Obsession of Those Who Chase Them," August 16, 1987,. *Los Angeles Times Magazine.*

Taylor, T. (2004) "Come Prepared to Stay Forever" Belle Gunness—"Lady Bluebeard," *Dead Men Do Tell Tales*, Retrieved from: http://www.prairieghosts.com/belle.html

Tulsa World (2007) *Volunteer Firefighter Admits to Arson*, Published October 13, 2007, Tulsa, Oklahoma.

United States Department of Justice (1998) *Serial Arsonist Pleads Guilty to Setting Eight Fires at Women's Health Clinics in California, Montana, Idaho, and Wyoming*, USDOJ Press Release, Tuesday, February 10, 1998.

United States Department of Justice (2005) *Three Charles County Subdivision Arson Defendants Sentenced*, Retrieved on December 5, 2005, http://www.usdoj.gov/usao/md

United States Fire Administration (2003) *Special Report: Firefighter Arson*, USFA-TR-141/January 2003, Emmitsburg, Maryland.

Villa, B. and Salcido, J. (2004) *Case File #404-00018-3310-999*, Los Angeles: Los Angeles County Sheriff's Department.

Wainwright, R. (2006), *Look at What I've Done*, Retrieved from: www.smh.com.au/news/national/look-at-what-ive-done/2006/01/06

Wambaugh, J. (2002) *Fire Lover*, New York: William Morrow-Harper Collins Publishers.

Warner, G. and Herbeck, D. (2009) "2 NY EMTs Charged with Arson," *EMS1.com*, June 29, 2009, Retrieved from: http://www.ems1.com/fire-ems/articles/505921-2-NY-EMTs-charged-with-arson/

Wheaton, S. (2001) "Personal Accounts: Memoirs of a Compulsive Firesetter," *Psychiatric Services*, Vol. 52, pp. 1035-6, August 2001.

Williams, D.L. (2005) *Understanding the Arsonist: From Assessment to Confession*, Tucson, AZ: Lawyers & Judges Publishing Company, Inc.

Wood, D. (2009) "Arson Suspect Described as Bi-Polar," *The Record*, May 27, 2009, Kitchener, Ontario, Canada.

INDEX

Made in the USA
Lexington, KY
24 September 2014